The Collected Poems of C. S. Lewis

The Collected Poems *of* C. S. Lewis

A Critical Edition

EDITED BY DON W. KING

The Kent State University Press

KENT, OHIO

Library of Congress Catalog Card Number 2013043209
ISBN 978-1-60635-202-1 (hardcover)
ISBN 978-1-60635-411-7 (paperback)
Manufactured in the United States of America

LIBRARY OF CONGRESS CATALOGING-IN-PUBLICATION DATA
Lewis, C. S. (Clive Staples), 1898–1963.
[Poems]
The collected poems of C.S. Lewis : a critical edition / edited by Don W. King.
pages cm
Includes bibliographical references and index.
ISBN 978-1-60635-202-1 (hardcover) ∞
I. King, Don W., 1951– editor of compilation. II. Title.
PR6023.E926 2014
821'.912—dc23
2013043209

19 18 17 16 15 5 4

To Walter Hooper

Contents

Acknowledgments

I have many people to thank for helping make this book a reality. First, I thank Joyce Harrison, Mary Young, and the staff at Kent State University Press. I have received full support and assistance from Joyce, Mary, and KSUP. I also owe debts of gratitude to the staff of the Marion E. Wade Center, particularly Laura Schmidt, Heidi Truty, Christopher W. Mitchell, and Marjorie L. Mead, who encouraged my research and provided invaluable assistance during my many visits to the Wade Center. At Montreat College, Library Director Elizabeth Pearson and her staff, especially Nathan King, Martha Martin, Lynn Holman, and Sue Diehl, have been endlessly patient and helpful in securing materials. I am also grateful to Marshall Flowers, Provost of Montreat College, for granting me a sabbatical, and the Appalachian College Association for awarding me a summer research grant; both the sabbatical and the research grant were crucial to bringing this book to print.

Many people provided essential help in the considerable work of finding Lewis's poems, securing accurate texts of them, translating specific parts of them, and obtaining permissions. Rachel Churchill of the C. S. Lewis Company was very helpful in securing permission to publish the poems appearing in this collection. Thanks as well to Ron Hussey of Houghton, Mifflin, and Harcourt. Lewis scholars Michael Ward, David Downing, Bruce Edwards, and Joe Christopher gave me valuable advice and suggestions. A. T. Reyes endlessly (and tirelessly) aided me by offering translations of many of Lewis's Latin words, phrases, and, in one case, an entire poem. Each of you has my gratitude. Perhaps above all, I owe much to Walter Hooper for his generosity with his time, expertise, and encouragement; for several poems of Lewis's that I sought for this collection, he was the only person holding holographs of them, and in every instance he kindly sent me copies.

Many thanks are due as well to my student assistants, Mary Willis Bertram, Molly-Kate Garner, Corrie Greene, and Mackenzie May. I especially thank my research and editorial assistant, Alyssa Klaus, who worked many hours helping me compile, edit, and "scrub" the manuscript. Finally, I owe my wife, Jeanine, a great debt for tolerating the many hours I spent away from her while working on this book.

Introduction

Why Lewis's Poetry Matters

I have not bowed in any other shrine
From babyhood, nor sought another god
To worship and with faithless footsteps trod
In any flower-strown path, save only thine
Dear poesy.
—C. S. Lewis, "Sonnet [1916]"

Although C. S. Lewis is best known as a prose writer for his clear, lucid literary criticism, his Christian apologetics, and his imaginative Ransom and Narnia novels, for the first two and a half decades of his life he considered himself a poet. During these years, Lewis modeled his verse upon older, traditional poetic forms, especially long, narrative poems and retellings of old myths, characterized by frequent archaisms and the use of traditional meters. Among the poetic works influencing him the most were Homer's *Iliad;* Thomas Malory's *Morte D'Arthur;* Edmund Spenser's *The Faerie Queen;* the anonymously written *Sir Gawain and the Green Knight;* John Milton's "Comus" and *Paradise Lost;* Percy Shelley's *Prometheus Unbound;* William Wordsworth's *The Prelude;* and William Morris's *Sigurd the Volsung.*

When *Spirits in Bondage: A Cycle of Lyrics* became the first of Lewis's works to be published (in 1919), the modest critical notices it received fueled his dreams of becoming a great poet. Accordingly, upon his return to Oxford after serving in the trenches in France during World War I, Lewis once more threw himself into writing poetry. Indeed, Owen Barfield recalls that anyone who met Lewis as a young man in the early 1920s during his student days at Oxford University, quickly learned that his "ruling passion was to become a great poet. At that time if you thought of Lewis you automatically thought of poetry."[1]

Yet despite Lewis's sustained, earnest, determined, and single-minded efforts at writing poetry through the mid-1920s, his reputation will always be based on his prose, both fiction and nonfiction. This fact begs the questions: Does Lewis's poetry matter? Why bother sifting through his verse if the real gold is to found elsewhere? Shouldn't we simply write off Lewis's poetry as adolescent self-indulgence? Didn't his commitment to older poetic forms and traditions hopelessly date his poetry? Didn't his antipathy to modernism isolate him to a poetic backwater, awash in pejoratives such as "tired, stale, traditional forms," "hackneyed, well-worn, tepid poetic diction," and, perhaps worst of all, "a late, late, Victorian *zeitgeist?*" Years ago, one of my friends expressed something of this view when he scoffed at Lewis's second published work, the long narrative poem *Dymer* (1926), relegating it to the ash heap of failed poetic aspirations. I suspect my friend is not alone, but I equally suspect that he and others who quickly dismiss Lewis's poetry reveal more about their own literary limitations than their understanding of Lewis's verse.

So, yes, I do think Lewis's poetry matters, both for biographical and literary reasons. Certain volumes, for instance, especially such early works as *Spirits in Bondage* and *Dymer,* offer unique insights into Lewis the atheist. In *Spirits in Bondage,* Lewis explores how the spirit of humankind—variously portrayed as either proud and indomitable or longing for beauty—is shackled by an earthly existence, one marked by suffering and theological uncertainty. Throughout the poems, we see Lewis disturbed by his sense that human life is directed by a malicious, capricious God. Lewis's theological dilemma is even more evident in *Dymer.* As Barfield argues, "it is practically the only place where the voice of the earlier Lewis [before his conversion to Christ] . . . is heard speaking not through the memory of the later Lewis but one could say in his own person."[2]

Perhaps more important is the literary significance of Lewis's devotion to poetry: it profoundly influenced his later prose. That Lewis, until well into his late twenties, saw himself primarily as a poet challenges us to make critical explorations of Lewis's prose from the perspective of his being a frustrated poet. Jerry Daniel points the way here when he notes that Lewis has "the soul of a poet . . . [and] all works were 'poetry' to him in the sense that the 'feel' or 'taste' was primary."[3] For instance, who can deny the poetic power of Lewis's prose in *Perelandra?* A close examination of Lewis's prose poetry throughout the Ransom trilogy reveals how his prose "works" like poetry.[4] In addition, the rhythm and cadence of his prose reflects his deeply felt poetic sensibility. Although some work has been done on his rhetorical use of metaphor, careful investigation of this technique in Lewis's prose shows that it is often motivated by poetic, rather than rhetorical, principles. *Mere Christianity* and *The Problem of Pain,* for example, are inspired at least partially by Lewis's poetic sensibilities, while *A Grief Observed* demonstrates that Lewis's prose imagery is inspired by his poetic imagination. Moreover, Lewis's early (and, as he later judges them to be, unhealthy) aspirations to achieve literary acclaim as a poet inform our understanding of why the danger of spiritual pride surfaces so often in his writings. From Rabadash in *The Horse and His Boy* to Orual in *Till We Have Faces,* from Screwtape in *The Screwtape Letters* to the damned in *The Great Divorce,* from Professor Weston in *Perelandra* to Mark Studdock in *That Hideous Strength,* Lewis examines the subtle yet powerful way in which humans are prone to pride. Can it be that he writes so convincingly of it because he knows so well its pull as a result of his early dreams of becoming a great poet?

Up until now I have considered only how a deeper understanding of Lewis's poetry might enhance our reading and appreciation of his prose. But what of the poetry itself? Has it been unjustly overlooked in the spirit of my friend who casually dismissed *Dymer?* More pointedly, didn't Lewis's traditional poetic vision put him at odds with modernism and the popular poets of the day, particularly T. S. Eliot and William Butler Yeats? Poet and theologian Malcolm Guite reflects with great insight on these questions:

> Lewis has sometimes been dismissed as archaic and eccentric, but in retrospect his efforts in poetry, as in other fields, are much more contemporary, much more keenly directed to the crises of modernity, than he has been given credit for. There are many and complex links between his work and that of his two great contemporaries, Yeats and Eliot. He is not perhaps a great poet in the same sense that they are, but he is a great deal better than the long neglect of his verse would imply. There is an internal coherence between all his efforts in every field. Taken together these efforts constitute an attempt at the redemptive reintegration of reason and imagination, the broken modes of our being and knowing. His poetry thus deserves to be reread, more widely studied, and anthologized.[5]

I agree completely with Guite. Since I first encountered Lewis's poetry more than thirty years ago, I have been fascinated by his verse. Initially this interest was confined to exploring yet another expression of Lewis's wide-ranging facility for writing in multiple literary genres. Eventually, however, I also came to appreciate how Lewis's poetry comments on, informs, and reflects key aspects of his "attempt at the redemptive reintegration of reason and imagination."

This long interest in Lewis's poetry led me to write *C. S. Lewis, Poet: The Legacy of His Poetic Impulse* (2001). When I wrote that book, I dreamed that one day I might be able to collect all of Lewis's poetry into one volume and offer the poems in chronological order. This book is the realization of that dream. A chronological reading of Lewis's poetry offers a fascinating insight into the "growth of [a poet's] mind."[6] Initially we see Lewis offering poetic retellings of Norse myths in the narrative style of Virgil and Milton. Then we see a rush of lyrics concerning nature's beauty, human suffering, and God's disconnection with both; many of the latter are hard-edged poems reflecting the influence of his great tutor, W. T. Kirkpatrick. After this we see Lewis's ten-year commitment to writing what he hoped would be his *opus magnum,* the ambitious but ultimately unsuccessful *Dymer.* Yet after the publication of *Dymer* and his realization that he would never be a great poet, Lewis wrote a collection of sixteen lyrics that he included in *The Pilgrim's Regress* (1933); as a group, these sixteen lyrics may be among his best poems. From this point forward until his death in 1963 Lewis continued writing and publishing poems. Often these poems appeared in journals and magazines under the pseudonym N. W., Lewis's Anglo-Saxon shorthand for *nat whilk*, "[I know] not whom." These later poems are occasional verse, burlesques, and erudite satire or contemplative or religious poems musing on the human condition, pain, suffering, pride, meaning, and the spiritual life. Finally, at the end of his life and after the death of his wife, Joy Davidman, we find a small group of poems marking the apex of his career as a poet, including three sonnets almost certainly dealing with Joy's cancer and subsequent death: "'Oh Doe not Die,'" "One Happier Look on Your Kind, Suffering Face," and "All This Is Flashy Rhetoric about Loving You."

A chronological reading of Lewis's poetry offers a broad overview of his work as a whole. For instance, the angry poet who blasphemes God in "De Profundis" from *Spirits in Bondage* is also the Christian allegorist tracing his journey to faith in *The Pilgrim's Regress*. The frustrated narrative poet who writes *Dymer* is also the imaginative novelist who writes the Ransom space trilogy. The self-doubting poet in "The Apologist's Evening Prayer" is also the buoyant, confident Christian apologist of *Mere Christianity*. The world-weary poet who writes "Scholars' Melancholy" is the same perceptive scholar who writes *English Literature in the Sixteenth Century, Excluding Drama*. The nature poet who laments "The Future of Forestry" is also the fantasy novelist who writes of the apocalyptic destruction of Narnian nature in *The Last Battle*. The ironic poet who worries about the deconstruction of language in "The Country of the Blind" is also the penetrating philosopher who writes *The Abolition of Man*. The mythopoeic poet who writes *The Queen of Drum* is also the realistic novelist who writes *Till We Have Faces*. And finally, the tender poet who writes "Love's as Warm as Tears" is the same broken-hearted memoirist who writes *A Grief Observed*.

Despite the importance of Lewis's poetry, until now it has been difficult to access all his verse in one place. Lewis's literary executor, Walter Hooper, made such access easier by seeing that *Spirits in Bondage* was republished in 1984. He also selected and edited the poems appearing in *Poems* (1964), *Narrative Poems* (1969), and *Collected Poems* (1994). Yet several of Lewis's poems remained difficult to access, especially those originally appearing in journals and magazines and omitted from republication in *Poems* and some that existed only in holographs. *The Collected Poems of C. S. Lewis* remedies this problem by gathering in one volume all of the poems previously published by Hooper together with others scattered in journals, magazines, and holographs (including twelve published here for the first time). I offer three caveats. First, this volume is not the complete poems of C. S. Lewis. While I believe it contains perhaps 95 percent of Lewis's original poems, I have omitted a number of poetic fragments and a few minor poems; moreover, there is always the possibility that a heretofore unknown Lewis poem of significance may be discovered. Second, I have not included Lewis's translation of portions of Virgil's *Aeneid*.[7] Third, this is not a variorum edition of Lewis's poetry. Although I did carefully sift through many differing drafts of the poems in order to ascertain the best possible version, I do not publish multiple versions of the poems.

In the end I have been directed by the following editorial principles. Perhaps the most important of these principles is my arrangement of the poems chronologically as they were written, so that readers can easily compare the poetry and the prose Lewis was simultaneously writing. In some cases this means a poem's published version may have appeared notably later than the date of its original composition; I indicate this by placing at the end of each poem first the date of composition and then the date(s) of publication, if any. In line with this principle, I have in several cases placed heretofore undated poems where I believe they were written chronologically; I note these and other cases where I cannot be sure of the dates of composition by following the date with a bracketed question mark.

Second, in most cases the versions of the poems I print here are those that first appeared in print. Accordingly, the versions of *Spirits in Bondage* and *Dymer* I publish here follow the first editions. Similarly, the sixteen poems from *The Pilgrim's Regress* are published as they appeared in the first edition of that work, while poems first published in periodicals appear in the form originally found in those journals and magazines. By adhering to this editorial principle, this collection sometimes offers different titles or phrasing from those found in Hooper's editions of Lewis's poems—*Poems, Narrative Poems,* and *Collected Poems.* In those books, he published what he believed to be the version of a poem Lewis intended, correctly noting that Lewis frequently tinkered with his poems even after they appeared in print. However, lacking a definitive way of knowing which version of each poem Lewis may have intended as the "final" one, I have thought it more judicious to publish here the version I know Lewis endorsed—the version that appeared in print during his lifetime. Following this editorial principle also means I often do not follow Hooper's titling of some poems. In general, I use the title given each poem on first publication. For poems not titled by Lewis (because they appeared after his death), I title the poem according to its first line. For readers familiar with Hooper's titles I indicate in the Bibliography of Poem Sources the instances where I am not using his titles.

Third, while I have retained Lewis's capitalization and British spelling variations in the poems and in all direct quotations from his prose (for instance, *honour* instead of *honor*), I have silently corrected obvious misspellings and made occasional minor changes in punctuation; in some instances, particularly in the case of certain narrative poems, I have indicated minor variations between Lewis's holograph version and the published version. In every case I have tried to provide a clean and precise text for each poem.

Lewis's poetry matters because it illustrates the degree to which writing poetry and being a poet were fundamental to his character. As a young poet, Lewis saw himself in the great tradition of the poets he so admired—Virgil, Dante, Milton, Wordsworth, and Yeats. While it is true that he will be best remembered for his prose rather than for his poetry, my heart did brighten while attending Lewis's investiture in Westminster Abbey's Poet's Corner on November 22, 2013. He could hardly have predicted that fifty years to the day of his death a stone honoring him would be placed in the floor of the abbey.[8] I think that had he been in the audience that day, he would have worn a wry—if slightly embarrassed—smile. *The Collected Poems of C. S. Lewis* demonstrates his lifelong commitment to poetry, revealing a dedicated, determined, and passionate poet at work.

Notes

1. Owen Barfield, "C. S. Lewis" lecture given at Wheaton College, Wheaton, Ill., Oct. 16, 1964.

2. Barfield, "C. S. Lewis" lecture.

3. Jerry Daniel, "The Taste of the Pineapple: A Basis for Literary Criticism," in *The Taste of the Pineapple: Essays on C. S. Lewis as Reader, Critic, and Imaginative Writer,* ed. Bruce L. Edwards (Bowling Green, Ohio: Bowling Green State Univ. Popular Press, 1988), 9, 11.

4. For example, see my "The Poetry of Prose: C. S. Lewis, Ruth Pitter, and *Perelandra,*" *Christianity and Literature* 49 (Spring 2000): 331–56; reprinted in *Plain to the Inward Eye: Essays on C. S. Lewis* (Abilene, Tex.: Abilene Christian Univ. Press, 2013).

5. Malcolm Guite, "Poet," in *The Cambridge Companion to C. S. Lewis,* ed. Robert MacSwain and Michael Ward (Cambridge, UK: Cambridge Univ. Press, 2010), 308.

6. As mentioned above, Lewis's poetry was profoundly influenced by Wordsworth's *The Prelude,* the poem Wordsworth spent most of his life writing and rewriting, and the one he described as "the poem on the growth of my own mind."

7. See the brilliant work done by A. T. Reyes in his *C. S. Lewis's Lost Aeneid: Arms and the Exile* (New Haven, Conn.: Yale Univ. Press, 2011).

8. The stone memorializing Lewis in Poet's Corner is inscribed with one of his most famous quotes: "I believe in Christianity as I believe that the sun has risen, not only because I see it, but because by it I see everything else" (C. S. Lewis, "Is Theology Poetry?" In *The Weight of Glory and Other Addresses* [1949; San Francisco, Calif.: HarperSanFrancisco, 2001], 140).

Poems

1907–1914

The Old Grey Mare

Round about the ladye's bower,
Round about the miller's tower,
Neath the shield
          and
5 O'er the field
Goes ye old grey mare.

Rushing in some dreadful fray,
SHE'S a living shield I say,
Rushing o'er the bloody field,
10 She WILL face the foeman's shield,

Dash against some warhorse stronge
Midst a battle's bloody throng.
Though her rider dight[1] in steels
The heavy thing she never feels.

15 When the bloody battle's over
Then is victory the rover.
For her feet there is the fen,
For her company the wren.
Far are known Knighthood,
20 But still more noble is the brood
Of the olde grey mare.

Round about the miller's tower,
Round about the ladye's bower,
Neath the shield
25   and
O'er the field
Goes ye old grey mare.
(1907–9; 1970)

Descend to Earth, Descend, Celestial Nine

I

Descend to earth, descend, celestial Nine[2]
And sing the ancient legend of the Rhine:[3]
What races first upon the world did dwell
In earliest days, descend Oh Muse and tell.
5 Who did the mighty hills inhabit, who
The earth's deep clefts: narrate the story true.
Upon the mountain tops in happy light
Abode the gods with majesty and might,
Whom Wotan ruled as chief.[4] The sluggish Rhine
10 Rhine maidens sheltered,[5] nymphs of form divine,
Who for their sire a noted treasure held,
The Rhinegold,[6] and in watch of this they dwelled.
Beneath the river's bed a hollow cave
To Nibelungen welcome shelter gave,[7]
15 A stunted race who never see the light,
Of hideous visage and of puny height:
Abide they thus in corners dark and deep,
Like ants which through a tunell'd city creep.
And cunning they, and full of vicious greed
20 Live that they may their base ambitions feed.
Their king, a petty despot, Alberich[8]
With bloodshot eyes and beard of volume which
The razor ne'er had known and to his feet
Reached almost, and the cave's smooth floor did meet,
25 One day ascended by a shaft whose mouth
Through the green Rhinebed rose and pointed south:
He stood: and through the water's shimmery sheen
The three fair maidens swimming could be seen.
Their beauty wakened in him base desire,
30 And kindled in his eyes an ugly fire,
And as they dive and circle in the dance
They hold the dwarf who stands as in a trance.
Their eyes, as through the ripples smooth they roam
Light on the ugly, rapt, and gazing gnome.
35 They see the purpose in his face and mock,
Laughing down on him from a lofty rock:
"Does Alberich indulge in dreams of love

And steer his mind through thoughts his state above?"
The words the passion in him urge on more,
40 And darts he forward from the pumice shore,
With arms outstretched to catch the laughing forms,
Who with fresh mirth elude his passion storms.
Then love gave place to anger. With a cry
He rushes forth; they to the surface fly.
45 Then for a moment mirth gives place to fear
And laughter changes to the frightened tear.
This mood prevails for but a little while
And soon return the scorn and mocking smile.
They tantalize with dance the tiny king,
50 The waters wide with wanton laughter ring.
Then darts the ugly imp with wanton eyes,
They dive and swim and to the surface rise:
As now he almost seems to grasp the maids,
And merrily they fly before his raids.
55 Anon the nymphs, made frail by easy life,
Grow faint and weary of the heated strife:
Alberich glories in his sinews strong
And knows he may maintain the chase for long:
For as they whirl and circle, laughter dies
60 And joy from weary countenances flies,
In vain they seek by wiles the dwarf t'elude
Nor longer can resist his sallies rude.
To one, as in despair the maidens swim,
A scheme suggests itself by which the whim
65 Of Alberich the base they may evade:
Above them in a cleft the treasure laid
Would tantalize the dwarf far more than they.
And with this thought she upwards wends her way
And, drawing back the curtain which obscures
70 The Rhinegold, by a call the dwarf allures,
Who, glancing upward through the water cold,
With greedy eyes espied the glint of gold.
As eagerly he sees the metal shine
No more he heeds the maids of form divine.
75 The glimmer and the gold his senses please
And up he dashes, arms outstretched to seize
The hoard. But like a dreamer in his sleep
He sinks repulsed and floundering in the deep

By force invisible, and does not reach
80 The gold. The nymphs with loud unguarded speech
Thus to each other: "Knows he not the key
By which alone the hoard his own may be?
Knows he not as he tries to grasp in vain
The treasure, that who would the Rhinegold gain
85 Must first curse love before his hands may hold
The glistening and so much desired gold?
And he, should he but gain the pile he wants
(If there be truth in legendary vaunts)
If to a RING he forge it by the art
90 Of goldsmith, then to rule shall be his part;
Whoe'er the treasure keeps and wears the RING
Shall rule the world, an everlasting king.
But Alberich, the basest slave of sense
Will never frame the destined curse: and hence
95 The treasure ne'er will gain." The greedy gnome,
As eagerly he through the waves did roam
To hear the maidens' voice, did not appear
And yet their every word his open ear
Drank in: And with a cry of triumph fierce
100 He upwards strove the tepid waves to pierce.
Then cursed he love; nor did the force this time
Repulse the squalid king of Nibelheim.
He clutched the pile, and with a mournful cry
The maids beheld their hope of safety die.
105 And with lugubrious strokes, no longer quick,
They swim away. The darkness gathers thick,
And Alberich with gait of triumph proud
Approaches through the soft and sedgy shroud,
And at the tunnel's mouth he stops and calls
110 Down to th'infernal kingdom of the trolls.
"Come up ye dwarfs, come up and greet your king;
For he has gained the Rhinegold and the ring."
The Nibelungs come up, an ugly throng
With tattered garb and muscles coarse and strong.
115 The darkness thickens at the dwarfs' approach
And noxious fumes upon the light encroach.
With joy they gather round like busy ants
And bear the treasure to their secret haunts;
Beneath the rolling Rhine the pile they lay
120 In jet black caves, far from the light of day.

II

The darkest hour it was before the light
Of dawn had burst upon the silent night;
The mountain of the gods enveloped stood,
Surrounded by the dense, mysterious shroud.
5 Then rose the sun upon the fertile hill,
Which beareth fruit although no ploughman till,
And touched with fire, Valhalla's stately hall,[9]
Tinging each buttress and each turret wall:
Reared by the hands of giants was the place
10 Fit home for members of th'immortal race.
For Wotan, chief of all the gods, desired
A hold of strength, and Logie[10] him inspired
(The god of fire, who Wotan most advised
And by his cunning many a scheme devised)
15 To compact with the mighty giants twain,
Fasolt and Fafnir,[11] monsters of the plain
To rear a hall. And as their price they claim
The goddess fair of love, to whom the name
Was Freia. Wotan gave a sad consent
20 To sacrifice which he had never meant;
And trusted Logie's wisdom to regain
The captive from the giants of the plain.
Thus, as the dawn was breaking, lay the god
Before the castle on the verdant sod;
25 The light caressed with gentle touch his form,
His noble visage, free from passion's storm,
His golden beard, and arms and limbs divine.
As on the herbage lay the god supine
Closed were his eyes, and sweet, refreshing sleep
30 The mighty king in soft embrace did keep.
Some paces off another form reclined
Of tender beauty like a mountain hind,
Twas Frika, Wotan's everlasting spouse.
Then Wotan did himself from dreams arouse,
35 And, rising, turned and viewed his noble home,
Let his dark eye o'er every cornice roam.
Then with majestic anthem greets the hall:
"Fit shelter for the lord and king of all!
Valhall! My home! Oh be thou strong and blessed,
40 Standing so firmly by the light caressed
See! How vermilion grows each stony point.

How flames like fire each wooden beam and joint:
Yet grim foreboding in my heart prevails,
Whispering fearful, half unuttered tales."
45 Then turning to the goddess, Wotan cried:
"Awake, Oh Fricka:[12] wake, my holy bride.
Come: let us enter our new built abode,
And taste the fruits which Logie's wit hath sowed
In Walhall's hall we'll dwell in peace for aye."
50 And Fricka, waking, said: "I know not why,
The name seems strange: and unaccustomed fears
Rise in my heart and urge the burning tears.
Can all be well, if Logie you inspires
To sell a goddess for your own desires?
55 Freia, bring Freia back, with her departs
Our happiness from faint and sickened hearts."
To whom the god with gravity replies:
"Ah, wipe the sorrow from those streaming eyes;
I did not wish the goddess fair to sell
60 But power of Logie's speech thou knowest well.
Advised by him—and let this bring you cheer—
I somehow hope to save our Freia dear.
By counsels smooth and words we will regain
The loved one from the monsters of the plain."
65 He spoke. And at that moment from below,
With those quick steps which terror's anguish shew
Freia herself came with dishevelled hair
And bloodless cheeks, and all her visage fair
Was strained with fear as o'er the turf she trod,
70 Full eagerly: and now she eyed the god.
"False traitor! Thou should'st my protection be
Oh save me from the monsters' grasp." Thus she.
And even as she spoke, with heavy tread
Approached the cumbrous objects of her dread.
75 With slow and awkward gait the giants move,
And slowly dog the goddess fair of love.
First comes Fasolt, the kindlier of the two,
Armed with a mighty tree like weapon, who
For her own sake the goddess sad desires:
80 But Fafnir a far different plan inspires,
Reflects he thus as up his way he wends:
"'Tis Freia who the golden apples tends,

Of which the gods immortal eat and live.
Were she not there the duteous care to give,
85 The gods must some day pass in death away,
I, with Fasolt, will hold unbounded sway
O'er all the world." As thus the giant thought,
Him one more pace before great Wotan brought.
Thus halting near the god the monster stands
90 Towering o'er him with his spread out hands.
Then thus with voice of thunder he addressed
The god: "Oh mighty lord of Valhall blessed.
We come the bargained price you owe to claim,
Fulfill your vows or yield t'eternal shame."
95 Then troubled thoughts on Wotan's brain encroach,
For he expects the god of fire's approach,
By whose aid only can he hope to gain
A triumph o'er the monsters of the plain.
He glances round and falters in his speech,
100 Retreating with a step from Fafnir's reach.
The giant sees the step, and on his brow
The anger grows. Then: "Dost remember how
I reared for you Valhalla's stately hall
And likewise could remove your home, your all?"
105 Said he. The prudent god, composed, replies:
"Fafnir! Suspect me not of ugly lies.
While I the woeful news to Freia tell,
I'll send you two of those who round me dwell,
Immortal gods, with converse to beguile
110 The space of time." He speaketh such things while
The molten glow of anger in the eyes
Of Fafnir quickened as he heard the lies.
Then leading Freia, Wotan inward goes.
To twain of the immortal gods he shows
115 His plans, and tells them how with words to cheat
The giants while he waits the god of heat.
The two were Froh, the laughing god of joy,
And Donner, god of thunder.[13] They employ
The time with oily words and counsels fair.
120 Fasolt, the lover, scarce delay can bear.
Thus the four great ones grouped together stood,
The giants' anger boiling in their blood:
Opposed to Fafnir stood the god of joy,

A laughing, fair, and well appointed boy.
125 And Donner stood and wielded in his hand
A mighty mallet which might crush a land,
With louder rhetoric and clumsier speech
To Fasolt patience he desires to teach:
In whose blue eyes the fire flames fiercer still,
130 Nor can he more control his yearning will,
His conversation flags and terser grow
His short replies: his twitching fingers shew
How tense his longing. Then at last he cries:
"No more of this. Arise, Oh Fafnir, rise.
135 And let us take the goddess in our hands
And bear her off from Walhall's wordy lands."
Thus speaking, both the giants think t'advance,
And Donner sees their harsh and meaning glance;
The god of thunder did no more delay
140 But sought to check their onslaught by a way
Of reasoning so sure that none could stand
Against its power—the mallet in his hand.
Ah! Ne'er the giant had aris'n again
Did but that blow descend with stunning pain;
145 But as the god for his fierce stroke drew back,
And in the effort every bone did crack,
Valhalla's door with creaking groanings oped,
And Wotan brought the friend for whom he'd hoped;
For by the hand he led a slender god,
150 In burning robe, in burning sandals shod:
His frame was thin, nor was his stature great,
His raven eyes with varied thoughts dilate.
He counts and counts again his every wile,
And whispers in his master's ear the while.
155 Then Wotan sees the mallet raised to strike
And rushes in between th'opponents like
A flash of lightning. Grasps he Donner's arm,
And stays the blow and rectifies the harm.
Then turns the god to Loge and enquires:
160 "Where have you been? What thought your brain inspires?"
To whom Red Fire replying, forward stands:
"Obedient have I been to your commands.
And scoured the stretching earth from end to end
To find what might our sorry bargain mend

165 And love replace: but useless was the task,
I could not find the substitute you ask.
Nor found I any mortal high or low
Who Freia's gentle favour would forgo.
But while I searched for one decided thing,
170 I many others found of moment, King.
One thing there was; which threatened all the earth
With downfall dire; and this new power's birth
I will relate. In yonder wand'ring Rhine,
Three maidens dwelled, you know, of form divine;
175 Who in their keeping held a hoard of gold,
Which they have guarded from the days of old.
But this mysterious virtue has the thing:
Whoe'er shall forge the metal to a ring
All earth shall rule—aye, gods as well as men.
180 How would it fare with mighty Walhall then?
But all was well. The nymphs dreamed not of power,
Nor pondered aught beyond the fleeting hour.
Thus far 'twas well: but only for a time,
Until the king of hollow Nibelheim
185 Ascending, stole the treasure from the maids:
They, helpless victims, fell before his rage.
I pitied them and—pray forgive me, king—
I did therein an uncommanded thing,
Exceeding thy high mandates: I did swear
190 Valhall assistance to their cause would bear."
Thus did narrate th'intriguing god of fire,
And did a thought great Fafnir's brain inspire.
Forward he dashed, and cried: "I beg thee, stay.
And hear my words." And Wotan answered: "Say
195 Fafnir what things you wish. Our ears are oped."
Fasolt thus hotly: "I had fondly hoped
Freia to gain: But since you do not choose
To give her up, I will not therefore lose
My whole reward. Freia to thee I'll give,
200 (So may she always in Valhalla live).
Give me that treasure which the god of fire
Hath told us of: for that I most desire."
"The treasure," answered Wotan, "is not mine;
The greedy dwarfs who stole it from the Rhine
205 Will doubtless hold it dearer than their lives.

And if a god with Nibelungen strives
Who shall prevail? Although our mighty arms
And pow'r divine secure us from alarms
Of martial foes: the cunning gnomes may snare
210 Our person by their wiles, did we but dare
Their noisome caverns where in gloom they dwell;
I fear their hidden, untried depths of hell."
Then answered Loge with a hidden sneer:
"'Tis not alone to face the regions drear
215 Of Nibelheim, descending from above
Is needful. But the hero must curse love
To gain the gold." Then Wotan stood aghast
Although the passion of his youth was past,
And doted he on power, he could not make
220 His lips the curse to frame and love forsake.
So casts he on the ground a troubled eye:
The giants see he fears to make reply
"Accept you not the liberal terms we make?
So be it. Freia then we justly take."
225 So Fafnir spoke; but Wotan, plunged in thought
Scarce heard the words, nor saw what sense they brought.
Then the two giants can restrain no more
Their purpose, but they open wide the door
Of Valhall: and bring forth the goddess sad.
230 Oh Freia, thou who once more glad than all
In freedom roamed, nor did one care appall
Thy gentle breast, what sorrow now you bear!
Nor do the giants in their haste forbear
To one of Asgard's great immortal race
235 To offer sacrilege and durance base:
Freia they lead away: with mournful tread,
Herself she sadly suffers to be led,
Nor strives with petty strength the fates to move,
Resigned, descending from the realms above.
240 Then Logie to his master turned and said:
"A gloomy day for Asgard dawns ahead:
Think not with impious words that I would strive
The righteous sorrow from your heart to drive,
I know your grief—indeed I share your pain.
245 But if Valhalla ere would raise again
Her haughty head above the hated clouds,

And cleanse her from the woe which now enshrouds
Her stately halls, we must to warfare turn,
Nor let the sorrow more our spirits burn.
250 For think of this: she is not here to tend
The golden apples. Who the want may mend?
By these alone the gods immortal live."
He spoke. And Wotan studious ear did give.
And all the gods who stood around did quake,
255 And frigid fear their every bone did shake;
Should Wotan not the goddess fair regain,
No more the gods immortal, free from pain,
Could hope to dwell: and thus on every hand
In speechless agony th'immortals stand.
260 And as they stand, a deathlike mist descends,
And with these words the god his thoughts now ends:
"No more of this: we do but waste the time.
Let us descend to tunneled Nibelheim:
There may we gain the treasure and the RING
265 The one will gain our Freia, one a king
Of all the world for aye myself will make,
If I but love will curse and love forsake."

III

Guide me, my muse, down yonder sloping way,
Far lead me from the happy light of day.
Let us descend by clefts, where fathoms deep
The Nibelungs their hollow city keep.
5 Here, in the regions of eternal night,
By pumice rocks enclosed: where never light
With shining radiance spreads its warming ray,
Nor morning dawns, nor differs night from day:
And hidden from the winds and waves and storms,
10 There dwells the race of small ungainly forms,
More hideous far than fancy can devise.
And in all cunning knowledge are they wise:
Ready to plot and scheme for others' harm.
And here they dwell secure from all alarm:
15 Dark is the cave, suffused with ruddy glow,
And rocky arches propped on pillars low
Support its roof of clay. And in the light
Of some red furnace gleaming through the night,

A goldsmith's forge of tiny size is seen,
20 The glare returning with a brighter sheen
From every burnished point. And heated air
Resounds with wild mysterious whispers there,
And taps of naked feet on earthy floors,
And creaking of the hinges and the doors
25 Of dark and unknown side apartments few
Would dare to penetrate. And waters blue
With phosphorescent glare, in one weird coin[14]
Rush down the world's internal lake to join.
Then in the firelight's ruddy glow appeared
30 A tiny dwarf of visage dark and weird:
'Twas Alberich, the king of Nibelheim,
And by the ear he dragged another—Mime,[15]
A larger dwarf of uglier visage yet,
And in his eyes the tears of rage were wet;
35 Nor was his chin adorned by flowing beard
Like that of Alberich at whom he leered
—Now spitefully, by hidden hatred shook,
Now with a cringing and submissive look.
To him with rage began the angry king:
40 "You idle dog! You worse than useless thing!
Have you not learned my mandates to obey,
And execute my words without delay?
Nor idly sit, yourself with peace to gorge:
Where is the headgear that I bade you forge,
45 The cap, the Tarnhelm[16] from the stolen gold?
Hast thou forgot the crafts thou knew of old?"
Then Mime's shrill voice through all the caverns rang:
"'Tis wrong that you should bitterly harangue
Your most obedient slave. The cap you bade
50 The cunning smith to forge, that cap is made.
Nor does the work disgrace my stablished art:
Full well have I fulfilled my humble part."
Thus, honey in his mouth, but in his brain
Hatred, the fruit of long endured pain,
55 The smith stooped down towards the pumice floor
And picked a bundle from amongst the store
Of instruments that to the forging trade
Pertain: the pack was in rich cloth arrayed,
And tenderly he did unfold the wrap;

60 Then in the firelight gleamed the golden cap.
"Behold," he cried, "the work is here to see:
Which willingly, my king, I give to thee."
Then Alberich, with eager hands acquired
The trinket which his heart so much desired:
65 His eyes with secret triumph glistened while
He placed it on his head and with a smile
The goldsmith gnome surveyed. But not alone
The fact that such a headgear was his own,
So finely wrought, so well with gems arrayed,
70 And to the proper form so fitly made,
That with such joy inspired him, but he knew,
That if the legend of the Rhine were true,
Which for the Tarnhelm—so the cap was named—
This virtue for the golden helmet claimed;
75 Whoe'er the headgear wore, at any time
What form he wished could take. And therefore Mime,
Who thought the cap must hold some power divine
Was loath to forge the metal of the Rhine
To that which would his hated king endow
80 With powers new. The other gladly now,
The cap upon its head, its virtue tried:
As standing by his cunning servant's side
One instant he was seen, the next the air
Was empty: to the loathing smith's despair
85 A scourge unseen his trembling limbs did greet,
And empty air upon his back did beat.
In vain he falls in terror on the ground,
And pity begs with noisy wailing sound:
Then, still invisible, the cruel king
90 Through the dark cave his unseen path did wing,
And leaves the smith in tears upon the floor.
Then opened from behind the cavern's door—
Ye gods! What light, what radiancy divine,
Fails to recite this earthly pen of mine,
95 Which that dark cavern flooded as the forms
Of two fair gods appeared. Their presence warms
The cavern with a glow it n'er had known;
Leaps out the furnace then to meet its own,
(For Logie and his master, Wotan, came
100 The gold they wished by stealth or arms to claim).

That furnace which before with ruddy beams
Had lit the place, now over feeble seems
Compared with that great, more than mortal light
Which from th'immortal places broke the night.
105 And like as when a housewife with a lamp
Invades some cellar full of stores and damp,
The rats with evil petterings haste away,
Recoiling from the glare in wild dismay:
So crowds of Nibelungen, right and left,
110 To hidden caves rush off. Alone, bereft
Of terror by his pain, the smith lies prone,
His wounds and sad existence does bemoan.
Then Wotan, drawing nearer, kindly says:
"Explain, good dwarf, what grief your soul dismays."
115 And eagerly the moaning dwarf returned,
"Long has the wish for fitting vengeance burned
In this poor soul of mine. Didst thou but know
What tyranny I daily undergo
From Alberich's hand, the hateful king,
120 The owner of the thrice accursed ring,
Then would your hearts be moved. I pray you hear
My tale of woe. Nor spurn the crushed out tear.
I daily live in terror of my lord,
Alternate blows receive of scourge and sword."
125 So spoke he, weeping; then the god of fire
Said: "If you, dwarf, deliverance desire
From your tormentor, listen to my words:
We come to conquer wealth, but not with swords.
By cunning shifts and wiles we seek to gain
130 The Rhinegold. And if you to cruel pain
Would bid farewell to aye and free become,
Help us to gain the treasure of your home."
As Mime, the cunning smith, would make reply
The caverns shudder with a painful cry,
135 And from the darkest corners of the place,
The members of the Nibelungen race,
Rush wearily with cries and tears of woe:
The lights of fire and gods their driver show,
The squalid king approaches; whip in hand,
140 Before him drives a Nibelungen band.
Then holds he high above his head the ring,

And yearns for all the triumph it will bring:
And mighty schemes revolve his tiny breast,
A swelling heart in narrow body pressed;
145 And all his being trembles with delight,
Grasping the gold, with golden headgear dight.
As thus he stands in rapt and joyous pose,
The gods their presence in these words disclose:
"Hail, mighty king. We know your sterling worth,
150 Nor, being wise, despise your dwarfish birth.
We come our due respect as brother kings
To pay. Valhalla worthy homage brings."
And Alberich in scorn does make reply:
"'Tis false, ye gods: and hast thou thought that I
155 Like some young child, by honeyed words deceived
Imagine I have homage true received?
Ye lying race of gods. I loathe ye all,
As you despise my body dark and small
And puny height, so I a fiercer shame
160 Impute to Asgard's oft repeated name.
What virtue have you in your godly pow'r,
What though Valhalla's mountains dimly tower
O'er all the ages? Didst thou by thine own
Unaided power this gain? No: 'tis well known,
165 The dark unknowable which men call fate
Set up the immortal objects of our hate:
Supplied them with dominion undeserved,
With immortality their throne preserved;
Thus tyrants helped by destiny, a blind
170 Unthinking power, they left all woes behind,
And lived forever in their haughty home.
Now of these tyrants lying, twain have come
To offer homage as they say. Do gods
Descend the dark and unfrequented roads
175 That lead to my dark realm, respects to pay
To Alberich? Or leave the glowing day
To seek the caverns of a king they hate?
Or doth the eagle with the beetle mate?
Am I a child that I should thus believe
180 Ye come love-laden spirits to relieve
With kindly words? Nay: never was there yet
A god but did all misery beget

With lofty schemes. The price of Asgard's good
Is running rivulets of human blood.
185 To better your estate ye gladly slay
Crowds of the bad: the good alike dismay.
Through all the ages war has been between
Thy race and mine. And do th'immortals mean
These words of homage as an ill timed jest,
190 Or do the dotards really strive their best
My spirit to deceive? Whiche're it be,
I care not!! Get ye gone from mine and me,
But stay. Before the hated schemers go,
To them their coming ruin I would show:
195 Although devoid of power my person seems,
The golden pile that in yon crevice gleams
Hath made me lord of all. Nay, start not so,
Ye did not deem a prince to meet below.
The ring this Nibelungen finger wears,
200 The Tarnhelm which this wrinkled forehead bears
My kingdom they set up. Ah! what a jest.
The power fate, which once of all its best
Gifts to Valhalla's gave, that very same
Fate hath prepared its downfall and its shame:
205 The ring hath made me monarch of ye all,
Valhalla's stately realms I will enthrall:
From harms I always easily escape,
The Tarnhelm gives me power to change my shape.
And when the world's broad kingdom is my joy,
210 Schemes for your torture will my brain employ:
I once to gain this ring sweet love did curse,
Now I will not than Asgard's race be worse:
Your doom, mendacious tyrant, learn and hear,
Ye also shall curse love." And at this jeer
215 The rage swelled up in Wotan's godly heart;
Forgets the god to play his subtler part,
And, like as when the hounds with barking stand
About the antlered deer, on either hand,
And vex the mighty monarch of the glades
220 Who, for a time, resists their paltry raids
With only lazy strength. Then rears his head
Above the throng, the meadow swims with red
And curdling gore as charges he the throng,

Invades their ribs with cruel horns and strong:
225 Not otherwise than this, Valhalla's king
Rages upon the owner of the ring.
And as he rushes forward to the blow,
And gleaming eyes their owner's passion shew,
And upwards Wotan did his weapon raise,
230 Loge the prudent, Loge far more wise,
Seizes his master's arm and softly says:
"Reserve your anger, king, for other days,"
But, turning to the dwarf, he gaily sneers:
"No doubt to thee, your scheme sublime appears;
235 You taunted us with deeming you a child
When we our homage on your spirit piled;
Accept you then, who are in wisdom great,
That we believe the legend you dictate?
Prove you the power you say the Tarnhelm grants,
240 Change thou thy shape. Fulfill your empty vaunts."
The crafty Nibelung raised his hoary head,
And answered with a look of hate and dread,
"Still rave the dotard gods? And think ye, friends,
I do not know your avaricious ends:
245 Shall I a small and feeble beast become,
That you may bear the treasure from my home?"
The baffled Wotan raised his haughty eyes,
And faltered twixt his fury and surprise;
But Loge, speaking calmly, said: "My friend,
250 If this in truth be of your power the end,
Lying were those who told us of your might,
You are not than mere men in better plight.
So fare thee well. We go to Walhall's hall."
Then in a trice the cunning, crafty Troll
255 Forgot his plans, and as a mortal will
When moved by pride, performed his office ill.
Stung to the quick by Loge's taunting words,
He answers, "Think not dazzling pomp and swords
And gleaming halls and tessellated courts
260 And armour bright and giant reared forts
Alone mean power. Nay, in this gloomy cave
Lies more concealed than Asgard's host would brave.
Credit ye not my words? Then I will give
A sign by which your quavering faith may live."

265 And with this bitter word once more he set
The Tarnhelm on his head. His fingers met
And clasped each other till the flesh grew white
About the knuckles, trying that he might
Compress his willing spirit, every thought,
270 Into the wish the golden Tarnhelm brought.
Ha! Wild, unprecedented, weird event
That through the godlike forms a shiver sent;
For looked they once, and in the ruddy glow
The furnace cast across that cavern low,
275 Saw they the uncouth Niblung's figure stand,
Solid in form and breathing close at hand;
Then looked again—Oh! horror that they saw!
E'en as the snow before the sun doth thaw
And leaveth streams where stood the solid mass,
280 E'en so the gods beheld their victim pass.
Slow into air dissolved the dwarfish flesh,
Melted the bones and teeth to take afresh
A body new. And in the troubled air
Hovered the spirit like a mass of fair
285 Yet fetid vapour, and alone the eyes
Dissolved not in the common mass. Surprise
Seized hold upon the gods when once again
With groanings like some animal in pain
The members in the glow ferment around
290 Those steadfast orbs of light, and all is bound
Into one solid whole. Fear Wotan rocks,
When stands where stood the dwarf a vicious fox.
And thrice he oped his lips and thrice surprise
The Father's speech did bar. The gleaming eyes
295 That did the fox's evil face adorn
Upon great Wotan flashed with haughty scorn,
But Loge of the cool foreknowing brain
Renewed the smile which on his lips had lain
Before the dark event, and said, "Oh king
300 I now believe the power of your ring.
Forgive my foolish words, my scornful smiles,
These were to hide my awe, transparent wiles;
I pay, oh mighty Niblung just, to you
The reverend homage which is all your due.
305 The warriors which Valhalla's chambers hold

Do not such marvels of your power behold:
A novel joy, this rapturous, trembling fear,
Unknown delights that Nibelheim doth bear!
Show us again, great dwarf, your wondrous might,
310 And let us taste again this fierce delight."
Once more the ruddy fox's limbs convulsed
In effort of desire. The sight repulsed
The watching gods who knew what was to come
Knew the dread secrets of the Niblung home;
315 Drank they with greedy eyes the wondrous sight
And pondered on it as the ruddy light
Revealed the coming change. Once more the mass
Of snowy fog before the dwarf did pass
Into which melted slowly every part,
320 The shining claws, the palpitating heart.
And still the ugly spirit hovered o'er
The shifting whirlwind, gathering more and more
Its specks of dust together, and the eyes
Above the ruin of the form arise.
325 Great golden orbs of light with lustrous sheen,
And where the dwarf in form of fox had been
There writhed a slimy toad upon the floor.
Then Wotan darted forward with a roar
Of triumph, and his garment gathered round
330 His godly waist. And to the pumice ground
He pinned the fragile reptile with his foot.
Again the effort of desire did shoot
Through Alberich's frame—it was too late!
The Tarnhelm on his brows no longer sate:
335 For Loge—scheming god—had seized the toy,
And god a god embraced in solemn joy.
Ah! sight of pleasure and of woe!—The cave
In deepest gloom was wrapped and hidden save
The scarlet oblong which the furnace cast
340 Across the earthen floor, and with its last
Expiring rays by distance dimmed alit
The farthest corners of the squalid pit.
And in the light two godly forms embraced
Each other, and each other gladly faced,
345 And Wotan's golden locks seemed brighter yet
As every hair the gleaming firelight met,

And Loge, skillful, fair and slight withal
Enraptured stood before his master tall.
Beneath the other's foot, in dismal plight,
350 —A contrast to the other pleasant sight—
The reptile sought its bleeding limbs to tear
From under that proud foot that crushed them there.
Then turned the mighty gods and Loge grasped
The toad in his strong hand and up they passed:
355 Up winding clefts the rocks had rent apart
In deep convulsions of the earth's deep heart,
Up funnels long, down which the freshening breeze
Odourous with the scent of lands and seas
Unnumbered, swept to choking Nibelheim.
360 The gods laughed loud, for, having been a time
In that foul den whose secrets few would dare
Rejoiced once more to breathe the upper air.

IV

To that dim shadow land of unknown space
Where twilit dwells the great immortal race—
I speak of Asgard, that mysterious hall
Which is the home of gods: that mountain tall
5 On which it stands, I speak of—to that shore
The gods their toad-formed victim gladly bore.
And as they neared the godly place on high
A thousand voices filled the azure sky:
Across its depth a thousand wondrous things
10 Floated at ease or hastened with their wings;—
The flying steeds that bear the Valkyrie maids[17]
And mighty serve them at their bloody raids.
As through the twilight winged the gods their way
In the last light of the departing day.
15 Out flew the warrior maidens bravely armed,
And music shrill the listening ear alarmed
—The music of the storm: the failing light
Revealed the lovely forms in armour dight.
And first of all that eerie cavalcade,
20 Whom every Valk'rie duteously obeyed,
Great Wotan's daughter rode, Brunhilda named,
Whose beauty would the fair of earth have shamed.
Then clashed a thousand spears. A joyous shout

Through and above the storms wild song rang out,
25 The multitude of Valk'ries joyous cheer,
As sound of joy to gods; no man may hear
That cry and live: thus sing they when they bear
The bravest warriors from the battle sore
To live in Asgard's bliss for evermore.
30 So, with this mede,[18] the flying train drew nigh
Through the resounding fathoms of the sky
Sweet in the twilight. And the gates of gold
Upon the well poised hinges open rolled
And gave admittance to the gods. They went
35 Onwards and upwards with the eyes intent
Of all the gods and heroes on their path,
And on the reptile which in frenzied wrath
Quaked in their iron grasp, and as they neared
The hall of Clouds, a radiant form appeared—
40 Fricka—great Wotan's spouse—she comes and leaves
The hall where cloudy fates she softly weaves.
Her stance is sad, her eyes betray her woe:
But Wotan loudly calls to her
(caetera desunt.)
(1912–13; 2001)

Quam Bene Saturno

Alas! what happy days were those[19]
When Saturn ruled a peaceful race,
Or yet the foolish mortals chose
With roads to track the world's broad face.

5 No haughty keel proud ocean spurned,
The breeze filled out no swelling sails,
No daring prow had outward turned
To face old Neptune's angry gales;

It sought to gain no foreign land,
10 Took produce from no distant shore.
The horse endured no bit's command
No yoke the sturdy oxen wore.

No door enclosed the happy home,
No landmark in the meadows fair
15 Bade whose there by chance might roam
The boundaries framed by men beware.

The wholesome nectar of the bees
From oaks poured down its golden wave,
The cattle, eager then to please,
20 Unasked their milk to mortals gave.

No clashing phalanx battle waged
Nor war the nations rent apart,
No man with man in anger raged
Nor plied the smith his savage art.

25 But now . . . With Jove our haughty lord
No peace we know but many a wound:
And famine, slaughter, fire and sword
With grim array our path surround.
(1913; 1913)

Carpe Diem

When, in haughty exultation, thou durst laugh in Fortune's face,[20]
Or when thou hast sunk down weary, trampled in the ceaseless race,
Dellius, think on this I pray thee; but the twinkling of an eye,
May endure thy pain or pleasure; for, thou knowest, thou shalt die,
5 Whether on some breeze-kissed upland with a flask of mellow wine
Thou hast all the world forgotten, stretched beneath the friendly pine,
Or, in foolish toil consuming all the springtime of thy life,
Thou hast worked for useless silver and endured the bitter strife:
Still unchanged thy doom remaineth. Thou art set towards thy goal,
10 Out into the empty breezes soon shall flicker forth thy soul.
Here, then, by the plashing streamlet, fill the tinkling glass, I pray,
Hither bring the short-lived garlands, and be happy—for today.
(1913; 1973)

In Winter When the Frosty Nights Are Long

In winter when the frosty nights are long
And sedge is stiff about the frozen meres,
One night above a volume of old song
Of legendary loves and magic fears
5 Sweetened by long elapse of slumbering years,
I nodded in the frosty firelight beam
And fell on sleep and straightway dreamed a dream.

I thought it was a luminous summer night,
And in the star-flecked welkin[21] overhead
10 A fading sickle of soft golden light
Its wonder over all the landscape spread,
While fleecy clouds athwart its paleness sped:
Ten thousand thousand points of light did peep
Out of the boundless heaven's velvet deep.

15 Meseemed I stood upon a goodly plain
Full of soft streams and meadows deep in corn,
While the far thunder of a foaming main
Across the calm, delicious air was born.
Beyond the plain, a mountain waste forlorn
20 Clear seen beneath the trembling silver light,
Rose, and yet rose with height still piled on height.

Higher than mountains seemed, than Alpine peaks
Or fabled mountains spied from the moon,
And tortured into grim fantastic freaks
25 Of rock: o'erhanging cliffs that seemed to swoon
Towards me, ready with vast ruin soon
To fall and whelm the plain, and vallies steep
Engulphed with icy torrents swift and deep.

The eye could hardly reach, and senses failed
30 In gazing on those unimagined . . .
(1913–14; 1998)

Loki Bound

"This is the awful city of the gods,[22]
Founded on high to overlook the world;
And yonder gabled hall, whose golden roof
Returns the sinking sun's red glare again
5 With twofold force, is Valhall. Yonder throne
That crowns th'eternal city's highest peak
Is Odin's throne, whence once the impious Frey
With ill-starred passion eyed the demon maid.
Fair is the city while the mellow light
10 Caresses every bulwark, while the cliffs,
Some, standing forth, with borrowed splendour shine,
Whilst others in the purple shade retire.
Aye surely, too, it seems impregnable,
Perched high above all fiends and monsters dire,
15 Out of their reach—yet if my soul speak sooth,
Not long shall she be fair, not long have peace.
For soon the red birds' cry at Ragnavik[23]
Shall muster all the sons of night for war,
And the fierce brood from Surtur[24] sprung shall come
20 And plant their grisly hosts about her walls.
And I shall shed no tear at Asgard's fall:
Nay rather will I join the demon band,
And with my monster children at my back
Defy my erstwhile masters. For know this,
25 All mortals, that tho' I enjoy the name,
The glory, and the hollow, hollow pomp,
The worship and the common reverence paid
To gods, yet I have never been of them.
For, in the dawn of all, ere time began,
30 Or haughty Asgard overlooked the world
Or men had come to being, and when still
Great Ymer's[25] corpse lay wallowing in the gulf,
I walked with Odin through the shapeless void.
Ah! We were brothers then, and then we pledged
35 Eternal friendship in those earlier times
—Fool that I was! But as we looked around,
And viewed the wild chaotic waste, the sun
The moon, the stars, all ignorant of their tasks,

Knowing not each his place, then Odin told
40 How he would build a world, a home for man,
And lay the Ocean round it like a cloak;
Confining to its utmost marge the vast
Uncomely giants and the monsters fell;
And over all that lived create the gods
45 Companions to himself, and he proposed
To make the conjuring dwarfs and beasts and men,
Building for each its habitation meet.
But even in that early age I saw
The awful error and injustice dread.
50 Then, knowing what I knew, addressed the god.
'Odin! and who art thou to make a soul
And force it into being? Who art thou
To bring forth men to suffer in the world
Without their own desire? Remember this,
55 In all the universe the harshest law,
No soul must ever die: it can but change
Its form and thro' the myriad years
Must still drag on for aye its weary course,
Enduring dreadful things for thy caprice.'
60 He answered darkly, with uncertain words
Hiding his thoughts. And when I would have called
The new made universe to sleep again,
Me he forbade, and with his magic power
Bound as his slave, bound me to work for him.
65 Thus, therefore have I lived thro' all these years,
Forced to obey the mighty criminal,
The father of injustice, he who makes
Sorrow and pain on earth, in heaven strife.
But not for ever shall his rule endure,
70 And even now in plans unknown to him
I set on foot destruction for the gods.
In Asgard, stone on stone shall not be left
And all the gods shall perish—haste that day.
Let all of them such pains as they have caused
75 Soon taste in full and learn what sorrow is!
Curse them, the light-souled gods! Yea, curses on them!
What form is this that glistens up aloft,
Athwart the gathering darkness? What that cry
Echoing wild across the riven clouds?

80 Lo! The bald ravens flutter down to earth:
'Tis Odin that I see. The cloud grey steed
Flies through the storm clouds, and upon his back
The grim creator of the world is borne."[26]
....

85 F[asholt]. "Hail strangers! Who are ye that sit alone
Thus brooding in the cruel winter night?
Nay, answer not; for I perceive myself,
Ye are the high gods' kinsfolk, and ye wait
Doubtless to watch the building of my wall.
90 Well, rest assured of this: it shall be done,
For I am bent on gaining that dear prize,
To cheer my lonely home in Jottumheim."[27]
....

"Yonder, over the hill, the pale precursor of Billing[28]
95 Paints with a ghostly line of white that corner of heaven:
Down in the silent woods, to the Westward, buried in shadow,
Tho' it be still dark night, yet every bird hath awoken.

Borne on the chill night breeze, a restless whisper ariseth,
Where they are stirring below, chattering down in the thickets.
100 Now, with a ruddier tint, the roofs of adorable mansions
Gleam in the city above, high in impregnable Asgard.

Lo! He is coming at last, the sun, and wherever he touches
Mountain or wall with his rays, with his life giving breath he ignites it.
Now from the vale and the hill, from the throat of many a songster
105 Poureth the song of the dawn, the song that is old as the mountain.

Gone is the night of our fear: let us greet the day with rejoicing.
Praising, each from her heart, the Norns[29] that have pitied our sorrow.
Who cometh hither in haste, so wild and so eager for tidings?
Surely over the brow of the mountain Loki appeareth."[30]
110 ....

O[din]. "So be it then. The day
Of doom at last has fallen. Wo is me,
Never again as in the days of yore,
To clasp thy hands in friendship, or to walk
115 Together through the chaos, as of old
Ere yet the worlds were builded! Thou alone
Couldest be my friend, or understand. For these—

Gods, men, or beasts—what are they but my self,
Mirrored again in myriad forms? Alas,
120 How weary is my soul . . . .
But let us come,
Oh, maidens, and repair to heaven's halls."[31]
(Exeunt Odin and Chorus).[32]
(1914; 2001)

Ovid's "Pars estis pauci"

I

Of the host whom I NAMED[33]
As friends, ye alone
Dear few! were ashamed
In troubles unknown
5 To leave me deserted; but boldly ye cherished my cause as your own.

II

My thanks shall endure
—The poor tribute I paid
To a faith that was pure—
Till my ashes be laid
10 In the urn; and the Stygian boatmen I seek, an impalpable shade.

III

But nay! For the days
Of a mortal are few;
Shall they limit your praise?
Nay rather to you
15 Each new generation shall offer—if aught be remembered—your due.

IV

For the lofty frame
That my VERSES ENFOLD,
Men still shall acclaim
Thro' ages untold:
20 And still shall they speak of your virtue; your honour they still shall uphold.
(1914; 1974, 1998)

1. Clothed, adorned.

2. The Muses, the nine classical goddesses of the arts and sciences.

3. For the influence of Richard Wagner's *Der Ring des Nibelungen (The Ring of the Nibelung)* upon this poem, see chapter 5, "Renaissance," in Lewis's autobiography, *Surprised by Joy: The Shape of My Early Life* (London: Geoffrey Bles, 1955); hereafter, *SJ*.

4. Wotan was the chief god in Richard Wagner's opera cycle *Der Ring des Nibelungen.*

5. The Rhine maidens were the three guardians of the Rhinegold.

6. The Rhinegold was a powerful lump of gold, accessible only to one who is willing to renounce love.

7. The Nibelungen were a race of dwarves. Lewis uses alternate spellings in the poem, specifically *Nibelung* and *Niblung,* in order to preserve the meter.

8. Alberich is the misshapen king of the Nibelung.

9. Valhalla, meaning "hall of the slain" in Old Norse, lies in Asgard and is the home of Wotan. Sometimes in the poem Lewis spells this *Walhalla.*

10. In Norse mythology, Logie is the scheming, clever god of fire. *Logie* is Lewis's variant spelling of *Loki.* He also employs a second variant, *Loge,* in order to preserve the meter.

11. The giants who had built Valhalla for Wotan; he had promised (falsely) to give them Freia, sister of his wife Frika, in return.

12. Wotan's wife; Lewis spells her name either *Frika* or *Fricka.*

13. Froh is the twin of Freia and the brother of Donner, god of thunder.

14. Angle.

15. Weak, cowardly brother of Alberich.

16. Magical headpiece that allows the wearer to change appearance, including the ability to become invisible.

17. In Norse mythology, the Valkyrie, whose name in Old Norse means literally "choosers of the slain," are beautiful young warrior maidens who choose the men doomed to die in battle and bring them to Valhalla.

18. Reward or prize.

19. The Latin title of this poem comes from Tibullus 1.3.35 and means "How well they lived when Saturn [was king]." The poem celebrates the benevolent rule of Saturn in the days of the Titans, before the successful rebellion of Jove.

20. The title of this poem is Latin for "Seize the day."

21. Firmament or sky.

22. Loki, the subject of this poem (of which only fragments survive), is a rebel, bitterly resentful that Odin (the Norse version of Wotan) had created mortals without their permission. For more on Loki, see also note 10 above.

23. Sometimes called Gotterdammerung, *Ragnavik* (Lewis's variant spelling of the name *Ragnarok,* which translates literally as "doom of the gods") in Norse mythology comprises a train of events that will mark end of the cosmos.

24. Surtur is chief of the fire gods.

25. In Norse mythology, Ymer was an elemental being, the primordial giant from whose body came the race of frost giants.

26. About the first eighty-three lines, Warren Lewis writes: "Loki's opening speech, for which 'sombre and eerie' music is required, reads thus." See the eleven-volume unpublished

manuscript, of "The Lewis Papers: Memoirs of the Lewis Family, 1850–1930" (hereafter, "LP"), edited by Warren Lewis and available in the Warren H. Lewis Papers, Marion E. Wade Center, Wheaton College, Wheaton, Ill. (hereafter, the Wade Center); quotation, 4:218.

27. In Norse mythology, Jottumheim is the homeland of the rock and frost giants. Warren Lewis writes about these eight lines: "The entry of Fasholt, for which 'bluff, swinging' music is asked, is handled thus" ("LP" 4:219).

28. A giant.

29. In Norse mythology, the Norns are three fates, female beings who shape the destiny of gods and men.

30. Warren Lewis writes about these sixteen lines: "Then follows the episode of the maddened horse and Fasholt's exit, after which succeeds the following song for the chorus which is obviously the 'dawn music' referred to" ("LP" 4:219).

31. Warren Lewis writes about these twelve lines: "The drama closes with Loki's rejection of Odin's proffered pardon and friendship, and a short final speech by Odin, for which Clive asks 'some inexpressibly sad, yearning little theme'" ("LP" 4:220).

32. Later in *SJ* Lewis reflected on the importance of *Loki Bound:*

> Norse in subject and Greek in form . . . as classical as any Humanist could have desired, with Prologues, Parodos, Epeisodia, Stasima, Exodus, Stichomythia, and (of course) one passage in trochaic *septenarii*—with rhyme. I never enjoyed anything more. The content was significant. My Loki was not merely malicious. He was against Odin because Odin had created a world though Loki had clearly warned him this was a wanton cruelty. Why should creatures have the burden of existence forced on them without their consent? The main contrast in my play was between the sad wisdom of Loki and the brutal orthodoxy of Thor. Odin was partly sympathetic; he could at least see what Loki meant and there had been old friendship between those two before cosmic politics forced them apart. Thor was the real villain, Thor with his hammer and his threats, who was always egging Odin on against Loki and always complaining that Loki did not sufficiently respect the major gods; to which Loki replied "I pay respect to wisdom not to strength." Thor was, in fact, the symbol of the Bloods though I see that more clearly now than I did at the time. Loki was a projection of myself; he voiced that sense of priggish superiority whereby I was, unfortunately, beginning to compensate myself for my unhappiness. The other feature of *Loki Bound* which may be worth commenting on is the pessimism. I was at this time living, like so many Atheists or Antitheists, in a whirl of contradictions. I maintained that God did not exist. I was also very angry with God for not existing. I was equally angry with Him for creating a world (114–15).

33. The title of this poem comes from Ovid's *Ex Ponto* 3.2.25. The complete phrase in Latin is *pars estis pauci melior,* which means, "you few are a better group," referring to several loyal friends who remained dedicated to and supportive of him during his exile.

Poems

1915–1919

Poems from "Early Poems: English Verses Made by C. S. Lewis"[1]

My Western Garden

I know a garden where the West-Winds blow;
Far hence it lies, and few there be that know,
And few that tread the road that leads thereto.

Its gladsome glades are girt about with mists,
5 And o'er its sward a slumberous streamlet twists,
Flowing like Lethe,[2] soundless; thence who lists

May drink his full, and naught remember more.
Methinks my garden must be by the shore
Of some vast nameless Ocean; for the roar

10 Of waters always murmurs through its bow'rs;
Faint flakes of foam lie crisp on all the flow'rs,
And salt spray mingles with the drowsy show'rs.

No chart will guide thee to that twilit land,
Nor mariner hath reached that Ocean's strand,
15 For space it knoweth not, nor Time's rough hand.

But 'tis the home of those faint dreams that keep,
The shadowy country, neither Life nor Sleep,
Which parts full wakening from the voiceless deep.

Scant need hath any man to wreck of woe,
20 Or joy, of hate or love, so he may go,
And shelter in the garden that I know—
—But few they be that find the road thereto.
(Easter 1915; 2004)

A Death Song

I am weary of Summer weather,
And fain would I hide me away
From the golden gorse, from the heather,
The flower-dight meades, and the day

5 That lingers o'er long. Yet the laughter
Of man and of beast, over hill
And dale, in the days that come after
Shall sink to a sob and be still,

When Lugh[3] is no longer in heaven;
10 —They are fools and they know not the best
Of the gifts that the wise gods have given,
And toil they love better than rest.

As they sigh for the fierce Summer season
Of labour and lust, so at last
15 They falter and fear without reason
When the tale of their life-days is past;

For they know not that rest on the bosom
—The kind cold bosom of Night,
Is more than the swift-withered blossom
20 And feverish joy of the Light.
(Easter 1915; 2004)

The Hills of Down

I will abide
    And make my dwelling here
What so betide,
    Since there is more to fear
5 Out yonder. Though
    This world is drear and wan,
I dare not go
    To dreaming Avalon,
Nor look what lands
10   May lie beyond the last
Strange sunset strands
    That gleam when day is past
I' the yearning West,
    Nor seek some faery town
15 Nor Cloud-Land, lest
    I lose the hills of Down,
    The long, low hills of Down!

Not I alone,
    If I were gone, must weep;
20 Themselves would moan
    From glen to topmost steep.
Cold, snow-pure wells
    Sweet with the Springtide's scent,
Forsaken fells
25   —That only I frequent—
And uplands bare
    Would call for me above,
Were I not there
    To roam the hills I love.
30 For I alone
    Have loved their loneliness;
None else hath known
    Nor seen the goodliness
Of the green hills of Down,
35 —The soft, low hills of Down!
(Easter 1915; 1994)[4]

Against Potpourri

I saw one garner in a bowl to keep
The drowsy leaves that mid-June roses weep,
Weep for the passing of the glad young year—
And musing gazed upon the crumpled heap,
5 And told half dreaming every fragrant tear.

These were no worser weeds than those they say
Sad Proserpine[5] was culling on that day
When, plucking such to deck her maiden bower,
Herself by swarthy Dis[6] was born away—
10 A harsher hand to pluck a fairer flower.

Methought: the phantom of each broken bloom,
Midst fellow-ghosts, throughout the winter's gloom,
Here in this bowl, upon some carven shelf,
They'll set to breathe across a firelit room
15 Some lingering magic of its summer self.

They ween, it may be, in these leaves to bind
Some remnant of dead Summers left behind
For a memorial. Folly! Though they shed
Some fragrance yet, there is no man shall find
20 Delight and beauty here among the dead.

There lurks among these wraiths no magic scent
To conjure back to earth old seasons spent:
These tidings only shall they yield at last.
—That where the leaves ye did not gather went,
25 Their full-blown summer beauty too hath passed.

Why do ye garner then the leaves that fall?
They should be left to weave the dead year's pall
And dance upon the Autumn's frosty breath.
For but one flower shall outlive them all—
30 The eternal poppy, deathless weed of death!
(Summer 1915; 1994)[7]

To the Gods of Old Time

Creeds that have flourished and faded! Gods that have waxen and waned,
Gods of the innocent altars! And Gods whose houses are stained
With the blood of the victims they gave you; since over and dead is your day
And a-down on the river of ages ye sail in your glory away;
5 Come tell me, I pray you, what token, remembrance of good or of ill
Ye have left to the race of the men-folk, to quicken your people or kill?

Thou wast great for a season, oh Isis![8] Thy love, he was lord in the land
Of Pharaoh. Come say did it sicken, or prosper then under his hand?
Did they that bowed before Baäl,[9] fare better than ye did or worse?
10 Did your friends wax great at your blessing, your foes fall faint at your curse?
And ye that cried to Astarté;[10] what gat ye of evil or good?
Did she fashion your hearts to her fancy? Or order the tide of your blood
That the cold grew warm, and the fevered ran cold? Or ye that of yore
Put trust in the man-slayer Arës,[11] or called in your need upon Thor[12]
15 At the turn of the tide in a battle, what lot did they give to the fight?
Were your targets the defter to parry? Your swords, were they surer to smite?
Tho' Gods that were merry and awful, and chaste and lewd we have seen,
Yet tell me, for all your teaching, if ever an age there hath been
When the prophet ceased from his preaching; the saint turned not to his cell,
20 And the happy and humble-hearted did otherwise aught than well;
When the wandering blood stayed steadfast, and the hot fool held from his lust,
Or the warrior fain of battle did suffer his war-gear rust?
There was no such age among ages, since ever all years began,
Though your temples were high as the heavens: albeit your altars ran
25 In blood as deep as the oceans: ye turned no whit from its path
The heart of man that ye flattered with love, and affrighted with wrath!
Hear then the end of the story! The sands of the slumbering years,
Have left but a ghost of your glory, too little for laughter or tears
And all that the high boasts hide is a barren shadow of might
30 Ye are Νμκτδs παῖδες 'άπαιδες,[13] childless children of night!
(Summer 1915; 2004)

The Town of Gold

Last night to sleep I laid me down
And dreamed I saw a golden town:
A phantom city of the night
Whose dwellings glittered fair and bright,
5 And bastions of furbished gold
Beneath did burn and on the height
Of every tower and gable old
Shone the shimmering sapphire cold.
Meseemed it were a dear delight
10 In such a burg as that to dwell,
And ever move among and see
Those dwellings wrought so wonderly.
But lo! A marvelous thing to tell,
I saw the folk go up and down
15 The roadways of my golden town;
Their cheeks were wan, their brows were wet,
Their feet went hurrying, evermore,
And rested not: their eyes were set
Forever on the golden floor.
20 They looked not on their left or right
To see the city good and fair;
And when I wondered at the sight,
How all these laboured everywhere
And wrought, and ceased not from their moil,
25 A voice came to me from the night
To tell me how that city hight
Which said:
This is the town of toil,
This is the home of them that set
30 Their hearts upon the cheerless gold,
And when 'tis gotten they forget
To cease their labour and behold
The thing they sought: but evermore
Their eyes are bended on the floor
35 Their cheeks are pale, a ghastly sweat
Is on their brows, as up and down
The roadways of their golden town
They hasten alway.

So it spoke
40 Therewith, in loathing and affright
At that strange city of the night.
Out of my slumbers I awoke.
(Summer 1915; 2004)

The Wood Desolate (near Bookham)

Night! Black night![14]
Oh Christ but the air bites cold!
The sad beasts shiver
Where dank mists quiver
5 Across the frozen wold,
In the chill moon's churlish light
By night, Black night!

Down! Deep down!
Like the site of a sick soul's dream,
10 Lurks low the hollow
Where none dare follow
The slot of a soundless stream,
That far and far from the town
Hurries down, deep down!

15 Bare! Stark bare!
Are the lonely-huddling trees,
Whose dead leaves cover
As skeletons over
The ways where wanderers freeze
20 If they stop for a moment there
By the branches bending bare!

Haste! Haste away!
There are lights in the lattices lit:
It is ill to tarry
25 Where swart bats carry
A message of fear as they flit,
And I ween the dread hollow is fey,
So away let us haste! Away!
(Summer 1915; 2004)

Anamnesis

The living laugh of the thunder[15]
  That shivers the shuddering air
The billows that break them thereunder,
  On cold cliffs barren and bare,
5 The sob of the sad surf wailing
  A dirge for the fugitive tide,
The sight of the sea-mews trailing
  To where their kindred abide
Beyond the bounds of the ocean
10 When sunset calls to us soft,
The glory and joy in the motion
  Of clouds that hurtle aloft
As feathers that Holda[16] hath shaken—
  Who hath measured? Hath understood
15 The memories strange they awaken,
  The song that they set in our blood?
Who hath loosened the bands of Orion?
  Hath bruisèd the dragon's head?
Or broken the jaws of the lion?
20 Or who at any time said
What secret thing they betoken
  Or measured their might in the scales,
Or told what wraith is awoken
  What voice in our spirit that wails?
25 Though we bid our souls to be sober
  And bury them deep in our flesh.
And chill as a cheerless October
  When winter reneweth afresh
Our days be waxen, yet never
30 The souls will be still, but again
She laugheth and languisheth ever,
  And even as the bubbles of rain
That roll on the lattice and mingle
  And change drawing nigh into one,
35 Or as wavelets that wed on the shingle
  Our hearts go outward; and run
To the sights of beauty and wonder
  Of terror or pain or delight—
The sunset, the foam and the thunder—

40 And out of the fathomless night
Of the past, a shadow floats o'er us
Of things that have been, and are not;
We are bounded behind and before us
With darkness, and who may wot
45 What time, what shore we remember
What strand of the uttermost years
That we thrill as a smouldering ember
New-kindled, to laughter or tears?
Who hath loosened the bands of Orion
50 Or gathered him ghosts from the dead
And trampled on Time, the lion,
To walk with the years that are sped?
(Summer 1915; 2004)

A Prelude

When casements creak and night-winds shriek
And window-panes are patterned o'er
With many a fair fantastic freak
Of felon Frost, and while the door
5 Is rattling restless on his hinge
And cheerful fires leap up amain
The chamber roof with flame to tinge—
I turn me on my bed again.

And then once more forgotten lore
10 And ancient stories old in time
And goodly names long covered o'er
With slumbering ages crusted rime
And worthy lays that did beguile
The kings of old, dance through my brain
15 To stately measures strange, the while
I turn me on my bed again.

Full plain by night each faery wight
Before my drowsy eyes I see,
And sorcerer, and lady white
20 And churl or clown of low degree,

While dusky galleys past me sail
Full-freighted on a faery main,
And silken merchants bid me hail
That turn me on my bed again.

25 And there I wiss were nought amiss
Were I content with faery lore
To con, and faery lips to kiss
And faery songs to murmur o'er,
But I must moil and labour long
30 With tongue untaught and careful pain
To beat my fancies into song,
And toss upon my bed again.

By midnight chimes in winter times
When tempests shook and shivered near
35 Upon my bed I wrought these rhymes—
Ill-done, may hap, and held too dear:
But foolish dreams will not be still,
Till one last dream hold longer reign,
Nor cease their silly songs, until
40 We turn to longer rest again.
(Summer 1915; 1994)[17]

Ballade of a Winter's Morning

The rain is pattering on the leads,
The wasted garden wan and bare
Is flooded o'er its flowerless beds;
So think no more to wander there
5 But rather by this cheerful glare
Draw up beside me, friend by friend
A snugly cushioned easy chair—
A merry morning we shall spend!

And though the rain be on the leads
10 And far-off hills a mantle wear
Of drifting mist about their heads,

Though out to sea the sirens blare
Where ships like pallid phantoms fare
And through the steaming fog-banks wend
15 A chilly way, we'll laugh at care
And make us merry friend by friend!

The rain is pattering on the leads,
But we this crackling blaze will share
And take fit books for drowsy heads
20 To bend above in easy-chair—
Old tomes full oft re-read with care,
Where hoary rhymes and legends blend
With noble pictures rich and rare
To make us merry friend by friend.

25 And while the rain is on the leads
What song-craft sweet shall be our fare?
—The tale where Spenser's magic sheds
A slumberous sweetness on the air
Of charmèd lands,[18] and Horace fair,[19]
30 And Malory who told the end
Of Arthur,[20] and the trumpet-blare
Of him who sang Patroklos' friend.[21]

The rain will cease upon the leads
All soon enough, the garden bare
35 Will blossom in those flowerless beds
When Spring returns with kindly care:
The years shall wax and wither there
Till other feet about it wend
And other lips shall call it fair
40 Than thine or mine, oh friend, my friend.

L'Envoi

So while the wind-foot seasons wear
Be glad, and when towards the end
Adown the dusky ways we fare,
We'll tread them bravely, friend by friend.
(Christmas 1915; 1994)[22]

Sonnet to John Keats

When Pope and Johnson slaughtered poesy,[23]
Long time the fruitless flight of year on year
Was barrenly forlorn, and dark and drear
As some wan Autumn day-break; till in thee
5 A new, sweet pipe from out of faërie
Began to sound, and ere in doubt and fear
Mid deafness cold and coarse, barbarian jeer
It hushed its ditty, for all time to be
It left an echo from the eternal strands
10 That lie about this pool of place and time,
That we might stretch towards them groping hands
And, sailing in a ship of golden rhyme
As though in Mananayne's[24] enchanted boat
Thro sunset seas to Happy Islands float.
(Christmas 1915; 2004)

Yet More of the Wood Desolate

As in the utter places of the earth
Cold awful stillness holds unending reign,
Save when the worm that spans the ocean's girth
And holds our little nations in a chain
5 Heaves up his grisly head twixt strand and strand
And hurls the foam-white waves deep-thundering back to land;

So was there stillness in my gloomy wood
That afternoon. The Autumn day was done,
And through the naked trees, as red as blood
10 The angry splendours of the fading sun
Were streaming, when I sat forlorn, apart,
With claspèd fingers numb, and cold, and sick at heart.

Whiles I thus sat, a down the windless ways
Like the first sob at some grand music's birth,
15 Winter's first breath was born, and in amaze,
Because my soul was sad and far from earth,
Strange things I saw beyond our mortal ken—
Mine eyes were holden not as are the eyes of men.

Soft in the slumbering glade it sighed, and stirred
20 The yellow leaves that lay in drifted piles
Of death: and faint as charmèd bugle heard
O'er leagues of mist in nameless faery isles
The breath blew on and mild and lovingly
It played about my brow and through the hair of me.

25 So when I felt that breeze as cold as death
Playing about my brow, I raised mine eyes
And oh! My God, my soul nigh swooned, my breath
Faltered and failed in fear and strange surprise,
For there, from out her northern summer home
30 Those eyes beheld the Ladie of the Winter come.

Yea, even I beheld the wondrous thing,
And through the wood I watched the Ladie go,
—Of awful form and faultless fashioning
Of limb; with misty weed as wan as snow
35 That girdled was about her shoulders fair
And floating far behind her chilled the shuddering air.

As some wise pigeon on a manor's roof
Throughout a dreaming summer afternoon,
Loiters alone from all his kin aloof
40 Bright in his rainbow throat and rose-red shoon,
Pondering some memory fond of amorous love
And tells and tells again his secret evermore.

Even so she moved, in suchlike slumberous wise
And like a cloud all down the wildwood passed,
45 Gazing around with beautiful, wild eyes
That turned all things to death whereso she cast
Her glance: for golden leaves she turned to brown,
And they that lingered yet on branch fell fluttering down.

And then it seemed she came to me and said
50 With kind caress and kiss of bloodless mouth;
Lay down fond life: the summer days are dead,
The silly birds are set towards the south
And whither they are gone thou canst not go,
—Behold, these lifeless leaves nor moil nor sorrow know.

55 Slumber! And I will fold thee in these arms
And both thy weary eyes fast bounden hold,
In darkness sweet, and scare with potent charms—
The throng of fevered ills thou had'st of old—
The troubling Fear and Hope and Joy and Woe,
60 That, as these lifeless leaves no travail thou shalt know.

Oh come and slumber where no wakenings are!
Cast off thy summer soul! Lay down thy head,
And let the world fade farther and yet more far
Out of thy ken! And if they call it "Dead,"
65 How is it worse than sleep they covet so,
That makes them as these leaves nor moil nor grief to know?

Oh come and slumber where no wakenings are!
And I thy soul in fragrant dreams will steep
Which nevermore life's foolish sounds shall mar;
70 Thy slumber shall be like an ocean deep
Wherein no wavelets stir nor breezes blow
And on whose foamless breast no travail thou shalt know.

Oh come and slumber where no wakenings are!
Lie down where sighs the west-winds's drowsy breath
75 On poppied meades beyond the shadowy bar
That sunders barren life from blissful death,
Come to that land and rest thee, even so
As these pale leaves that wind and rain no more shall know.

She spake: and as that prophet for his king
80 Turned back the dial-shadow, so all time
Ceased for me, till it seemed a little thing
To hearken and obey her trancèd rhyme.
But she passed by and swept the woods along,
Though in the frosty air yet hung her deathly song.

85 But when that lingering cadence died away,
Then woke the heart within me, as from sleep.
I saw the passing of that cheerless day
And heard the far-off plaint of chilly sheep
In frosty grass, and knew that I was cold,
90 And in the work-day world, and eve was waxen old.

So I arose and gat me home again.
But ever, as upon my way I went,
Rang in mine ears the Winter Ladie's strain,
Until I almost would my days were spent
95 That I into the darkness calm might go,
—But ah! towards the sea the weary streams are slow!
(Christmas 1915; 2004)

The Wind

Now make an end of craven, sad complaint!
Come forth! Come forth! The wind is on the fells,
Laughing aloud to quicken hearts that faint—
A secret from some world of mirth he tells
5 And shakes for joy about the whispering dells.

Come forth! Come forth! And leave unhappy care,
Old carking thought and riddles none may know,
To roam instead on boisterous hill-tops bare,
And hear the windy paean of the crow
10 Chime to the cheerful lisp of brooks below.

Come forth! And with mad, unwearied feet,
For all this mad, young world is dancing now—
The pines up on the sky-line bend to meet
The grasses fluttering on the mountain-brow,
15 And buffet each his fellow, bough to bough.

Beneath the flying wisps of feathery cloud
That drive so fast athwart the headlong sky,
The stormed-tossed birds, with voices raised aloud
In garrulous strife or sport go tumbling by
20 And hold their frenzied revelry on high.

Come forth! Come forth! And who shall think today
On human fate and all the tears of Things,
And wisdom, made to steal our joys away?
For while the glad North-Easter shouts and rings
25 About our ears, we'll wear the hearts of kings!

All hail! Oh fair and lovely world! All hail!
All hail! Oh winsome world so blithe and free!
From thy frore northern wastes and icebergs pale
Down to the borders of thine utmost sea—
30 Forgive me that I erst spake ill of thee!
(Christmas 1915; 2004)

New Year's Eve

Yea! We are down, we are broken; the host of the ages goes over
And smothers our laughter and groans with the murmur of mutable years;
Each of them stalks to her end in the web that her destiny wove her,
Red for a raiment of blood, or grey for a garment of tears.
5 We know not the goal of their going, what guerdon we have for our sorrow,
Nor why their feet be of iron, and stony the way that they tread,
Nor if we may look for good tidings and joy of a merciful morrow,
And if there be rest for the souls they have trampled when all shall have sped.
The beetle we crush on the pavement is slain: but we hear not its chiding,
10 No tale of the limbs that are twisted, breast-shattered and broken brain;
And we too? How shall we also cry out to the Thing that is guiding
The years? Shall it hear if we call it? Or hearing, reck of our pain?
Shall a man then pray to the whirlwind, or reason his cause with the thunder?
Shall the winds of the North give an ear to his pleading, or pity his woe?
15 Even so! Our desire is as nought, to the years and their Master: but under
Their heels we are crushed and forever unmoved on their journey they go.
But since this our last old stepdame is weak and her life-day is waning,
Come let us bid her God-speed, or ever she goes on her way,
Clasping the claw that hath torn us: and utter no curse or complaining,
20 For we—we are pitiless too, we have done worse deeds in our day.
(Christmas 1915; 2004)

Laus Mortis

Past the surge and solemn sound of ocean,[25]
Where his river like a dragon curled
Rolls forever with untroubled motion
Round the last lone beaches of the world,

5 Near the full-toned tide a cloudy glade is
Where no wandering sunbeam ever rests;
'Tis the wone[26] of old horse-mastering Hades—
Lord of many thralls and many guests.

Only through the silvery birches quiver
10 Pallid lights more faint than marish-fires,
Where the soft, wan wraiths to Lethe river
Throng to quench their sorrows and desires.

Shadowy hunters there may hunt for shadows
Driving boar and deer through brake and fell,
15 Phantom lovers greet in darkling meadows
On the cold dew-sprinkled asphodel.

Time this people knoweth not, nor treason
Of his guile that steals swift joys away,
Nor this garish pomp of changing season
20 And the interflow of night and day.

These are free alike from joy and sorrow
Love and hate and thoughts that laugh and weep
Dreams may not affright, nor conquering morrow
Break the undawning twilight of their sleep.

25 Sad these hither beaches, where the shingle
Slowly sinks in weed and whispering sedge
Where sea-birds and saddened waters mingle
Songs of sighing at the cold sea's edge.

Cut thy shallop from the shores asunder
30 Child of man, and drift towards the West
Where the pale lights gleam, and drifting wonder
Why so long thou tarriedst from thy rest.
(Easter 1916; 1994)[27]

In His Own Image

Whip me the stunted bards and burn their verse![28]
Misshapen goblins, whipping-boys of fate
Abortions, whose pale sneer and maniac curse
Sit well on lips whose only love is hate.

5 When in the stricken pass of Roncevaux[29]
The good knight Roland, sorely battle-worn
Among the paynim traïtors, will not blow
One blast of succour on his ivory horn.

When in his deathly thirst and burning pain
10 At Zutphen by the Spanish ball o'erthrown,
Young Sydney gives the proffered cup again
To one whose need is greater than his own;[30]

When from the tent where crouching mortals fight
Their desperate cause with death: and all about
15 Rages the horror of the undawning night,
A very gallant gentleman goes out;

I laugh to scorn philosophers that jibe,
Poets and satirists with venomed pen,
Cynics and priests and all the embittered tribe
20 That curse through dwarfish lips the sons of men.
(Easter 1916; 2004)

Sonnet

The clouds are red behind us and before,
The Morrigan[31] is passing through the land
With such a torch of battle in her hand
And such a stare of horror as she wore
5 When to Cuchulain,[32] dauntless knight of yore,
She came in all her wrath, beside the strand
Of that ill river; in such case we stand
In this great darkened world afflicted sore.
But though all else the fates may loose and bind

10 Yet still the sons of men in every plight,
May call their manhood's high estate to mind
And bid their mood be most when least their might,
Or rouse with deeds too high for loftiest rhyme
The echoing trump of unforgetful time.
(Easter 1916; 2004)

Loneliness

Oh! I am weary of the flowers
Untrodden in the lonely vales,
And weary of the shuddering gales
That blow the leaves in eddying showers
5 From solemn trees in shadowy places;
And though I wander all the day
Whiling empty hours away,
Yet no gleam of woodland faces
Through the tangled glen will greet
10 These sad eyes that fain would meet
Flying over stream and lawn
The twinkle of an Oread's feet[33]
Far away, so white and fleet,
Or find old Pan[34] amid the dawn
15 Piping measures shrill and sweet.
But hence! Be gone, unquiet dream,
Leasing false of fabled lore
More fickle than the witch-fire's beam;
The faery people nevermore
20 Shall haunt by holy pool and stream
Or revel on the sad, sea-shore.
For dull and dead is the leaping fountain
And empty all the woodland dusk,
A monstrous mass the purple mountain
25 And meaningless the scent of musk.
Seek no more i' the barren earth
—This dreary puzzle fair-arrayed,
This mask of senseless atoms made—
For any spark of living worth!
30 I tell you, but one spirit dwells

In all the glory of the fells
In all the flowers of the glade—
Ev'n a wan and shrouded maid,
Pale as any priestess sworn
35 To some virgin goddess old.
And when I wander all forlorn
Through the misty Autumn's gold,
Then she watches my distress
Smiles on me and follows near
40 To whisper counsel in my ear,
"Weep not, for none will pity thee
Nor pray, for there is none to hear,"
And thus and thus will counsel she
The ghostly lady, Loneliness.
(Easter 1916; 2004)

The Little Golden Statuette

If fragrant wealth of tangled hair
And living things all warm and fair,
  Dure not beyond a moment's space
But waste and wither everywhere;

5 Then were it better far to mould
Or chisel from refinèd gold
  A faultless limb and luring face
Whose tale was not so swiftly told;

And wiser were the Gods to set
10 A little golden statuette
  To dream forever in the sun
And feel no taint of mortal fret,

Than thus to prison and in-mesh
A spirit in unquiet flesh,—
15 A thing whose work is never done
Whose hunger dies to wax afresh.

We envy sore this image sweet,
The dance of its unwearied feet
    Frozen in joy, its eyes afar
20 Still set its unknown love to greet.

We deem them wise that wrought thee so!
But of their counsel who may know
    That made us men-folk as we are,
Dear golden thing, unlearned of woe?
(Easter 1916; 2004)

Sonnet

I have not bowed in any other shrine
From babyhood, nor sought another god
To worship and with faithless footsteps trod
In any flower-strown path, save only thine
5 Dear poesy. Not Pallas' love divine
Nor red Lyaeus with his ivied rod
Nor Ares with his stern feet brazen-shod
To crush, no Aphrodite's[35] maddening wine
Have turned me back from following after thee
10 And suing still thy flying tracks of song
If but for some curt season thou mayst be
Gracious of heart to him that wooed thee long,
    And grant the lowliest burden of my cry,
    —To make one worthy song before I die.
(Summer 1916; 2001)[36]

Sonnet to Sir Philip Sydney

Oh stainless knight of God, oh fresh young flower
Of manhood pure and faultless chivalry,
Before thy memory still we bow the knee
And turn towards thee in this darkened hour,
5 Who didst not dream in any rose-sweet bower
Sequestered, all thy days, but even as we
Didst battle in the selfsame troublous sea
And loved the terrible voices of its power;
For though in shepherd tale and amorous song
10 We hear the silver chimes of old romance,
Yet not the less the singer's arm was strong
To break in real lists no fabled lance,
  Treading a nobler path than Milton trod,
  To justify the ways of man to God.
(Summer 1916; 1994)[37]

Exercise on an Old Theme

In antique books of wits divine
  Sweet love I oft have read,
Filling this hungry heart of mine
  With gestes of heroes dead.

5 I know the tale of Malory
  And Arthur sore bestead,
In that last battle of the sea,
  —But Arthur's knights are dead.

I know of Tristan's[38] joy and pain
10 That in the wildwood fled,
And still the thought comes back again,
  The loves of old are dead.

Beneath a carrion crowded sky
  The plains of Troy were red,
15 But the ravens rent Patroklos' eye.[39]
  And the Priamid is dead.[40]

And I remember Brynhild old[41]
To craven Gunther wed,[42]
—But the worms know well her hair of gold,
20 For Odin's child is dead.

Their lives and loves and fabled pain
Are all in darkness sped,
And still they leave us one refrain,
—The knights of old are dead.
(Summer 1916; 2004)

Of Ships

Although they tell us that the days are fled
Wherein men loved the labour that they wrought
And fashioned answering beauties to the thought
Before the maker's joy was wholly dead,

5 I think that we have still a happy toil,
Albeit in one craft only, to us left,
One that a burdened age has not yet reft
Nor all our golden tyranny can spoil.

On a boat's deck this morning I was borne
10 Dead slow between the Twins.[43] And there I heard,
More tunable than song of any bird,
A thousand hammers ringing in the morn.

A thousand hammers ringing all for joy
Because the soul of a ship is still the same
15 As when among his father's shipwrights came,
To watch the work, Odysseus, then a boy,

He loved to see the master galley grow
And felt, perhaps, in dreams the spicy breeze
Of lotus-isles, and thought on endless seas
20 That nearest down to the ocean-river flow.

And so today, be it a liner tall,
Black collier, or some galleon of old Spain,
Or some old battered tramp all seamed with pain
The man of honest heart shall love them all.

25 *Argo* or *Golden Hind* or *Mary Lee*,[44]
From every country where man's foot has trod,
Sure they're all ships to brave the winds of God
And have their business in his glorious sea.
(Christmas 1916; 1994)[45]

Couplets

Oh friend, the spring is mad to-day; the trees
Like wintry waves are tossing in the breeze
With rushing music round us and above
The sun is bright on those green hills we love
5 Where now the fresh wind revels and makes mirth
O'er heathery wastes and comfortable earth
But newly-cloven, rich and kind and brown.
There hidden far from this gray careful town
And lifted high towards the rapid clouds
10 We'll see beneath us these unwholesome shrouds
Of hanging mist, these wreaths of dreary smoke,
And all this turmoil of the enthralled folk
That labour. In that place, full well I know
That many an ambling journey we can go;
15 I know the little copses newly dressed
In baby green—time out of mind possessed
By fairy men who nightly habit there
And through long years have made their dwelling fair
With happy toil: nearby the earthy gods
20 Have left their cloven print in the dewy sods
That we may mark with wonder and chaste dread
At hour of noon, when, with our limbs outspread,
Lazily in the whispering grass we lie
To gaze our full upon the windy sky
25 Far, far away, and kindly, friend with friend.
To talk the old, old talk that has no end,

Roaming without a name, without a chart
The unknown garden of another's heart.

I think, if it be truth, as some have taught
30 That these frail seeds of being are not caught
And blown upon the cosmic winds in vain
After our death, but bound in one again
Somewhere, we know not how, they thrive and live
Forever, and the proud gods will not give
35 The comfortable doom of quiet sleep,
Then doubt not but that from the starry deep
And utmost spaces lit by suns unknown
We should return again whence we were flown,
Leaving the bauble of a sainted crown
40 To walk and talk upon the hills of Down.[46]
(Christmas 1916; 1979, 1994)[47]

Hylas

Surely by now I must be dead:[48]
It seems so very long ago
When by the sedgy bank I fled
And heard the cold green river flow
5 With summer murmuring o'er his bed.
I fell. A horrid gloom of night
Covered my eyes, and in my head
There came a singing. . . .
Stay! A light
10 Is trembling yonder into birth,
A moving mass of gold and green
That trembles with a watery sheen,
Aye me! The squalid Charon's firth![49]
Farewell, oh happy glorious earth,
15 Hail and farewell oh comrades dear.
For whom, oh cruel! even now
Ship *Argo* heaves her quivering prow
Above the foam; the joyous cheer
Rises at every bending oar
20 Rises above the loud waves roar . . .

And I shall follow nevermore
The wise prince Jason and the rest
Who sail upon the glorious quest . . .

There comes a murmur in the gloom
25 —Haply my friends about the tomb—
A moving in the shadow dim,
A scent of hair: a smooth, cold limb,
Ah God! . . .
(Christmas 1916; 2004)

Decadence

Oh Galahad![50] My Galahad!
The world is old and very sad,
    The world is old and gray with pain
And all the ways thereof are bad.

5 The bows of story stand unstrung,
The stock from whence the heroes sprung
    Is dead and shall not flower again
And all the song of them is sung.

But off the merry coast of Spain
10 Still hoves[51] the island of Cockayne,[52]
    Where I have found a castle fair
Beside the music of the main.

Where all night long the reddening moon
Swings low towards the warm lagoon
15   To hear the sea-maids singing there
Among the surf a slumberous tune.

There neither hail nor sleet doth fall
Nor any tempest comes at all,
    Nor hate and labour, love and pain,
20 Nor shall the trumps of battle call,

Till from his healing slumber freed
Pale Arthur wake to win the mead
Of glory and go forth again
To help the Brethons[53] at their need.
(Christmas 1916; 2004)[54]

MHΔÈN 'ÁTAN

Some praise the golden mean. Oh peasant law![55]
Made for the hornet-haunted tribe that wail
On this side Styx,[56] cast out from either pale,
The very dross of the world, whom Dante saw,
5 Children of nothing, wisps of windborn straw
Who leave unto the afterborn no tale
Of good or evil. We with fuller sail
Praising excess our compass wider draw.
The journey is so swift and we would taste
10 Somewhat of every city we pass by;
Now to the right, now to the left we haste
Seeking our sport: the others forward ply
Steadily, safely on the beaten way:
And both lie down together at close of the day.
(Easter 1917; 2004)

Ballade on a Certain Pious Gentleman

Oh you are godly, you are wise
You are stuffed full of virtues rare,
Your face is set to one sole prize,
Your bargain driven for heavenly ware:
5 We see and envy, if we dare,
And lowly pray that even we
Some day the grace of God may share
Beside thee, oh mine enemy.

From little, cold and beady eyes
10 From hands like claws to clutch and tear.

What matters it if men surmise
One human frailty lurking there?
'Tis half a virtue, sure, to spare
To grind to pinch that God may be
15 Praised for the money's hoarded fair
Beside thee, oh mine enemy.

Elected, elder of the skies
Lord God Almighty's special care,
Above archangels born to rise,
20 Predestined, 'umble, spotless heir;
No dross of human love to bear
No sinful pity hinders thee—
No child a careless smile could wear
Beside thee, oh mine enemy.

L'Envoy

25 And when you climb the starry stair
(While the wise saints come out to see!)
'Faith, I'd be sooner damned than fare
Beside thee, oh mine enemy!
(Easter 1917; 2004)

Circe—A Fragment

Her couch was of the mighty sea-beast's tusk[57]
With gold and Tyrian scarlet overlaid
Set in a chamber where the wafted musk
With scent of pines a wanton medley made
5 Born on the breeze of every breath that played
Through the wide-pillared arches of her hall.
And there the echoing cool and peaceful shade
Of pallid marble vault and floor and wall
Hung like a tender dream about her palace all.

10 Without, the unbeclouded afternoon
Of an eternal summer drenched with light

Her drifting island, ready half to swoon
Beneath such heavy burden of delight:
The drunken bees forgot their toilsome flight.
15 To slumber in the countless, drooping flowers,
And in the wide blue sea no foam cap white
Was seen, save where it wore the leaden hours
Booming about the rocks and faint green Nereid bowers.[58]
(Easter 1917; 1994)[59]

Exercise

Where are the magic swords
That elves of long ago
Smithied beneath the snow
For heroes' rich rewards?

5 Where are the crowns of gold
That kings for worship wore,
And the banners that they bore
In the battle-edge of old?

Where are the chargers true
10 That bore them in their day,
Bayard and Gringolet
And cloudy Sleipnir too?[60]

Where are the speaking birds
That warned and taught our sires?
15 Where are the dead desires,
And long forgotten words,

The loves, the wisdoms high
The sorrows, where are they?
They are nothing at all today.
20 They are less than you and I.
(Easter 1917; 1994)[61]

Despoina, Bear with Me

Despoina,[62] bear with me
A little longer yet:
In fevered curse and fret
I have borne me evilly.
5 Speaking with madman's breath
Words full of wind and pride,
When I grew dim-eyed
Being near to death.

Morning has come, has come
10 Open the window, sweet,
Day hounds upon the feet
Of night. Lo, I am dumb
I shall not speak again.
(Fall 1917 [?]; 2004)

Poems from Spirits in Bondage: A Cycle of Lyrics *(1919)*[63]

[Epigraph]

The land where I shall never be
The love that I shall never see.[64]

Prologue

As of old Phoenician men, to the Tin Isles sailing[65]
Straight against the sunset and the edges of the earth,
Chaunted loud above the storm and the strange sea's wailing,
Legends of their people and the land that gave them birth—
5 Sang aloud to Baal-Peor,[66] sang unto the horned maiden,
Sang how they should come again with the Brethon treasure laden,[67]
Sang of all the pride and glory of their hardy enterprise,
How they found the outer islands, where the unknown stars arise;
And the rowers down below, rowing hard as they could row,
10 Toiling at the stroke and feather through the wet and weary weather,
Even they forgot their burden in the measure of a song,
And the merchants and the masters and the bondmen all together,
Dreaming of the wondrous islands, brought the gallant ship along;

So in mighty deeps alone on the chainless breezes blown
15 In my coracle of verses I will sing of lands unknown,
Flying from the scarlet city where a Lord that knows no pity
Mocks the broken people praying round his iron throne,
—Sing about the Hidden Country fresh and full of quiet green.
Sailing over seas uncharted to a port that none has seen.
(Fall 1918 [?]; 1919)

Part I
The Prison House

1

Satan Speaks

I am Nature, the Mighty Mother,
I am the law: ye have none other.

I am the flower and the dewdrop fresh,
I am the lust in your itching flesh.

5 I am the battle's filth and strain,
I am the widow's empty pain.

I am the sea to smother your breath,
I am the bomb, the falling death.

I am the fact and the crushing reason
10 To thwart your fantasy's new-born treason.

I am the spider making her net,
I am the beast with jaws blood-wet.

I am a wolf that follows the sun
And I will catch him ere day be done.
(Spring 1918 [?]; 1919)

2

French Nocturne

(Monchy-Le-Preux)

Long leagues on either hand the trenches spread[68]
And all is still; now even this gross line
Drinks in the frosty silences divine,
The pale, green moon is riding overhead.

5 The jaws of a sacked village, stark and grim,
Out on the ridge have swallowed up the sun,
And in one angry streak his blood has run
To left and right along the horizon dim.

There comes a buzzing plane: and now, it seems
10 Flies straight into the moon. Lo! where he steers
Across the pallid globe and surely nears
In that white land some harbour of dear dreams!

False, mocking fancy! Once I too could dream,
Who now can only see with vulgar eye
15 That he's no nearer to the moon than I
And she's a stone that catches the sun's beam.

What call have I to dream of anything?
I am a wolf. Back to the world again,
And speech of fellow-brutes that once were men
20 Our throats can bark for slaughter: cannot sing.
(Spring 1918 [?]; 1919)

3

The Satyr

When the flowery hands of spring[69]
Forth their woodland riches fling,
    Through the meadows, through the valleys
Goes the satyr carolling.

5 From the mountain and the moor,
Forest green and ocean shore
    All the faerie kin he rallies
Making music evermore.

See! the shaggy pelt doth grow
10 On his twisted shanks below,
    And his dreadful feet are cloven
Though his brow be white as snow—

Though his brow be clear and white
And beneath it fancies bright,
15   Wisdom and high thoughts are woven
And the musics of delight,

Though his temples too be fair
Yet two horns are growing there
    Bursting forth to part asunder
20 All the riches of his hair.

Faerie maidens he may meet
Fly the horns and cloven feet,
    But, his sad brown eyes with wonder
Seeing—stay from their retreat.
(Summer 1916; 1919)

4

Victory

Roland is dead, Cuchulain's crest is low,[70]
The battered war-gear wastes and turns to rust,
And Helen's eyes and Iseult's lips are dust[71]
And dust the shoulders and the breasts of snow.

5 The faerie people from our woods are gone,
No Dryads[72] have I found in all our trees.
No Triton[73] blows his horn about our seas
And Arthur[74] sleeps far hence in Avalon.

The ancient songs they wither as the grass
10 And waste as doth a garment waxen old,
All poets have been fools who thought to mould
A monument more durable than brass.

For these decay: but not for that decays
The yearning, high, rebellious spirit of man
15 That never rested yet since life began
From striving with red Nature and her ways.

Now in the filth of war, the baresark[75] shout
Of battle, it is vexed. And yet so oft
Out of the deeps, of old, it rose aloft
20 That they who watch the ages may not doubt.

Though often bruised, oft broken by the rod,
Yet, like the phœnix, from each fiery bed
Higher the stricken spirit lifts its head
And higher—till the beast become a god.
(Easter 1916; 1919)

5

Irish Nocturne

Now the grey mist comes creeping up[76]
From the waste ocean's weedy strand
And fills the valley, as a cup
Is filled of evil drink in a wizard's hand;
5 And the trees fade out of sight,
Like dreary ghosts unhealthily,
Into the damp, pale night,
Till you almost think that a clearer eye could see
Some shape come up of a demon seeking apart
10 His meat, as Grendel sought in Harte
The thanes that sat by the wintry log[77]—
Grendel or the shadowy mass
Of Balor,[78] or the man with the face of clay,
The grey, grey walker who used to pass
15 Over the rock-arch nightly to his prey.
But here at the dumb, slow stream where the willows hang,
With never a wind to blow the mists apart,
Bitter and bitter it is for thee, O my heart,
Looking upon this land, where poets sang,
20 Thus with the dreary shroud
Unwholesome, over it spread,
And knowing the fog and the cloud
In her people's heart and head
Even as it lies for ever upon her coasts
25 Making them dim and dreamy lest her sons should ever arise
And remember all their boasts;
For I know that the colourless skies
And the blurred horizons breed
Lonely desire and many words and brooding and never a deed.
(Easter 1917; 1919)

6

Spooks

Last night I dreamed that I was come again
Unto the house where my belovèd dwells
After long years of wandering and pain.

And I stood out beneath the drenching rain
5 And all the street was bare, and black with night,
But in my true love's house was warmth and light.

Yet I could not draw near nor enter in,
And long I wondered if some secret sin
Or old, unhappy anger held me fast;

10 Till suddenly it came into my head
That I was killed long since and lying dead—
Only a homeless wraith that way had passed.

So thus I found my true love's house again
And stood unseen amid the winter night
15 And the lamp burned within, a rosy light,
And the wet street was shining in the rain.
(Fall 1918 [?]; 1919)[79]

7

Apology

If men should ask,[80] Despoina,[81] why I tell
Of nothing glad nor noble in my verse
To lighten hearts beneath this present curse
And build a heaven of dreams in real hell,

5 Go you to them and speak among them thus:
"There were no greater grief than to recall,
Down in the rotting grave where the lithe worms crawl,
Green fields above that smiled so sweet to us."

Is it good to tell old tales of Troynovant[82]
10 Or praises of dead heroes, tried and sage,
Or sing the queens of unforgotten age,
Brynhild and Maeve and virgin Bradamant?[83]

How should I sing of them? Can it be good
To think of glory now, when all is done,
15 And all our labour underneath the sun
Has brought us this—and not the thing we would?

All these were rosy visions of the night,
The loveliness and wisdom feigned of old.
But now we wake. The East is pale and cold,
20 No hope is in the dawn, and no delight.
(Fall 1917 [?]; 1919)

8

Ode for New Year's Day

Woe unto you, ye sons of pain that are this day in earth,[84]
Now cry for all your torment: now curse your hour of birth
And the fathers who begat you to a portion nothing worth.
And Thou, my own belovèd, for as brave as ere thou art,
5 Bow down thine head, Despoina,[85] clasp thy pale arms over it,
Lie low with fast-closed eyelids, clenched teeth, enduring heart,
For sorrow on sorrow is coming wherein all flesh has part.
The sky above is sickening, the clouds of God's hate cover it,
Body and soul shall suffer beyond all word or thought,
10 Till the pain and noisy terror that these first years have wrought
Seem but the soft arising and prelude of the storm
The fiercer still and heavier with sharper lightnings fraught
Shall pour red wrath upon us over a world deform.

Thrice happy, O Despoina, were the men who were alive
15 In the great age and the golden age when still the cycle ran
On upward curve and easily, for then both maid and man
And beast and tree and spirit in the green earth could thrive.
But now one age is ending, and God calls home the stars
And looses the wheel of the ages and sends it spinning back
20 Amid the death of nations, and points a downward track,
And madness is come over us and great and little wars.
He has not left one valley, one isle of fresh and green
Where old friends could forgather amid the howling wreck.
It's vainly we are praying. We cannot, cannot check
25 The Power who slays and puts aside the beauty that has been.

It's truth they tell, Despoina, none hears the heart's complaining
For Nature will not pity, nor the red God lend an ear.
Yet I too have been mad in the hour of bitter paining
And lifted up my voice to God, thinking that he could hear
30 The curse wherewith I cursed Him because the Good was dead.
But lo! I am grown wiser, knowing that our own hearts
Have made a phantom called the Good, while a few years have sped
Over a little planet. And what should the great Lord know of it
Who tosses the dust of chaos and gives the suns their parts?

35 Hither and thither he moves them; for an hour we see the show of it:
Only a little hour, and the life of the race is done.
And here he builds a nebula, and there he slays a sun
And works his own fierce pleasure. All things he shall fulfill,
And O, my poor Despoina, do you think he ever hears
40 The wail of hearts he has broken, the sound of human ill?
He cares not for our virtues, our little hopes and fears,
And how could it all go on, love, if he knew of laughter and tears?

Ah, sweet, if a man could cheat him! If you could flee away
Into some other country beyond the rosy West,
45 To hide in the deep forests and be for ever at rest
From the rankling hate of God and the outworn world's decay!
(Easter 1917 [?]; 1919)

9

Night

After the fret and failure of this day,[86]
And weariness of thought, O Mother Night,
Come with soft kiss to soothe our care away
And all our little tumults set to right;
5 Most pitiful of all death's kindred fair,
Riding above us through the curtained air
On thy dusk car, thou scatterest to the earth
Sweet dreams and drowsy charms of tender might
And lovers' dear delight before to-morrow's birth.
10 Thus art thou wont thy quiet lands to leave
And pillared courts beyond the Milky Way,
Wherein thou tarriest all our solar day
While unsubstantial dreams before thee weave
A foamy dance, and fluttering fancies play
15 About thy palace in the silver ray
Of some far, moony globe. But when the hour,
The long-expected comes, the ivory gates
Open on noiseless hinge before thy bower
Unbidden, and the jewelled chariot waits
20 With magic steeds. Thou from the fronting rim

Bending to urge them, whilst thy sea-dark hair
Falls in ambrosial ripples o'er each limb,
With beautiful pale arms, untrammelled, bare
For horsemanship, to those twin chargers fleet
25 Dost give full rein across the fires that glow
In the wide floor of heaven, from off their feet
Scattering the powdery star-dust as they go.
Come swiftly down the sky, O Lady Night,
Fall through the shadow-country, O most kind,
30 Shake out thy strands of gentle dreams and light
For chains, wherewith thou still art used to bind
With tenderest love of careful leeches' art
The bruised and weary heart
In slumber blind.
(Summer 1916; 1919)[87]

10

To Sleep

I will find out a place for thee, O Sleep[88]—
A hidden wood among the hill-tops green,
Full of soft streams and little winds that creep
    The murmuring boughs between.

5 A hollow cup above the ocean placed
Where nothing rough, nor loud, nor harsh shall be,
But woodland light and shadow interlaced
    And summer sky and sea.

There in the fragrant twilight I will raise
10 A secret altar of the rich sea sod,
Whereat to offer sacrifice and praise
    Unto my lonely god:

Due sacrifice of his own drowsy flowers,
The deadening poppies in an ocean shell
15 Round which through all forgotten days and hours
    The great seas wove their spell.

So may he send me dreams of dear delight
And draughts of cool oblivion, quenching pain,
And sweet, half-wakeful moments in the night
20   To hear the falling rain.

And when he meets me at the dusk of day
To call me home for ever, this I ask—
That he may lead me friendly on that way
    And wear no frightful mask.
(Easter 1916; 1919)

11

In Prison

I cried out for the pain of man,
I cried out for my bitter wrath
Against the hopeless life that ran
For ever in a circling path
5 From death to death since all began;
Till on a summer night
I lost my way in the pale starlight
And saw our planet, far and small,
Through endless depths of nothing fall
10 A lonely pin-prick spark of light,
Upon the wide, enfolding night,
With leagues on leagues of stars above it,
And powdered dust of stars below—
Dead things that neither hate nor love it
15 Nor even their own loveliness can know,
Being but cosmic dust and dead.
And if some tears be shed,
Some evil God have power,
Some crown of sorrows sit
20 Upon a little world for a little hour—
Who shall remember? Who shall care for it?
(Spring 1918 [?]; 1919)

12

De Profundis

Come let us curse our Master ere we die,[89]
For all our hopes in endless ruin lie.
The good is dead. Let us curse God most High.

Four thousand years of toil and hope and thought
5 Wherein men laboured upward and still wrought
New worlds and better, Thou hast made as naught.

We built us joyful cities, strong and fair,
Knowledge we sought and gathered wisdom rare.
And all this time you laughed upon our care,

10 And suddenly the earth grew black with wrong,
Our hope was crushed and silenced was our song,
The heaven grew loud with weeping. Thou art strong.

Come then and curse the Lord. Over the earth
Gross darkness falls, and evil was our birth
15 And our few happy days of little worth.

Even if it be not all a dream in vain
—The ancient hope that still will rise again—
Of a just God that cares for earthly pain,

Yet far away beyond our labouring night,
20 He wanders in the depths of endless light,
Singing alone his musics of delight;

Only the far, spent echoes of his song
Our dungeons and deep cells can smite along,
And Thou art nearer. Thou art very strong.

25 O universal strength, I know it well,
It is but froth of folly to rebel,
For thou art Lord and hast the keys of Hell.

Yet I will not bow down to thee nor love thee,
For looking in my own heart I can prove thee,
30 And know this frail, bruised being is above thee.

Our love, our hope, our thirsting for the right,
Our mercy and long seeking of the light,
Shall we change these for thy relentless might?

Laugh then and slay. Shatter all things of worth,
35 Heap torment still on torment for thy mirth—
Thou art not Lord while there are Men on earth.
(Spring 1918 [?]; 1919)

13

Satan Speaks

I am the Lord your God: even he that made
Material things, and all these signs arrayed
Above you and have set beneath the race
Of mankind, who forget their Father's face
5 And even while they drink my light of day
Dream of some other gods and disobey
My warnings, and despise my holy laws,
Even tho' their sin shall slay them. For which cause,
Dreams dreamed in vain, a never-filled desire
10 And in close flesh a spiritual fire,
A thirst for good their kind shall not attain,
A backward cleaving to the beast again.
A loathing for the life that I have given,
A haunted, twisted soul for ever riven
15 Between their will and mine—such lot I give
While still in my despite the vermin live.
They hate my world! Then let that other God
Come from the outer spaces glory-shod,
And from this castle I have built on Night
20 Steal forth my own thought's children into light,
If such an one there be. But far away
He walks the airy fields of endless day,
And my rebellious sons have called Him long

And vainly called. My order still is strong
25 And like to me nor second none I know.
Whither the mammoth went this creature too shall go.
(Spring 1918 [?]; 1919)

14

The Witch

Trapped amid the woods with guile
They've led her bound in fetters vile
To death, a deadlier sorceress
Than any born for earth's distress
5 Since first the winner of the fleece
Bore home the Colchian witch to Greece[90]—
Seven months with snare and gin
They've sought the maid o'erwise within
The forest's labyrinthine shade.
10 The lonely woodman half afraid
Far off her ragged form has seen
Sauntering down the alleys green,
Or crouched in godless prayer alone
At eve before a Druid stone.
15 But now the bitter chase is won,
The quarry's caught, her magic's done,
The bishop's brought her strongest spell
To naught with candle, book, and bell;
With holy water splashed upon her,
20 She goes to burning and dishonour
Too deeply damned to feel her shame,
For, though beneath her hair of flame
Her thoughtful head be lowly bowed
It droops for meditation proud
25 Impenitent, and pondering yet
Things no memory can forget,
Starry wonders she has seen
Brooding in the wildwood green
With holiness. For who can say
30 In what strange crew she loved to play,
What demons or what gods or old

Deep mysteries unto her have told
At dead of night in worship bent
At ruined shrines magnificent,
35 Or how the quivering will she sent
Alone into the great alone
Where all is loved and all is known,
Who now lifts up her maiden eyes
And looks around with soft surprise
40 Upon the noisy, crowded square,
The city oafs that nod and stare,
The bishop's court that gathers there,
The faggots and the blackened stake
Where sinners die for justice' sake?
45 Now she is set upon the pile,
The mob grows still a little while,
Till lo! before the eager folk
Up curls a thin, blue line of smoke.
"Alas!" the full-fed burghers cry,
50 "That evil loveliness must die!"
(Summer 1918 [?]; 1919)

15

Dungeon Grates

So piteously the lonely soul of man
Shudders before this universal plan,
So grievous is the burden and the pain,
So heavy weighs the long, material chain
5 From cause to cause, too merciless for hate,
The nightmare march of unrelenting fate,
I think that he must die thereof unless
Ever and again across the dreariness
There came a sudden glimpse of spirit faces,
10 A fragrant breath to tell of flowery places
And wider oceans, breaking on the shore
For which the hearts of men are always sore.
It lies beyond endeavour; neither prayer
Nor fasting, nor much wisdom winneth there,
15 Seeing how many prophets and wise men

Have sought for it and still returned again
With hope undone. But only the strange power
Of unsought Beauty in some casual hour
Can build a bridge of light or sound or form
20 To lead you out of all this strife and storm;
When of some beauty we are grown a part
Till from its very glory's midmost heart
Out leaps a sudden beam of larger light
Into our souls. All things are seen aright
25 Amid the blinding pillar of its gold,
Seven times more true than what for truth we hold
In vulgar hours. The miracle is done
And for one little moment we are one
With the eternal stream of loveliness
30 That flows so calm, aloof from all distress
Yet leaps and lives around us as a fire
Making us faint with overstrong desire
To sport and swim for ever in its deep—
Only a moment.
35 O! but we shall keep
Our vision still. One moment was enough,
We know we are not made of mortal stuff.
And we can bear all trials that come after,
The hate of men and the fool's loud bestial laughter
40 And Nature's rule and cruelties unclean,
For we have seen the Glory—we have seen.
(Spring 1918 [?]; 1919)

16

The Philosopher

Who shall be our prophet then,[91]
Chosen from all the sons of men
To lead his fellows on the way
Of hidden knowledge, delving deep
5 To nameless mysteries that keep
Their secret from the solar day!
Or who shall pierce with surer eye
This shifting veil of bittersweet

And find the real things that lie
10 Beyond this turmoil, which we greet
With such a wasted wealth of tears?
Who shall cross over for us the bridge of fears
And pass in to the country where the ancient Mothers dwell?
Is it an elder, bent and hoar
15 Who, where the waste Atlantic swell
On lonely beaches makes its roar,
In his solitary tower
Through the long night hour by hour
Pores on old books with watery eye
20 When all his youth has passed him by,
And folly is schooled and love is dead
And frozen fancy laid abed,
While in his veins the gradual blood
Slackens to a marish flood?
25 For he rejoiceth not in the ocean's might,
Neither the sun giveth delight,
Nor the moon by night
Shall call his feet to wander in the haunted forest lawn.
He shall no more rise suddenly in the dawn
30 When mists are white and the dew lies pearly
Cold and cold on every meadow,
To take his joy of the season early,
The opening flower and the westward shadow,
And scarcely can he dream of laughter and love,
35 They lie so many leaden years behind.
Such eyes are dim and blind,
And the sad, aching head that nods above
His monstrous books can never know
The secret we would find.
40 But let our seer be young and kind
And fresh and beautiful of show,
And taken ere the lustyhead
And rapture of his youth be dead,
Ere the gnawing, peasant reason
45 School him over-deep in treason
To the ancient high estate
Of his fancy's principate,
That he may live a perfect whole,

A mask of the eternal soul,
50 And cross at last the shadowy bar
To where the ever-living are.
(Easter 1917; 1919)

17

The Ocean Strand

O leave the labouring roadways of the town,[92]
The shifting faces and the changeful hue
Of markets, and broad echoing streets that drown
The heart's own silent music. Though they too
5 Sing in their proper rhythm, and still delight
The friendly ear that loves warm human kind,
Yet it is good to leave them all behind,
Now when from lily dawn to purple night
Summer is queen,
10 Summer is queen in all the happy land.
Far, far away among the valleys green
Let us go forth and wander hand in hand
Beyond those solemn hills that we have seen
So often welcome home the falling sun
15 Into their cloudy peaks when day was done—
Beyond them till we find the ocean strand
And hear the great waves run,
With the waste song whose melodies I'd follow
And weary not for many a summer day,
20 Born of the vaulted breakers arching hollow
Before they flash and scatter into spray.
On, if we should be weary of their play
Then I would lead you further into land
Where, with their ragged walls, the stately rocks
25 Shut in smooth courts and paved with quiet sand
To silence dedicate. The sea-god's flocks
Have rested here, and mortal eyes have seen
By great adventure at the dead of noon
A lonely nereid drowsing half a-swoon
30 Buried beneath her dark and dripping locks.
(Christmas 1916; 1919)

18

Noon

Noon! and in the garden bower[93]
The hot air quivers o'er the grass,
The little lake is smooth as glass
And still so heavily the hour
5 Drags, that scarce the proudest flower
Pressed upon its burning bed
Has strength to lift a languid head:
—Rose and fainting violet
By the water's margin set
10 Swoon and sink as they were dead
Though their weary leaves be fed
With foam-drops of the pool
Where it trembles dark and cool,
Wrinkled by the fountain spraying
15 O'er it. And the honey-bee
Hums his drowsy melody
And wanders in his course a-straying
Through the sweet and tangled glade
With his golden mead o'erladen,
20 Where beneath the pleasant shade
Of the darkling boughs a maiden
—Milky limb and fiery tress,
All at sweetest random laid—
Slumbers, drunken with the excess
25 Of the noontide's loveliness.
(Christmas 1915; 1919)[94]

19

Milton Read Again
(In Surrey)

Three golden months while summer on us stole[95]
I have read your joyful tale another time,
Breathing more freely in that larger clime
And learning wiselier to deserve the whole.

5 Your Spirit, Master,[96] has been close at hand
And guided me, still pointing treasures rare,
Thick-sown where I before saw nothing fair
And finding waters in the barren land,

Barren once thought because my eyes were dim.
10 Like one I am grown to whom the common field
And often-wandered copse one morning yield
New pleasures suddenly; for over him

Falls the weird spirit of unexplained delight,
New mystery in every shady place,
15 In every whispering tree a nameless grace,
New rapture on the windy seaward height.

So may she come to me, teaching me well
To savour all these sweets that lie to hand
In wood and lane about this pleasant land
20 Though it be not the land where I would dwell.
(Easter 1917; 1919)

20

Sonnet

The stars come out; the fragrant shadows fall[97]
About a dreaming garden still and sweet,
I hear the unseen bats above me bleat
Among the ghostly moths their hunting call,
5 And twinkling glow-worms all about me crawl.
Now for a chamber dim, a pillow meet
For slumbers deep as death, a faultless sheet,
Cool, white and smooth. So may I reach the hall
With poppies strewn where sleep that is so dear
10 With magic sponge can wipe away an hour
Or twelve and make them naught. Why not a year,
Why could a man not loiter in that bower
Until a thousand painless cycles wore,
And then—what if it held him evermore?
(Christmas 1915; 1919)

21

The Autumn Morning

See! the pale autumn dawn[98]
Is faint, upon the lawn
That lies in powdered white
Of hoar-frost dight.

5 And now from tree to tree
The ghostly mist we see
Hung like a silver pall
To hallow all.

It wreathes the burdened air
10 So strangely everywhere
That I could almost fear
This silence drear

Where no one song-bird sings
And dream that wizard things
15 Mighty for hate or love
Were close above.

White as the fog and fair
Drifting through middle air
In magic dances dread
20 Over my head.

Yet these should know me too
Lover and bondman true,
One that has honoured well
The mystic spell

25 Of earth's most solemn hours
Wherein the ancient powers
Of dryad, elf, or faun
Or leprechaun

Oft have their faces shown
30 To me that walked alone
Seashore or haunted fen
Or mountain glen.

Wherefore I will not fear
To walk the woodlands sere
35 Into this autumn day
Far, far away.
(Summer 1916; 1919)

Part II
Hesitation

22

L'apprenti Sorcier

Suddenly there came to me[99]
The music of a mighty sea
That on a bare and iron shore
Thundered with a deeper roar
5 Than all the tides that leap and run
With us below the real sun:
Because the place was far away,
Above, beyond our homely day,
Neighbouring close the frozen clime
10 Where out of all the woods of time,
Amid the frightful seraphim
The fierce, cold eyes of Godhead gleam,
Revolving hate and misery
And wars and famines yet to be.
15 And in my dream I stood alone
Upon a shelf of weedy stone,
And saw before my shrinking eyes
The dark, enormous breakers rise,
And hover and fall with deafening thunder
20 Of thwarted foam that echoed under
The ledge, through many a cavern drear,
With hollow sounds of wintry fear.
And through the waters waste and grey,
Thick-strown for many a league away,
25 Out of the toiling sea arose
Many a face and form of those
Thin, elemental people dear
Who live beyond our heavy sphere.
And all at once from far and near,
30 They all held out their arms to me,
Crying in their melody,
"Leap in! Leap in, and take thy fill

Of all the cosmic good and ill,
Be as the Living ones that know
35 Enormous joy, enormous woe,
Pain beyond thought and fiery bliss:
For all thy study hunted this,
On wings of magic to arise,
And wash from off thy filmèd eyes
40 The cloud of cold mortality,
To find the real life and be
As are the children of the deep!
Be bold and dare the glorious leap,
Or to thy shame, go, slink again
45 Back to the narrow ways of men."
So all these mocked me as I stood
Striving to wake because I feared the flood.
(Easter 1917; 1919)

23

Alexandrines

There is a house that most of all on earth I hate.
Though I have passed through many sorrows and have been
In bloody fields, sad seas, and countries desolate,
Yet most I fear that empty house where the grasses green
5 Grow in the silent court the gaping flags between,
And down the moss-grown paths and terrace no man treads
Where the old, old weeds rise deep on the waste garden beds.
Like eyes of one long dead the empty windows stare
And I fear to cross the garden, I fear to linger there,
10 For in that house I know a little, silent room
Where Someone's always waiting, waiting in the gloom
To draw me with an evil eye, and hold me fast—
Yet thither doom will drive me and He will win at last.
(Fall 1918 [?]; 1919)

24

In Praise of Solid People

Thank God that there are solid folk
Who water flowers and roll the lawn,
And sit and sew and talk and smoke,
And snore all through the summer dawn.

5 Who pass untroubled nights and days
Full-fed and sleepily content,
Rejoicing in each other's praise,
Respectable and innocent.

Who feel the things that all men feel,
10 And think in well-worn grooves of thought,
Whose honest spirits never reel
Before man's mystery, overwrought.

Yet not unfaithful nor unkind,
With work-day virtues surely staid,
15 Theirs is the sane and humble mind,
And dull affections undismayed.

O happy people! I have seen
No verse yet written in your praise,
And, truth to tell, the time has been
20 I would have scorned your easy ways.

But now thro' weariness and strife
I learn your worthiness indeed,
The world is better for such life
As stout, suburban people lead.

25 Too often have I sat alone
When the wet night falls heavily,
And fretting winds around me moan,
And homeless longing vexes me

For lore that I shall never know,
30 And visions none can hope to see,

Till brooding works upon me so
A childish fear steals over me.

I look around the empty room,
The clock still ticking in its place,
35 And all else silent as the tomb,
Till suddenly, I think, a face

Grows from the darkness just beside.
I turn, and lo! it fades away,
And soon another phantom tide
40 Of shifting dreams begins to play,

And dusky galleys past me sail,
Full freighted on a faerie sea;
I hear the silken merchants hail
Across the ringing waves to me

45 —Then suddenly, again, the room,
Familiar books about me piled,
And I alone amid the gloom,
By one more mocking dream beguiled.

And still no nearer to the Light,
50 And still no further from myself,
Alone and lost in clinging night
—(The clock's still ticking on the shelf).

Then do I envy solid folk
Who sit of evenings by the fire,
55 After their work and doze and smoke,
And are not fretted by desire.
(Christmas 1916 [?]; 1919)

Part III

The Escape

25

Song of the Pilgrims

O Dwellers at the back of the North Wind,[100]
What have we done to you? How have we sinned
Wandering the Earth from Orkney unto Ind?[101]

With many deaths our fellowship is thinned,
5 Our flesh is withered in the parching wind,
Wandering the earth from Orkney unto Ind.

We have no rest. We cannot turn again
Back to the world and all her fruitless pain,
Having once sought the land where ye remain.

10 Some say ye are not. But, ah God! we know
That somewhere, somewhere past the Northern snow
Waiting for us the red-rose gardens blow:

—The red-rose and the white-rose gardens blow
In the green Northern land to which we go,
15 Surely the ways are long and the years are slow.

We have forsaken all things sweet and fair,
We have found nothing worth a moment's care
Because the real flowers are blowing there.

Land of the Lotus fallen from the sun,
20 Land of the Lake from whence all rivers run,
Land where the hope of all our dreams is won!

Shall we not somewhere see at close of day
The green walls of that country far away,
And hear the music of her fountains play?

25 So long we have been wandering all this while
By many a perilous sea and drifting isle,
We scarce shall dare to look thereon and smile.

Yea, when we are drawing very near to thee,
And when at last the ivory port we see
30 Our hearts will faint with mere felicity:

But we shall wake again in gardens bright
Of green and gold for infinite delight,
Sleeping beneath the solemn mountains white,

While from the flowery copses still unseen
35 Sing out the crooning birds that ne'er have been
Touched by the hand of winter frore and lean;

And ever living queens that grow not old
And poets wise in robes of faerie gold
Whisper a wild, sweet song that first was told

40 Ere God sat down to make the Milky Way.
And in those gardens we shall sleep and play
For ever and for ever and a day.

Ah, Dwellers at the back of the North Wind,
What have we done to you? How have we sinned,
45 That ye should hide beyond the Northern wind?

Land of the Lotus, fallen from the Sun,
When shall your hidden, flowery vales be won
And all the travail of our way be done?

Very far we have searched; we have even seen
50 The Scythian waste that bears no soft nor green,
And near the Hideous Pass our feet have been.

We have heard the Syrens singing all night long
Beneath the unknown stars their lonely song
In friendless seas beyond the Pillars strong.[102]

55 Nor by the dragon-daughter of Hypocras[103]
Nor the vale of the Devil's head[104] we have feared to pass,
Yet is our labour lost and vain, alas!

Scouring the earth from Orkney unto Ind,
Tossed on the seas and withered in the wind,
60 We seek and seek your land. How have we sinned?

Or is it all a folly of the wise,
Bidding us walk these ways with blinded eyes
While all around us real flowers arise?

But, by the very God, we know, we know
65 That somewhere still, beyond the Northern snow
Waiting for us the red-rose gardens blow.
(Easter 1917; 1919)

26

Song

Faeries must be in the woods
Or the satyrs' laughing broods—
Tritons in the summer sea,
Else how could the dead things be
5 Half so lovely as they are?
How could wealth of star on star
Dusted o'er the frosty night
Fill thy spirit with delight
And lead thee from this care of thine
10 Up among the dreams divine,
Were it not that each and all
Of them that walk the heavenly hall
Is in truth a happy isle,
Where eternal meadows smile,
15 And golden globes of fruit are seen
Twinkling through the orchards green;
Where the Other People go
On the bright sward to and fro?
Atoms dead could never thus

20 Stir the human heart of us
Unless the beauty that we see
The veil of endless beauty be,
Filled full of spirits that have trod
Far hence along the heavenly sod
25 And seen the bright footprints of God.
(May 1918; 1919)[105]

27

The Ass

I woke and rose and slipt away
To the heathery hills in the morning grey.

In a field where the dew lay cold and deep
I met an ass, new-roused from sleep.

5 I stroked his nose and I tickled his ears,
And spoke soft words to quiet his fears.

His eyes stared into the eyes of me
And he kissed my hands of his courtesy.

"O big, brown brother out of the waste,
10 How do thistles for breakfast taste?

"And do you rejoice in the dawn divine
With a heart that is glad no less than mine?

"For, brother, the depth of your gentle eyes
Is strange and mystic as the skies:

15 "What are the thoughts that grope behind,
Down in the mist of a donkey mind?

"Can it be true, as the wise men tell,
That you are a mask of God as well,

"And, as in us, so in you no less
20 Speaks the eternal Loveliness,

"And words of the lips that all things know
Among the thoughts of a donkey go?

"However it be, O four-foot brother,
Fair to-day is the earth, our mother.

25 "God send you peace and delight thereof,
And all green meat of the waste you love,

"And guard you well from violent men
Who'd put you back in the shafts again."

But the ass had far too wise a head
30 To answer one of the things I said,

So he twitched his fair ears up and down
And turned to nuzzle his shoulder brown.
(Easter 1915 [?]; 1919)

28

Ballade Mystique

The big, red house is bare and lone[106]
The stony garden waste and sere
With blight of breezes ocean blown
To pinch the wakening of the year;
5 My kindly friends with busy cheer
My wretchedness could plainly show.
They tell me I am lonely here—
What do they know? What do they know?

They think that while the gables moan
10 And casements creak in winter drear
I should be piteously alone
Without the speech of comrades dear;
And friendly for my sake they fear,

It grieves them thinking of me so
15 While all their happy life is near—
What do they know? What do they know?

That I have seen the Dagda's throne[107]
In sunny lands without a tear
And found a forest all my own
20 To ward with magic shield and spear,
Where, through the stately towers I rear
For my desire, around me go
Immortal shapes of beauty clear:
They do not know, they do not know.

L'ENVOI

25 The friends I have without a peer
Beyond the western ocean's glow,
Whither the faerie galleys steer,
They do not know: how should they know?
(Easter 1917; 1919)[108]

29

Night

I know a little Druid wood[109]
Where I would slumber if I could
And have the murmuring of the stream
To mingle with a midnight dream,
5 And have the holy hazel trees
To play above me in the breeze,
And smell the thorny eglantine;
For there the white owls all night long
In the scented gloom divine
10 Hear the wild, strange, tuneless song
Of faerie voices, thin and high
As the bat's unearthly cry,
And the measure of their shoon
Dancing, dancing, under the moon,
15 Until, amid the pale of dawn
The wandering stars begin to swoon. . . .

Ah, leave the world and come away!
The windy folk are in the glade,
And men have seen their revels, laid
20 In secret on some flowery lawn
Underneath the beechen covers.
Kings of old, I've heard them say,
Here have found them faerie lovers
That charmed them out of life and kissed
25 Their lips with cold lips unafraid,
And such a spell around them made
That they have passed beyond the mist
And found the Country-under-wave. . . .

Kings of old, whom none could save!
(Easter 1916; 1919)

30

Oxford

It is well that there are palaces of peace
And discipline and dreaming and desire,
Lest we forget our heritage and cease
The Spirit's work—to hunger and aspire:

5 Lest we forget that we were born divine,
Now tangled in red battle's animal net,
Murder the work and lust the anodyne,
Pains of the beast 'gainst bestial solace set.

But this shall never be: to us remains
10 One city that has nothing of the beast,
That was not built for gross, material gains,
Sharp, wolfish power or empire's glutted feast.

We are not wholly brute. To us remains
A clean, sweet city lulled by ancient streams,
15 A place of vision and of loosening chains,
A refuge of the elect, a tower of dreams.

She was not builded out of common stone
But out of all men's yearning and all prayer
That she might live, eternally our own,
20 The Spirit's stronghold—barred against despair.
(Spring 1918 [?]; 1919)

31

Hymn (For Boys' Voices)

All the things magicians do
Could be done by me and you
Freely, if we only knew.

Human children every day
5 Could play at games the faeries play
If they were but shown the way.

Every man a God would be
Laughing through eternity
If as God's his eye could see.

10 All the wizardries of God—
Slaying matter with a nod,
Charming spirits with his rod,

With the singing of his voice
Making lonely lands rejoice,
15 Leaving us no will nor choice,

Drawing headlong me and you
As the piping Orpheus drew
Man and beast the mountains through,[110]

By the sweetness of his horn
20 Calling us from lands forlorn
Nearer to the widening morn—

All that loveliness of power
Could be man's peculiar dower,
Even mine, this very hour;

25 We should reach the Hidden Land
And grow immortal out of hand,
If we could but understand!

We could revel day and night
In all power and all delight
30 If we learned to think aright.
(Spring 1918 [?]; 1919)

32

"Our Daily Bread"

We need no barbarous words nor solemn spell[111]
To raise the unknown. It lies before our feet;
There have been men who sank down into Hell
In some suburban street,

5 And some there are that in their daily walks
Have met archangels fresh from sight of God,
Or watched how in their beans and cabbage-stalks
Long files of faerie trod.

Often me too the Living voices call
10 In many a vulgar and habitual place,
I catch a sight of lands beyond the wall,
I see a strange god's face.

And some day this will work upon me so
I shall arise and leave both friends and home
15 And over many lands a pilgrim go
Through alien woods and foam,

Seeking the last steep edges of the earth
Whence I may leap into that gulf of light
Wherein, before my narrowing Self had birth,
20 Part of me lived aright.
(Fall 1918 [?]; 1919)

33

How He Saw Angus the God

I heard the swallow sing in the eaves and rose[112]
All in a strange delight while others slept,
And down the creaking stair, alone, tip-toes,
So carefully I crept.

5 The house was dark with silly blinds yet drawn,
But outside the clean air was filled with light,
And underneath my feet the cold, wet lawn
With dew was twinkling bright.

The cobwebs hung from every branch and spray
10 Gleaming with pearly strands of laden thread,
And long and still the morning shadows lay
Across the meadows spread.

At that pure hour when yet no sound of man,
Stirs in the whiteness of the wakening earth,
15 Alone through innocent solitudes I ran
Singing aloud for mirth.

Till I had found the open mountain heath
Yellow with gorse, and rested there and stood
To gaze upon the misty sea beneath,
20 Or on the neighbouring wood,

—That little wood of hazel and tall pine
And youngling fir, where oft we have loved to see
The level beams of early morning shine
Freshly from tree to tree.

25 Though in the denser wood there's many a pool
Of deep and night-born shadow lingers yet
Where the new-wakened flowers are damp and cool
And the long grass is wet.

In the sweet heather long I rested there
30 Looking upon the dappled, early sky,
When suddenly, from out the shining air
A god came flashing by.

Swift, naked, eager, pitilessly fair,
With a live crown of birds about his head,
35 Singing and fluttering, and his fiery hair,
Far out behind him spread,

Streamed like a rippling torch upon the breeze
Of his own glorious swiftness: in the grass
He bruised no feathery stalk, and through the trees
40 I saw his whiteness pass.

But, when I followed him beyond the wood,
Lo! he was changed into a solemn bull
That there upon the open pasture stood
And browsed his lazy full.
(Christmas 1916; 1919)

34

The Roads

I stand on the windy uplands among the hills of Down[113]
With all the world spread out beneath, meadow and sea and town,
And ploughlands on the far-off hills that glow with friendly brown.

And ever across the rolling land to the far horizon line,
5 Where the blue hills border the misty west, I see the white roads twine,
The rare roads and the fair roads that call this heart of mine.

I see them dip in the valleys and vanish and rise and bend
From shadowy dell to windswept fell, and still to the West they wend,
And over the cold blue ridge at last to the great world's uttermost end.

10 And the call of the roads is upon me, a desire in my spirit has grown
To wander forth in the highways, 'twixt earth and sky alone,
And seek for the lands no foot has trod and the seas no sail has known:

—For the lands to the west of the evening and east of the morning's birth,
Where the gods unseen in their valleys green are glad at the ends of earth
15 And fear no morrow to bring them sorrow, nor night to quench their mirth.
(Easter 1916; 1919)

35

Hesperus

Through the starry hollow[114]
Of the summer night
I would follow, follow
Hesperus the bright,
5 To seek beyond the western wave
His garden of delight.

Hesperus the fairest
Of all gods that are,
Peace and dreams thou bearest
10 In thy shadowy car,
And often in my evening walks
I've blessed thee from afar.

Stars without a number,
Dust the noon of night,
15 Thou the early slumber
And the still delight
Of the gentle twilit hours
Rulest in thy right.

When the pale skies shiver,
20 Seeing night is done,
Past the ocean-river,
Lightly thou dost run,
To look for pleasant, sleepy lands,
That never fear the sun.

25 Where, beyond the waters
Of the outer sea,
Thy triple crown of daughters

That guards the golden tree
Sing out across the lonely tide
30 A welcome home to thee.

And while the old, old dragon
For joy lifts up his head,
They bring thee forth a flagon
Of nectar foaming red,
35 And underneath the drowsy trees
Of poppies strew thy bed.

Ah! that I could follow
In thy footsteps bright,
Through the starry hollow
40 Of the summer night,
Sloping down the western ways
To find my heart's delight!
(Christmas 1916; 1919)

36

The Star Bath

A place uplifted towards the midnight sky[115]
Far, far away among the mountains old,
A treeless waste of rocks and freezing cold,
Where the dead, cheerless moon rode neighbouring by—
5 And in the midst a silent tarn there lay,
A narrow pool, cold as the tide that flows
Where monstrous bergs beyond Varanger stray,[116]
Rising from sunless depths that no man knows;
Thither as clustering fireflies have I seen
10 At fixèd seasons all the stars come down
To wash in that cold wave their brightness clean
And win the special fire wherewith they crown
The wintry heavens in frost. Even as a flock
Of falling birds, down to the pool they came.
15 I saw them and I heard the icy shock
Of stars engulfed with hissing of faint flame

—Ages ago before the birth of men
Or earliest beast. Yet I was still the same
That now remember, knowing not where or when.
(Summer 1916; 1919)[117]

37

Tu Ne Quæsieris

For all the lore of Lodge and Myers[118]
I cannot heal my torn desires,[119]
Nor hope for all that man can speer
To make the riddling earth grow clear.
5 Though it were sure and proven well
That I shall prosper, as they tell,
In fields beneath a different sun
By shores where other oceans run,
When this live body that was I
10 Lies hidden from the cheerful sky,
Yet what were endless lives to me
If still my narrow self I be
And hope and fail and struggle still,
And break my will against God's will,
15 To play for stakes of pleasure and pain
And hope and fail and hope again,
Deluded, thwarted, striving elf
That through the window of my self
As through a dark glass scarce can see
20 A warped and masked reality?[120]
But when this searching thought of mine
Is mingled in the large Divine,
And laughter that was in my mouth
Runs through the breezes of the South,
25 When glory I have built in dreams
Along some fiery sunset gleams,
And my dead sin and foolishness
Grow one with Nature's whole distress,
To perfect being I shall win,
30 And where I end will Life begin.
(Fall 1918 [?]; 1919)

38

Lullaby

Lullaby! Lullaby![121]
There's a tower strong and high
Built of oak and brick and stone,
Stands before a wood alone.
5 The doors are of the oak so brown
As any ale in Oxford town,
The walls are builded warm and thick
Of the old red Roman brick,
The good grey stone is over all
10 In arch and floor of the tower hall.
And maidens three are living there
All in the upper chamber fair,
Hung with silver, hung with pall,
And stories painted on the wall.
15 And softly goes the whirring loom
In my ladies' upper room,
For they shall spin both night and day
Until the stars do pass away.
But every night at evèning
20 The window open wide they fling,
And one of them says a word they know
And out as three white swans they go,
And the murmuring of the woods is drowned
In the soft wings' whirring sound,
25 As they go flying round, around,
Singing in swans' voices high
A lonely, lovely lullaby.
(Fall 1917 [?]; 1919)

39

World's Desire

Love, there is a castle built in a country desolate,[122]
On a rock above a forest where the trees are grim and great,
Blasted with the lightning sharp—giant boulders strewn between,
And the mountains rise above, and the cold ravine
5 Echoes to the crushing roar and thunder of a mighty river
Raging down a cataract. Very tower and forest quiver
And the grey wolves are afraid and the call of birds is drowned,
And the thought and speech of man in the boiling water's sound.
But upon the further side of the barren, sharp ravine
10 With the sunlight on its turrets is the castle seen,
Calm and very wonderful, white above the green
Of the wet and waving forest, slanted all away,
Because the driving Northern wind will not rest by night or day.
Yet the towers are sure above, very mighty is the stead,
15 The gates are made of ivory, the roofs of copper red.

Round and round the warders grave walk upon the walls for ever
And the wakeful dragons couch in the ports of ivory,
Nothing is can trouble it, hate of the gods nor man's endeavour,
And it shall be a resting-place, dear heart, for you and me.

20 Through the wet and waving forest with an age-old sorrow laden
Singing of the world's regret wanders wild the faerie maiden,
Through the thistle and the brier, through the tangles of the thorn,
Till her eyes be dim with weeping and her homeless feet are torn.
Often to the castle gate up she looks with vain endeavour,
25 For her soulless loveliness to the castle winneth never.

But within the sacred court, hidden high upon the mountain,
Wandering in the castle gardens lovely folk enough there be,
Breathing in another air, drinking of a purer fountain
And among that folk, beloved, there's a place for you and me.
(Fall 1917 [?]; 1919)

40

Death in Battle

Open the gates for me,[123]
Open the gates of the peaceful castle, rosy in the West,
In the sweet dim Isle of Apples[124] over the wide sea's breast,
Open the gates for me!

5 Sorely pressed have I been
And driven and hurt beyond bearing this summer day,
But the heat and the pain together suddenly fall away,
All's cool and green.

But a moment agone,
10 Among men cursing in fight and toiling, blinded I fought,
But the labour passed on a sudden even as a passing thought,
And now—alone!

Ah, to be ever alone,
In flowery valleys among the mountains and silent wastes untrod,
15 In the dewy upland places, in the garden of God,
This would atone!

I shall not see
The brutal, crowded faces around me, that in their toil have grown
Into the faces of devils—yea, even as my own—
20 When I find thee,

O Country of Dreams!
Beyond the tide of the ocean, hidden and sunk away,
Out of the sound of battles, near to the end of day,
Full of dim woods and streams.
(Fall 1917 [?]; 1919)

Also from 1915–1919

Nimue

There was none stirring in the hall that night,[125]
The dogs slept in the ashes, and the guard
Drowsily nodded in the warm fire-light,
Lulled by the rain and wearied of his ward,
5 Till, hearing one that knocked without full hard,
Half-dazed he started up in aged fear
And rubbed his eyes and took his tarnished spear
And hobbled to the doorway and unbarred.
(September 18, 1919; 1979)

Notes

1. From 1915 until the publication of *Spirits in Bondage* in 1919, Lewis was actively engaged in writing lyric poetry. Many of these poems, including versions later published in *Spirits in Bondage,* appear in a holograph manuscript, "Early Poems: English Verses Made by Clive Staples Lewis and Copied by His Friend Joseph Arthur Greeves: Belfast in the Year 1917" (hereafter, "Early Poems"). The original is held by the Linen Hall Library, Belfast, Ireland, and a photocopy, catalogued CSL / MS-41 / X, is available in the Wade Center. For many reasons, "Early Poems" is a critical source of information about Lewis's poetry of this period, especially since it includes the date each poem was written. See the Bibliography of Poem Sources for detailed information on this manuscript.

2. In Greek mythology, Lethe is a river in Hades that induces oblivion.

3. Lugh was the Celtic lord of skill and craftsmen.

4. Warren Lewis confirms Easter 1915 as the date of composition in "LP" 4:306–7. The poem was first published in *The Collected Poems of C. S. Lewis,* ed. Walter Hooper (London: Fount, 1994), 229–30 (hereafter, *CP*).

5. Proserpine was the daughter of Ceres, who was taken by Pluto to become the queen of Hades.

6. Dis is another name for Pluto.

7. Warren Lewis confirms summer 1915 as the date of composition in "LP" 5:14; "Against Potpourri" was first published in *CP,* 231–32.

8. Wife of Osiris, Isis was the Egyptian mother goddess.

9. Ancient Middle Eastern fertility god.

10. Ancient Middle Eastern fertility goddess.

11. Greek god of war.

12. Norse god of thunder.

13. The ending of the poem is appended with this comment: "Pronounced 'nuktos paidîs apaidês' to rhyme with 'hide is' above. The author, I believe, is Sophocles. The literal translation follows in the second half of the line."

14. Bookham was the village in Surrey (often referred to as Great and Little Bookham) where Lewis was tutored by W. T. Kirkpatrick from 1914 until 1917.

15. Anamnesis is the philosophical idea, explored by Plato in his *Meno, Phaedo,* and *Phaedrus,* that humans are born with knowledge from past incarnations and that learning is simply rediscovering such knowledge within themselves.

16. In Germanic myth, Holda was a goddess who protected agriculture and women's crafts.

17. Warren Lewis confirms summer 1915 as the date of composition in "LP" 5:15; the poem was first published in *CP,* 233–34.

18. This refers to Edmund Spenser's *The Fairy Queene* (1590, 1596).

19. This refers to Horace's *Odes.*

20. This refers to Thomas Malory's *Le Morte d'Arthur* (1485).

21. This refers to Homer's *Iliad.*

22. Warren Lewis confirms Christmas 1915 as the date of composition in "LP" 5:46–47; the poem was first published in *CP,* 234–35.

23. Alexander Pope (1688–1744) and Samuel Johnson (1709–1784)

24. In Irish mythology, Mannanan was a god of the sea.

25. The Latin title of this poem means "praise of death."

26. The term *wone* means "a place of habitation."

27. Warren Lewis confirms the Easter 1916 date of composition in "LP" 5:73; the poem was first published in *CP*, 236–37.

28. Immediately following the title of this poem, Lewis included this note: "[And God saw that the wickedness of man was great . . . and that every imagination of his heart was but of evil, and that continually—Genesis. There is no more pitiful thing that moves on the face of all-nurturing earth than the sons of men—Homer. The most pernicious race of little vermin—Swift]."

29. The battle of Roncevaux Pass in 778, a minor battle between part of Charlemagne's army and the Basques, was elevated to a heroic conflict between Christians and Muslims in the eleventh-century epic poem *Song of Roland* (*Le chanson de Roland*), in which Roland, a valiant young vassal of Charlemagne, is defeated by the Saracens.

30. This refers to the Battle of Zutphen, fought on Sept. 22, 1586, between Spanish forces and those of the United Provinces of the Netherlands, supported by English troops. English soldier and poet Sir Philip Sidney (*Astrophel and Stella*, *The Defence of Poesy*, and *The Countess of Pembroke's Arcadia*) was mortally wounded during the battle.

31. Morrigan is the Celtic goddess of death; her name has been variously interpreted to mean "great queen" or "phantom queen."

32. Best known for his single-handed defense of Ulster, Cuchulain was one of the greatest heroes of Irish mythology and legend. Cuchulain had earned the wrath of Morrigan when he stopped her (unknowingly) from stealing one of his cows. As a result she prophesied his death in battle, which eventually occurred.

33. Oreads were mountain nymphs in Greek mythology.

34. Pan was the Greek god of shepherds and flocks, of mountain wilds, hunting, and rustic music.

35. In Greek mythology, the Pallas referred to here is either the spearing-brandishing Titan or to Pallas Athena, the goddess of wisdom. Lyaeus, more familiarly known as Dionysus in Greek religion and mythology, is the god of fertility and wine. Ares is the Greek god of war, while Aphrodite is the Greek goddess of love.

36. First published in Don W. King, *C. S. Lewis, Poet: The Legacy of His Poetic Impulse* (Kent, Ohio: Kent State Univ. Press, 2001), 321–22.

37. Warren Lewis confirms the summer 1916 date of composition in "LP" 5:123; the poem was first published in *CP*, 237.

38. This alludes to the Celtic story of the adulterous love between the Cornish knight Tristan and the Irish princess Isolde. Sent by King Mark, his uncle, Tristan was to bring Isolde to the king for marriage. However, during the journey Tristan and Isolde drank a love potion that caused them to fall hopelessly in love with each other.

39. Patroklos was the beloved friend of Achilles in the *Ilaid*.

40. In Greek mythology, Priam (here given as Priamid) was the king of Troy.

41. Brynhild or Brynhilda, the daughter of Odin, was a Valkyrie who was revived from an enchanted sleep by Sigurd.

42. Because of a magical device, Brynhilda unknowingly married Gunther while believing she was marrying Sigurd.

43. This refers to the Gemini constellation.

44. *Argo* was the ship in which Jason and the Argonauts sailed to retrieve the Golden Fleece. The *Golden Hind* was the ship in which Sir Francis Drake circumnavigated the globe (1577–80).

45. Warren Lewis confirms Christmas 1916 as the date of composition in "LP" 5:170; the poem was first published in *CP,* 238–39.

46. This refers to County Down, one of Northern Ireland's six counties and the location of Belfast, where Lewis was born and spent his early life.

47. Warren Lewis confirms Christmas 1916 as the date of composition in "LP" 5:171–72; the poem was first published in *CP,* 240–41. Lines 21–28 also appear on the dedication page of *They Stand Together: The Letters of C. S. Lewis to Arthur Greeves (1914–1963),* ed. Walter Hooper (New York: Macmillan, 1979).

48. The speaker of these verses is the youth Hylas, in Greek mythology a servant to Heracles, who was abducted by water nymphs.

49. In Greek mythology, Charon is the ferryman of the dead, who carries souls to Hades.

50. Lewis's nickname for Arthur Greeves.

51. Archaic word meaning "rises."

52. A mythical Utopian land.

53. This refers to Britons, natives of Brittany in northwest France.

54. The first stanza appears later in a letter Lewis wrote to Arthur Greeves on Mar. 6, 1917, published in *Collected Letters of C. S. Lewis,* Volume 1: *Family Letters 1905–1931* (hereafter, *CL* 1), ed. Walter Hooper (London: Harper Collins, 2000), 288–89.

55. The title of this poem means "nothing in excess," and is one of the gnomic sayings carved at the entrance of the temple of Apollo in Delphi.

56. In Greek mythology, this is the river of hate, one of the rivers surrounding Hades.

57. In Homer's Odyssey, Circe was the witch who temporarily enchanted many of Odysseus's mariners, turning them into pigs, before helping them to return home.

58. In Greek mythology, the Nereids were sea nymphs.

59. Warren Lewis confirms Easter 1917 as the date of composition in "LP" 5:197; the poem was first published in *CP,* 241.

60. Three legendary horses: Bayard is a magical bay horse in romances derived from the twelfth-century French chanson de geste *Quatre fils Aymon;* Gringolet is the name of Gawain's horse in the Arthurian legends; and Sleipnir is the name of Odin's horse in Norse mythology.

61. Warren Lewis confirms Easter 1917 as the date of composition in "LP" 5:197–98; the poem was first published in *CP,* 242.

62. In Greek mythology, Despoina (Greek word for "mistress" and perhaps a pun on "despot" since the masculine Greek equivalent is *despotes*) was the daughter of Demeter and Poseidon. Here Lewis appears to be using the name to denote an idealized woman.

63. Except for those appearing in "Early Poems," no manuscript or holograph versions exist of the poems appearing in Lewis's *Spirits in Bondage* (hereafter, *SB*), which he published under the pseudonym Clive Hamilton. The text presented here is based on the first edition, published on Mar. 20, 1919: Clive Hamilton [C. S. Lewis], *Spirits in Bondage: A Cycle of Lyrics* (London: William Heinemann, 1919). Many early drafts of poems that later appear in *Spirits in Bondage* are founded in "Early Poems." Accordingly, whenever possible I date poems appearing in *Spirits in Bondage* using the dating found in "Early Poems"; in cases when the date is uncertain, I note this with a question mark. In order to maintain the integrity of Lewis's ordering of *Spirits in Bondage,* I have not listed the poems from that work in chronological order. Other sources consulted regarding the dating of these poems include Walter Hooper's preface to a later edition of *Spirits in Bondage* (New York: Harcourt Brace Jovanovich, 1984); *CL* 1; Warren Lewis's notes in the eleven-volume unpublished manuscript, "The Lewis Papers:

Memoirs of the Lewis Family, 1850–1930" ("LP"), available in the Warren H. Lewis Papers, Wade Center; and my article "Lost but Found: The 'Missing' Poems of C. S. Lewis's *Spirits in Bondage*," *Christianity and Literature* 53 (Winter 2004): 163–201.

64. Lewis draws this epigraph from Andrew Lang's *History of English Literature from Beowulf to Swinburne* (London: Longmans, Green and Co., 1912). Regarding Edgar Allan Poe, Lang wrote: "Poe has been more admired on the Continent, and translated into more languages than any poet of America. His works were admirably rendered into French by Charles Baudelaire, himself an adorer of 'The love whom I shall never meet, / The land where I shall never be'" (579).

65. The British Isles were called the Tin Isles during the Roman occupation of England.

66. Moabite god that demanded the sacrifice of first-born children.

67. Tin.

68. Monchy-Le-Preux is a French village six miles south of Arras, site of major action during World War I.

69. An early version of this poem appears in "Early Poems."

70. An early version of "Victory," entitled "Ad Astra," appears in "Early Poems." For information on Roland, see note 29, above, to "In His Own Image." For information on Cuchulain, see note 32, above, to "Sonnet [The clouds are red behind and before]."

71. Helen, wife of Menelaus, the King of Sparta, was pursued by the Trojan prince, Paris (with the blessing of Aphrodite); their elopement set into motion the Trojan War. For information on Iseult (also known as Isolde), see note 38, above, to "Exercise on an Old Theme."

72. Tree nymphs.

73. In Greek mythology, a demigod who was the messenger of the sea and the son of Poseidon, god of the sea, and Amphitrite, goddess of the sea.

74. In Arthurian legend, Arthur was the king who united Britain in a peaceful golden age, while Avalon is the island where Arthur's sword, Excalibur, was forged, and where he was brought to die after being mortally wounded by Mordred.

75. *Baresark,* meaning "frenzied," is a variant of *berserk* (literally "bare shirt").

76. An early version of this poem appears in "Early Poems."

77. Grendel was the man-eating monster in the old English heroic poem *Beowulf.* Harte is a variant of *Heorot,* the feasting hall of the king of the Danes, Hrothgar, in *Beowulf.* In the story Grendel prevents Hrothgar and his thanes from enjoying fellowship in Heorot.

78. In Celtic mythology, Balor, king of a demonic race of giants, had a huge eye that killed anything it looked on.

79. I base the date of composition for this poem on Walter Hooper's contention, in the preface to the 1984 edition of *Spirits in Bondage,* that Lewis sent his publisher, William Heinemann, "'Our Daily Bread,' 'The Autumn Morning,' 'Alexandrines,' 'Tu Ne Quaesieris,' and 'Spooks' [to replace] five poems in the original manuscript" that Heinemann did not want to include (xxxiv). The five Heinemann wanted replaced were "To Sir Philip Sydney," "Ballade on a Certain Pious Gentleman," "Sonnet," "Retreat," and "In Venusberg." If Hooper is correct, all but "The Autumn Morning" (dated in "Early Poems" to summer 1916) may date to sometime in the fall of 1918, since Heinemann's letter to Lewis is dated Oct. 8, 1918. For a fuller discussion of this matter, see Don W. King, "Lost but Found: The 'Missing' Poems of C. S. Lewis's *Spirits in Bondage*" *Christianity and Literature* 53 (Winter 2004): 163–201, especially footnote 15, 195–96.

80. An early version of this poem, titled "If men Should Ask," appears in "Early Poems."

81. For more on Despoina, see note 62, above, to "Despoina, Bear with Me."

82. Troy.

83. For more on Brynhild, see note 41, above, to "Exercise on an Old Theme." Queen Maeve is best known from the Irish legend The Cattle Raid of Cooley. In the story she initiated the plan to steal Ulster's prize stud bull. The French heroine Bradamant was one of the greatest female knights in literature; an expert fighter, she carried a magical lance that unhorsed anyone it touched.

84. Two poems found in "Early Poems," "Ode" and "Tho' Its Truth They Tell," contribute versions of lines that later appear in "Ode for New Year's Day." Specifically, versions of lines 1–21 and 43–46 from "Ode" and versions of lines 26–42 from "Tho' Its Truth They Tell" were reworked by Lewis into what became "Ode for New Year's Day."

85. For more on Despoina, see note 62, above, to "Despoina, Bear with Me."

86. An early version of this poem appears in "Early Poems."

87. Warren Lewis dates this poem to Easter 1916; see "LP" 5:72.

88. An early version of this poem, titled "A Hymn," appears in "Early Poems."

989. The Latin title of this poem means "out of the depths" and is an ironic allusion to Psalms 130:1–2: "Out of the depths have I cried unto thee, O LORD. Lord, hear my voice: let thine ears be attentive to the voice of my supplications."

90. In Greek mythology, Medea was the witch who agreed to assist Jason in his quest for the Golden Fleece on the condition that he marry her.

91. An early version of this poem appears in "Early Poems."

92. An early version of this poem appears in "Early Poems."

93. An early version of this poem appears in "Early Poems."

94. Warren Lewis confirms Christmas 1915 as the date of composition in "LP" 5:45–46.

95. An early version of this poem appears in "Early Poems." The reference to Surrey suggests Lewis wrote the poem while living in Bookham and being tutored by W. T. Kirkpatrick; see note 14, above, to "The Wood Desolate (near Bookham)."

96. John Milton (1608–1674).

97. An early version of this poem appears in "Early Poems."

98. An early version of this poem appears in "Early Poems."

99. An early version of this poem appears in "Early Poems." The French title means "the sorcerer's apprentice."

100. An early version of this poem appears in "Early Poems."

101. The Orkney Islands lie off the northern coast of Scotland; Ind refers to India, or, more generally, the end of the world.

102. In Greek mythology, alluring, dangerous creatures that were part-women and part-bird, whose beautiful songs caused passing sailors to jump into the water and drown. In Homer's *Odyssey,* Odysseus saved his men by putting wax in their ears and having himself tied to mast of the ship. The Pillars of Heracles were two promontories marking the entrance to the Strait of Gibraltar: the Rock of Gibraltar to the north and an unspecified North African peak to the south.

103. This is a reference to a passage in chapter 4, "Of the Way from Constantinople to Jerusalem. Of Saint John the Evangelist. And of the Daughter of Ypocras, transformed from a Woman to a Dragon" of *The Marvellous Adventures of Sir John Maundevile, Kt* (1895): "And then pass Men through the Isles of Colos and of Lango (Cos), of the which Isles Ypocras was Lord. And some men say that in the Isle of Lango is yet the Daughter of Ypocras, in Form and Likeness of a Great Dragon, that is 100 Fathom of great length."

104. This is a reference to a passage in chapter 28, "Of the Devil's Head in the Valley Perilous. And of the Customs of Folk in diverse Isles that be about in the Lordship of Prester

John," of *The Marvellous Adventures of Sir John Maundevile, Kt:* "Beside that Isle of Mistorak upon the left Side nigh to the River of Pison is a marvellous Thing. There is a Vale between the Mountains, that endureth nigh a 4 Mile. And some call it the Vale Enchanted, some call it the Vale of Devils, and some call it the Vale Perilous."

105. For the dating of this poem, see *CL* 1:372–73 and "Early Poems."

106. An early version of this poem, titled "Ballade Mystical," appears in "Early Poems."

107. Dagda was the Irish-Celtic god of the earth and ruler over life and death.

108. Warren Lewis confirms Easter 1917 as the date of composition in "LP" 9:255.

109. An early version appears in "Early Poems."

110. In Greek mythology, Orpheus was a semi-divine poet and minstrel who tried to rescue his dead wife from the Underworld.

111. The title of this poem is an allusion to Matthew 6:9–13 (Authorized [King James] Version): "Our Father which art in heaven, Hallowed be thy name. Thy kingdom come, Thy will be done in earth, as it is in heaven. Give us this day our daily bread. And forgive us our debts, as we forgive our debtors. And lead us not into temptation, but deliver us from evil: For thine is the kingdom, and the power, and the glory, for ever. Amen."

112. An early version of this poem, titled "How I Saw Angus the God," appears in "Early Poems." In Irish mythology, Angus was the god of love; he often had four birds flying about his head (perhaps symbolizing kisses), who inspired love in all who heard them.

113. An early version of this poem appears in "Early Poems." For more on the hills of Down, see note 46, above, to "Couplets."

114. An early version of this poem appears in "Early Poems." In Greek mythology, Hesperus, the planet Venus, is the son of the dawn goddess Eos. It is often known as the evening star.

115. An early version of this poem appears in "Early Poems."

116. A peninsula in Norway.

117. Warren Lewis confirms summer 1916 as the date of composition in "LP" 5:122–23.

118. At different times, Joseph Lodge and Fredrick Myers served as president of the Society for Psychical Research.

119. The Latin title of this poem, which means "You should not ask," constitutes the opening words to Ode 11 in Book I of Horace's *Odes.*

120. Perhaps a veiled reference to the biblical passage "For now we see through a glass, darkly; but then face to face: now I know in part; but then shall I know even as also I am known" (1 Corinthians 13:12 [King James Bible, Authorized Version, Cambridge Edition, hereafter, AV]).

121. An early version of this poem appears in "Early Poems."

122. An early version of this poem, titled "Oh There Is a Castle Built," appears in "Early Poems."

123. An early version of this poem, titled "My Own Death Song," appears in "Early Poems." First published in *Reveille* 3 (Feb. 1919): 508, under the pseudonym Clive Hamilton.

124. Avalon, the mysterious island where Arthur's sword, Excalibur, was forged and where he was taken to recover from wounds after his fight with Mordred. Here Lewis intended the Isle of Apples to represent a paradisal retreat from the brutality of the battlefield.

125. This poem did not appear in *Spirits in Bondage.* Lewis first mentions it in a 1919 letter to Arthur Greeves, giving its first stanza, which is all that survives. It was not published until 1979. In Arthurian legend, Nimue is one of the Ladies of the Lake, who later enchants and entraps the wizard Merlin.

Poems

1920–1925

Oh That a Black Ship

Oh that a black ship now were bearing me
    Between the stars of the sky
And the answering stars of the sea!—
    And the wind to throb, and I
5   On the decks to be sitting, awake
    Watching the foamdrops break
    In fire from her prow:
Passing a moon-drencht island, pale, a Hesperian clime
    Where the apple hangs on the bough
10   And the blood-red life, with no repining
    Is full of shouting, a giant, terrible, shining,
Till the guttering of the candle and the gathering home of time.[1]
(1920; 2000)

Heart-breaking School

        Heart-breaking school[2]
Received me, where an ogre hearted man held rule,
Secret and irresponsible, out of the call
Of men's reproach, like Cyclops in his savage hall:
5 For at his gate no neighbour went in, nor his own
Three fading daughters easily won out alone,
Nor if they did, dared wag their tongues, but, in a trice
Their errand done, whisked home again, three pattering mice,
Pale, busy, meek: more pitiable far than we
10 From whom he ground the bread of his adversity,
Himself a theme for pity: for within him boiled
The spirit of Gengis Khan or Timur,[3] ever foiled
And forced back to the dogs-eared Virgil and the desk
To earn his food: ridiculous, old, poor, grotesque,
15 A man to be forgiven. Here let him pass, by me
Forgiven: and let the memory pass. Let me not see
Under the curled moustaches on the likerous, red,
Moist lips, the flat Assyrian smile we used to dread
When in the death-still room the weeping of one boy
20 Gave the starved dragon inklings of ancestral joy,
Antediluvian taste of blood.
(1920–23 [?]; 1998)

…ey Sent Me to Another Place

… me to another place,[4]
…chool. But I retrace
…ere I found;[5] one master dear,
…e bird of memory sings. More clear
…rmament of the world within.
… at my ear begin
…Dionysiac drum to knock,
Like goat foot dancers thudding on the thin soiled rock
Of blue volcanic country, where the hammered hills
10 Grow hot like metal, and metallic sunshine fills
The basin of the burning sky till the blue is dark,
And the small insects' shadow is as deep and stark
As the jagg'd rocks: and from on high the Olympians throw
The thunderbolt, and quakings from the gods below
15 Trouble the earth: and gods in the leaf shaking mountains
Cluster, and in cold water glens and sacred fountains
Gods and half gods and sons of gods, and all the crew
Of Maenads[6] in the mountain tread the bloodied dew
In honour of the beautiful and beastlike son
20 Of Semele[7]—Then cold Platonic forms: the One
Arching forever above all height; the long process
From lovely, up through lovelier things, to Loveliness
Herself, and in herself, abstract, alone, complete—
Then Sabine woods and worshipped river heads and neat
25 Virgilian farms, and cattle, and the care of bees,[8]
The old pieties of temperate Numa's time.[9] All these,
An old man with a honey-sweet and singing voice
Led me among; an innocent old man whose choice
Once made to dwell with beauty and melodious thought,
30 Unchanged, from early youth to sad old age, had brought
The spirit gently ripening onward to the place
Where courage droops. "Μή ζοίην μετ' ἀμουσίας![10]
Gentlemen (for he chose to call us urchins so)
Let us not rest save where the springs of beauty flow."
35 Therefore the ancient beauty brought him clear delight
Each day, and all day long, and in the wakeful night
Forgetfulness of the unhappy thousand things
Age thinks of, making equal to the wealth of Kings
His poverty. Oh Master, may the earth be green

40 Above thy grave! Far hidden in the lands unseen,
Far off now, and mature among the ghosts, yet fare
Well and thrice well forevermore and everywhere.
(1920–23 [?]; 1998)

Old Kirk, Like Father Time Himself

Old Kirk, like Father Time himself, was coming after,[11]
With clouds of cheap tobacco smoke, with claps of laughter,
My third and greatest teacher who of old had taught
My father; then my brother; and now I was brought
5 A solitary pupil where he lived alone
With few books and no friends, and in his garden, sown
Up to the gates with green utilitarian kale,
Laboured all day, a tall, gnarled shape, hirsute and hale
As Charon:[12] crude antiquity: a leathery, lean
10 Northeaster of a man whose seventy years had seen,
Unflinching, many hopes destroyed. He drew his blood
From the brave, bitter Presbyterian race who stood
For Calvin to the gallow's foot. But Kirk allowed
No God in the world, nor spirit in man. He did not shroud
15 That unbelief in pious frauds, as teachers love.
He thought the reverence owed to boys was Truth. He drove
With lance in rest and loud Have-at-thee on the foe,
Hammer of priests and kings, true lineage of Rousseau,
Hume, and Voltaire.[13] And all the enlightenment's gay din
20 Of onset rang about his veteran ears, and in
And out of season (Covenanter still) he preached
The word of death.
But mark this well: his daring reached
Never so far as to forbid each seventh day
25 A Presbyterian shift of suits from rusty grey
To rusty black. He gardened differently clad
On Sundays. Such peculiar praise the Mighty had
One day in seven from this redoubtable, whose boast
Of reason meant to shake the Throne. On the iron coast
30 Of such a man, with noise of yeasty waves, the young
Spring-swellings of my uncorrected mind were flung
So often that even now I see him as he spoke
Fling up his arm, and hear him from the cloud of smoke

Break in. "I hear you well enough. Stop there! I hear!
35 Have you read this—and that—and the other?—Hah! I fear
You've got no facts. Give me the FACTS!" Repeated shame
Silenced my babbling: months wore on, and I became
Aware how the discourse of men (what none before
Of all my teachers showed me) asks for something more
40 Than lungs and lips. Across my landscape, like the dawn,
Some image of the sovereignty of truth was drawn,
And how to have believed an unproved thing by will
Pollutes the mind's virginity; how reasons kill
Beloved supposals: day makes dry lesser lights,
45 And mountain air is med'cinal. Oh Attic nights
And rigour of debate! Shrewd blows. Parry and thrust.
No quarter. And above us like a battle dust
Fine particles of poets and philosophers
Went flying in the midnight room. I had my spurs
50 Of intellectual knighthood in that bannered field
From Kirk's strong hand. He first hung on my maiden shield
Who now is dead, and died without hope, like a beast.
Let tongue and pen betray me if I break the least
Of the oaths he then administered, the glittering laws
55 Of battle; blameless champion of a pitiful cause.
(1920–23 [?]; 1998)

The Carpet Rises in the Draught

The carpet rises in the draught. The little scarlet leaf,
That's blown in from the window sill, is wicked past belief:
That old face in the picture there is bad as bad can be,
And thro' its chromolithic eyes it says strange things to me.
5 Beyond this room, if I went out, there's thirty feet or more
Of passage thro' the empty house and many an open door
And many an empty room that's full of breeze and sunless light
With empty beds for visitors all neat and cold and white.
And sometimes now a door will bang and then at other whiles
10 A little bit of wind gets lost—strays in beneath the tiles
And among beams and water pipes it makes a fretting sound
Behind the walls, between the laths it wheezes round around,
There's so much room about a house. . . .
(1922–23 [?]; 1998)

The Tale of Psyche Is Unjustly Told

The tale of Psyche is unjustly told[14]
And half the truth concealed by all who hold
With Apuleius.[15] Famous poets sing
That once upon a time there lived a king
5 Whose daughter was so fair that from the sky
Venus beheld her with an evil eye;
And afterwards, for Venus' hate, they say
By singing priests the girl was led away
And left upon the hills in fetters where
10 An old, big sacred serpent kept his lair
Among grey rocks. So far they tell it right:
Only—it was no fabled Venus' spite
That drove them to this thing; but summer rains
Withheld and harvest withering on the plains.
15 The streams were low, and in the starving tribe
Ran murmurs that of old a dearer bribe
Had charmed the rain. Forgotten customs then
Stirred in their sleep below the hearts of men
Thrusting up evil heads. The priests began
20 To feed their god, the sacred snake, with man,
—Prisoners at first, then slaves. But this was vain
They must give more, give all, to get the rain,
Give the land's best and first—give anything—
Even to the royal blood. Now let the king
25 Deny them, and within the hour he's dead.
"What? Shall the king be spared? Our sons have bled
To build his throne. His turn has come today.
Children are dying. Lead the girl away."
—I think it was like that.
30 What follows next
I take for truth; but who can read the text?
In the worst hour, close to the serpent's den,
At twilight and in chains, and when the men
Had left her (and they went in haste, to leave

35 The silent place)—that moment I believe
When fear had done his worst in the girl's heart
That some strange helper came and took her part.
They talk of the wind spirit opening wide
His cloudy arms—and on the mountain side
40 Palaces rising—music in the air—
The bed in the dark room—the lover there
Whose face must not be seen. Amidst it all
Something is lost, but not without recall,
Blurred in the tale, yet somehow told enough.
45 But what comes after this is poorer stuff
And slander; for across the tale, they bring
Two ugly elder daughters of the king,
Two Cinderella's sisters, who must come
To visit Psyche in her secret home
50 And envy it: and for no other cause
Tempt her to break that fairy country's laws
—Which leads to her undoing. But all this
Is weighted on one side and told amiss.
It's like the work of some poetic youth,
55 Angry, and far too certain of the truth,
Mad from the gleams of vision that claim to find
Bye ways to something missed by all mankind.
He thinks that only envy or dull eyes
Keep all men from believing in the prize
60 He holds in secret. In revenge he drew
—For portrait of us all—the sisters two,
Misunderstanding them: and poets since
Have followed.
Now I say there was a prince
65 Twin brother to this Psyche, fair as she,
And prettier than a boy would choose to be,
His name was Jardis. Older far than these
Was Caspian who had rocked them on her knees,
The child of the first marriage of the king.

....

70 But when I rest my eyes
Upon that house, I see far otherwise.
First, it is weeping shapes: then these begin
To come apart. And here is Psyche's twin,

A brother, not a sister, fair as she
75 And prettier than a boy would choose to be,
Reading his book, self pleased in hazy thought.
Now, on my life, I'll guess it's he that taught
The story, as we have it, to the world.[16]
(1923; 2001)

The Silence of the Night

The silence of the night upon the stroke[17]
Of midnight like a bubble snapt and broke
Into ten thousand clamours. Forests wide
With leagues of oaks whipt over to one side
5 Came roaring out of slumber, scattering birds
Like dead leaves up the sky. Half spoken words
Snatched from the lips of shepherds that lay out
Rose wheeling and became a giant's shout
Over six counties. In his turret room
10 Hippolytus[18] woke shrieking in a gloom
That staggered like a ship: the clothes were blown
Out of his clutching hand. With ocean tone
The seven-mile-crested waves of air were hurled
Against his walls. The doors of half the world
15 Seemed banging in his ears. The hollow halls
Echoed like caves beneath him. On the walls
His hanging helmet clanged and on the floor
He heard the carpets flap. Then more and more
Came other noises through the wuthering wind,
20 Cat calls that raised the hair and drums that dinned,
Struck cymbals, screaming voices and the sounds
Of divine beasts at mort and gaining hounds
Baying their thirst, that nearer, nearer rang
Now in the street, now at the door. He sprang
25 Naked from rest, quivering from heel to head
Dry mouthed. The dogs that slept about his bed
Crouched whimpering at the door with fangs laid bare
In foam, and on their backs the roughening hair
Rose stiff. With fingers fumbling round about
30 The straining latch he loosened and thrust out
The chamber door into the wind, hard pressed,

Labouring with shoulder weight and panting breast
Choked like a fish upstream, then, for a space
Dizzied with moonlight stabbing his flushed face,
35 Then—forward, where the dogs before him went
Flat eared and nosing on a fiercer scent
Than earthly quarry has. In haste he passed
Blind labyrinths of the house and came at last
Forth on the street. None stirred. As clear as noon
40 Showed every stone and tile. That night the moon
Had slipt her moorings and with one huge eye
Through headlong clouds flooded the ruined sky
Low blazing to the earth. Immense and blind,
As if at dawn his shadow lurched behind,
45 A monstrous escort up the empty street,
Measuring uneven strides. And now his feet
Fell on cool grass; wide fields before him lay,
Hedgerows with flowers shut up and ghostly may
A faintest perfume fluttering the dim air.
50 The great hill-voice was calling everywhere
Breathing sharp strength upon him. Now each limb
Ran riot, charged with god. Through coverts dim,
Up slopes where the uncounted daisies sleep,
Slant woods and the high tracks of wandering sheep,
55 Up winding glen, riven gulley, cragg'd ascent,
—The wild goat's path—bleeding and mired he went
Up to the hills, away.

Then suddenly
Running beside the prince there seemed to be
60 Innumerable hordes of beast and man.
Under his feet the little foxes ran;
Wings smote upon his temples. Often he felt
The hoarse breathed mountain bear with shaggy pelt
Brushing his thighs. Women with skirts caught up
65 And revellers fresh crowned from the full cup
And maudlin pipe, ancients with silver head,
Young children, priests, merchants, and maids unwed
Ran there with labouring breath, wide gaping mouth,
Some naked, wounded some, all parched with drouth
70 In the burning throat; but fiercer burned the fire
In heart and bloodshot eye, the insane desire
Fixed towards the cloven passes and the bare

Storm-fostering heights. Around them everywhere
The houseless hills made carnival; the trees
75 Strained with the mimic noise of raging seas
In orgy to the wind. Green boulders torn
From mossy rest down the full streams were borne
Breaking the greenwood. Break. Break everything,
Break the old world for life is on the wing
80 To strange adventures. Dian's out tonight.[19]
Brothers, how fair you are. See, red and white,
See, the ghost hounds before us in the dales,
The moon dogs. Onward now. The spirit fails,
The brain cracks. Earth reels under us. Faster yet,
85 Lead, Goddess, lead. The bracken dewy wet
Gleams diamonds and the white enormous moon
Dazzles the eyes and fills the heavens. Now soon
She will be here herself, the Cold-of-the-Air
The freezing Chastity, the haggard fair;
90 Mania is in her feet, and in her face
The hopes of the long dead. We of the chase
See but her shoulders. Lead. Lead on the pack.
Brothers, I have grown hound. I smell the track
I am all nose—Look. Look; with flanks of snow
95 See where the quarry flies—it is a doe—
It is a lion—it's a man[20]—

....

But soon his feet
Ran in the singing grass, by leaping hedges
That flogged the entangled stars, by reeds' and sedges'
100 Dry treble in steep glens: upward to where
On the higher slopes the huge ninth wave of air
Caught him behind the knees. Holm oak like bows
Bends double. The leaves race. Among them goes
Head-over-heels the king—one pace in thirty
105 Touching the earth by luck—through clean and dirty
A king of the dead leaves. Oh night, be dumb,
Cover his shame. Whisper it not in Drum
How Majesty scuds breechless, blown away
Like washing from the line: up past the grey
110 And niggard grass of the heights, further than sheep
Climb furtherest, through the pines and heathery steep
Up to the moon, straight on.

There suddenly
Crowding the nine leagues ridge, the king could see
115 Innumerable hordes—beast, woman, man.
Nuzzling his feet, tongues out, the foxes ran,
Wings lashed him in the face. Often he felt
The wheezy mountain bear with icy pelt
Brushing his side. But the men—alas for Drum.
120 Why should my lord Archbishop home hither come
Showing his teeth so yellow, and except
His mitre, bare as an egg? And now he has leapt
The chasm. . . . [21]
....
The rough breathed mountain bear with icy pelt
125 Brushing him. Then came whinney and drumm'd hoof
And over his head a momentary roof
Of darkness: and he ducked: and square between
The vast moon and his eyes, one moment seen,
Dead black the alighting horse appeared—a shape
130 Well known—his horse—how should the brute escape?
Was he not stalled—are the grooms mad? And now
Flicking irreverent hoofs at our dread brow.
Oats are the devil.
The men—alas for Drum.
135 Why should my lord Archbishop hither have come,
Showing his teeth so tawny, bare except
His mitre and soft beard? And now he's leapt
The crevasse (eighty years upon his shoulder)
Laughing, amid young lads, and no lad bolder,
140 Nor, by the Lord, none fairer. Who'd have thought it?
What has alighted on his limbs? He caught it
Out of the moon. He spread both hands and dipped.
(1923; 2001)

Joy

Today was all unlike another day.
The long waves of my sleep near morning broke
On happier beaches, tumbling lighted spray
Of soft dreams filled with promises. As I woke,
5 Like a huge bird, Joy with the feathery stroke
Of strange wings brushed me over. Sweeter air
Came never from dawn's heart. The misty smoke
Cooled it upon the hills. It touched the lair
Of each wild thing and woke the wet flowers everywhere.

10 I looked from the eastward window. In my thought
I boasted that this mood could never die,
"Here the new life begins. My quarry is caught.
Here is my kingdom won, and here am I."
Shape after shape the fleeted clouds swam by,
15 Snow-pinnacled or flushed with early red.
The standing pools, new married to the sky,
Shone on the moors. All earth, before me spread,
Called to my feet to wander whither the wind led.

A crooked land of ever-changing lines
20 And mountain labyrinths hard to understand,
A land of sudden gorse and slanted pines
And far withdrawn blue valleys—a clean land
Washed with the rains, decked with the flowery hand
Of northern spring, cooled with the streams that wind
25 Through moss and primrose down to the sea sand.
Like Christian when his burden dropt behind,[22]
I was set free. Pure colour purified my mind.

We do not know the language Beauty speaks,
She has no answer to our questioning,
30 And ease to pain and truth to one who seeks
I know she never brought and cannot bring.
But, if she wakes a moment, we must fling
Doubt at her feet, not answered, yet allayed.
She beats down wisdom suddenly. We cling
35 Fast to her flying skirts and she will fade,
Even at the kiss of welcome, into deepest shade.

We have no gift but tears for sacrifice.
She will not stay. But those were bitterer tears
If time's recording measure could suffice
40 To count the endless flash when she appears.
It is not to be weighed with empty years
And hours—they are consumed in that swift birth.
And I—I had forgotten the dull fears,
The waiting and the days that have no worth
45 When I returned, alone, through a grey evening earth.

And then I knew that this was all gone over.
I shall not live like this another day.
Tomorrow I'll go wandering, a poor lover
Of earth, rejected, outcast every way,
50 And see not, hear not. Rapture will not stay
Longer than this, lest mortals grow divine
And old laws change too much. The sensitive ray
Of Beauty, her creative vision fine,
Pass. I am hers, but she will not again be mine.
(1924; 1924)

West Germanic to Primitive Old English

From *W. GMNC* to *Primitive O.E.*
Vowel Changes.

AU, AI, Ă, Ã, EU, IU. When Hors and Hengist turned the prow
From home, they brought germanic AU
And AI from Baltic woods afar
And short Ă and the longer Ã
5 And EU and its companion IU;
Through all whose fates I mean to see you.

A > Ǣ The short Ă soon began to wag,
WĂGAN turned to WÆGN, DĂGS turned to DǢG;
Or, by a following nasal bitten,
10 More often as an "O" was written;
Ã nasalised (in some cold lough),
Followed by X, became an ŌH;
Said Hengist "BRÃXTA, DÃHTA ought-ter
Be rather sounded BROHTE, ÞOHTE."
15 To whom thus Hors replied with scorn . . .

(1925?; 1969)

Notes

1. For the context of this poem, see Lewis's letter to Leo Baker [Aug. 14?, 1920], *CL* 1:506.

2. This poem concerns Robert Capron, headmaster of Wynyard School, in Watford, Hertfordshire, where Lewis was a pupil from 1908 to 1910; in *SJ,* Capron becomes the tyrannical Oldie of Belsen. The end of Warren Lewis's lengthy recollection of Capron's brutality in "LP" provides an apt preface to his brother's poem: "Robert Capron is dismissed . . . contemptuously, by Clive Lewis in a fragmentary autobiographical poem from which I have been permitted to use the following excerpt" ("LP" 3:41).

3. Timur (1336–1405), also known as Tamburlaine, was a Turkish conqueror, chiefly remembered for the barbarity of his conquests.

4. This forty-two-line alexandrine panegyric honors Henry Wakelyn Smith, Lewis's favorite teacher at Malvern College, where he enrolled in Sept. 1913. In *SJ,* Smith became Smewgy and Malvern became Wyvern. Warren Lewis notes that "the memory of [Smewgy] was to be the only pleasant one which Clive . . . brought away with him after his short stay at Malvern, and the [excerpt from the] unfinished autobiographical poem . . . shows vividly the impression which Mr. Smith was capable of making on a clever and sensitive boy" ("LP" 3:262).

5. These lines are perhaps an echo of Dante's *Inferno,* canto 1, lines 8–9: "Yet there I gained such good, that, to convey / The tale, I'll write what else I found therewith" (Trans. Dorothy L. Sayers [London: Penguin Classics, 1949]).

6. In Greek mythology, maenads are female followers of Dionysus; their name, from the Greek for "raving ones," describes the frenzied ecstacy of their dancing, inspired by Dionysus, god of the wine harvest and ecstacy.

7. In Greek mythology, Semele was a mortal princess and, by Zeus, the mother of Dionysus.

8. This refers to the mountainous country east of the Tiber River.

9. Numa Pompilius (753–673 B.C.) of the Sabine tribe was the second king of Rome (715–673 B.C.), having succeeded Romulus.

10. In *SJ,* Lewis comments on this Greek phrase: "'Never let us live with *amousia,*' was one of [Smewgy's] favorite maxims: *amousia,* the absence of the Muses" (112).

11. In Sept. 1914, Lewis was sent to study under W. T. Kirkpatrick, his greatest teacher. In this fifty-four-line extract of alexandrines, Lewis presents a vivid picture of Kirkpatrick (immortalized as "The Great Knock" in *SJ*), describing him with both wit and respect.

12. In Greek mythology, Charon is the traditional ferryman of the dead, who transports them to the underworld.

13. Jean-Jacques Rousseau (1712–1778), David Hume (1711–1776), and Voltaire (François-Marie Arouet) (1694–1778) insisted on the importance of human freedom and reason.

14. Warren Lewis writes: "It will perhaps be remembered that in this year [1923] Clive describes himself as being very full of the idea of re-writing the story of Cupid and Psyche. To what state of completion the scheme was brought is not known, but I have found the following draft in one of his note books" ("LP" 8:163). Then he adds: "This note book contains six or seven other drafts of the first thirty odd lines of the poem" ("LP" 8:164). In a diary entry for Sept. 9, 1923, Lewis wrote: "My head was very full of my old idea of a poem on my own version of the Cupid and Psyche story in which Psyche's sister would not be jealous, but unable to see anything by moors when Psyche showed her the Palace. I have tried it twice before, once in couplets and once in ballad form" (C. S. Lewis, *All My Road Before Me: The Diary of C. S. Lewis, 1922–27* [London: Collins, 1991], 266).

15. Lucius Apuleius (A.D. 125–180) was a Latin writer best known for *The Golden Ass,* a novel encompassing several stories, of which one of the most famous was his version of the well-known tale of Cupid and Psyche. When Lewis later published his own retelling of the Cupid and Psyche story in *Till We Have Faces: A Myth Retold* (London: Geoffrey Bles, 1956), he included a note at the end giving a summary of Apuleius's version of the story and detailing his own alterations.

16. Warren Lewis says these nine lines are "another version of the last six lines."

17. "The Silence of the Night" is a ninety-five-line fragment, in heroic couplets, concerning Hippolytus, possibly the source poem for Lewis's later narrative poem *The Queen of Drum.* Warren Lewis says it was written in 1923, about the same time as "The Tale of Psyche Is Unjustly Told" ("LP" 8:164).

18. Lewis's use of Hippolytus—in Greek mythology, the son of Theseus—may suggest that he was reading Euripides' *The Bacchae* around the time these lines were composed.

19. Goddess of the moon, the hunt, and virgins.

20. Warren Lewis writes: "In the same note book is what appears to be another beginning of the same poem; in this version however 'Hippolytus' becomes 'The King of Drum.' The storm and the hero's awaking are told in much the same, often THE same language as in the version above, but the poem is in a lighter vein. After the hero's entry into the moonlit street it continues" ("LP" 8:166).

21. Warren Lewis says the following eighteen lines constitute another fragment of the same poem ("LP" 8:167).

22. This refers to the scene in John Bunyan's *The Pilgrim's Progress* (1678) when the protagonist, Christian, stands in front of the Cross and the "burden of sin" that he had been carrying falls off his back.

Poems

1926

Dymer (1926)

Preface by the Author to the 1950 Edition

At its original appearance in 1926, *Dymer,* like many better books, found some good reviews and almost no readers. The idea of disturbing its repose in the grave now comes from its publishers, not from me, but I have a reason for wishing to be present at the exhumation. Nearly a quarter of a century has gone since I wrote it, and in that time things have changed both within me and round me; my old poem might be misunderstood by those who now read it for the first time.

I am told that the Persian poets draw a distinction between poetry which they have "found" and poetry which they have "brought": if you like, between the given and the invented, though they wisely refuse to identify this with the distinction between good and bad. Their terminology applies with unusual clarity to my poem. What I "found," what simply "came to me" was the story of a man who, on some mysterious bride, begets a monster: which monster, as soon as it has killed its father, becomes a god. This story arrived, complete, in my mind somewhere about my seventeenth year. To the best of my knowledge I did not consciously or voluntarily invent it, nor was it, in the plain sense of that word, a dream. All I know about it is that there was a time when it was not there, and then presently a time when it was. Every one may allegorise it or psychoanalyse it as he pleases: and if I did so myself my interpretations would have no more authority than anyone else's.

The Platonic and totalitarian state from which Dymer escapes in Canto I was a natural invention for one who detested the state in Plato's *Republic* as much as he liked everything else in Plato, and who was, by temperament, an extreme anarchist. I put into it my hatred of my public school and my recent hatred of the army. But I was already critical of my own anarchism. There had been a time when the sense of defiant and almost drunken liberation which fills the first two acts of *Siegfried* had completely satisfied me.[1] Now, I thought, I knew better. My hero therefore must go through his Siegfried moment in Cantos I and II and find in Canto IV what really comes of that mood in the end. For it seemed to me that two opposite forces in man tended equally to revolt. The one criticises and at need defies civilisation because it is not good enough, the other stabs it from below and behind because it is already too good for total baseness to endure. The hero who dethrones a tyrant will therefore be first fêted and afterwards murdered by the rabble who feel a disinterested hatred of order and reason as such. Hence, in Canto IV, Bran's revolt which at once parodies and punishes Dymer's. It will be remembered that, when I wrote, the first horrors of the Russian Revolution were still fresh in every one's mind;[2] and in my own country,

Ulster, we had had opportunities of observing the daemonic character of popular political "causes."

In those days the new psychology was just beginning to make itself felt in the circles I most frequented at Oxford. This joined forces with the fact that we felt ourselves (as young men always do) to be escaping from the illusions of adolescence, and as a result we were much exercised about the problem of fantasy or wishful thinking. The "Christiana Dream" as we called it (after Christiana Pontifex in Butler's novel),[3] was the hidden enemy whom we were all determined to unmask and defeat. My hero, therefore, had to be a man who had succumbed to its allurements and finally got the better of them. But the particular form in which this was worked out depended on two peculiarities of my own history.

(1) From at least the age of six, romantic longing—*Sehnsucht*—had played an unusually central part in my experience. Such longing is in itself the very reverse of wishful thinking: it is more like thoughtful wishing. But it throws off what may be called systems of imagery. One among many such which it had thrown off for me was the Hesperian or Western Garden system, mainly derived from Euripides, Milton, Morris, and the early Yeats.[4] By the time I wrote *Dymer* I had come, under the influence of our common obsession about Christiana Dreams, into a state of angry revolt against that spell. I regarded it as the very type of the illusions I was trying to escape from. It must therefore be savagely attacked. Dymer's temptation to relapse into the world of fantasy therefore comes to him (Canto VII) in that form. All through that canto I am cutting down my own former "groves and high places" and biting the hand that had fed me. I even tried to get the sneer into the metre; the archaic spelling and accentuation of *countrie* in vii. 23 is meant as parody. In all this, as I now believe, I was mistaken. Instead of repenting my idolatry I spat upon the images which only my own misunderstanding greed had ever made into idols. But "the heresies that men leave are hated most" and lovers' quarrels can be the bitterest of all.

(2) Several years before I wrote the poem, back in my teens, when my mind, except for a vigilant rejection of Christianity, had no fixed principles, and everything from strict materialism to theosophy could find by turns an entry, I had been, as boys are, temporarily attracted to what was then called "the Occult." I blundered into it innocently enough. In those days every one was reading Maeterlinck,[5] and I wanted to improve my French. Moreover, from Yeats's early poetry it was natural to turn to his prose; and there I found to my astonishment that Yeats, unlike other romantic poets, really and literally believed in the sort of beings he put into his poems. There was no question here of "symbolism": he believed in magic. And so for a time *Rosa Alchemica* took its turn (along with Voltaire, Lucretius, and Joseph McCabe) among my serious books.[6] You will understand that this period had ended a long time (years are longer at that age) before I set about writing *Dymer*. By then, so far as I was anything, I was an idealist, and for an idealist all supernaturalisms were equally illusions, all "spirits" merely symbols of "Spirit" in the metaphysical sense, futile

and dangerous if mistaken for facts. I put this into vii. 8. I was now quite sure that magic or spiritism of any kind was a fantasy and of all fantasies the worst. But this wholesome conviction had recently been inflamed into a violent antipathy. It had happened to me to see a man, and a man whom I loved, sink into screaming mania and finally into death under the influence, as I believed, of spiritualism.[7] And I had also been twice admitted to the upper room in Yeats's own house in Broad Street.[8] His conversation turned much on magic. I was overawed by his personality, and by his doctrine half fascinated and half repelled because of the fascination.

The angel in the last canto does not of course mean that I had any Christian beliefs when I wrote the poem, any more (*si parva licet componere magnis*)[9] than the conclusion of *Faust,* Part II, means that Goethe was a believer.

This, I think, explains all that the reader might want explained in my narrative. My hero was to be a man escaping from illusion. He begins by egregiously supposing the universe to be his friend and seems for a time to find confirmation of his belief. Then he tries, as we all try, to repeat his moment of youthful rapture. It cannot be done; the old Matriarch sees to that. On top of his rebuff comes the discovery of the consequences which his rebellion against the City has produced. He sinks into despair and gives utterance to the pessimism which had, on the whole, been my own view about six years earlier. Hunger and a shock of real danger bring him to his senses and he at last accepts reality. But just as he is setting out on the new and soberer life, the shabbiest of all brides is offered him; the false promise that by magic or invited illusion there may be a short cut back to the one happiness he remembers. He relapses and swallows the bait, but he has grown too mature to be really deceived. He finds that the wish-fulfilment dream leads to the fear-fulfilment dream, recovers himself, defies the Magician who tempted him, and faces his destiny.

The physical appearance of the Magician in vi. 6–9 owes something to Yeats as I saw him. If he were now alive I would ask his pardon with shame for having repaid his hospitality by such freedom. It was not done in malice, and the likeness is not, I think, in itself, uncomplimentary.

Since his great name here comes before us, let me take the opportunity of saluting his genius: a genius so potent that, having first revivified and transmuted that romantic tradition which he found almost on its death-bed (and invented a new kind of blank verse in the process), he could then go on to weather one of the bitterest literary revolutions we have known, embark on a second career, and, as it were with one hand, play most of the moderns off the field at their own game. If there is, as may be thought, a pride verging on insolence in his later work, such pride has never come so near to being excusable. It must have been difficult for him to respect either the mere Romantics who could only bewail a lost leader or the mere moderns who could see no difference between *On Baile's Strand* and the work of Richard le Gallienne.[10]

Some may be surprised at the strength of the anti-totalitarian feeling in a poem written so long ago. I had not read *Brave New World* or *Land Under England* or *The*

Aerodrome:[11] nor had we yet tasted the fruits of a planned economy in our own lives. This should be a warning for critics who attempt to date ancient texts too exactly on that kind of internal evidence.

1950 C. S. L.

> "Nine nights I hung upon the Tree,
> wounded with the spear, as an offering to
> Odin, myself sacrificed to myself."
> —*Havamal*[12]

Dymer

Canto I

1

You stranger, long before your glance can light
Upon these words, time will have washed away
The moment when I first took pen to write,
With all my road before me—yet today,
5 Here, if at all, we meet; the unfashioned clay
Ready to both our hands; both hushed to see
That which is nowhere yet come forth and be.

2

This moment, if you join me, we begin
A partnership where both must toil to hold
10 The clue that I caught first. We lose or win
Together; if you read, you are enrolled.
And first, a marvel—Who could have foretold
That in the city which men called in scorn
The Perfect City, Dymer could be born?

3

15 There you'd have thought the gods were smothered down
Forever, and the keys were turned on fate.
No hour was left unchartered in that town,
And love was in a schedule and the State
Chose for eugenic reasons who should mate
20 With whom, and when. Each idle song and dance
Was fixed by law and nothing left to chance.

4

For some of the last Platonists had founded
That city of old. And mastery they made
An island of what ought to be, surrounded
25 By this gross world of easier light and shade.
All answering to the master's dream they laid
The strong foundations, torturing into stone
Each bubble that the Academy had blown.

5

This people were so pure, so law-abiding,
30 So logical, they made the heavens afraid:
They sent the very swallows into hiding
By their appalling chastity dismayed:
More soberly the lambs in spring time played
Because of them: and ghosts dissolved in shame
35 Before their common-sense—till Dymer came.

6

At Dymer's birth no comets scared the nation,
The public crêche engulfed him with the rest,
And twenty separate Boards of Education
Closed round him. He was passed through every test,
40 Was vaccinated, numbered, washed and dressed,
Proctored, inspected, whipt, examined weekly,
And for some nineteen years he bore it meekly.

7

For nineteen years they worked upon his soul,
Refining, chipping, moulding and adorning.
45 Then came the moment that undid the whole—
The ripple of rude life without a warning.
It came in lecture-time one April morning
—Alas for laws and locks, reproach and praise,
Who ever learned to censor the spring days?

8

50 A little breeze came stirring to his cheek.
He looked up to the window. A brown bird
Perched on the sill, bent down to whet his beak
With darting head—Poor Dymer watched and stirred
Uneasily. The lecturer's voice he heard
55 Still droning from the dais. The narrow room
Was drowsy, over-solemn, filled with gloom.

9

He yawned, and a voluptuous laziness
Tingled down all his spine and loosed his knees,
Slow-drawn, like an invisible caress.

60 He laughed—The lecturer stopped like one that sees
A Ghost, then frowned and murmured, "Silence, please."
That moment saw the soul of Dymer hang
In the balance—Louder then his laughter rang.

10

The whole room watched with unbelieving awe,
65 He rose and staggered rising. From his lips
Broke yet again the idiot-like guffaw.
He felt the spirit in his finger tips,
Then swinging his right arm—a wide ellipse
Yet lazily—he struck the lecturer's head.
70 The old man tittered, lurched and dropt down dead.

11

Out of the silent room, out of the dark
Into the sun-stream Dymer passed, and there
The sudden breezes, the high hanging lark
The milk-white clouds sailing in polished air,
75 Suddenly flashed about him like a blare
Of trumpets. And no cry was raised behind him.
His class sat dazed. They dared not go to find him.

12

Yet wonderfully some rumour spread abroad—
An inarticulate sense of life renewing
80 In each young heart—He whistled down the road:
Men said: "There's Dymer"—"Why, what's Dymer doing?"
"I don't know"—"Look, there's Dymer,"—far pursuing
With troubled eyes—A long mysterious "Oh"
Sighed from a hundred throats to see him go.

13

85 Down the white street and past the gate and forth
Beyond the wall he came to grassy places.
There was a shifting wind to West and North
With clouds in heeling squadron running races.
The shadows following on the sunlight's traces
90 Crossed the whole field and each wild flower within it
With change of wavering glories every minute.

14

There was a river, flushed with rains, between
The flat fields and a forest's willowy edge.
A sauntering pace he shuffled on the green,
95 He kicked his boots against the crackly sedge
And tore his hands in many a furzy hedge.
He saw his feet and ankles gilded round
With buttercups that carpeted the ground.

15

He looked back then. The line of a low hill
100 Had hid the city's towers and domes from sight;
He stopt: he felt a break of sunlight spill
Around him sudden waves of searching light.
Upon the earth was green, and gold, and white
Smothering his feet. He felt his city dress
105 An insult to that April cheerfulness.

16

He said: "I've worn this dust heap long enough,
Here goes!" And forthwith in the open field
He stripped away that prison of sad stuff:
Socks, jacket, shirt and breeches off he peeled
110 And rose up mother-naked with no shield
Against the sun: then stood awhile to play
With bare toes dabbling in cold river clay.

17

Forward again, and sometimes leaping high
With arms outspread as though he would embrace
115 In one act all the circle of the sky:
Sometimes he rested in a leafier place,
And crushed the wet, cool flowers against his face:
And once he cried aloud, "Oh world, oh day,
Let, let me,"—and then found no prayer to say.

18

120 Up furrows still unpierced with earliest crop
He marched. Through woods he strolled from flower to flower,
And over hills. As ointment drop by drop

Preciously meted out, so hour by hour
The day slipped through his hands: and now the power
125 Failed in his feet from walking. He was done,
Hungry and cold. That moment sank the sun.

19

He lingered—Looking up, he saw ahead
The black and bristling frontage of a wood
And over it the large sky swimming red
130 Freckled with homeward crows. Surprised he stood
To feel that wideness quenching his hot mood,
Then shouted, "Trembling darkness, trembling green,
What do you mean, wild wood, what do you mean?"

20

He shouted. But the solitude received
135 His noise into her noiselessness, his fire
Into her calm. Perhaps he half believed
Some answer yet would come to his desire.
The hushed air quivered softly like a wire
Upon his voice. It echoed, it was gone:
140 The quiet and the quiet dark went on.

21

He rushed into the wood. He struck and stumbled
On hidden roots. He groped and scratched his face.
The little birds woke chattering where he fumbled.
The stray cat stood, paw lifted, in mid-chase.
145 There is a windless calm in such a place.
A sense of being indoors—so crowded stand
The living trees, watching on every hand:

22

A sense of trespass—such as in the hall
Of the wrong house, one time, to me befell.
150 Groping between the hatstand and the wall—
A clear voice from above me like a bell,
The sweet voice of a woman asking "Well?"
No more than this. And as I fled I wondered
Into whose alien story I had blundered.

23

155 A like thing fell to Dymer. Bending low,
Feeling his way he went. The curtained air
Sighed into sound above his head, as though
Stringed instruments and horns were riding there.
It passed and at its passing stirred his hair.
160 He stood intent to hear. He heard again
And checked his breath half-drawn, as if with pain.

24

That music could have crumbled proud belief
With doubt, or in the bosom of the sage
Madden the heart that had outmastered grief,
165 And flood with tears the eyes of frozen age
And turn the young man's feet to pilgrimage—
So sharp it was, so sure a path it found,
Soulward with stabbing wounds of bitter sound.

25

It died out on the middle of a note,
170 As though it failed at the urge of its own meaning.
It left him with life quivering at the throat,
Limbs shaken and wet cheeks and body leaning,
With strain towards the sound and senses gleaning
The last, least, ebbing ripple of the air,
175 Searching the emptied darkness, muttering "Where?"

26

Then followed such a time as is forgotten
With morning light, but in the passing seems
Unending. Where he grasped the branch was rotten,
Where he trod forth in haste the forest streams
180 Laid wait for him. Like men in fever dreams
Climbing an endless rope, he labored much
And gained no ground. He reached and could not touch.

27

And often out of darkness like a swell
That grows up from no wind upon blue sea,
185 He heard the music, unendurable

In stealing sweetness wind from tree to tree.
Battered and bruised in body and soul was he
When first he saw a little lightness growing
Ahead: and from that light the sound was flowing.

28

190 The trees were fewer now: and gladly nearing
That light, he saw the stars. For sky was there,
And smoother grass, white flowered—a forest clearing
Set in seven miles of forest, secreter
Than valleys in the tops of clouds, more fair
195 Than greenery under snow or desert water
Or the white peace descending after slaughter.

29

As some who have been wounded beyond healing
Wake, or half wake, once only and so bless
Far off the lamplight travelling on the ceiling.
200 A disk of pale light filled with peacefulness
And wonder if this is the C.C.S.,[13]
Or home, or heaven, or dreams—then sighing win
Wise, ignorant death before the pains begin:

30

So Dymer in the wood-lawn blessed the light,
205 A still light, rosy, clear, and filled with sound.
Here was some pile of building which the night
Made larger. Spiry shadows rose all round,
But through the open door appeared profound
Recesses of pure light—fire with no flame—
210 And out of that deep light the music came.

31

Tip-toes he slunk towards it where the grass
Was twinkling in a lane of light before
The archway. There was neither fence to pass
Nor word of challenge given, nor bolted door,
215 But where it's open, open evermore,
No knocker and no porter and no guard,
For very strangeness entering in grows hard.

32

Breathe not! Speak not! Walk gently. Someone's here,
Why have they left their house with the door so wide?
220 There must be someone. . . . Dymer hung in fear
Upon the threshold, longing and big-eyed.
At last he squared his shoulders, smote his side
And called, "I'm here. Now let the feast begin.
I'm coming now. I'm Dymer," and went in.

Canto II

1

More light. Another step, and still more light
Opening ahead. It swilled with soft excess,
His eyes yet quivering from the dregs of night,
And it was nowhere more and nowhere less:
5 In it no shadows were. He could not guess
Its fountain. Wondering round around he turned:
Still on each side the level glory burned.

2

Far in the dome to where his gaze was lost
The deepening roof shone clear as stones that lie
10 In-shore beneath pure seas. The aisles, that crossed
Like forests of white stone their arms on high,
Past pillar after pillar dragged his eye
In unobscured perspective till the sight
Was weary. And there also was the light.

3

15 Look with my eyes. Conceive yourself above
And hanging in the dome: and thence through space
Look down. See Dymer, dwarfed and naked, move,
A white blot on the floor, at such a pace
As boats that hardly seem to have changed place
20 Once in an hour when from the cliffs we spy
The same ship always smoking towards the sky.

4

The shouting mood had withered from his heart;
The oppression of huge places wrapped him round.
A great misgiving sent its fluttering dart
25 Deep into him—some fear of being found,
Some hope to find he knew not what. The sound
Of music, never ceasing, took the role
Of silence and like silence numbed his soul.

5

Till, as he turned a corner, his deep awe
30 Broke with a sudden start. For straight ahead,
Far off, a wild eyed, naked man he saw
That came to meet him: and beyond was spread
Yet further depth of light. With quickening tread
He leaped towards the shape. Then stopped and smiled
35 Before a mirror, wondering like a child.

6

Beside the glass, unguarded, for the claiming,
Like a great patch of flowers upon the wall
Hung every kind of clothes: silk, feathers flaming,
Leopard skin, furry mantles like the fall
40 Of deep mid-winter snows. Upon them all
Hung the faint smell of cedar, and the dyes
Were bright as blood and clear as morning skies.

7

He turned from the white spectre in the glass
And looked at these. Remember, he had worn
45 Thro' winter slush, thro' summer flowers and grass
One kind of solemn stuff since he was born,
With badge of year and rank. He laughed in scorn
And cried, "Here is no law, nor eye to see,
Nor leave of entry given. Why should there be?

8

50 "Have done with that—you threw it all behind.
Henceforth I ask no licence where I need.
It's on, on, on, though I go mad and blind,
Though knees ache and lungs labour and feet bleed,

Or else—it's home again: to sleep and feed,
55 And work, and hate them always and obey
And loathe the punctual rise of each new day."

9

He made mad work among them as he dressed,
With motley choice and litter on the floor,
And each thing as he found it seemed the best.
60 He wondered that he had not known before
How fair a man he was. "I'll creep no more
In secret," Dymer said. "But I'll go back
And drive them all to freedom on this track."

10

He turned towards the glass. The space looked smaller
65 Behind him now. Himself in royal guise
Filled the whole frame—a nobler shape and taller,
Till suddenly he started with surprise,
Catching, by chance, his own familiar eyes,
Fevered, yet still the same, without their share
70 Of bravery, undeceived and watching there.

11

Yet, as he turned, he cried, "The rest remain. . . .
If they rebelled . . . if they should find me here,
We'd pluck the whole taut fabric from the strain,
Hew down the city, let live earth appear!
75 —Old men and barren women whom through fear
We have suffered to be masters in our home,
Hide! hide! for we are angry and we come."

12

Thus feeding on vain fancy, covering round
His hunger, his great loneliness arraying
80 In facile dreams until the qualm was drowned,
The boy went on. Through endless arches straying
With casual tread he sauntered, manly playing
At manhood lest more loss of faith betide him,
Till lo! he saw a table set beside him.

13

85 When Dymer saw this sight, he leaped for mirth,
He clapped his hands, his eye lit like a lover's.
He had a hunger in him that was worth
Ten cities. Here was silver, glass and covers.
Cold peacock, prawns in aspic, eggs of plovers,
90 Raised pies that stood like castles, gleaming fishes
And bright fruit with broad leaves around the dishes.

14

If ever you have passed a café door
And lingered in the dusk of a June day,
Fresh from the road, sweat-sodden and foot-sore,
95 And heard the plates clink and the music play,
With laughter, with white tables far away,
With many lights—conceive how Dymer ran
To table, looked once round him, and began.

15

That table seemed unending. Here and there
100 Were broken meats, bread crumbled, flowers defaced
—A napkin, with white petals, on a chair,
—A glass already tasted, still to taste.
It seemed that a great host had fed in haste
And gone: yet left a thousand places more
105 Untouched, wherein no guest had sat before.

16

There in the lonely splendour Dymer ate,
As thieves eat, ever watching, half in fear.
He blamed his evil fortune. "I come late.
Whose board was this? What company sat here?
110 What women with wise mouths, what comrades dear
Who would have made me welcome as the one
Free-born of all my race and cried, 'Well done!'"

17

Remember, yet again, he had grown up
On rations and on scientific food,
115 At common boards, with water in his cup,
One mess alike for every day and mood:

But here, at his right hand, a flagon stood.
He raised it, paused before he drank, and laughed.
"I'll drown their Perfect City in this draught."

18

120 He fingered the cold neck. He saw within,
Like a strange sky, some liquor that foamed blue
And murmured. Standing now with pointed chin
And head thrown back, he tasted. Rapture flew
Through every vein. That moment louder grew
125 The music and swelled forth a trumpet note.
He ceased and put one hand up to his throat.

19

Then heedlessly he let the flagon sink
In his right hand. His staring eyes were caught
In distance, as of one who tries to think
130 A thought that is still waiting to be thought.
There was a riot in his heart that brought
The loud blood to the temples. A great voice
Sprang to his lips unsummoned, with no choice.

20

"Ah! but the eyes are open, the dream is broken!
135 To sack the Perfect City? . . . a fool's deed
For Dymer! Folly of follies I have spoken!
I am the wanderer, new born, newly freed . . .
A thousand times they have warned me of men's greed
For joy, for the good that all desire, but never
140 Till now I knew the wild heat of the endeavour.

21

"Some day I will come back to break the City,
—Not now. Perhaps when age is white and bleak
—Not now. I am in haste. Oh God, the pity
Of all my life till this, groping and weak,
145 The shadow of itself! But now to seek
That true most ancient glory whose white glance
Was lost through the whole world by evil chance!

22

"I was a dull, cowed thing from the beginning.
Dymer the drudge, the blackleg who obeyed.
150 Desire shall teach me now. If this be sinning,
Good luck to it! Oh splendour long delayed,
Beautiful world of mine, oh world arrayed
For bridal, flower and forest, wave and field,
I come to be your lover. Loveliest, yield!

23

155 "World, I will prove you. Lest it should be said
There was a man who loved the earth: his heart
Was nothing but that love. With doting tread
He worshipt the loved grass: and every start
Of every bird from cover, the least part
160 Of every flower he held in awe. Yet earth
Gave him no joy between his death and birth.

24

"I know my good is hidden at your breast.
There is a sound of great good in my ear,
Like wings. And, oh! this moment is the best;
165 I shall not fail—I taste it—it comes near.
As men from a dark dungeon see the clear
Stars shining and the filled streams far away,
I hear your promise booming and obey.

25

"This forest lies a thousand miles, perhaps,
170 Beyond where I am come. And farther still
The rivers wander seaward with smooth lapse,
And there is cliff and cottage, tower and hill.
Somewhere, before the world's end, I shall fill
My spirit at earth's pap. For earth must hold
175 One rich thing sealed as Dymer's from of old.

26

"One rich thing—or, it may be, more than this . . .
Might I not reach the borders of a land
That ought to have been mine? And there, the bliss
Of free speech, there the eyes that understand,

180 The men free grown, not modelled by the hand
Of masters—men that know, or men that seek,
—They will not gape and murmur when I speak."

27

Then, as he ceased, amid the farther wall
He saw a curtained and low lintelled door;
185 —Dark curtains, sweepy fold, night-purple pall,
He thought he had not noticed it before.
Sudden desire for darkness overbore
His will, and drew him towards it. All was blind
Within. He passed. The curtains closed behind.

28

190 He entered in a void. Night-scented flowers
Breathed there, but this was darker than the night
That is most black with beating thunder showers,
—A disembodied world where depth and height
And distance were unmade. No seam of light
195 Showed through. It was a world not made for seeing,
One pure, one undivided sense of being.

29

Through darkness smooth as amber, warily, slowly
He moved. The floor was soft beneath his feet.
A cool smell that was holy and unholy,
200 Sharp like the very spring and roughly sweet
Blew towards him: and he felt his fingers meet
Broad leaves and wiry stems that at his will
Unclosed before and closed behind him still.

30

With body intent he felt the foliage quiver
205 On breast and thighs. With groping arms he made
Wide passes in the air. A sacred shiver
Of joy from the heart's centre oddly strayed
To every nerve. Deep sighing, much afraid,
Much wondering, he went on: then, stooping, found
210 A knee-depth of warm pillows on the ground.

31

And there it was sweet rapture to lie still,
Eyes open on the dark. A flowing health
Bathed him from head to foot and great goodwill
Rose springing in his heart and poured its wealth
215 Outwards. Then came a hand as if by stealth
Out of the dark and touched his hand: and after
The beating silence budded into laughter:

32

—A low grave laugh and rounded like a pearl,
Mysterious, filled with home. He opened wide
220 His arms. The breathing body of a girl
Slid into them. From the world's end, with the stride
Of seven-league boots came passion to his side.
Then, meeting mouths, soft-falling hair, a cry,
Heart-shaken flank, sudden cool-folded thigh:

33

225 The same night swelled the mushroom in earth's lap
And silvered the wet fields: it drew the bud
From hiding and led on the rhythmic sap
And sent the young wolves thirsting after blood,
And, wheeling the big seas, made ebb and flood
230 Along the shores of earth: and held these two
In dead sleep till the time of morning dew.

Canto III

1

He woke, and all at once before his eyes
The pale spires of the chestnut-trees in bloom
Rose waving and, beyond, dove-coloured skies;
But where he lay was dark and, out of gloom,
5 He saw them, through the doorway of a room
Full of strange scents and softness, padded deep
With growing leaves, heavy with last night's sleep.

2

He rubbed his eyes. He felt that chamber wreathing
New sleepiness around him. At his side
10 He was aware of warmth and quiet breathing.
Twice he sank back, loose limbed and drowsy eyed;
But the wind came even there. A sparrow cried
And the wood shone without. Then Dymer rose,
—"Just for one glance," he said, and went, tip-toes,

3

15 Out into crisp grey air and drenching grass.
The whitened cobweb sparkling in its place
Clung to his feet. He saw the wagtail pass
Beside him and the thrush: and from his face
Felt the thin-scented winds divinely chase
20 The flush of sleep. Far off he saw, between
The trees, long morning shadows of dark green.

4

He stretched his lazy arms to their full height,
Yawning, and sighed and laughed, and sighed anew:
Then wandered farther, watching with delight
25 How his broad naked footprints stained the dew,
—Pressing his foot to feel the cold come through
Between the spreading toes—then wheeling round
Each moment to some new, shrill forest sound.

5

The wood with its cold flowers had nothing there
30 More beautiful than he, new waked from sleep,
New born from joy. His soul lay very bare
That moment to life's touch, and pondering deep
Now first he knew that no desire could keep
These hours for always, and that men do die
35 —But oh, the present glory of lungs and eye!

6

He thought: "At home they are waking now. The stair
Is filled with feet. The bells clang—far from me.
Where am I now? I could not point to where
The City lies from here," . . . then, suddenly,

40 "If I were here alone, these woods could be
A frightful place! But now I have met my friend
Who loves me, we can talk to the road's end."

7

Thus, quickening with the sweetness of the tale
Of his new love, he turned. He saw, between
45 The young leaves where the palace walls showed pale
With chilly stone: but far above the green,
Springing like cliffs in air, the towers were seen,
Making more quiet yet the quiet dawn.
Thither he came. He reached the open lawn.

8

50 No bird was moving here. Against the wall
Out of the unscythed grass the nettle grew.
The doors stood open wide, but no footfall
Rang in the colonnades. Whispering through
Arches and hollow halls the light wind blew . . .
55 His awe returned. He whistled—then, no more,
It's better to plunge in by the first door.

9

But then the vastness threw him into doubt.
Was this the door that he had found last night?
Or that, beneath the tower? Had he come out
60 This side at all? As the first snow falls light
With following rain before the year grows white,
So the first, dim foreboding touched his mind,
Gently as yet, and easily thrust behind.

10

And with it came the thought, "I do not know
65 Her name—no, nor her face." But still his mood
Ran blithely as he felt the morning blow
About him, and the earth-smell in the wood
Seemed waking for long hours that must be good
Here, in the unfettered lands, that knew no cause
70 For grudging—out of reach of the old laws.

11

He hastened to one entry. Up the stair,
Beneath the pillared porch, without delay,
He ran—then halted suddenly: for there
Across the quiet threshold something lay,
75 A bundle, a dark mass that barred the way.
He looked again and lo, the formless pile
Under his eyes was moving all the while.

12

And it had hands, pale hands of wrinkled flesh,
Puckered and gnarled with vast antiquity,
80 That moved. He eyed the sprawling thing afresh,
And bit by bit (so faces come to be
In the red coal) yet surely, he could see
That the swathed hugeness was uncleanly human,
A living thing, the likeness of a woman.

13

85 In the centre a draped hummock marked the head;
Thence flowed the broader lines with curve and fold
Spreading as oak roots do. You would have said
A man could hide among them and grow old
In finding a way out. Breasts manifold
90 As of the Ephesian Artemis might be
Under that robe.[14] The face he did not see.

14

And all his being answered, "Not that way!"
Never a word he spoke. Stealthily creeping
Back from the door he drew. Quick! No delay!
95 Quick, quick, but very quiet!—backward peeping
Till fairly out of sight. Then shouting, leaping,
Shaking himself he ran—as puppies do
From bathing—till that door was out of view.

15

Another gate—and empty. In he went
100 And found a courtyard open to the sky;
Amidst it dripped a fountain. Heavy scent

Of flowers was here; the foxglove standing high
Sheltered the whining wasp. With hasty eye
He travelled round the walls. One doorway led
105 Within: one showed a further court ahead.

16

He ran up to the first—a hungry lover,
And not yet taught to endure, not blunted yet,
But weary of long waiting to discover
That loved one's face. Before his foot was set
110 On the first stair, he felt the sudden sweat,
Cold on his sides. That sprawling mass in view,
That shape—the horror of heaviness—here too.

17

He fell back from the porch. Not yet—not yet—
There must be other ways where he would meet
115 No watcher in the door. He would not let
The fear rise, nor hope falter, nor defeat
Be entered in his thoughts. A sultry heat
Seemed to have filled the day. His breath came short,
And he passed on into that inner court.

18

120 And (like a dream) the sight he feared to find
Was waiting here. Then cloister, path and square
He hastened through: down paths that ended blind,[15]
Traced and retraced his steps. The thing sat there
In every door, still watching, everywhere,
125 Behind, ahead, all round—So! Steady now,
Lest panic comes. He stopped. He wiped his brow.

19

But, as he strove to rally, came the thought
That he had dreamed of such a place before
—Knew how it all would end. He must be caught
130 Early or late. No good! But all the more
He raged with passionate will that overbore
That knowledge: and cried out, and beat his head,
Raving, upon the senseless walls, and said,

20

“Where? Where? Dear, look once out. Give but one sign.
135 It’s I, I, Dymer. Are you chained and hidden?
What have they done to her? Loose her! She is mine.
Through stone and iron, haunted and hag-ridden,
I’ll come to you—no stranger, nor unbidden,
It’s I. Don’t fear them. Shout above them all.
140 Can you not hear? I’ll follow at your call.”

21

From every arch the echo of his cry
Returned. Then all was silent, and he knew
There was no other way. He must pass by
That horror: tread her down, force his way through,
145 Or die upon the threshold. And this too
Had all been in a dream. He felt his heart
Beating as if his throat would burst apart.

22

There was no other way. He stood a space
And pondered it. Then, gathering up his will,
150 He went to the next door. The pillared place
Beneath the porch was dark. The air was still,
Moss on the steps. He felt her presence fill
The threshold with dull life. Here too was she.
This time he raised his eyes and dared to see.

23

155 Pah! Only an old woman! . . . but the size,
The old, old matriarchal dreadfulness,
Immovable, intolerable . . . the eyes
Hidden, the hidden head, the winding dress
Corpselike . . . The weight of the brute that seemed to press
160 Upon his heart and breathing. Then he heard
His own voice, strange and humbled, take the word.

24

“Good Mother, let me pass. I have a friend
To look for in this house. I slept the night
And feasted here—it was my journey’s end,

165 —I found it by the music and the light,
And no one kept the doors, and I did right
To enter—did I not? Now, Mother, pray,
Let me pass in . . . good Mother, give me way."

25

The woman answered nothing: but he saw
170 The hands, like crabs, still wandering on her knee.
"Mother, if I have broken any law,
I'll ask a pardon once: then let it be,
—Once is enough—and leave the passage free.
I am in haste. And though it were a sin
175 By all the laws you have, I must go in."

26

Courage was rising in him now. He said,
"Out of my path, old woman. For this cause
I am new born, new freed, and here new wed,
That I might be the breaker of bad laws.
180 The frost of old forbiddings breaks and thaws
Wherever my feet fall. I bring to birth
Under its crust the green, ungrudging earth."

27

He had started, bowing low: but now he stood
Stretched to his height. His own voice in his breast
185 Made misery pompous, firing all his blood.
"Enough," he cried. "Give place. You shall not wrest
My love from me. I journey on a quest
You cannot understand, whose strength shall bear me
Through fire and earth. A bogy will not scare me.

28

190 "I am the sword of spring; I am the truth.
Old night put out your stars, the dawn is here,
The sleeper's wakening, and the wings of youth.
With crumbling veneration and cowed fear
I make no truce. My loved one, live and dear,
195 Waits for me. Let me in! I fled the City,
Shall I fear you or . . . Mother, ah, for pity."

29

For his high mood fell shattered. Like a man
Unnerved, in bayonet-fighting, in the thick,
—Full of red rum and cheers when he began,
200 Now, in a dream, muttering: "I've not the trick.
It's no good. I'm no good. They're all too quick.
There! Look there! Look at that!" So Dymer stood,
Suddenly drained of hope. It was no good.

30

He pleaded then. Shame beneath shame. "Forgive.
205 It may be there are powers I cannot break.
If you are of them, speak. Speak. Let me live.
I ask so small a thing. I beg. I make
My body a living prayer whose force would shake
The mountains. I'll recant—confess my sin—
210 But this once let me pass. I must go in.

31

"Yield but one inch, once only from your law;
Set any price—I will give all, obey
All else but this, hold your least word in awe,
Give you no cause for anger from this day.
215 Answer! The least things living when they pray
As I pray now bear witness. They speak true
Against God. Answer! Mother, let me through."

32

Then when he heard no answer, mad with fear
And with desire, too strained with both to know
220 What he desired or feared, yet staggering near,
He forced himself towards her and bent low
For grappling. Then came darkness. Then a blow
Fell on his heart, he thought. There came a blank
Of all things. As the dead sink, down he sank.

33

225 The first big drops are rattling on the trees,
The sky is copper dark, low thunder pealing.
See Dymer with drooped head and knocking knees
Comes from the porch. Then slowly, drunkly reeling,

Blind, beaten, broken, past desire of healing,
230 Past knowledge of his misery, he goes on
Under the first dark trees and now is gone.

Canto IV

1

First came the peal that split the heavens apart
Straight overhead. Then silence. Then the rain;
Twelve miles of downward water like one dart,
And in one leap were launched along the plain,
5 To break the budding flower and flood the grain,
And keep with dripping sound an undersong
Amid the wheeling thunder all night long.

2

He put his hands before his face. He stooped
Blind with his hair. The loud drops' grim tattoo
10 Beat him to earth. Like summer grass he drooped,
Amazed, while sheeted lightning large and blue
Blinked wide and pricked the quivering eyeball through.
Then, scrambling to his feet, with downward head
He fought into the tempest as chance led.

3

15 The wood was mad. Soughing of branch and straining
Was there: drumming of water. Light was none
Nor knowledge of himself. The trees' complaining
And his own throbbing heart seemed mixed in one,
One sense of bitter loss and beauty undone;
20 All else was blur and chaos and rain-stream
And noise and the confusion of a dream.

4

Aha! . . . Earth hates a miserable man:
Against him even the clouds and winds conspire.
Heaven's voice smote Dymer's ear-drum as he ran,
25 Its red throat plagued the dark with corded fire
—Barbed flame, coiled flame that ran like living wire
Charged with disastrous current, left and right
About his path, hell-blue or staring white.

5

Stab! Stab! Blast all at once. What's he to fear?
30 Look there—that cedar shrivelling in swift blight
Even where he stood! And there—ah, that came near!
Oh, if some shaft would break his soul outright,
What ease so to unload and scatter quite
On the darkness this wild beating in his skull
35 Too burning to endure, too tense and full.

6

All lost: and driven away: even her name
Unknown. O fool, to have wasted for a kiss
Time when they could have talked! An angry shame
Was in him. He had worshipt earth, and this
40 —The venomed clouds fire spitting from the abyss,
This was the truth indeed, the world's intent
Unmasked and naked now, the thing it meant.

7

The storm lay on the forest a great time
—Wheeled in its thundery circuit, turned, returned.
45 Still through the dead-leaved darkness, through the slime
Of standing pools and slots of clay storm-churned
Went Dymer. Still the knotty lightning burned
Along black air. He heard the unbroken sound
Of water rising in the hollower ground.

8

50 He cursed it in his madness, flung it back,
Sorrow as wild as young men's sorrows are,
Till, after midnight, when the tempest's track
Drew off, between two clouds appeared one star.
Then his mood changed. And this was heavier far,
55 When bit by bit, rarer and still more rare,
The weakening thunder ceased from the cleansed air;

9

When leaves began to drip with dying rain
And trees showed black against the glimmering sky,
When the night-birds flapped out and called again

60 Above him: when the silence cool and shy
Came stealing to its own, and streams ran by
Now audible amid the rustling wood
—Oh, then came the worst hour for flesh and blood.

10

It was no nightmare now with fiery stream
65 Too horrible to last, able to blend
Itself and all things in one hurrying dream;
It was the waking world that will not end
Because hearts break, that is not foe nor friend,
Where sane and settled knowledge first appears
70 Of work day desolation, with no tears.

11

He halted then, footsore, weary to death,
And heard his heart beating in solitude,
When suddenly the sound of sharpest breath
Indrawn with pain and the raw smell of blood
75 Surprised his sense. Near by to where he stood
Came a long whimpering moan—a broken word,
A rustle of leaves where some live body stirred.

12

He groped towards the sound. "What, brother, brother,
Who groaned?"—"I'm hit. I'm finished. Let me be."
80 —"Put out your hand, then. Reach me. No, the other."
—"Don't touch. Fool! Damn you. Leave me."—"I can't see.
Where are you?" Then more groans. "They've done for me.
I've no hands. Don't come near me. No, but stay,
Don't leave me . . . oh my God! Is it near day?"

13

85 —"Soon now, a little longer. Can you sleep?
I'll watch for you."—"Sleep, is it? That's ahead,
But none till then. Listen, I've bled too deep
To last out till the morning. I'll be dead
Within the hour—sleep then. I've heard it said
90 They don't mind at the last, but this is Hell.
If I'd the strength—I have such things to tell."

14

All trembling in the dark and sweated over
Like a man reared in peace, unused to pain,
Sat Dymer near him in the lightless cover,
95 Afraid to touch and shamefaced to refrain.
Then bit by bit and often checked again
With agony the voice told on. (The place
Was dark, that neither saw the other's face.)

15

"There is a City which men call in scorn
100 The Perfect City—eastward of this wood—
You've heard about the place. There I was born.
I'm one of them, their work. Their sober mood,
The ordered life, the laws, are in my blood
—A life . . . well, less than happy, something more
105 Than the red greed and lusts that went before.

16

"All in one day one man and one blow
Brought ruin on us all. There was a boy
—Blue eyes, large limbs, were all he had to show,
You need no greater prophets to destroy.
110 He seemed a man asleep. Sorrow and joy
Had passed him by—the dreamiest, safest man,
The most obscure, until this curse began.

17

"Then—how or why it was, I cannot say,
This Dymer, this fool baby pink-and-white,
115 Went mad beneath his quiet face. One day,
With nothing said, he rose and laughed outright
Before his master: then, in all our sight,
Even where we sat to watch, he struck him dead
And screamed with laughter once again and fled.

18

120 "Lord! how it all comes back. How still the place is,
And he there lying dead . . . only the sound
Of a bluebottle buzzing . . . sharpened faces

Strained, gaping from the benches all around . . .
The dead man hunched and quiet with no wound,
125 And minute after minute terror creeping
With dreadful hopes to set the wild heart leaping.

19

"Then one by one at random (no word spoken),
We slipt out to the sunlight and away.
We felt the empty sense of something broken
130 And comfortless adventure all that day.
Men loitered at their work and could not say
What trembled at their lips or what new light
Was in girls' eyes. Yet we endured till night.

20

"Then . . . I was lying awake in bed,
135 Shot through with tremulous thought, lame hopes, and sweet
Desire of reckless days—with burning head.
And then there came a clamour from the street,
Came nearer, nearer, nearer—stamping feet
And screaming song and curses and a shout
140 Of 'Who's for Dymer, Dymer?—Up and out!'

21

"We looked out from our window. Thronging there
A thousand of our people, girls and men,
Raved and reviled and shouted by the glare
Of torches and of bonfire blaze. And then
145 Came tumult from the street beyond: again
'Dymer!' they cried. And farther off there came
The sound of gun-fire and the gleam of flame.

22

"I rushed down with the rest. Oh, we were mad!
After this, it's all nightmare. The black sky
150 Between the housetops framed was all we had
To tell us that the old world could not die
And that we were no gods. The flood ran high
When first I came, but after was the worse,
Oh, to recall . . . ! On Dymer rest the curse!

23

155 "Our leader was a hunchback with red hair
—Bran was his name. He had that kind of force
About him that will hold your eyes fast there
As in ten miles of green one patch of gorse
Will hold them—do you know? His lips were coarse
160 But his eyes like a prophet's—seemed to fill
The whole face. And his tongue was never still.

24

"He cried: 'As Dymer broke, we'll break the chain.
The world is free. They taught you to be chaste
And labour and bear orders and refrain.
165 Refrain? From what? All's good enough. We'll taste
Whatever is. Life murmurs from the waste
Beneath the mind . . . who made the reasoning part
The jailer of the wild gods in the heart?'

25

"We were a ragtail crew—wild-haired, half dressed,
170 All shouting, 'Up, for Dymer! Up away!'
Yet each one always watching all the rest
And looking to his back. And some were gay
Like drunk men, some were cringing, pinched and grey
With terror dry on the lip. (The older ones
175 Had had the sense enough to bring their guns.)

26

"The wave where I was swallowed swelled and broke,
After long surge, into the open square.
And here there was more light: new clamour woke.
Here first I heard the bullets sting the air
180 And went hot round the heart. Our lords were there
In barricade with all their loyal men.
For every one man loyal Bran led ten.

27

"Then charge and cheer and bubbling sobs of death,
We hovered on their front. Like swarming bees
185 Their spraying bullets came—no time for breath.

I saw men's stomachs fall out on their knees;
And shouting faces, while they shouted, freeze
Into black, bony masks. Before we knew
We're into them . . . 'Swine!'—'Die, then'—'That's for you.'

28

190 "The next that I remember was a lull
And sated pause. I saw an old, old man
Lying before my feet with shattered skull,
And both my arms dripped red. And then came Bran
And at his heels a hundred murderers ran,
195 With prisoners now, clamouring to take and try them
And burn them, wedge their nails up, crucify them.

29

"God! . . . Once the lying spirit of a cause
With maddening words dethrones the mind of men,
They're past the reach of prayer. The eternal laws
200 Hate them. Their eyes will not come clean again,
But doom and strong delusion drive them then
Without ruth, without rest . . . the iron laughter
Of the immortal mouths goes hooting after.

30

"And we had firebrands too. Tower after tower
205 Fell sheathed in thundering flame. The street was like
A furnace mouth. We had them in our power!
Then was the time to mock them and to strike,
To flay men and spit women on the pike,
Bidding them dance. Wherever the most shame
210 Was done the doer called on Dymer's name.

31

"Faces of men in torture . . . from my mind
They will not go away. The East lay still
In darkness when we left the town behind
Flaming to light the fields. We'd had our will:
215 We sang, 'Oh, we will make the frost distil
From Time's grey forehead into living dew
And break whatever has been and build new.'

32

"Day found us on the border of this wood,
Blear-eyed and pale. Then the most part began
220 To murmur and to lag, crying for food
And shelter. But we dared not answer Bran.
Wherever in the ranks the murmur ran
He'd find it—'You, there, whispering. Up, you sneak,
Reactionary, eh? Come out and speak.'

33

225 "Then there'd be shrieks, a pistol shot, a cry,
And someone down. I was the third he caught.
The others pushed me out beneath his eye,
Saying, 'He's here; here, Captain.' Who'd have thought,
My old friends? But I know now. I've been taught . . .
230 They cut away my two hands and my feet
And laughed and left me for the birds to eat.

34

"Oh, God's name! If I had my hands again
And Dymer here . . . it would not be my blood.
I am stronger now than he is, old with pain,
235 One grip would make him mine. But it's no good,
I'm dying fast. Look, Stranger, where the wood
Grows lighter. It's the morning. Stranger dear,
Don't leave me. Talk a little while. Come near."

35

But Dymer, sitting hunched with knee to chin,
240 Close to the dying man, answered no word.
His face was stone. There was no meaning in
His wakeful eyes. Sometimes the other stirred
And fretted, near his death; and Dymer heard,
Yet sat like one that neither hears nor sees.
245 And the cold east whitened beyond the trees.

Canto V

1

Through bearded cliffs a valley has driven thus deep
Its wedge into the mountain and no more.
The faint track of the farthest-wandering sheep
Ends here, and the grey hollows at their core
5 Of silence feel the dulled continuous roar
Of higher streams. At every step the skies
Grow less and in their place black ridges rise.

2

Hither, long after noon, with plodding tread
And eyes on earth, grown dogged, Dymer came,
10 Who all the long day in the woods had fled
From the horror of those lips that screamed his name
And cursed him. Busy wonder and keen shame
Were driving him, and little thoughts like bees
Followed and pricked him on and left no ease.

3

15 Now, when he looked and saw this emptiness
Seven times enfolded in the idle hills,
There came a chilly pause to his distress,
A cloud of the deep world despair that fills
A man's heart like the incoming tide and kills
20 All pains except its own. In that broad sea
No hope, no change, and no regret can be.

4

He felt the eternal strength of the silly earth,
The unhastening circuit of the stars and sea,
The business of perpetual death and birth,
25 The meaningless precision. All must be
The same and still the same in each degree—
Who cared now? And he smiled and could forgive,
Believing that for sure he would not live.

5

Then, where he saw a little water run
30 Beneath a bush, he slept. The chills of May

Came dropping and the stars peered one by one
Out of the deepening blue, while far away
The western brightness dulled to bars of grey.
Half-way to midnight, suddenly, from dreaming
35 He woke wide into present horror, screaming.

6

For he had dreamt of being in the arms
Of his beloved and in quiet places;
But all at once it filled with night alarms
And rapping guns: and men with splintered faces,
40 —No eyes, no nose, all red—were running races
With worms along the floor. And he ran out
To find the girl and shouted: and that shout

7

Had carried him into the waking world.
There stood the concave, vast, unfriendly night,
45 And over him the scroll of stars unfurled.
Then wailing like a child he rose upright,
Heart-sick with desolation. The new blight
Of loss had nipt him sore, and sad self-pity
Thinking of her—then thinking of the City.

8

50 For, in each moment's thought, the deeds of Bran,
The burning and the blood and his own shame,
Would tease him into madness till he ran
For refuge to the thought of her; whence came
Utter and endless loss—no, not a name,
55 Not a word, nothing left—himself alone
Crying amid that valley of old stone,

9

"How soon it all ran out! And I suppose
They, they up there, the old contriving powers,
They knew it all the time—for someone knows
60 And waits and watches till we pluck the flowers,
Then leaps. So soon—my store of happy hours
All gone before I knew. I have expended
My whole wealth in a day. It's finished, ended.

10

"And nothing left. Can it be possible
65 That joy flows through and, when the course is run,
It leaves no change, no mark on us to tell
Its passing? And as poor as we've begun
We end the richest day? What we have won,
Can it all die like this? . . . Joy flickers on
70 The razor-edge of the present and is gone.

11

"What have I done to bear upon my name
The curse of Bran? I was not of his crew,
Nor any man's. And Dymer has the blame—
What have I done? Wronged whom? I never knew.
75 What's Bran to me? I had my deed to do
And ran out by myself, alone and free.
—Why should earth sing with joy and not for me?

12

"Ah, but the earth never did sing for joy . . .
There is a glamour on the leaf and flower
80 And April comes and whistles to a boy
Over white fields: and, beauty has such power
Upon us, he believes her in that hour,
For who could not believe? Can it be false,
All that the blackbird says and the wind calls?

13

85 "What have I done? No living thing I made
Nor wished to suffer harm. I sought my good
Because the spring was gloriously arrayed
And the blue eyebright misted all the wood.
Yet to obey that springtime and my blood,
90 This was to be unarmed and off my guard
And gave God time to hit once and hit hard.

14

"The men built right who made that City of ours,
They knew their world. A man must crouch to face
Infinite malice, watching at all hours,
95 Shut nature out—give her no moment's space

For entry. The first needs of all our race
Are walls, a den, a cover. Traitor I
Who first ran out beneath the open sky.

15

"Our fortress and fenced place I made to fall,
100 I slipt the sentries and let in the foe.
I have lost my brothers and my love and all.
Nothing is left but me. Now let me go.
I have seen the world stripped naked and I know.
Great God, take back your world. I will have none
105 Of all your glittering gauds but death alone."

16

Meanwhile the earth swung round in hollow night.
Souls without number in all nations slept,
Snug on her back, safe speeding towards the light,
Hours tolled, and in damp woods the night beast crept,
110 And over the long seas the watch was kept
In black ships, twinkling onward, green and red:
Always the ordered stars moved overhead.

17

And no one knew that Dymer in his scales
Had weighed all these and found them nothing worth.
115 Indifferently the dawn that never fails
Troubled the east of night with gradual birth,
Whispering a change of colours on cold earth,
And a bird woke, then two. The sunlight ran
Along the hills and yellow day began.

18

120 But stagnant gloom clung in the valley yet;
Hills crowded out a third part of the sky,
Black-looking, and the boulders dripped with wet:
No bird sang. Dymer, shivering, heaved a sigh
And yawned and said: "It's cruel work to die
125 Of hunger"; and again, with cloudy breath
Blown between chattering teeth, "It's a bad death."

19

He crouched and clasped his hands about his knees
And hugged his own limbs for the pitiful sense
Of homeliness they had—familiars these,
130 This body, at least, his own, his last defence.
But soon his morning misery drove him thence,
Eating his heart, to wander as chance led
On, upward, to the narrowing gully's head.

20

The cloud lay on the nearest mountain-top
135 As from a giant's chimney smoking there,
But Dymer took no heed. Sometimes he'd stop,
Sometimes he hurried faster, as despair
Pricked deeper, and cried out: "Even now, somewhere,
Bran with his crew's at work. They rack, they burn,
140 And there's no help in me. I've served their turn."

21

Meanwhile the furrowed fog rolled down ahead,
Long tatters of its vanguard smearing round
The bases of the crags. Like cobweb shed
Down the deep combes it dulled the tinkling sound
145 Of water on the hills. The spongy ground
Faded three yards ahead: then nearer yet
Fell the cold wreaths, the white depth gleaming wet.

22

Then after a long time the path he trod
Led downward. Then all suddenly it dipped
150 Far steeper, and yet steeper, with smooth sod.
He was half running now. A stone that slipped
Beneath him, rattled headlong down: he tripped,
Stumbled and clutched—then panic, and no hope
To stop himself, once lost upon that slope.

23

155 And faster, ever faster, and his eye
Caught tree-tops far below. The nightmare feeling
Had gripped him. He was screaming: and the sky
Seemed hanging upside down. Then struggling, reeling,

With effort beyond thought he hung half kneeling,
160 Halted one saving moment. With wild will
He clawed into the hillside and lay still,

24

Half hanging on both arms. His idle feet
Dangled and found no hold. The moor lay wet
Against him and he sweated with the heat
165 Of terror, all alive. His teeth were set.
"By God, I will not die," said he. "Not yet."
Then slowly, slowly, with enormous strain,
He heaved himself an inch: then heaved again,

25

Till saved and spent he lay. He felt indeed
170 It was the big, round world beneath his breast,
The mother planet proven at his need.
The shame of glad surrender stood confessed,
He cared not for his boasts. This, this was best,
This giving up of all. He need not strive;
175 He panted, he lay still, he was alive.

26

And now his eyes were closed. Perhaps he slept
Lapt in unearthly quiet—never knew
How bit by bit the fog's white rearguard crept
Over the crest and faded, and the blue
180 First brightening at the zenith trembled through,
And deepening shadows took a sharper form
Each moment, and the sandy earth grew warm.

27

Yet, dreaming of blue skies, in dream he heard
The pure voice of a lark that seemed to send
185 Its song from heights beyond all height. That bird
Sang out of heaven, "The world will never end,"
Sang from the gates of heaven, "Will never end,"
Sang till it seemed there was no other thing
But bright space and one voice set there to sing.

28

190 It seemed to be the murmur and the voice
Of beings beyond number, each and all
Singing I AM. Each of itself made choice
And was: whence flows the justice that men call
Divine. She keeps the great worlds lest they fall
195 From hour to hour, and makes the hills renew
Their ancient youth and sweetens all things through.

29

It seemed to be the low voice of the world
Brooding alone beneath the strength of things,
Murmuring of days and nights and years unfurled
200 Forever, and the unwearied joy that brings
Out of old fields the flowers of unborn springs,
Out of old wars and cities burned with wrong,
A splendour in the dark, a tale, a song.

30

The dream ran thin towards waking, and he knew
205 It was but a bird's piping with no sense.
He rolled round on his back. The sudden blue,
Quivering with light, hard, cloudless and intense,
Shone over him. The lark still sounded thence
And stirred him at the heart. Some spacious thought
210 Was passing by too gently to be caught.

31

With that he thrust the damp hair from his face
And sat upright. The perilous cliff dropped sheer
Before him, close at hand, and from his place
Listening in mountain silence he could hear
215 Birds crying far below. It was not fear
That took him, but strange glory, when his eye
Looked past the edge into surrounding sky.

32

He rose and stood. Then lo! the world beneath
—Wide pools that in the sun-splashed foot hills lay,
220 Sheep-dotted downs, soft-piled, and rolling heath,
River and shining weir and steeples grey

And the green waves of forest. Far away
Distance rose heaped on distance: nearer hand,
The white roads leading down to a new land.

Canto VI

1

The sun was high in heaven and Dymer stood
A bright speck on the endless mountain-side,
Till, blossom after blossom, that rich mood
Faded and truth rolled homeward, like a tide
5 Before whose edge the weak soul fled to hide
In vain, with ostrich head, through many a shape
Of coward fancy, whimpering for escape.

2

But only for a moment; then his soul
Took the full swell and heaved a dripping prow
10 Clear of the shattering wave-crest. He was whole.
No veils should hide the truth, no truth should cow
The dear self-pitying heart. "I'll babble now
No longer," Dymer said. "I'm broken in.
Pack up the dreams and let the life begin."

3

15 With this he turned. "I must have food today,"
He muttered. Then among the cloudless hills
By winding tracks he sought the downward way
And followed the steep course of tumbling rills
—Came to the glens the wakening mountain fills
20 In springtime with the echoing splash and shock
Of waters leaping cold from rock to rock.

4

And still, it seemed, that lark with its refrain
Sang in the sky and wind was in his hair
And hope at heart. Then once, and once again,
25 He heard a gun fired off. It broke the air
As a stone breaks a pond, and everywhere

The dry crags echoed clear: and at the sound
Once a big bird rose whirring from the ground.

5

In half an hour he reached the level land
30 And followed the field-paths and crossed the stiles,
Then looked and saw, near by, on his left hand
An old house, folded round with billowy piles
Of dark yew hedge. The moss was on the tiles,
The pigeons in the yard, and in the tower
35 A clock that had no hands and told no hour.

6

He hastened. In warm waves the garden scent
Came stronger at each stride. The mountain breeze
Was gone. He reached the gates; then in he went
And seemed to lose the sky—such weight of trees
40 Hung overhead. He heard the noise of bees
And saw, far off, in the blue shade between
The windless elms, one walking on the green.

7

It was a mighty man whose beardless face
Beneath grey hair shone out so large and mild
45 It made a sort of moonlight in the place.
A dreamy desperation, wistful-wild,
Showed in his glance and gait: yet like a child,
An Asian emperor's only child, was he
With his grave looks and bright solemnity.

8

50 And over him there hung the witching air,
The wilful courtesy, of the days of old,
The graces wherein idleness grows fair;
And somewhat in his sauntering walk he rolled
And toyed about his waist with seals of gold,
55 Or stood to ponder often in mid-stride,
Tilting his heavy head upon one side.

9

When Dymer had called twice, he turned his eye:
Then, coming out of silence (as a star
All in one moment slips into the sky
60 Of evening, yet we feel it comes from far),
He said, "Sir, you are welcome. Few there are
That come my way": and in huge hands he pressed
Dymer's cold hand and bade him in to rest.

10

"How did you find this place out? Have you heard
65 My gun? It was but now I killed a lark."
"What, Sir," said Dymer, "shoot the singing bird?"
"Sir," said the man, "they sing from dawn till dark,
And interrupt my dreams too long. But hark . . .
Another? Did you hear no singing? No?
70 It was my fancy, then . . . pray, let it go.

11

"From here you see my garden's only flaw.
Stand here, Sir, at the dial." Dymer stood.
The Master pointed; then he looked and saw
How hedges and the funeral quietude
75 Of black trees fringed the garden like a wood,
And only, in one place, one gap that showed
The blue side of the hills, the white hill-road.

12

"I have planted fir and larch to fill the gap,"
He said, "because this too makes war upon
80 The art of dream. But by some great mishap
Nothing I plant will grow there. We pass on . . .
The sunshine of the afternoon is gone.
Let us go in. It draws near time to sup
—I hate the garden till the moon is up."

13

85 They passed from the hot lawn into the gloom
And coolness of the porch: then, past a door
That opened with no noise, into a room

Where green leaves choked the window and the floor
Sank lower than the ground. A tattered store
90 Of brown books met the eye: a crystal ball:
And masks with empty eyes along the wall.

14

Then Dymer sat, but knew not how nor where,
And supper was set out before these two,
—He saw not how—with silver old and rare
95 But tarnished. And he ate and never knew
What meats they were. At every bite he grew
More drowsy and let slide his crumbling will.
The Master at his side was talking still.

15

And all his talk was tales of magic words
100 And of the nations in the clouds above,
Astral and aerish tribes who fish for birds
With angles. And by history he could prove
How chosen spirits from earth had won their love,
As Arthur, or Usheen:[16] and to their isle
105 Went Helen for the sake of a Greek smile.

16

And ever in his talk he mustered well
His texts and strewed old authors round the way,
"Thus Wierus writes,"[17] and "Thus the Hermetics tell,"[18]
"This was Agrippa's view,"[19] and "Others say
110 With Cardan,"[20] till he had stolen quite away
Dymer's dull wits and softly drawn apart
The ivory gates of hope that change the heart.

17

Dymer was talking now. Now Dymer told
Of his own love and losing, drowsily.
115 The Master leaned towards him, "Was it cold,
This spirit, to the touch?"—"No, Sir, not she,"
Said Dymer. And his host: "Why this must be
Aethereal, not aereal! Oh my soul,
Be still . . . but wait. Tell on, Sir, tell the whole."

18

120 Then Dymer told him of the beldam too,
The old, old, matriarchal dreadfulness.
Over the Master's face a shadow drew,
He shifted in his chair and "Yes" and "Yes,"
He murmured twice. "I never looked for less!
125 Always the same . . . that frightful woman shape
Besets the dream-way and the soul's escape."

19

But now when Dymer made to talk of Bran,
A huge indifference fell upon his host,
Patient and wandering-eyed. Then he began,
130 "Forgive me. You are young. What helps us most
Is to find out again that heavenly ghost
Who loves you. For she was a ghost, and you
In that place where you met were ghostly too.

20

"Listen! for I can launch you on the stream
135 Will roll you to the shores of her own land . . .
I could be sworn you never learned to dream,
But every night you take with careless hand
What chance may bring? I'll teach you to command
The comings and the goings of your spirit
140 Through all that borderland which dreams inherit.

21

"You shall have hauntings suddenly. And often,
When you forget, when least you think of her
(For so you shall forget) a light will soften
Over the evening woods. And in the stir
145 Of morning dreams (oh, I will teach you, Sir)
There'll come a sound of wings. Or you shall be
Waked in the midnight murmuring, 'It was she.'"

22

"No, no," said Dymer, "not that way. I seem
To have slept for twenty years. Now—while I shake
150 Out of my eyes that dust of burdening dream,

Now when the long clouds tremble ripe to break
And the far hills appear, when first I wake,
Still blinking, struggling towards the world of men,
And longing—would you turn me back again?

23

155 "Dreams? I have had my dream too long. I thought
The sun rose for my sake. I ran down blind
And dancing to the abyss. Oh, Sir, I brought
Boy-laughter for a gift to Gods who find
The martyr's soul too soft. But that's behind.
160 I'm waking now. They broke me. All ends thus
Always—and we're for them, not they for us.

24

"And she—she was no dream. It would be waste
To seek her there, the living in that den
Of lies." The Master smiled. "You are in haste!
165 For broken dreams the cure is, Dream again
And deeper. If the waking world, and men,
And nature marred your dream—so much the worse
For a crude world beneath its primal curse."

25

—"Ah, but you do not know! Can dreams do this,
170 Pluck out blood-guiltiness upon the shore
Of memory—and undo what's done amiss,
And bid the thing that has been be no more?"
—"Sir, it is only dreams unlock that door,"
He answered with a shrug. "What would you have?
175 In dreams the thrice-proved coward can feel brave.

26

"In dreams the fool is free from scorning voices.
Grey-headed whores are virgin there again.
Out of the past dream brings long-buried choices,
All in a moment snaps the tenfold chain
180 That life took years in forging. There the stain
Of oldest sins—how do the good words go?—
Though they were scarlet, shall be white as snow."

27

Then, drawing near, when Dymer did not speak,
"My little son," said he, "your wrong and right
185 Are also dreams: fetters to bind the weak
Faster to phantom earth and blear the sight.
Wake into dreams, into the larger light
That quenches these frail stars. They will not know
Earth's bye-laws in the land to which you go."

28

190 —"I must undo my sins,"—"An earthly law,
And, even in earth, the child of yesterday.
Throw down your human pity; cast your awe
Behind you; put repentance all away.
Home to the elder depths! for never they
195 Supped with the stars who dared not slough behind
The last shred of earth's holies from their mind."

29

"Sir," answered Dymer, "I would be content
To drudge in earth, easing my heart's disgrace,
Counting a year's long service lightly spent
200 If once at the year's end I saw her face
Somewhere, being then most weary, in some place
I looked not for that joy—or heard her near
Whispering, 'Yet courage, friend,' for one more year."

30

"Pish," said the Master. "Will you have the truth?
205 You think that virtue saves? Her people care
For the high heart and idle hours of youth;
For these they will descend our lower air,
Not virtue. You would nerve your arm and bear
Your burden among men! Look to it, child:
210 By virtue's self vision can be defiled.

31

"You will grow full of pity and the love of men,
And toil until the morning moisture dries
Out of your heart. Then once, or once again

It may be you will find her: but your eyes
215 Soon will be grown too dim. The task that lies
Next to your hand will hide her. You shall be
The child of earth and gods you shall not see."

32

Here suddenly he ceased. Tip-toes he went.
A bolt clicked—then the window creaked ajar,
220 And out of the wet world the hedgerow scent
Came floating; and the dark without one star
Nor shape of trees nor sense of near and far,
The undimensioned night and formless skies
Were there, and were the Master's great allies.

33

225 "I am very old," he said. "But if the time
We suffered in our dreams were counting age,
I have outlived the ocean and my prime
Is with me to this day. Years cannot gauge
The dream-life. In the turning of a page,
230 Dozing above my book, I have lived through
More ages than the lost Lemuria knew.[21]

34

"I am not mortal. Were I doomed to die
This hour, in this half-hour I interpose
A thousand years of dream: and, those gone by,
235 As many more, and in the last of those,
Ten thousand—ever journeying towards a close
That I shall never reach: for time shall flow,
Wheel within wheel, interminably slow.

35

"And you will drink my cup and go your way
240 Into the valley of dreams. You have heard the call.
Come hither and escape. Why should you stay?
Earth is a sinking ship, a house whose wall
Is tottering while you sweep; the roof will fall
Before the work is done. You cannot mend it.
245 Patch as you will, at last the rot must end it."

36

Then Dymer lifted up his heavy head
Like Atlas on broad shoulders bearing up
The insufferable globe. "I had not said,"
He mumbled, "Never said I'd taste the cup.
250 What, is it this you give me? Must I sup?
Oh lies, all lies . . . Why did you kill the lark?
Guide me the cup to lip . . . it is so dark."

Canto VII

1

The host had trimmed his lamp. The downy moth
Came from the garden. Where the lamplight shed
Its circle of smooth white upon the cloth,
Down mid the rinds of fruit and broken bread,
5 Upon his sprawling arms lay Dymer's head;
And often, as he dreamed, he shifted place,
Muttering and showing half his drunken face.

2

The beating stillness of the dead of night
Flooded the room. The dark and sleepy powers
10 Settled upon the house and filled it quite;
Far from the roads it lay, from belfry towers
And hen-roosts, in a world of folded flowers,
Buried in loneliest fields where beasts that love
The silence through the unrustled hedgerows move.

3

15 Now from the Master's lips there breathed a sigh
As of a man released from some control
That wronged him. Without aim his wandering eye,
Unsteadied and unfixed, began to roll.
His lower lip dropped loose. The informing soul
20 Seemed fading from his face. He laughed out loud
Once only: then looked round him, hushed and cowed.

4

Then, summoning all himself, with tightened lip,
With desperate coolness and attentive air,
He touched between his thumb and finger tip,
25 Each in its turn, the four legs of his chair,
Then back again in haste—there!—that one there
Had been forgotten . . . once more! . . . safer now;
That's better! and he smiled and cleared his brow.

5

Yet this was but a moment's ease. Once more
30 He glanced about him like a startled hare,
His big eyes bulged with horror. As before,
Quick!—to the touch that saves him. But despair
Is nearer by one step; and in his chair
Huddling he waits. He knows that they'll come strong
35 Again and yet again and all night long;

6

And after this night comes another night
—Night after night until the worst of all.
And now too even the noonday and the light
Let through the horrors. Oh, could he recall
40 The deep sleep and the dreams that used to fall
Around him for the asking. But, somehow,
Something's amiss . . . sleep comes so rarely now.

7

Then, like the dog returning to its vomit,
He staggered to the bookcase to renew
45 Yet once again the taint he had taken from it,
And shuddered as he went. But horror drew
His feet, as joy draws others. There in view
Was his strange heaven and his far stranger hell,
His secret lust, his soul's dark citadel:—

8

50 Old Theogmagia,[22] Demonology,
Cabbala,[23] Chemic Magic, Book of the Dead,[24]
Damning Hermetic rolls that none may see

Save the already damned—such grubs are bred [25]
From minds that lose the Spirit and seek instead
55 For spirits in the dust of dead men's error,
Buying the joys of dream with dreamland terror.

9

This lost soul looked them over one and all
Now sickened at the heart's root; for he knew
This night was one of those when he would fall
60 And scream alone (such things they made him do)
And roll upon the floor. The madness grew
Wild at his breast, but still his brain was clear
That he could watch the moment coming near.

10

But, ere it came, he heard a sound, half groan,
65 Half muttering, from the table. Like a child
Caught unawares that thought it was alone,
He started as in guilt. His gaze was wild,
Yet pitiably with all his will he smiled,
—So strong is shame, even then. And Dymer stirred,
70 Now waking, and looked up and spoke one word:

11

"Water!" he said. He was too dazed to see
What hell-wrung face looked down, what shaking hand
Poured out the draught. He drank it thirstily
And held the glass for more. "Your land . . . your land
75 Of dreams," he said. "All lies! . . . I understand
More than I did. Yes, water. I've the thirst
Of hell itself. Your magic's all accursed."

12

When he had drunk again he rose and stood,
Pallid and cold with sleep. "By God," he said,
80 "You did me wrong to send me to that wood.
I sought a living spirit and found instead
Bogys and wraiths." The Master raised his head
Calm as a sage and answered, "Are you mad?
Come, sit you down. Tell me what dream you had."

13

85 —"I dreamed about a wood . . . an autumn red
Of beech-trees big as mountains. Down between—
The first thing that I saw—a clearing spread,
Deep down, oh, very deep. Like some ravine
Or like a well it sank, that forest green
90 Under its weight of forest—more remote
Than one ship in a landlocked sea afloat.

14

"Then through the narrowed sky some heavy bird
Would flap its way, a stillness more profound
Following its languid wings. Sometimes I heard
95 Far off in the long woods with quiet sound
The sudden chestnut thumping to the ground,
Or the dry leaf that drifted past upon
Its endless loiter earthward and was gone.

15

"Then next . . . I heard twigs splintering on my right
100 And rustling in the thickets. Turning there
I watched. Out of the foliage came in sight
The head and blundering shoulders of a bear,
Glistening in sable black, with beady stare
Of eyes towards me, and no room to fly
105 —But padding soft and slow the beast came by.

16

"And—mark their flattery—stood and rubbed his flank
Against me. On my shaken legs I felt
His heart beat. And my hand that stroked him sank
Wrist-deep upon his shoulder in soft pelt.
110 Yes . . . and across my spirit as I smelt
The wild thing's scent, a new, sweet wildness ran
Whispering of Eden-fields long lost by man.

17

"So far was well. But then came emerald birds
Singing about my head. I took my way
115 Sauntering the cloistered woods. Then came the herds,

The roebuck and the fallow deer at play
Trooping to nose my hand. All this, you say,
Was sweet? Oh, sweet! . . . do you think I could not see
That beasts and wood were nothing else but me?

18

120 " . . . That I was making everything I saw,
Too sweet, far too well fitted to desire
To be a living thing? Those forests draw
No sap from the kind earth: the solar fire
And soft rain feed them not: that fairy brier
125 Pricks not: the birds sing sweetly in that brake
Not for their own delight but for my sake!

19

"It is a world of sad, cold, heartless stuff,
Like a bought smile, no joy in it."—"But stay;
Did you not find your lady?"—"Sure enough!
130 I still had hopes till then. The autumn day
Was westering, the long shadows crossed my way,
When over daisies folded for the night
Beneath rook-gathering elms she came in sight."

20

—"Was she not fair?"—"So beautiful, she seemed
135 Almost a living soul. But every part
Was what I made it—all that I had dreamed—
No more, no less: the mirror of my heart,
Such things as boyhood feigns beneath the smart
Of solitude and spring. I was deceived
140 Almost. In that first moment I believed.

21

"For a big, brooding rapture, tense as fire
And calm as a first sleep had soaked me through
Without thought, without word, without desire . . .
Meanwhile above our heads the deepening blue
145 Burnished the gathering stars. Her sweetness drew
A veil before my eyes. The minutes passed
Heavy like loaded vines. She spoke at last.

22

"She said, for this land only did men love
The shadow-lands of earth. All our disease
150 Of longing, all the hopes we fabled of,
Fortunate islands or Hesperian seas
Or woods beyond the West, were but the breeze
That blew from off those shores: one farspent breath
That reached even to the world of change and death.

23

155 "She told me I had journeyed home at last
Into the golden age and the good countrie
That had been always there. She bade me cast
My cares behind forever:—on her knee
Worshipped me, lord and love—oh, I can see
160 Her red lips even now! Is it not wrong
That men's delusions should be made so strong?

24

"For listen, I was so besotted now
She made me think that I was somehow seeing
The very core of truth . . . I felt somehow,
165 Beyond all veils, the inward pulse of being.
Thought was enslaved, but oh, it felt like freeing
And draughts of larger air. It is too much!
Who can come through untainted from that touch?

25

"There I was nearly wrecked. But mark the rest:
170 She went too fast. Soft to my arms she came.
The robe slipped from her shoulder. The smooth breast
Was bare against my own. She shone like flame
Before me in the dusk, all love, all shame—
Faugh!—and it was myself. But all was well,
175 For, at the least, that moment snapped the spell.

26

"As when you light a candle, the great gloom
Which was the unbounded night, sinks down, compressed
To four white walls in one familiar room,

So the vague joy shrank wilted in my breast
180 And narrowed to one point, unmasked, confessed;
Fool's paradise was gone: instead was there
King Lust with his black, sudden, serious stare.

27

"That moment in a cloud among the trees
Wild music and the glare of torches came.
185 On sweated faces, on the prancing knees
Of shaggy satyrs fell the smoky flame,
On ape and goat and crawlers without name,
On rolling breast, black eyes and tossing hair,
On old bald-headed witches, lean and bare.

28

190 "They beat the devilish tom-tom rub-a-dub;
Lunging, leaping, in unwieldy romp,
Singing Cotytto [26] and Beelzebub,
With devil dancers' mask and phallic pomp,
Torn raw with briers and caked from many a swamp
195 They came, among the wild flowers dripping blood
And churning the green mosses into mud.

29

"They sang, 'Return! Return! We are the lust
That was before the world and still shall be
When your last law is trampled into dust,
200 We are the mother swamp, the primal sea
Whence the dry land appeared. Old, old are we.
It is but a return . . . it's nothing new,
Easy as slipping on a well-worn shoe.'

30

"And then there came warm mouths and finger-tips
205 Preying upon me, whence I could not see,
Then . . . a huge face, low browed, with swollen lips
Crooning, 'I am not beautiful as she,
But I'm the older love; you shall love me
Far more than Beauty's self. You have been ours
210 Always. We are the world's most ancient powers.'

31

"First flatterer and then bogy—like a dream!
Sir, are you listening? Do you also know
How close to the soft laughter comes the scream
Down yonder?" But this host cried sharply, "No.
215 Leave me alone. Why will you plague me? Go!
Out of my house! Begone."—"With all my heart,"
Said Dymer. "But one word before we part."

32

He paused, and in his cheek the anger burned:
Then turning to the table, he poured out
220 More water. But before he drank he turned—
Then leaped back to the window with a shout
For there—it was no dream—beyond all doubt
He saw the Master crouch with levelled gun
Cackling in maniac voice, "Run, Dymer, run!"

33

225 He ducked and sprang far out. The starless night
On the wet lawn closed round him every way.
Then came the gun-crack and the splash of light
Vanished as soon as seen. Cool garden clay
Slid from his feet. He had fallen and he lay
230 Face downward among leaves—then up and on
Through branch and leaf till sense and breath were gone.

Canto VIII

1

When next he found himself no house was there,
No garden and great trees. Beside a lane
In grass he lay. Now first he was aware
That, all one side, his body glowed with pain:
5 And the next moment and the next again
Was neither less nor more. Without a pause
It clung like a great beast with fastened claws;

2

That for a time he could not frame a thought
Nor know himself for self, nor pain for pain,
10 Till moment added on to moment taught
The new, strange art of living on that plane,
Taught how the grappled soul must still remain,
Still choose and think and understand beneath
The very grinding of the ogre's teeth.

3

15 He heard the wind along the hedges sweep,
The quarter striking from a neighbouring tower.
About him was the weight of the world's sleep;
Within, the thundering pain. That quiet hour
Heeded it not. It throbbed, it raged with power
20 Fit to convulse the heavens; and at his side
The soft peace drenched the meadows far and wide.

4

The air was cold, the earth was cold with dew,
The hedge behind him dark as ink. But now
The clouds broke and a paler heaven showed through
25 Spacious with sudden stars, breathing somehow
The sense of change to slumbering lands. A cow
Coughed in the fields behind. The puddles showed
Like pools of sky amid the darker road.

5

And he could see his own limbs faintly white
30 And the blood black upon them. Then by chance
He turned . . . and it was strange; there at his right
He saw a woman standing, and her glance
Met his: and at the meeting his deep trance
Changed not, and while he looked the knowledge grew
35 She was not of the old life but the new.

6

"Who is it?" he said. "The loved one, the long lost."
He stared upon her. "Truly?"—"Truly indeed."
"Oh, lady, you come late. I am tempest-tossed,

Broken and wrecked. I am dying. Look, I bleed.
40 Why have you left me thus and given no heed
To all my prayers?—left me to be the game
Of all deceits?"—"You should have asked my name."

7

—"What are you, then?" But to his sudden cry
She did not answer. When he had thought awhile
45 He said: "How can I tell it is no lie?
It may be one more phantom to beguile
The brain-sick dreamer with its harlot smile."
"I have not smiled," she said. The neighbouring bell
Tolled out another quarter. Silence fell.

8

50 And after a long pause he spoke again:
"Leave me," he said. "Why do you watch with me?
You do not love me. Human tears and pain
And hoping for the things that cannot be,
And blundering in the night where none can see,
55 And courage with cold back against the wall,
You do not understand."—"I know them all.

9

"The gods themselves know pain, the eternal forms.
In realms beyond the reach of cloud, and skies
Nearest the ends of air, where come no storms
60 Nor sound of earth, I have looked into their eyes
Peaceful and filled with pain beyond surmise,
Filled with an ancient woe man cannot reach
One moment though in fire; yet calm their speech."

10

"Then these," said Dymer, "were the world I wooed . . .
65 These were the holiness of flowers and grass
And desolate dews . . . these, the eternal mood
Blowing the eternal theme through men that pass.
I called myself their lover—I that was
Less fit for that long service than the least
70 Dull, workday drudge of men or faithful beast.

11

"Why do they lure to them such spirits as mine,
The weak, the passionate, and the fool of dreams?
When better men go safe and never pine
With whisperings at the heart, soul-sickening gleams
75 Of infinite desire, and joy that seems
The promise of full power? For it was they,
The gods themselves that led me on this way.

12

"Give me the truth! I ask not now for pity.
When gods call, can the following them be sin?
80 Was it false light that lured me from the City?
Where was the path—without it or within?
Must it be one blind throw to lose or win?
Has heaven no voice to help? Must things of dust
Guess their own way in the dark?" She said, "They must."

13

85 Another silence: then he cried in wrath,
"You came in human shape, in sweet disguise
Wooing me, lurking for me in my path,
Hid your eternal cold with woman's eyes,
Snared me with shows of love—and all was lies."
90 She answered, "For our kind must come to all
If bidden, but in the shape for which they call."

14

"What," answered Dymer. "Do you change and sway
To serve us, as the obedient planets spin
About the sun? Are you but potter's clay
95 For us to mould—unholy to our sin
And holy to the holiness within?"
She said, "Waves fall on many an unclean shore,
Yet the salt seas are holy as before.

15

"Our nature is no purer for the saint
100 That worships, nor from him that uses ill
Our beauty, can we suffer any taint.

As from the first we were, so are we still:
With incorruptibles the mortal will
Corrupts itself, and clouded eyes will make
105 Darkness within from beams they cannot take."

16

"Well . . . it is well," said Dymer. "If I have used
The embreathing spirit amiss . . . what would have been
The strength of all my days I have refused
And plucked the stalk, too hasty, in the green,
110 Trusted the good for best, and having seen
Half-beauty, or beauty's fringe, the lowest stair,
The common incantation, worshipped there."

17

But presently he cried in his great pain,
"If I had loved a beast it would repay,
115 But I have loved the Spirit and loved in vain.
Now let me die . . . ah, but before the way
Is ended quite, in the last hour of day,
Is there no word of comfort, no one kiss
Of human love? Does it all end in this?"

18

120 She answered, "Never ask of life and death.
Uttering these names you dream of wormy clay
Or of surviving ghosts. This withering breath
Of words is the beginning of decay
In truth, when truth grows cold and pines away
125 Among the ancestral images. Your eyes
First see her dead: and more, the more she dies.

19

"You are still dreaming, dreams you shall forget
When you have cast your fetters, far from here.
Go forth, the journey is not ended yet.
130 You have seen Dymer dead and on the bier
More often than you dream and dropped no tear,
You have slain him every hour. Think not at all
Of death lest into death by thought you fall."

20

He turned to question her, then looked again,
135 And lo! the shape was gone. The darkness lay
Heavy as yet and a cold, shifting rain
Fell with the breeze that springs before the day.
It was an hour death loves. Across the way
The clock struck once again. He saw near by
140 The black shape of the tower against the sky.

21

Meanwhile above the torture and the riot
Of leaping pulse and nerve that shot with pain,
Somewhere aloof and poised in spectral quiet
His soul was thinking on. The dizzied brain
145 Scarce seemed her organ: link by link the chain
That bound him to the flesh was loosening fast
And the new life breathed in unmoved and vast.

22

"It was like this," he thought. "Like this, or worse
For him that I found bleeding in the wood . . .
150 Blessings upon him . . . there I learned the curse
That rests on Dymer's name, and truth was good.
He has forgotten now the fire and blood,
He has forgotten that there was a man
Called Dymer. He knows not himself nor Bran.

23

155 "How long have I been moved at heart in vain
About this Dymer, thinking this was I . . .
Why did I follow close his joy and pain
More than another man's? For he will die,
The little cloud will vanish and the sky
160 Reigns as before. The stars remain and earth
And Man, as in the years before my birth.

24

"There was a Dymer once who worked and played
About the City; I sloughed him off and ran.
There was a Dymer in the forest glade
165 Ranting alone, skulking the fates of man.

I cast him also, and a third began
And he too died. But I am none of those.
Is there another still to die . . . Who knows?"

25

Then in his pain, half wondering what he did,
170 He made to struggle towards that belfried place.
And groaning down the sodden bank he slid
And groaning in the lane he left[27] his trace
Of bloodied mire: then halted with his face
Upwards, towards the gateway, breathing hard
175 —An old lych-gate before a burial-yard.

26

He looked within. Between the huddling crosses,
Over the slanted tombs and sunken slate
Spread the deep quiet grass and humble mosses,
A green and growing darkness, drenched of late,
180 Smelling of earth and damp. He reached the gate
With failing hand. "I will rest here," he said,
"And the long grass will cool my burning head."

Canto IX

1

Even as he heard the wicket clash behind
Came a great wind beneath that seemed to tear
The solid graves apart; and deaf and blind
Whirled him upright like smoke, through towering air,
5 Whose levels were as steps of a sky stair.
The parching cold roughened his throat with thirst
And pricked him at the heart. This was the first.

2

And as he soared into the next degree,
Suddenly all round him he could hear
10 Sad strings that fretted inconsolably
And ominous horns that blew both far and near.
There broke his human heart, and his last tear
Froze scalding on his chin. But while he heard
He shot like a sped dart into the third.

3

15 And its first stroke of silence could destroy
The spring of tears forever and compress
From off his lips the curved bow of the boy
Forever. The sidereal loneliness
Received him, where no journeying leaves the less
20 Still to be journeyed through: but everywhere,
Fast though you fly, the centre still is there.

4

And here the well-worn fabric of our life
Fell from him. Hope and purpose were cut short,
—Even the blind trust that reaches in mid-strife
25 Towards some heart of things. Here blew the mort
For the world spirit herself. The last support
Was fallen away—Himself, one spark of soul,
Swam in unbroken void. He was the whole,

5

And wailing: "Why hast Thou forsaken me?
30 Was there no world at all, but only I
Dreaming of gods and men?" Then suddenly
He felt the wind no more: he seemed to fly
Faster than light but free; and scaled the sky
In his own strength—as if a falling stone
35 Should wake to find the world's will was its own.

6

And on the instant, straight before his eyes
He looked and saw a sentry shape that stood
Leaning upon its spear, with hurrying skies
Behind it and a moonset red as blood.
40 Upon its head were helmet and mailed hood
And shield upon its arm and sword at thigh,
All black and pointed sharp against the sky.

7

Then came the clink of metal, the dry sound
Of steel on rock, and challenge: "Who comes here?"
45 And as he heard it, Dymer at one bound

Stood in the stranger's shadow, with the spear
Between them. And his human face came near
That larger face. "What watch is this you keep?"
Said Dymer, "On the edge of such a deep."

8

50 And answer came, "I watch both night and day
This frontier . . . there are beasts of the upper air
As beasts of the deep sea . . . one walks this way
Night after night, far scouring from his lair,
Chewing the cud of lusts which are despair
55 And fill not, while his mouth gapes dry for bliss
That never was."—"What kind of beast is this?"

9

"A kind of things escaped that have no home,
Hunters of men. They love the spring uncurled,
The will worn down, the wearied hour. They come
60 At night-time when the mask is off the world
And the soul's gate ill-locked and the flag furled
—Then, softly, a pale swarm, and in disguise
Flit past the drowsy watchman, small as flies."

10

"I'll see this aerish beast whereof you speak.
65 I'll share the watch with you."—"Nay, little One,
Begone. You are of earth. The flesh is weak . . ."
—"What is the flesh to me? My course is run,
All but some deed still waiting to be done,
Some moment I may rise on, as the boat
70 Lifts with the lifting tide and steals afloat.

11

"You are a spirit, and it is well with you,
But I am come out of great folly and shame,
The sack of cities, wrongs I must undo . . .
But tell me of the beast, and whence it came;
75 Who were its sire and dam? What is its name?"
—"It is my kin. All monsters are the brood
Of heaven and earth, and mixed with holy blood."

12

—"How can this be?"—"My son, sit here awhile.
There is a lady in that primal place
80 Where I was born, who with her ancient smile
Made glad the sons of heaven. She loved to chase
The springtime round the world. To all your race
She was a sudden quivering in the wood
Or a new thought springing in solitude.

13

85 "Till, in prodigious hour, one swollen with youth,
Blind from new broken prison, knowing not
Himself nor her, nor how to mate with truth,
Lay with her in a strange and secret spot,
Mortal with her immortal, and begot
90 This walker-in-the-night."—"But did you know
This mortal's name?"—"Why . . . it was long ago.

14

"And yet, I think, I bear the name in mind;
It was some famished boy whom tampering men
Had crippled in their chains and made him blind
95 Till their weak hour discovered them: and then
He broke that prison. Softly!—it comes again,
I have it. It was Dymer, Little One,
Dymer's the name. This spectre is his son."

15

Then, after silence, came an answering shout
100 From Dymer, glad and full: "Break off! Dismiss !
Your watch is ended and your lamp is out.
Unarm, unarm. Return into your bliss.
You are relieved, Sir. I must deal with this
As in my right. For either I must slay
105 This beast or else be slain before the day."

16

"So mortal and so brave?" that other said,
Smiling, and turned and looked in Dymer's eyes,
Scanning him over twice from heel to head

—Like an old sergeant's glance, grown battle wise
110 To know the points of men. At last, "Arise,"
He said, "and wear my arms. I can withhold
Nothing; for such an hour has been foretold."

17

Thereat, with lips as cold as the sea-surge,
He kissed the youth, and bending on one knee
115 Put all his armour off and let emerge
Angelic shoulders marbled gloriously
And feet like frozen speed and, plain to see,
On his wide breast dark wounds and ancient scars,
The battle honours of celestial wars.

18

120 Then like a squire or brother born he dressed
The young man in those plates, that dripped with cold
Upon the inside, trickling over breast
And shoulder: but without, the figured gold
Gave to the tinkling ice its jagged hold,
125 And the icy spear froze to Dymer's hand.
But where the other had stood he took his stand

19

And searched the cloudy landscape. He could see
Dim shapes like hills appearing, but the moon
Had sunk behind their backs. "When will it be?"
130 Said Dymer: and the other, "Soon now, soon.
For either he comes past us at night's noon
Or else between the night and the full day,
And down there, on your left, will be his way."

20

—"Swear that you will not come between us two
135 Nor help me by a hair's weight if I bow."
—"If you are he, if prophecies speak true,
Not heaven and all the gods can help you now.
This much I have been told, but know not how
The fight will end. Who knows? I cannot tell."
140 "Sir, be content," said Dymer. "I know well."

21

Thus Dymer stood to arms, with eyes that ranged
Through aching darkness: stared upon it, so
That all things, as he looked upon them, changed
And were not as at first. But grave and slow
145 The larger shade went sauntering to and fro,
Humming at first the snatches of some tune
That soldiers sing, but falling silent soon.

22

Then came steps of dawn. And though they heard
No milking cry in the fields, and no cock crew,
150 And out of empty air no twittering bird
Sounded from neighbouring hedges, yet they knew.
Eastward the hollow blackness paled to blue,
Then blue to white: and in the West the rare,
Surviving stars blinked feebler in cold air.

23

155 For beneath Dymer's feet the sad half-light
Discovering the new landscape oddly came,
And forms grown half familiar in the night
Looked strange again: no distance seemed the same.
And now he could see clear and call by name
160 Valleys and hills and woods. The phantoms all
Took shape, and made a world, at morning's call.

24

It was a ruinous land. The ragged stumps
Of broken trees rose out of endless clay
Naked of flower and grass: the slobbered humps
165 Dividing the dead pools. Against the grey
A shattered village gaped. But now the day
Was very near them and the night was past,
And Dymer understood and spoke at last.

25

"Now I have wooed and won you, bridal earth,
170 Beautiful world that lives, desire of men.
All that the spirit intended at my birth

This day shall be born into deed . . . and then
The hard day's labour comes no more again
Forever. The pain dies. The longings cease.
175 The ship glides under the green arch of peace.

26

"Now drink me as the sun drinks up the mist.
This is the hour to cease in, at full flood,
That asks no gift from following years—but, hist!
Look yonder! At the corner of that wood—
180 Look! Look there where he comes! It shocks the blood,
The first sight, eh? Now, sentinel, stand clear
And save yourself. For God's sake come not near."

27

His full-grown spirit had moved without command
Or spur of the will. Before he knew, he found
185 That he was leaping forward spear in hand
To where that ashen brute wheeled slowly round
Nosing, and set its ears towards the sound,
The pale and heavy brute, rough-ridged behind,
And full of eyes, clinking in scaly rind.

28

190 And now ten paces parted them: and here
He halted. He thrust forward his left foot,
Poising his straightened arms, and launched the spear,
And gloriously it sang. But now the brute
Lurched forward: and he saw the weapon shoot
195 Beyond it and fall quivering on the field.
Dymer drew out his sword and raised the shield.

29

What now, my friends? You get no more from me
Of Dymer. He goes from us. What he felt
Or saw from henceforth no man knows but he
200 Who has himself gone through the jungle belt
Of dying, into peace. That angel knelt
Far off and watched them close but could not see
Their battle. All was ended suddenly.

30

A leap—a cry—flurry of steel and claw,
205 Then silence. As before, the morning light
And the same brute crouched yonder; and he saw
Under its feet, broken and bent and white,
The ruined limbs of Dymer, killed outright
All in a moment, all his story done.
210 . . . But that same moment came the rising sun;

31

And thirty miles to Westward, the grey cloud
Flushed into answering pink. Long shadows streamed
From every hill, and the low hanging shroud
Of mist along the valleys broke and steamed
215 Gold-flecked to heaven. Far off the armour gleamed
Like glass upon the dead man's back. But now
The sentinel ran forward, hand to brow,

32

And staring. For between him and the sun
He saw that country clothed with dancing flowers
220 Where flower had never grown; and one by one
The splintered woods, as if from April showers,
Were softening into green. In the leafy towers
Rose the cool, sudden chattering on the tongues
Of happy birds with morning in their lungs.

33

225 The wave of flowers came breaking round his feet,
Crocus and bluebell, primrose, daffodil
Shivering with moisture: and the air grew sweet
Within his nostrils, changing heart and will,
Making him laugh. He looked, and Dymer still
230 Lay dead among the flowers and pinned beneath
The brute: but as he looked he held his breath;

34

For when he had gazed hard with steady eyes
Upon the brute, behold, no brute was there,
But someone towering large against the skies,
235 A wing'd and sworded shape, through whom the air

Poured as through glass: and its foam-tumbled hair
Lay white about the shoulders and the whole
Pure body brimmed with life, as a full bowl.

35

And from the distant corner of day's birth
240 He heard clear trumpets blowing and bells ring,
A noise of great good coming into earth
And such a music as the dumb would sing
If Balder[28] had led back the blameless spring
With victory, with the voice of charging spears,
245 And in white lands long-lost Saturnian years.[29]
(1916–25; 1926)

Notes

Originally published in 1926 under a pseudonym, *Dymer* was reprinted in 1950 under Lewis's own name. This preface appeared in that 1950 reprint (London: J. M. Dent, 1950). *Dymer* was later republished with Lewis's three other principal narrative poems in C. S. Lewis, *Narrative Poems* (hereafter, *NP*), ed. Walter Hooper (New York: Harcourt Brace Jovanovich, 1969).

1. *Siegfried* is the third of the four operas that constitute *Der Ring des Nibelungen* (*The Ring of the Nibelung*), by Richard Wagner. For Wagner's influence on Lewis, see chapter 5, "Renaissance," of his autobiography, *Surprised by Joy.*

2. Although Russia experienced more than one uprising at the beginning of the twentieth century, the term Russian Revolution generally refers to two uprisings in Feb. and Oct. 1917, near the end of World War I, which respectively overthrew the tzar and brought the Bolsheviks to power.

3. Christiana Pontifex is an important character in Samuel Butler's *The Way of All Flesh* (1903).

4. William Butler Yeats (1865–1939), fellow Irishman to Lewis, was the most important poet of the late nineteenth and early twentieth centuries. His hold on Lewis's imagination in the writing of *Dymer* is described below.

5. Belgian Maurice Maeterlinck (1862–1949) was a poet, playwright, and essayist who won the Nobel Prize for Literature in 1911 for his outstanding works of symbolist theatre.

6. Yeats's "Rosa Alchemica" (1897) is a short prose romance that forms one part of the mystical triptych, with "The Adoration of the Magi" and "The Tables of the Law." Titus Lucretius Carus (99–55 B.C.) was a Roman poet and philosopher whose only known work is a philosophical poem celebrating Epicureanism, *De rerum natura* (translated into English as *On the Nature of Things*). Joseph Martin McCabe (1867–1955), after serving as a Roman Catholic priest, renounced his faith and wrote about his experience in *Twelve Years in a Monastery* (1897).

7. Lewis is alluding here to John Hawkins Askins (1877–1923), a brother of Mrs. Janie Moore, often referred to as Doc. Lewis recounts his descent into madness in his diary, published as *All My Road Before Me* (London: Collins, 1991), 201–30. In *SJ* he adds: "It had been my chance to spend fourteen days, and most of the fourteen nights as well, in close contact with a man

who was going mad. He was a man whom I had dearly loved, and well he deserved love. And now I helped to hold him while he kicked and wallowed on the floor, screaming out that devils were tearing him and that he was that moment falling down into Hell. And this man, as I well knew, had not kept the beaten track. He had flirted with Theosophy, Yoga, Spiritualism, Psychoanalysis, what not?" (202–3).

8. For more on Lewis's visits to see Yeats, see his *CL* 1:524–34 and 564–66.

9. "If it be allowable to compare small things with great."

10. *On Baile's Strand* is a verse play by Yeats (1903; 1906). Richard Le Gallienne (1866–1947) was a popular writer and poet. Lewis's point is that Yeats was the greater writer, even if modernists were unable to realize that fact.

11. *Brave New World* (1932) is a dark futuristic novel by Aldous Huxley exploring the conflict between the interests of the individual and those of society. *Land Under England* (1935), by Joseph O'Neill, is a science-fiction account of a totalitarian society ruled by telepathic mind control. *The Aerodrome: A Love Story* (1941) is an antifascist novel by Rex Warner.

12. From Odin's High Song in the *Edda*, essentially a code of laws and ethics his people are to use to govern their conduct. The complete reference is:

I ween that I hung on the windy tree
Hung there for nights full nine:
With the spear I was wounded, and offered I was
To Othin, myself to myself,
On the tree that none may ever know
What root beneath it runs.

(*The Poetic Edda*, trans. Henry Adams Bellows [New York: The American-Scandinavin Foundation, 1923], 60). The windy tree refers to the "ash Yggdrasil (literally 'the Horse of Othin,' so called because of this story), on which Othin, in order to win the magic runes, hanged himself as an offering to himself, and wounded himself with his own spear" (*Poetic Edda*, 60).

13. This refers to the Casualty Clearing Stations common during World War I. These medical stations, manned by personnel of the British Royal Army Medical Corps, treated and sorted wounded troops for return to duty or evacuation.

14. In Greek mythology, Artemis is the goddess of chastity, virginity, the hunt, and the moon; the Roman version of this goddess is Diana.

15. In the first edition, instead of *ended* Lewis uses the word *needed*. Here I follow the 1950 edition.

16. Usheen (or Ossian) was the legendary greatest poet of Ireland. In *Oisín in Tir na nÓg*, his most famous tale, he is visited by a fairy woman, Níamh Chinn Óir ("Niamh of the golden hair" or "head") who announces she loves him and takes him away to Tir na nÓg ("the land of the young").

17. Johann Weyer (or Wierus) (1515–1588) was a Dutch physician, occultist, and demonologist, and a disciple and follower of Heinrich Cornelius Agrippa.

18. Hermeticism is the ancient doctrine that affirms that a single, true theology underlies all religions.

19. Heinrich Cornelius Agrippa von Nettesheim (1486–1535) was a German philosopher, theologian, and scholar specializing in occultism, alchemy, and medicine. See also note 17, above, on Wierus.

20. Italian doctor and mathematician Girolamo Cardan (1501–1576) wrote *Ars Magna,* the first Latin work devoted solely to algebra.

21. Lemuria was a legendary lost land, variously located in the Indian and Pacific oceans.

22. Ancient Athenian festival celebrating the marriage of Zeus and Hera.

23. Secret or occult doctrine.

24. *The Book of the Dead* is an ancient Egyptian funerary text.

25. In the first edition, Lewis uses the word *grules* instead of *grubs.* Here I follow the 1950 edition.

26. Cotytto is a Greek goddess of unbridled sexual activity.

27. In the first edition, Lewis instead uses the word *felt* instead of *left.* Here I follow the 1950 edition.

28. In Norse mythology, Balder was a son of the chief god Odin and his wife, the goddess Frigg, known as beautiful and just.

29. In "LP" 9:129–30, Lewis offers his own chronological account of the writing of *Dymer:*

The prose version of *Dymer*—1916 (?)
The "Redemption of Ask" (In two parts, Lucrece metre)—Oct.–Nov. 1918
The "Red Maid" (ballad)—1920
Dymer begun—Apr. 2, 1922
Canto I finished—May 11, 1922
Canto II finished—June 1, 1922
Canto III (A-version) abandoned—June 22, 1922
Canto III (B-version) finished—June 29, 1922
"Lyrical Epilogue" for *Dymer* attempted—July 8, 1922
Canto IV finished—Oct. 8, 1922
Canto V finished—Mar. 25, 1923
Canto V recopied and corrected—June 27, 1923
"Kirkian" stanzas for Canto VI done—June 28, 1923
"Kirkian" episode abandoned—June 29, 1923
Cantos VI and VII (A-version) finished (Village shop and boat)—Sept. 8, 1923
Cantos VI and VII condemned by Harwood—Oct. 21, 1923
Canto VI (B) finished (Old Welkin and boat)—Oct. (?) 1923
Canto III (C-version) finished (e cow version)—Jan. 22, 1924
Canto VI (C-version) finished—Mar. 25, 1924
Canto IX finished—Mar. 25, 1924
Canto VII (B-version) begun—Apr. 6, 1924
Fresh start on Canto VII (B-version)—Apr. 10, 1924
Canto VII (B-version) finished (Complete text now in existence; condemned)—Apr. 28, 1924
Canto VI (D-version) started—Apr. or May 1924
Canto VI (D-version) finished—Before May 23, 1924
Canto VII (C-version) and VIII—Long Vacation 1925 (?)
Accepted by Dent's—Apr. 1, 1926

As Lewis's chronology makes clear, from 1920 to 1926 he threw himself into composing *Dymer* with intensity and deliberate single-mindedness. His diary, *All My Road Before Me,* illustrates this in detail, as it contains more than seventy-five direct references to his writing of *Dymer.*

In these diary entries, he recounts an almost daily obsession with both his progress on the poem and his ambition to achieve fame as a poet. Moreover, during this composition process, he shifted from one canto to another, revising here and there as he saw the need. Often he was assisted in this process by the sympathetic but frank criticism of colleagues, including Leo Baker, Owen Barfield, Alfred Hamilton-Jenkin, Cecil Harwood, Rodney Pasley, and Arthur Greeves. For more on this, see King, *C. S. Lewis, Poet,* 1–26 and 108–36.

Poems

1927–1934

The Lord Is a Jealous God—A Careful Shepherd

The Lord is a jealous god—a careful shepherd,
Tenderly (ah how tenderly!) guards my life;
Allows no rival in me, wolf nor leopard,
—My throat is sacred to the butcher's knife.[1]
(Summer 1927 [?]; 2006)

The Hedgehog Moralised

Hedgehog hase ane sturne rynde
uppon his bak wha sall it se
bot wambe and brest after his kynde
bathe is softe as silk harde.
5 Þat ane signifyeþ to my mynde
fortitude al witerle
þat oþer as man iwriten finde
þe noble vertue of charitee

Whan þat he is idrad of fas
10 intill ane bal then torneþ he
what mister beste ojeins him gas
can nat gar him grue ne dee
his heued he ligges untill his tas
þat lowest to þat heizest sal bee
15 quhilk signifyeþ as in this cas
guid sheltrom is in humilitee.
EX
PLICI
T
(1927–28 [?]; 2001)

Thus Æ to Ĕ

Thus Æ to Ĕ they soon were fetchin,'
Cf. such forms as ÞÆC and ÞECCEAN.[2]
(1928 [?]; 2000)

Artless and Ignorant Is Andvāri

Artless and ignorant is Andvāri[3]
As a kneaded clod, if never he heard
Where is gold growing, the glory of Rhine!
A second sun, under still water
(Can it be Odin's eye?)[4] that upward shoots
Answering that other (or, from under earth,
Balder bringing the buried good?)[5]
Who knows the nature of that noble kind
Would not laugh lightly at the lover of it;
It holds inherent in it the heritage of nine worlds.
None shall reave it from Rhine, nor to ring twist it
Till he unlearn the law whereby Love made him
And spill himself for the sake of the gold.[6]
Ignorant and artless is Andvāri—
Never dwarf but was dull, daring only in greed.[7]
(June 1929 [?]; 2001)

Long at Lectures

Long at lectures
On Monday morning
I work till one! Hoihe!!
Piddling pupils
I in taking am engaged!!
Can your car
So swiftly over
Earth's back wander
From Oxford to London between one and 5:45?
Walawei! Hoo-ruddy-rah!!!!
Ho-hai!!!!!
!!
? !!!!
If so, call
For me at Magdalen
Were wisest rune
On Monday at one!
If you lie
On Tuesday night

20 In Magdalen's ancient College
You will meet Dyson
Dining with me
Of men the justest!!
[The whole scene explodes][8]
(October 1929 [?]; 2001)

Save Yourself. Run and Leave Me. I Must Go Back

Save yourself. Run and leave me. I must go back.
Though we have escaped the sentry and are past the wall,
Though returning means mockery and the whip and the rack,
Yet their sending is too strong; I must turn at their call.
5 Save yourself. Leave me. I must go back.
(1929–30 [?]; 1964)

I Woke from a Fool's Dream, to Find All Spent

I woke from a fool's dream, to find all spent
Except one little sixpence, worn and bent.
The same day, in the nick of time, I found
The market where my sixpence buys a pound.
5 Sirs, tell me was the bargain good or bad?
The price was cheap. The price was all I had.
(1929–1930 [?]; 1964)

Essence

Thoughts that go through my mind,
I dare not tell them;
The alphabet of kind
Lacks script to spell them.

5 Yet I remain. My will
Some things yet can;
Thought is still one, and still
I am called a man.

Oh of what kind, how far
10 Past fire's degree
Of pureness, past a star
In constancy;

Than light, which can possess
Its own outgoing,
15 How much more one, much less
Division knowing,

That essence must have been
Which still I call
My self, since—thus unclean—
20 It dies not all.

(1929–30 [?]; 1940)

The following poems appeared in The Pilgrim's Regress *(1933)*[9]

He Whom I Bow To

He whom I bow to only knows to whom I bow[10]
When I attempt the ineffable name, murmuring *Thou;*
And dream of Pheidian[11] fancies and embrace in heart
Meanings, I know, that cannot be the thing thou art.
5 All prayers always, taken at their word, blaspheme,
Invoking with frail imageries a folk-lore dream;
And all men are idolaters, crying unheard
To senseless idols, if thou take them at their word,
And all men in their praying, self-deceived, address
10 One that is not (so saith that old rebuke) unless
Thou, of mere grace, appropriate, and to thee divert
Men's arrows, all at hazard aimed, beyond desert.
Take not, oh Lord, our literal sense, but in thy great,
Unbroken speech our halting metaphor translate.
(1929–30 [?]; 1933)

You Rest Upon Me All My Days

You rest upon me all my days[12]
The inevitable Eye,
Dreadful and undeflected as the blaze
Of some Arabian sky;

5 Where, dead still, in their smothering tent
Pale travellers crouch, and, bright
About them, noon's long-drawn Astonishment
Hammers the rocks with light.

Oh, for but one cool breath in seven,
10 One air from northern climes,
The changing and the castle-clouded heaven
Of my old Pagan times!

But you have seized all in your rage
Of Oneness. Round about,

15 Beating my wings, all ways, within your cage,
I flutter, but not out.
(1929–30 [?]; 1933)

My Heart Is Empty

My heart is empty.[13] All the fountains that should run
With longing, are in me
Dried up. In all my countryside there is not one
That drips to find the sea.
5 I have no care for anything thy love can grant
Except the moment's vain
And hardly noticed filling of the moment's want
And to be free from pain.
Oh, thou that art unwearying, that dost neither sleep
10 Nor slumber, who didst take
All care for Lazarus in the careless tomb, oh keep
Watch for me till I wake.
If thou think for me what I cannot think, if thou
Desire for me what I
15 Cannot desire, my soul's interior Form, though now
Deep-buried, will not die,
—No more than the insensible dropp'd seed which grows
Through winter ripe for birth
Because, while it forgets, the heaven remembering throws
20 Sweet influence still on earth,
—Because the heaven, moved moth-like by thy beauty, goes
Still turning round the earth.
(1929–30 [?]; 1933)

Thou Only Art Alternative to God

Thou only art alternative to God,[14] oh, dark
And burning island among the spirits, tenth hierarch,
Wormwood, immortal Satan, Ahriman,[15] alone
Second to Him to whom no second else were known,
5 Being essential fire, sprung of His fire, but bound
Within the lightless furnace of thy Self, bricked round
To rage in the reverberated heat from seven

Containing walls: hence power thou hast to rival heaven.
Therefore, except the temperance of the eternal love
10 Only thy absolute lust is worth the thinking of.
All else is weak disguisings of the wishful heart,
All that seemed earth is Hell, or Heaven. God is: thou art:
The rest, illusion. How should man live save as glass
To let the white light without flame, the Father, pass
15 Unstained: or else—opaque, molten to thy desire,
Venus infernal starving in the strength of fire!

Lord, open not too often my weak eyes to this.
(1929–30 [?]; 1933)

God in His Mercy Made

God in His mercy made[16]
The fixèd pains of Hell.
That misery might be stayed,
God in his mercy made
5 Eternal bounds and bade
Its waves no further swell.
God in his mercy made
The fixèd pains of Hell.
(1929–30 [?]; 1933)

Nearly They Stood Who Fall

Nearly they stood who fall;[17]
Themselves as they look back
See always in the track
The one false step, where all
5 Even yet, by lightest swerve
Of foot not yet enslaved,
By smallest tremor of the smallest nerve,
Might have been saved.

Nearly they fell who stand,
10 And with cold after fear
Look back to mark how near

They grazed the Sirens' land,
Wondering that subtle fate,
By threads so spidery fine,
15 The choice of ways so small, the event so great,
Should thus entwine.

Therefore oh, man, have fear
Lest oldest fears be true,
Lest thou too far pursue
20 The road that seems so clear,
And step, secure, a hair's
Breadth past the hair-breadth bourne,
Which, being once crossed forever unawares,
Denies return.
(1929–30 [?]; 1933)

I Have Scraped Clean the Plateau

I have scraped clean the plateau from the filthy earth,[18]
Earth the unchaste, the fruitful, the great grand maternal,
Sprawling creature, lolling at random and supine,
The broad-faced, sluttish helot, the slave wife
5 Grubby and warm, who opens unashamed
Her thousand wombs unguarded to the lickerous sun.
Now I have scoured my rock clean from the filthy earth,
On it no root can strike and no blade come to birth,
And though I starve of hunger it is plainly seen
10 That I have eaten nothing common or unclean.

I have by fasting purged away the filthy flesh,
Flesh the hot, moist, salt scum, the obscenity
And parasitic tetter, from my noble bones.
I have torn from my breasts—I was an udder'd beast—
15 My child, for he was fleshly. Flesh is caught
By a contagion carried from impure
Generation to generation through the body's sewer.
And now though I am barren, yet no man can doubt
I am clean and my iniquities are blotted out.

20 I have made my soul (once filthy) a hard, pure, bright
Mirror of steel: no damp breath breathes upon it
Warming and dimming: it would freeze the finger
If any touched it. I have a mineral soul.
Minerals eat no food and void no excrement.
25 So I, borrowing nothing and repaying
Nothing, neither growing nor decaying,
Myself am to myself, a mortal God, a self-contained
Unwindowed monad,[19] unindebted and unstained.
(1929–30 [?]; 1933)

Because of Endless Pride

Because of endless pride[20]
Reborn with endless error,
Each hour I look aside
Upon my secret mirror
5 Trying all postures there
To make my image fair.

Thou givest grapes, and I,
Though starving, turn to see
How dark the cool globes lie
10 In the white hand of me,
And linger gazing thither
Till the live clusters wither.

So should I quickly die
Narcissus-like of want,
15 But, in the glass, my eye
Catches such forms as haunt
Beyond nightmare, and make
Pride humble for pride's sake.

Then and then only turning
20 The stiff neck round, I grow
A molten man all burning
And look behind and know
Who made the glass, whose light makes dark, whose fair
Makes foul, my shadowy form reflected there

25 That Self-Love, brought to bed of Love may die and bear
Her sweet son in despair.
(1929–30 [?]; 1933)

Iron Will Eat the World's Old Beauty Up

Iron will eat the world's old beauty up.[21]
Girder and grid and gantry will arise,
Iron forest of engines will arise,
Criss-cross of iron crochet. For your eyes
5 No green or growth. Over all, the skies
Scribbled from end to end with boasts and lies.
(When Adam ate the irrevocable apple, Thou
Saw'st beyond death the resurrection of the dead.)

Clamour shall clean put out the voice of wisdom,
10 The printing-presses with their clapping wings,
Fouling your nourishment. Harpy wings,
Filling your minds all day with foolish things,
Will tame the eagle Thought: till she sings
Parrot-like in her cage to please dark kings.
15 (When Israel descended into Egypt, Thou
Didst purpose both the bondage and the coming out.)

The new age, the new art, the new ethic and thought,
And fools crying, Because it has begun
It will continue as it has begun!
20 The wheel runs fast, therefore the wheel will run
Faster for ever. The old age is done,
We have new lights and see without the sun.
(Though they lay flat the mountains and dry up the sea,
Wilt thou yet change, as though God were a god?)
(1929–30 [?]; 1933)

Quick! The Black, Sulphurous, Never Quenched

Quick! The black, sulphurous, never quenched,[22]
Old festering fire begins to play
Once more within. Look! By brute force I have wrenched
Unmercifully my hands the other way.

5 Quick, Lord! On the rack thus, stretched tight,
Nerves clamouring as at nature's wrong,
Scorched to the quick, whipp'd raw—Lord, in this plight
You see, you see no man can suffer long.

Quick, Lord! Before new scorpions bring
10 New venom—ere fiends blow the fire
A second time—quick, show me that sweet thing
Which, 'spite of all, more deeply I desire.
(1929–30 [?]; 1933)

When Lilith Means to Draw Me

When Lilith means to draw me[23]
Within her secret bower,
She does not overawe me
With beauty's pomp and power,
5 Nor, with angelic grace
Of courtesy, and the pace
Of gliding ships, come veiled at evening hour.

Eager, unmasked, she lingers
Heart-sick and hunger sore;
10 With hot, dry, jewelled fingers
Stretched out, beside her door,
Proffers with gnawing haste
Her cup, whereof who taste,
(She promises no better) thirst far more.

15 What moves me, then, to drink it?
—Her spells, which all around
So change the land, we think it
A great waste where a sound

Of wind like tales twice told
20 Blusters, and cloud is rolled
Always above yet no rain falls to ground.

Across drab iteration
Of bare hills, line on line,
The long road's sinuation
25 Leads on. The witch's wine,
Though promising nothing, seems
In that land of no streams
To promise best—the unrelished anodyne.
(1929–30; 1933)

Once the Worm-laid Egg Broke in the Wood

Once the worm-laid egg broke in the wood.[24]
I came forth shining into the trembling wood,
The sun was on my scales, dew upon the grasses,
The cool, sweet grasses and the budding leaves.
5 I wooed my speckled mate. We played at druery[25]
And sucked warm milk dropping from the goats' teats.

Now I keep watch on the gold in my rock cave
In a country of stones: old, deplorable dragon,
Watching my hoard. In winter night the gold
10 Freezes through toughest scales my cold belly.
The jagged crowns and twisted cruel rings
Knobbly and icy are old dragon's bed.

Often I wish I hadn't eaten my wife,
Though worm grows not to dragon till he eat worm.
15 She could have helped me, watch and watch about
Guarding the hoard. Gold would have been the safer.
I could uncoil my weariness at times and take
A little sleep, sometimes when she was watching.

Last night under the moonset a fox barked,
20 Woke me. Then I knew I had been sleeping.
Often an owl flying over the country of stones
Startles me, and I think I must have slept.

Only a moment. That very moment a man
Might have come out of the cities, stealing, to get my gold.

25 They make plots in the towns to get my gold.
They whisper of me in a low voice, laying plans,
Merciless men. Have they not ale upon the benches,
Warm wife in bed, singing, and sleep the whole night?
But I leave not the cave but once in winter
30 To drink of the rock pool: in summer twice.

They feel no pity for the old, lugubrious dragon.
Oh, Lord, that made the dragon, grant me Thy peace!
But ask not that I should give up the gold,
Nor move, nor die; others would get the gold.
35 Kill, rather, Lord, the men and the other dragons
That I may sleep, go when I will to drink.
(1929–30 [?]; 1933)

I Have Come Back with Victory Got

I have come back with victory got [26]—
But stand away—touch me not
Even with your clothes. I burn red-hot.

The worm was bitter. When she saw
5 My shield glitter beside the shaw[27]
She spat flame from her golden jaw.

When on my sword her vomit spilt
The blade took fire. On the hilt
Beryl cracked, and bubbled gilt.

10 When sword and sword arm were all flame
With the very heat that came
Out of the brute, I flogged her tame.

In her own spew the worm died.
I rolled her round and tore her wide
15 And plucked the heart from her boiling side.

When my teeth were in the heart
I felt a pulse within me start
As though my breast would break apart.

It shook the hills and made them reel
20 And spun the woods round like a wheel.
The grass singed where I set my heel.

Behemoth is my serving man!
Before the conquered hosts of Pan,
Riding tamed Leviathan,
25 Loud I sing for well I can
RESVRGAM and IO PAEAN,[28]
IO, IO, IO PAEAN!!

Now I know the stake I played for,
Now I know what a worm's made for!
(1929–30 [?]; 1933)

I Am Not One that Easily Flits Past in Thought

I am not one that easily flits past in thought[29]
The ominous stream, imagining death made for nought.
This person, mixed of body and breath, to which concurred
Once only one articulation of thy word,
5 Will be resolved eternally: nor can time bring
(Else time were vain) once back again the self-same thing.
Therefore among the riddles that no man has read
I put thy paradox, Who liveth and was dead.
As Thou hast made substantially, thou wilt unmake
10 In earnest and for everlasting. Let none take
Comfort in frail supposal that some hour and place
To those who mourn recovers the wished voice and face.
Whom Thy great *Exit* banishes, no after age
Of epilogue leads back upon the lighted stage.
15 Where is Prince Hamlet when the curtain's down? Where fled
Dreams at the dawn, or colours when the light is sped?
We are thy colours, fugitive, never restored,
Never repeated again. Thou only art the Lord,

Thou only art holy. In the shadowy vast
20 Of thine Osirian wings Thou dost enfold the past.
There sit in throne antediluvian,[30] cruel kings,
There the first nightingale that sang to Eve yet sings,
There are the irrecoverable guiltless years,
There, yet unfallen, Lucifer among his peers.

25 For thou art also a deity of the dead, a god
Of graves, with necromancies in thy potent rod;
Thou art Lord of the unbreathable transmortal air
Where mortal thinking fails: night's nuptial darkness, where
All lost embraces intermingle and are bless'd,
30 And all die, but all are, while Thou continuest.
(1929–30 [?]; 1933)

Passing To-day by a Cottage, I Shed Tears

Passing to-day by a cottage, I shed tears[31]
When I remembered how once I had dwelled there
With my mortal friends who are dead. Years
Little had healed the wound that was laid bare.

5 Out, little spear that stabs. I, fool, believed
I had outgrown that local, unique sting,
I had transmuted away (I was deceived)
Into love universal the lov'd thing.

But Thou, Lord, surely knewest Thine own plan
10 When the angelic indifferences with no bar
Universally loved but Thou gav'st man
The tether and pang of the particular;

Which, like a chemic drop, infinitesimal,
Plashed into pure water, changing the whole,
15 Embodies and embitters and turns all
Spirit's sweet water to astringent soul.

That we, though small, may quiver with fire's same
Substantial form as Thou—nor reflect merely,
As lunar angel, back to thee, cold flame.
20 Gods we are, Thou hast said: and we pay dearly.
(1929–30 [?]; 1933)

I Know Not, I

I know not, I,[32]
    What the men together say,
How lovers, lovers die
    And youth passes away.

5 Cannot understand
    Love that mortal bears
For native, native land
    —All lands are theirs.

Why at grave they grieve
10   For one voice and face,
And not, and not receive
    Another in its place.

I, above the cone
    Of the circling night
15 Flying, never have known
    More or lesser light.

Sorrow it is they call
    This cup: whence my lip,
Woe's me, never in all
20   My endless days must sip.
(1929–30 [?]; 1933)

The Shortest Way Home

Is this your duty? Do not lay your ear
Back to your skull and snarl, bright tiger! Down.
Bruin! Grimalkin back![33] Did you not hear
    Man's voice and see man's frown?

5 Down, the whole pack, or else—so! now you are meek!
And then, alas, your eyes. Dumb, suffering brutes.
So bottomless is your pain, your strength so weak,
    It plucks at my heart-roots.

Oh courage. I'll come back when I've grown shepherd
10 To comfort and grown child to lead you all
Where there's green pasture growing for the leopard
And for the wolf a stall.

But not before the voyage on which I am bound
Has made its end and its beginning meet
15 When over and under earth I have travelled round
The whole heaven's milky street.
(1929–30 [?]; 1934)

They Tell Me, Lord that When I Seem

They tell me, Lord that when I seem
To be in speech with you,
Since but one voice is heard, it's all a dream,
One talker aping two.

5 Sometimes it is, yet not as they
Conceive it. Rather, I
Seek in myself the things I hoped to say,
But lo! my wells are dry.

Then, seeing me empty, you forsake
10 The listener's role and through
My dumb lips breathe and into utterance wake
The thoughts I never knew.

And thus you neither need reply
Nor can; thus, while we seem
15 Two talkers, thou are One forever, and I
No dreamer, but thy dream.
(1929–30 [?]; 1964)

Set on the Soul's Acropolis the Reason Stands

Set on the soul's acropolis the reason stands
A virgin, arm'd, commercing with celestial light,
And he who sins against her has defiled his own
Virginity: no cleansing makes his garment white;
5 So clear is reason. But how dark imagining,
Warm, dark, obscure and infinite, daughter of Night:
Dark is her brow, the beauty of her eyes with sleep
Is loaded, and her pains are long, and her delight.
Tempt not Athene. Wound not in her fertile pains
10 Demeter,[34] nor rebel against her mother-right.
Oh who will reconcile in me both maid and mother,
Who make in me a concord of the depth and height?
Who make imagination's dim exploring touch
Ever report the same as intellectual sight?
15 Then could I truly say, and not deceive,
Then wholly say, that I BELIEVE.
(1929–32 [?]; 1964)

Abecedarium Philosophicum

A is the Absolute: none can express it.[35]
The Absolute, Gentleman! Fill up! God bless it!
B is for Bergson who said: "It's a crime!
They've been and forgotten that Time is Time!"[36]
5 C is for Croce who said: "Art's a stuff
That means what it says (and that's little enough!)"[37]
And also for Cambridge, that kindest of nurses,
Where "tissues" write essays and "ganglia" verses.
D for Descartes who said: "God couldn't be
10 So complete if he weren't. So he is. Q.E.D."[38]
And also Democritus (Atoms and Void
Were the only two things the man really enjoyed).[39]
E is for Elis, where men lived and died.
They couldn't walk out of that town if they tried.[40]
15 F is for Fichte,[41] who tapped on the pane
And said: "Come in, my dear, I'm[42] just starting to rain!"
G is the Good. Now we say that a cup
Or a shoe or a ship may be good. . . . Oh, shut up!

All right, then, for Godwin who earns what he eats[43]
20 By hoodwinking all the Romantics but Keats.
H is for Hume who awoke Kant from nappin.'
He said: "There's no causes for things. They just happen."[44]
I am transcendent and I am empirical;
I am a slave and I am a miracle.
25 J is for Judgment. Identity please!
S's are S's and P's will be P's.
K is for Kant who said: "Things in themselves
Are no good till the forms of per
ception and judgment have
30 pickled and bottled and
labelled and sorted 'em
out into neat little
rows on the shelves."[45]
L is for Leibnitz who said: "It's the best
35 Of all possible worlds. I've examined the rest."[46]
(He also invented a nice calculation
To pull up fast trains—like a portable station.)
M is the Many, the Mortal, the Body,
The Formless, the Female, the Thoroughly Shoddy.
40 N is Not-Being which sinks even deeper,
More formless, more female, more footling—and cheaper.
But it's O for the One. Hallelujah! Callay!
Glory be! (and see also above under A);
For the One is all round like an accurate sphere
45 And its function is simple, my son—to cohere.
P is for Plato who held that Ideas
Were snobs who would only leave cards on their peers.
Q is for Quality—otherwise "Whatness"—
The gauntness of Ghent and totness of Totnes.
50 R was a Realist, having no doubt
That it's there in the Bank, though you can't draw it out.
And also the Rumpus they made, when they found
That it wasn't the Sun but the Earth that went round.
S is for Socrates. Gad, if he'd met
55 Santayana and Spengler and some of that set![47]
T is for St. Thomas who gave me a shock[48]
When he danced like a lady[49] and struck like a clock.[50]
U is Upstairs to the Ultimate Unity,
Where we'd all better go at the first opportunity.

60 But, pilgrims afflicted with weak Understandings,
Oh beware of the Un-Dings you meet on the landings!
V is for Vico whose Views were heretical;[51]
He thought Pithecanthropus wise and poetical.[52]
W stands for the Water whence Thales
65 Derived the whole Cosmus, beginning with Whales,
And also for Wells,[53] who thinks God is defensible,
If only he'd take his advice and be sensible.
X is for Xenophanes:[54] "Mouse is myolatrous,
Rhinocerotes are rhinocerolatrous,
70 Billy and Nanny-goats both are tragolatrous,
Therefore religion is auto-idolatrous!"
(The first of a very long series of scrimmages
As to which fashioned which after which of their images).[55]
Y is for Yoga—the subtle askesis
75 Of taking deep breaths in (which then one releases).
And Z? For poor Zeno who often felt faint,
When he heard you deny that Nonentity ain't.[56]
(1929–32 [?]; 1933)

You, Beneath Scraping Branches

You, beneath scraping branches, to the gate,
At evening, outward bound, have driven the last
Time of all times; the old, disconsolate,
Familiar pang you have felt as in the past.

5 Drive on and look not out. Though from each tree
Grey memories drop and dreams thick-dusted lie
Beneath; though every other place must be
Raw, new, colonial country till we die;

Yet look not out. Think rather, "When from France
10 And those old German wars we came back here,
Already it was the mind's swift, haunting glance
Towards the further past made that time dear."

Then to that further past, still up the stream
Ascend, and think of some divine first day
15 In holidays from school. Even there the gleam
Of earlier memory like enchantment lay.

Always from further back breathes the thin scent,
As of cold Eden wakenings on wet lawns;
And eldest hours had elder to lament
20 And dreamed of irrecoverable dawns.

No more's lost now than that whose loss made bright
Old things with older things' longer-lingering breath.
The past you mourn for, when it was in flight,
Lived, like the present, in continual death.
(1930; 1986)

In a Spring Season I Sailed Away

In a spring season I sailed away
Early at evening of an April night.
Master mariner of the men was I,
Eighteen in all. And every day
5 We had weather at will. White-topped the seas
Rolled, and the rigging rang like music,
While fast and fair the unfettered wind
Followed. Sometimes fine-sprinkling rain
Over our ship scudding sparkled for a moment
10 And was gone in a glance; then gleaming white
Of cloud-castles was unclosed, and the blue
Of bottomless heav'n, over the blowing waves
Blessed us returning. Half blind with her speed,
Foamy-throated, into the flash and salt
15 Of the seas rising our ship ran on
For ten days' time. Then came a turn of luck.
On the tenth evening too soon the light
Over working seas went beneath the sky line,
Darkness came dripping and the deafening storm
20 Upon wild waters, wet days and long,
Carried us, and caverned clouds immeasurable
Harried and hunted like a hare that ship
Too many days. Men were weary.
Then was a starless night when storm was worst,
25 The man of my mates whom most I loved
Cried "Lost!" and then he leaped. Alive no more
Nor dead either the dear-loved face
Was seen. But soon, after his strange going,

Worse than the weathers, came the word shouted,
30 "Breakers ahead of us," and out of black darkness,
Hell-white, appeared horrid torment
Of water at the walls of a wild country.
The cliffs were high, cluttered with splinters
Of basalt at the base, bare-toothed. We found
35 Sea-room too small; we must split for sure,
And I heeded not the helm. Their hearts broke there,
The men I loved. Mad-faced they ran
All ways at once, till the waves swallowed
Many a smart seaman. Myself, I leaped
40 And wondered as I went what-like was death,
Before the cold clasped me. But there came a sea
Lifting from under me, so large a wave
That far above the foam of the first rock-shelves
It bore me, and far above the spray,
45 Upward, upward, into the air's region,
Beyond the cliffs into a yawning dark.
Other echoes, earthlier sounding,
In closer space, shut out the clamourous waves.
Then backward drawn with a babble of stones,
50 Softly sounding, in its spent fury,
A dull, dragging, withdrawing sigh,
That wave returned into the wastes, its home,
And would have sucked me back as I sank wearied,
But that there was grass growing where I gripped the land,
55 And roots all rough: so that I wrestled, clinging,
Against the water's tug. The wave left me,
And I grovelled on the ground, greatly wearied.
How long I lay, lapped in my weariness,
Memory minds not. To me it seems
60 That for one full turn of the wheels above
I slept. Certainly when the sleep left me
There was calm and cool. No crashing of the sea,
But darkness all about. Dim-shadowed leaves
In mildest air moved above me,
65 And, over all, earth-scented smell
Sweetly stealing about the sea-worn man,
And faintly, as afar, fresh-water sounds,
Runnings and ripplings upon rocky stairs
Where moss grows most. Amidst it came,

70 Unearthly sweet, out of the air it seemed,
A voice singing to the vibrant string,
"Forget the grief upon the great water,
Card and compass and the cruel rain.
Leave that labour; lilies in the green wood
75 Toil not, toil not. Trouble were to weave them
Coats that come to them without care or toil.
Seek not the seas again; safer is the green wood,
Lilies that live there have labour not at all,
Spin not, spin not. Spent in vain the trouble were
80 Beauty to bring them that better comes by kind."
Then I started up and stood, staring in the darkness,
After the closing strain. The clouds parted
Suddenly. The seemly, slow-gliding moon
Swam, as it were in shallows, of the silver cloud,
85 Out into the open, and with orb'd splendour
She gleamed upon the groves of a great forest.
There were trees taller than the topmost spire
Of some brave minster, a bishop's seat;
Their very roots so vast that in
90 Their mossy caves a man could hide
Under their gnarl'd windings. And nearer hand
Ferns fathoms high, flowers tall like trees,
Trees bright like flowers: trouble it is to me
To remember much of that mixed sweetness
95 The smell and the sight and the swaying plumes
Green and growing, all the gross riches,
Waste fecundity of a wanton earth,[57]
—Gentle is the genius of that juicy wood—
Insatiable the soil. There stood, breast high,
100 In flowery foam, under the flame of moon,
One not far off, nobly fashioned.
Her beauty burned in my blood, that, as a fool,
Falling before her at her feet I prayed,
Dreaming of druery, and with many a dear craving
105 Wooed the woman under the wild forest.
She laughed when I told my love-business,
Witch-hearted queen. "A worthy thing,
Traveller, truly, my troth to plight
With the sea villain that smells of tar
110 Horny-handed, and hairy-cheeked."

Then I rose wrathfully; would have ravished the witch
In her empty isle, under that orb'd splendour.
    But she laughed louder, and a little way
She went back, beckoning with brows and eyes.
115 Like to lilies,[58] when she loosed her robe
Under broad moonshine,[59] her breasts appeared,
No maiden's breasts, but with milk swelling,
Like Rhea[60] unrobed, rich in offspring.
Her sign was not sent to the sea-wanderer:
120 Others answered. From the arch'd forest
Beasts came baying: the bearded ape,
The lion, the lamb, the long-sided,
Padding panther, and the purring cat,
The snake sliding, and the stepping horse,
125 Busy beaver, and the bear jog-trot,
The scurrying rat, and the squirrel leaping
On the branch above. Those beasts came all.
She grudged no grace to those grim ones. I
Saw how she suckled at her sweet fountains
130 The tribes that go dumb. Teeth she feared not,
Her nipple was not denied to the nosing worm.
I thought also that out of the thick foliage
I saw the branches bend towards her breast, thirsting,
Creepers climbing and the cups of flowers
135 Upward opening—all things that lived,
As for sap, sucking at her sweet fountains.
And as the wood milked her, witch-hearted queen,
I saw that she smiled, softly murmuring
As if she hushed a child. How long it was
140 These marvels stood, memory holds not,
—All was gone in a glance. Under the green forest
We two were alone, as from trance wakened.
She was far fairer than at the first seeing.
Then she struck the string and sang clearly
145 Another lay. Earth stood silent.
"You are too young in years. My yesterdays
Left behind me, are a longer tale
Than your histories hold. Far hence she lies
Who would learn gladlier of your love business.
150 Woven in wizardry, wearily she lingers,
Stiller and stiller, with the stone in her heart,

Crying; so cruelly creeps the bitter change on her,
—Happy the head is that shall harbour in that breast—
My dear daughter, that dieth away,
155 In the enchanter's chain. Who chooses best
Will adventure his life and advance far on
Into the cruel country. If he comes again
Bringing that beautiful one, out of bonds redeemed,
He shall win for reward a winsome love."
160 "This quarrel and quest, Queen," I answered,
"I will undertake though I earn my death
At the wizard's wiles. But of the way thither,
The councils, and the kind, of that crafty man,
Tell me truly." When she turned her face
165 Her teeth glittered. She tossed her head,
Nostrils widened, as a noble dame
In scorn, scoffing, at a shameful thing[61]—
"Eastward in the island the old one stands
Working wonders in the woeful shade
170 Of a grim garden that is growing there
Newly planted. That was the navel once
Of a sweet country, stol'n now from me,
Where he would be called a king. But he is cold at heart
And he has wrought ruin in those rich pleasances,
175 He has felled forests, put to flight my beasts,
Chaining with enchantment many a changeful stream,
Putting into prison all that his power reaches;
Life is loathsome to that lord;[62] and joy,
Abomination; and the bed of love
180 Eggs him with envy—outcast himself,
An old, ugly, ice-hearted wraith.
If I saw shaking the skin upon his throat,
Or the rheum dropping from his red eyelids,
Or his tongue mumbling in the toothless gums,
185 By loathing I should lose my life. Strong thief!
Once amid these waters, well was my country,
Living lonely in my land, a queen.
Truly, I cannot tell of a time before
I was ruling this realm. I am its right lady.
190 Ages after, that other came
Out of the ocean in an hour of storm,
Humble and homeless. At my hearth, kneeling,

Sweetly he besought me to save his life,
And grant him ground where he might grow his bread.[63]
195 All that he asked for, ill-starred I gave,
Pleased with pity, that I have paid dearly,
And easily won. But for each acre
That my bounty gave to the beggar, soon
He stole a second, till as a strong tyrant
200 He holds in his hand one half the land.
My flute he has stolen. Flowers loved it well
And rose upright at the ripple of the note
Sound-drenched, as if they drank,[64] after drought, sweet rain.
Grass was the greener for it, as at grey evening
205 After the sun's setting of a summer day,
When dusk comes near,[65] and the drooping, crushed
Stalks stand once more in the still twilight.
That reed of delight he ravished away,
Stole it stealthily. In a strange prison
210 It lies unloved; and of my life one half
With the flute followed, and I am faded now,
Mute the music. But a mightier woe
Followed the first one; with his fine weavings,
Cobwebby, clinging, and his cruel, thin
215 Enchanter's chains, he has charmed away
My only child out of my own country,
Into the grim garden, and will give her to drink
Heart-changing draughts.[66] He that tastes of them
Shall stand, a stone, till the stars crumble.
220 Of that drug drink not, lest, in his danger caught,
Moveless as marble thou remain. But take
This sword, seaman, and strike off his head.
Hasten, if haply, ere his hard threatenings
Or his lies' labyrinth, lapped about her,
225 Have driven her to drink that draught, in time,
You may redeem my dear."
Dawn was round me,
Cool and coloured, and there came a breeze
Brushing the grasses. Birds were chattering.
230 There was I only in the empty wood,
The woman away. One time I thought
It was a dream's burden; but, amid the dews sprinkled
At my feet, flashing, that fallow sword

Lay to my liking.[67] Lingeringly I weighed it,
235 Bright and balanced. That was the best weapon
That ever I owned. I ate in that place
My full upon the fruits the forest bore.
Then, among still shadows, slow-paced I went
Always eastward into the arch'd forest.
240 It was at the fifth furlong, forth I issued
From the dreaming wood into a down country.
All the island opened like a picture
Before my feet. Far-off the hills,
Long and limber, as it were lean greyhounds,
245 With level chines, lay beneath the sunrise.
Chalk made them pale. Never a church nor a rick
Nor smoke, nor the smell of a small homestead,
Rose upon the ridges. The rolling land
Climbed to the eastward—there was the clearest sky—
250 Heaving ever hillward, until high moorland
Shut off my seeing. The sorcerer's home,
My goal, was there as I guessed. Thither
I held my way and my heart lightened.
Over hedge, over ditch, over high, over low,
255 By waters and woods I went and ran,
And swung the sword as I swung my legs.
Laughing loudly, alone I walked,
Till many a mile was marched away.
Half-way in heav'n to his highest throne
260 The gold sun glittering had gained above,
When I looked and lo! in the long grasses
By a brook's margin a bright thing lay,
Reflecting the flame of floating sun,
Drawing my glances. As in danger, aside
265 I swerved in my step: a serpent I thought
Basking its belly in the bright morning
Lay there below me. But when I looked again,
Lo it never moved. Nearer gazing,
I found it was a flute, fashioned delicately,
270 Purely golden. When I picked it up
I could make with my mouth no music at all
And with my five fingers, failing always
Whatever tune I tried, testing that instrument.
Almost, in anger—for it irked me so—

275 I had flung the flute among the flowers and grass,
Let it lie there by the lapping stream.
Presently I put it in the pouch I bear
Set on my shoulder. It was my second thoughts.
    Over hedge, over ditch, over high, over low,
280 By waters and woods I went and ran,
And swung the sword as I swung my legs.
Laughing loudly alone I walked
Till many a mile was marched away.
    Bright above me on the bridge of noon
285 Sun was standing, shadows dwindled,
Heat was hovering in a haze that danced
Upon rocks about my road. I raised my eyes.
On the green bosom of a grassy hill,[68]
White, like wethers, in a wide circle,
290 Stones were standing; as on Salisbury Plain
Where wild men made for the worshipt sun
That old altar. On thither I went
Marching right among them. Man-shaped they were,
Now that I was nearer and could know their kind,
295 —Awful images, as it were an earlier race,
Nearer neighbours of the noble gods,
They were so quiet and cold. Kingly faces
There hushed my heart from its hard knockings.
    As I walked, wondering, in their wide consistory,
300 Through and through them, for the throng was great,
Fear stopped my breath. I found sitting
Lonely among the lifeless, but alive, a man,
His head hanging, and his hands were clasped,
His arms knotted, and from his eyes there came,
305 Sadly, without ceasing, slow tears and large.
Hunched and hairy was his whole body,
Durned and dwindled. Dwarflike he seemed,
But his ears bigger than any other man's.
He was grubby as if he had grown from the ground, plantlike,
310 Big of belly, and with bandy legs.
Shrublike his shape, shock-headed too,
As if a great gooseberry could go upon legs,
Or a mangel be a man. Amazed, I spoke.
"What little wight then, weeping among the stonemen,
315 Lives alone here? What is the load of care

That has dwelled in you, dwarf, and dwined you thus?"
Then the little man lifted up his eyebrows
And he spoke sadly. "Sorrow it is to me
To remember my mates. Men they were born
320 Who are now stone-silenced in this circle here,
By wizard's wand. Once they beat me,
Captain kicked me, and cook also,
Bosun boxed me on both my ears,
Cabin-boy, carpenter—all the crew of the *Well Away*—
325 Before they fell—she foundered here—
Into the wizard's hand. He worked them into stone,
That they move no more, on the main or on the shore.
Able seaman of old were they all,
Ranting and roaring when the rum was in
330 Like true British sailors. Trouble it is to me
To remember my mates—the men that they were!
I shall not meet their match. When the mate was drunk
It took all ten of their toughest men
In a strange seaport to shut him up.
335 Now they are stones, standing. He stopped their life,
Made them into marble, and of more beauty,
Fairer faces, and their form nobler,
Proud and princely. But the price was death.
They have bought beauty. That broke my heart."
340 "I am an enemy to that old sorcerer,
Dwarf," I answered. "Dwelling in the greenwood
Where the waves westward wash the sea-cliff,
I found, fairest of all flesh, the Queen
Who should rule this realm, for she is its right lady.
345 I am sent on her side. I shall save the land
From the enchanter's chain; so my charge bids me.
Lead me loyally where that lord dwelleth
In his ill garden, ice-hearted man."
The dwarf answered "She who dwells in the wood
350 Is the second fear in this strange country.
She has a wand also, that woman there;
Whom she chooses to change, she'll choke the voice
In his throat. Thickly, like a thing without sense,
Growling and grunting, grovelling four-foot,
355 He will pad upon paws. Pelt coats him round,
He is a brute beast then, once her bonds catch him.

The other half of my old shipmates
She bewitched in her wood. It is the way she deals.
Therefore I lurk alone in the land between
360 Twixt the devil and the deep. I am in dread of both,
Either the stone or the sty. But here I stay, hoping
Always, if ever such an hour should come,
To drink before I die out of the deep tankard,
And to eat ham and eggs in my home country
365 That is the weald of Kent. And I wish that I was there."
    Doubts came darkening and all grew dull within,
Cold and clouded with clinging dread,
At this new story. Noon was burning
Bright about us. I bade the dwarf
370 To lead me, though he was loth, to the lair of the mage.
Willingly he would not. But with words of threat,
With coaxings and with kicks, he must come at the last,
Following me; a faltering, faint-hearted guide.
    Over hedge, over ditch, over high, over low,
375 By waters and wood I went and ran
Till many a mile was marched away.
I swung no more my sword as I walked;
Little stomach to laugh had I,
And shuffling, and shaking on his shoulders his shaggy head, came the dwarf,
380 Cunningly catching all occasions to creep aside out of the way.
Every mile, he would be asking for another rest. If I had let him,
The task would have been interminable, the tale wanted an ending.
Day was dropping to the dazzling plain
Of the waves westward. Winging homeward
385 Came the flying flocks; flowers were closing,
Level light over the land was poured.
I looked to my left in a low valley
Among quiet flowers. Queen-like there stood
A marble maid, mild of countenance,
390 Her lips open, her limbs so lithe
Made for moving, that the marble death
Seemed but that moment to have swathed her round.
Her beauty made me bow as a brute to the earth.
To have won a word of her winsome mouth,
395 Scorn or sweetness, salutation,
Bidding or blessing, I would have borne great pain.
Longing bade me to lay my cheek

On the cool, carven countenance, and worshipping
To kiss the maid, if so she might come awake.
400 Awe forbade me, and her anger feared.
Then I was ware in a while of one behind;
There stood in stole that stately fell
And swept, beneath, the sward, a man.
The beard upon his bos'm, burnt-gold in hue
405 Grew to his girdle. That was the gravest man,[69]
Of amplest brow, and his eye steadiest,
And his mien mightiest, that I have met in earth.
Then I gathered more sure my grip upon the sword,
And for clear arm-play I cast aside
410 From shoulder my sack. The silly dwarf
Caught and kept it. He was cold at heart
Whimpering and woebegone. The wizard spoke:
"Second counsels, my son, are best.
If my art aid not, in empty land,
415 Lonely and longing for a lifeless stone,
Here you may harbour. What help is that?
Marble minds not a man's desire,
Cold lips comfort him neither with kiss nor speech,
Nor will her arms open. Eager lover,
420 Not even the art of this old master
Can wake, as you want, this woman here.
Chaste, enchanted, till the change of the world,
In beauty she abides. Nor breath, nor death,
Touches nor troubles her. You can be turned and made
425 Nearer to her nature; not she to yours
Ever. Only your own changing,
Boy, can bring you, where your bride waits you,
If you are love-learnëd to so large a deed.
You think, being a thrall, that it is thorough death
430 To be made marble and to move no limb.
Wise men are wary. Once only fools
Look before leaping. Lies were told you.
Fear was informer;[70] else you had freely craved,
If your master had been love, to be made even now
435 Like to the lady. It was your loins told you,
And your belly, and your blood, and your blind servants
Five, who are unfaithful. Fear had moved them.
Death they were in dread of. Death let them have;

For their fading and their fall is the first waking,
440 And their night the noon, of a new master,
Peace after pleasure. Passionless for the stonemen[71]
Life stands limpid. Left far behind
Is that race rushing over its roar'd cataracts,
The murmuring, mixed, much thwarted stream
445 Of the flesh, flowing with confusëd noise,
Perishing perpetually. Had you proved one hour
Their blessed life whose blood is stilled,
—How they hearken to the heavens raining
Starry influence in the still of night,
450 Feel the fingers, far below them
Of the earth's archon[72] in an ancient place
Moulding metals: how among them steals,
As the moon moves them when the month flows full,
Love and longing, that is unlike mortals'
455 Dreams of druery, drawn from further,
Nobler in nature—you would know 'tis small
Wonder if they will not to wander any more.
Life has left them, whoso looks without;
All things are other on their inner side.
460 This child that I have changed with the chalice of peace,
Was my own daughter. I, pondering much,
Gave her the greatest of gifts I knew.
Long she was in labour in a land of dread,
Tangled in torments. The toils had her,
465 And her wild mother, witch-hearted queen,
Delayed her in that lair. Long since it was
When the woman was my wife. Worse befell her
After, when she was evil. By arts she stole
The golden flute, that was a gift fashioned
470 For my dear daughter, and a daemon's work,
The earth's archon of old made it.
She took the toy. To touch the stops
Or to make with her mouth the music it held,
Art she had not. Envy moved her.
475 She was changed at heart. My child she stole,
Fled to the forests: found there comrades,
Beasts and brambles and brown shadows,
With whom she holds. Half this island
Wrongly she has ravished. I am its rightful lord.

480 Where she flung the flute as she fled thither,
No man knoweth. None the richer
Was the thief of her theft: but that she thinks it wealth
If another ail. She aches at heart.
Second counsels, oh son, are best.
485 All things are other on their inner side."
He spoke those words. They sped so well,
What for the maiden's love and the man's wisdom,
Awed and eager, I asked him soon
For a draught of that drink. Drought parched my throat.
490 Cold and crystal in the cup it glanced,
White like water. In the west, scarlet,
Day was dying. Dark night apace
Over[73] earth's eastern edge towards us
Came striding up. Stars, one or two,
495 Had lit their lamps. My lip was set
To the cold border of the cup. The dwarf
Cried out and crossed himself: "This is a crazy thing!
Dilly, dilly, as the duckwife said,
Come and let me kill you. Catch younger trouts, Sir,
500 Tickling, tickling, with no trouble at all."
"What meddling mite," said the man of spells,
"Creeps in my country? Clod! Earth thou art,
Unworthy to be worked to a white glory
Of stable stone. But stay not long,
505 Base, mid thy betters! Or into boggy peats,
Slave, I'll sing thee." But he skipped away
Light and limber, though his limbs were crook'd.
Out of the bag that he bore on his brown shoulder
—He had caught it and kept when I cast it away—
510 The dwarf deftly[74] drew the flute out,
Gold and glittering. Grinned while he spoke,
"All things, ogre, have another side.
I trust even now, by a trick I have learnt,
That I shall drink before I die out of a deep tankard
515 In the weald of Kent, will you, nill you!"
He laid his lip to the little flute.
Long and liquid,—light was waning—
The first note flowed. Then faster came,
Reedily, ripple-like, running as a watercourse,
520 Meddling of melodies, moulded in air,

Pure and proportional. Pattering as the rain-drops
Showers of it, scattering silverly, poured on us,
Charmed the enchanter that he was changed and wept,
At the pure, plashing, piping of the melody,
525 Coolly calling, clearer than a nightingale,
Defter and more delicate. Dainty the division of it,
True the trilling and the turns upon itself,
Sweet the descending. For it sang so well,
First he fluted off his flesh away
530 The shaggy hair; and from his shoulders next
Heaved by harmonies the hump away;
Then he unbandied, with a burst of beauty, his legs,
Standing straighter as the strain loudened.
I saw that the skin was smoother on his face
535 Than a five-year boy's. He was the fairest thing
That ever was on earth. Either shoulder
Was swept with wings; swan's down they were,
Elf-bright his eyes. Evening darkened,
The sun had set. Over the sward he danced,
540 With arms open, as an eager boy
Leaps towards his lover. I looked whither.
Noble creatures were coming near, and more
Stirring, as I saw them, out of stone bondage,
Stirring, and descending from their still places,
545 And every image shook, as an egg trembles
Over the breaking beak. Through the broad garden
—The dew drenched it—drawn, ev'n as moths,
To that elf's glimmering, his old shipmates
Moved to meet him. There, among, was tears,
550 Clipping and kissing. King they hailed him,
Men, once marble, that were his mates of old,
Fair in feature and of form godlike,
For the stamp of the stone was still on them
Carved by the wizard. They kept, and lived,
555 The marble mien. They were men weeping,
Round the dwarf dancing to his deft fingers.
Then was the grey garden as if the gods of heaven
On the carol dancing had come and chos'n
The flowers folded, for their floor to dance.
560 Close beside me, as when a cloud brightens
When, mid thin vapours, through comes the sun,

The marble maid, under mask of stone,
Shook and shuddered. As a shadow streams
Over the wheat waving, over the woman's face
565 Life came lingering. Nor was it long after
Down its blue pathways, blood returning
Moved, and mounted to her maiden cheek.
Breathing broadened her breast. Then light
From her eyes' opening all that beauty
570 Worked into woman. So the wonder was complete,
Set, precipitate, and the seal taken,
Clear and crystal the alchemic change,
Bright and breathing. In my breast faltering
My spirit was spent. Speech none I found,
575 Standing by[75] the stranger who was stone before.
But the wing'd wonder—wide rings they danced
Over the flowers folded to his fluting sweet—
Danced to my dear one. Druery he taught her,
Bent her, bowed her, bent never before,
580 Brought her, blushing as it were a bride mortal,
To hold to her heart my head as I kneeled,
Faint in that ferly:[76] frail, mortal man,
Till I was love-learnëd both to learn and teach
Love with that lady. Nor was it long after
585 That the man of spells moved and started
As one that wakes. "Weary it is to me
To remember much. Miseries innumerable
Have ruled in this realm. I will run quickly
West to the woodland, to the wild city,
590 Haply my love lives yet. Long time I've borne
Hate and hungering. Now is harvest come,
Now is the hour striking, the ice melting,
The bond broken, and the bride waiting."
All in order—the old one led—
595 On flowers folded, to flute music,
Forth we followed. No fays lightlier
Dance and double in their dew'd ringlet
On All Saints Eve. Earth-breathing scents
On mildest breeze moved towards us.
600 Cobwebs caught us. Clear-voiced, an owl
To his kind calling clove the darkness,[77]
The fox, further, was faint barking.

We came quickly to the country of downs
That lies so long between the land of dread
605 And the grim garden. Glory breaking
Unclosed the clouds. Clear and golden
Out into the open swam the orb'd splendour
Of a moon, marvellous. Magic called her.
Pale as paper, where she poured her ray
610 The downs lay drenched. Dark before us,
Stilly standing, was the stern frontier
Of the aisled forest. Out thence there came
Thunder, I thought it. Thick copses broke.
From dread darkness, with drumming hoofs,
615 Swept the centaurs, swift in onset,
Abreast, embattled, as a broad army,
To that elf's glimmering. They were his old shipmates,
Unenchanted, as those others were,
Bettered after beasthood. They had the brows of men,
620 Tongues to talk with, and, to touch the string,
Hands for harping. But the horse lingered,
And the mark of their might, as magic had wrought,
The stamp of that strength was still on them.
Hands for harping, hoofs for running,
625 Mighty stallions, that were men weeping
Round the dwarf dancing to his deft music.
First before them ran the fairest one,
Comeliest of the coursers; king-like his eye,
Proud his pawing and his pomp of speed,
630 Big and bearded. On his back riding—
Such courtesy he could—there came, so fair,
The lady of the land, lily-breasted,
Gentle and rejoicing. The magician's love
Made her beauty burn as a bright ruby
635 Or as a coal on fire, under cool moonlight,
And swam in her eyes till she swooned almost
Bending her body to his back on whom she rode.
And now full near those nations stood,
That king's courtiers whom he had carved in stone,
640 And the wide flung wings of the woman's horse,
Both as for battle; all the beauty of his,
The strength of hers. Straightway they fell
To talk, those two. Their tale was sweet

In all our ears. Earth stood silent.
645 Either answered other softly.
HIC: "My love's laughter is light falling
Through broad branches in brown woodland,
On a cold fountain, in a cave darkling,
A mild sparkling in mossy gloom."
650 ILLA: "But my lord's wisdom is light breaking,
And sound shaking, a sundered tomb."
HIC: "My love's looking is long dimness
And stars' influence. In strange darkness
Her eyes open their orb'd dreaming
655 As a huge, gleaming[78] mid-harvest moon."
ILLA: "But my lord's looking is the lance darted
Through mists parted when morn comes soon."
HIC: "Thy dear bosom is a deep garden
Between high hedges where heat burns not,
660 Where no rains ruin and no rimes harden,
A closed garden, where climbs no snake."
ILLA: "But thy dear valour is a deep, rolling,
And a tower tolling strong towns awake."
HIC: "My friend's beauty is the free springing
665 Of the world's welfare from the womb'd ploughland,
The green growing, the great mothering,
Her breast smothering with her brood unfurled."
ILLA: "But my friend's beauty is the form minted
Above heav'n, printed on the holy world."[79]
670 So they were singing. The song was done.
When either in arms other folded
Fondly and fairly, fire-red was she,
Fire-white the sage. The fields of air
Beamed more brightly. About the moon
675 More than a myriad mazy weavings
Of fire flickered. Far off there rolled
Summer thunder. The sage all mild
For the maid and for me his mouth opened,
"The air of earth this other two
680 Must breathe in breast. Now broad ocean
Smiles in sleeping and smoother winds
Favour, let us find them a ferry hence.
This elf also, even as he wished for,
Hoping, while he was helpless, for his home country,

685 Earth of England, unenchanted,
Let us send on the sea. He served us well,
MULTUM AMAVIT,[80] which is of most virtue,
In heav'n and here and in hell under us."
  Centaurs swiftly, when he said, were gone,
690 Glorying in gallop to the great forest.
Heaving hardily, whole trees they tore
From earth upward. Echoing ruin
Dinned in darkness. Down thence they hauled
Many an ancient oak. The orb'd splendour
695 Shone on their shoulders as they sweat naked
Under moon's mildness. Magic helped them,
The boat was built in the blink of an eye,
Long and limber, of line stately,
Fair in fashion. Out of the forest came
700 Spiders for spinning, speedily they footed,
Shooting like shuttles on the shadowy grass,
Backward and forward, brisk upon their spindle shanks,
And made for the mast a marvellous sail
Of shimmering web. That ship full soon
705 Over grass gliding, glorious stallions
With Heave! and Ho! hauled to the sea's rim,
A throng, dancing. They thrust her out
Into deep water. There was din of hoofs
In salt shallows and the spray cast up
710 Under moon, glancing. The maiden soon,
The elf also, I then, the third,
Were on board in the boat. Breathing mildly
Off the island—it arched our sail—
The breeze blew then, blest the fragrance[81]
715 Of flower and fruit, floating seaward,
Land-laden air. I long even now
To remember more of that mixed sweetness.
But fast and fair into the foamless bay
Onward and outward, under the orb'd splendour,
720 Our boat was borne. Back oft I gazed[82]
As the land lessened, lo! all that folk
Burned on the beaches as they were bright angels,
Light and lovely, and the long ridges
With their folds fleecy under the flame of moon
725 Swam in silver of swathing mist,

Elf-fair that isle. But on apace
We went on the wave. That wingëd boy
Held firm the helm. Ahead, far on,
Like floor unflawed, the flood, moon-bright,
730 Stretched forth the twinkling streets of ocean
To the rim of the world. No ripple at all
Nor foam was found, save the furrow we made,
The stir at our stern, and the strong cleaving
Of the throbbing prow. We thrust so swift,
735 Moved with magic, that a mighty curve
Upward arching from either bow
Rose, all rainbowed; as a rampart stood
Bright about us. As the book tells us,
Walls of water, and a way between,
740 Were reared and rose at the Red Sea ford,
On either hand, when Israel came
Out of Egypt to their own country.
(August 1930; 1969)

I Will Write Down the Portion that I Understand

I will write down the portion that I understand
Of twenty years wherein I went from land to land.
At many bays and harbours I put in with joy
Hoping that there I should have built my second Troy
5 And stayed. But either stealing harpies drove me thence,
Or the trees bled, or oracles, whose airy sense
I could not understand, yet must obey, once more
Sent me to sea to follow the retreating shore
Of this land which I call at last my home, where most
10 I feared to come; attempting not to find whose coast
I ranged half round the world, with vain design to shun
The last fear whence the last security is won.
Oh perfect life, unquivering, self-enkindled flame
From which my fading candle first was lit, oh name
15 Too lightly spoken, therefore left unspoken here,
Terror of burning, nobleness of light, most dear
And comfortable warmth of the world's beating side,
Feed from thy unconsumed what wastes in me, and guide
My soul into the silent places till I make

20 A good end of this book for after-travellers' sake.
In times whose faded chronicle lies in the room
That memory cannot turn the key of, they to whom
I owe this mortal body and terrestrial years,
Uttered the Christian story to my dreaming ears.
25 And I lived then in Paradise, and what I heard
Ran off me like the water from the water-bird;
And what my mortal mother told me in the day
At night my elder mother nature wiped away;
And when I heard them telling of my soul, I turned
30 Aside to read a different lecture whence I learned
What was to me the stranger and more urgent news,
That I had blood and body now, my own, to use
For tasting and for touching the young world, for leaping
And climbing, running, wearying out the day, and sleeping—
(1932; 1974, 1998)

When the Year Dies in Preparation for the Birth

When the year dies in preparation for the birth[83]
Of other seasons, not the same, on the same earth,
Then saving and calamity together make
The Advent gospel, telling how the heart will break
5 With dread, and stars, unleaving from the rivelled sky,
Scatter on the wind of man's Redemption drawing nigh,
Man's doom and his Redeeming and the wreck of man.
Therefore it was in Advent that the Quest began;
In wail of wind the flower of the Britons all
10 Went out, and desolation was in Arthur's hall,
And stillness in the City of Legions. Then the Queen
Expected their returning when the woods were green;
But leaves grew large, and heaviness of August lay
Upon the woods. The Guinever began to say,
15 "Autumn will bring them home again." But autumn passed
With all its brown solemnities, and weathers fast
Came driving down the valley of the Usk[84] with hail
At Advent, and the hearts of men began to fail,
And Lucan said, "If summer brings the heathen men
20 From over-seas, or trouble of Picts[85] beyond the wall,
Britain will break. The Sangrail[86] has betrayed us all,

According to the prophecy Pelles[87] the king
Once made, that at the moving of this holy thing
Our strength would fail." But Arthur, who was daily less
25 Of speech, through all these winter days, gave answer,[88] "Yes.
I know it, and I knew it when they rode away."
The year turned round and bettered, and the coloured May
Crept up the valley of the Usk, and softening green
Rounded the form of forests. But this year the Queen
30 Said nothing of the knights'[89] return; and it became
A custom in that empty court never to name
The fear all felt, and not to listen any more
For rumours, nor to watch the roads, nor pace the shore;
Patience, most like conspiracy, had hushed them all,
35 Women, old men, and boys.
That year was heavy fall
Of snows. And when amid its silence Gawain, first
Defeat from the long Quest, came riding home, their thirst
For news he could not or he would not satisfy.
40 He was unlike the Gawain they had known, with eye
Unfrank, and voice ambiguous, and his answers short.
Gulfs of unknowing lay between him and the court,
Unbreakable misunderstandings. To the King,
He answered, No; he had not seen the holy thing.
45 And, No; he had heard no news of Launcelot and the rest,
But, for his own part, he was finished with the Quest
And now asked leave to journey North and see his own
Estates. And this was granted, and he went, alone,
Leaving a hollow-heartedness in every man
50 And, in the Queen, new fear. Then, with the spring, began
The home-coming of heroes from the Quest, by two's
And three's, unlike their expectation, without news,
A dim disquiet of defeated men, and all
Like Gawain, changed irrelevant in Arthur's hall,
55 Strange to their wives, unwelcome to their[90] stripling boys.
Ladies of Britain mourned the losing of their joys:
"What have they eaten, or in what forgetful land
Were their adventures? Now they do not understand
Our speech. They talk to one another in a tongue
60 We do not know. Strange sorrows and new jests, among
Themselves, they have. The Sangrail has betrayed us all."
So leaf by leaf the old fellowship of Arthur's hall

Felt Autumn's advent. New divisions came, and new
Allyings: till, of all the Table Round, those few
65 Alone who had not ridden on the dangerous Quest
Now bore the name of courteous and were loved the best,
Mordred,[91] or Kai,[92] or Caliburn,[93] or Agravaine.[94]
And the Queen understood it all. And the drab pain,
Now for two years familiar in her wearied side,
70 Stirred like a babe within her. Every nerve woke wide
To torture, with low-moaning pity of self, with tears[95]
At dawn, with[96] midnight jealousies; and dancing fears
Touched with their stabs and quavers and low lingerings
Her soul, as a musician plays the trembling strings;
75 And loud winds from the cruel countries of despair
Came roaring through her, breaking down, and laying bare,
Till naked to the changing of the world she stood
At Advent. And no tidings now could do her good
Forever: the heart failing in her breast for fear
80 —Of Launcelot dead—of Launcelot daily drawing near
And bringing her the sentence that she knew not of,
The doom, or the redeeming, or the change of love.
Yet, like a thief surprising her, the moment came
At last, of his returning. The tormented flame
85 Leaned from the candle guttering in the noisy gloom
Of wind and rain, where Guinever amid her room
Stood with scared eyes at midnight on the windy floor,
Thinking, forever thinking. From beyond her door
Came foot of sentry and change of countersign; and then
90 A murmur of their rough-mouthed talk between the men
She heard, that in one moment like an arrow flew
Into the deepest crimson of her heart and slew
Hopes and half-doubts and self-deceits; and told the Queen
That Launcelot already had returned—had been
95 Three days now in the city and sent to her no word.
The rain was gone, the sky was pale, when next she stirred,
Having no memory of the passing of that night,
And in her cold, small fingers took her pen to write,
And wrote five words, and sent it by her aged nurse.
100 Then the cold hours began their march again, not worse,
Not better, never-ending. And that night he came,
Out of the doorway's curtained darkness to the flame
Of candlelight and firelight. And the curtains fell

Behind him, and they stood alone, with all to tell,
105 Not like that Launcelot tangled in the boughs of May
Long since, nor like the Guinever he kissed that day,
But he was pale, with pity in his face writ wide,
And she a haggard woman, holding to her side
A pale hand pressed, asking "What is it?" Slowly then
110 He came to her and took her by the hand, as men
Take tenderly a daughter's or a mother's hand
To whom they bring bad news she will not understand.
So Launcelot led the Queen and made her sit: and all
This time he saw her shoulders move and her tears fall,
115 And he himself wept not, but sighed. Then, like a man
Who ponders, in the fire he gazed; and so began
Presently, looking always in the fire, the tale
Of his adventures seeking for the Holy Grail.[97]

How Launcelot and his shining horse had gone together
120 So far that at the last they came to springy weather;
The sharpened buds like lances were on every tree,
The little hills went past him like the waves of the sea,
The white, new castles, blazing on the distant fields
Were clearer than the painting upon new-made[98] shields.
125 Under high forests many days he rode, and all
The birds made shrill with marriage songs their shadowy hall
Far overhead. But afterwards the sun withdrew,
And into barren countries, having all gone through
The fair woods and the fortunate, he came at last.
130 He sees about him noble beeches overcast[99]
And aged oaks revealing to the rainless sky
Shagg'd nakedness of roots uptorn. He passes by
Forsaken wells and sees the buckets red with rust
Upon the chains. Dry watercourses filled with dust
135 He crosses over; and villages on every side
Ruined he sees, and jaws of houses gaping wide,
And abbeys showing ruinously the peeling gold
In roofless choirs and, underneath, the churchyard mould
Cracking and far subsiding into dusty caves
140 That let the pale light in upon[100] the ancient graves.
All day he journeys in a land of ruin and bones
And rags; and takes his rest at night among the stones
And broken things; till, after many leagues he found

A little stone-built hermitage in barren ground.
145 And at his door the hermit stands, so pined and thin
The bone-face is scarce hidden by the face of skin.
"Now fair, sweet friend," says Launcelot, "Tell me, I pray
How all this countryside has fallen into decay?"
The good man does not look on Launcelot at all,
150 But presently his loud, high voice comes like the call
Of a sad horn that blows to prayer in Pagan lands:
"This is the daughter of Babylon who gnaws her hands
For thirst and hunger. Nine broad realms in this distress
Are lying for the sake of one man's heedlessness
155 Who came to the King Fisherman, who saw the Spear
That burns with blood, who saw the Sangrail drawing near,
Yet would not ask for whom it served. Until there come
The Good Knight who will kneel and see, yet not be dumb,
But ask, the Wasted Country shall be still accursed
160 And the spell upon the Fisher King unreversed,
Who now lies sick and languishing and near to death."[101]
So far the hermit's voice pealed on: and then his breath
Rattled within the dry pass of his throat: his head
Dropped sideways, and the slender trunk stands upright, dead,
165 And tall against the lintel of the narrow door.
And Launcelot alighted there, and in the floor
Of that low house scraped in the dust a shallow grave
And laid the good man in it, praying God to save
His soul; and for himself such grace as may prevail
170 To come to the King Fisherman and find the Grail.
Then up he climbed and rode again, and from his breath
The dust was cleared, and from his mind the thought of death,
And in the country of ruin and rags he came so far
That over the grey moorland, like a shining star,
175 He sees a valley, emerald with grass, and gleam
Of water, under branches, from a winding stream,
A respite in the[102] wilderness, a pleasant place,
Struck with the sun. His charger sniffs and mends his pace,
And down[103] they go, and by labyrinthine[104] paths, until
180 They reach the warm green country, sheltered by the hill.
Jargon of birds angelical warbles above,
And Launcelot throws this mail'd hood back, and liquid love
Wells in his heart. He looks all round the quartered sky
And wonders in what region Camelot may lie

185 Singing "The breezes here have passed my lady's mouth
And stol'n a paradisal fragrance of the South."
Singing "All gentle hearts should worship her and sing
The praises of her pity and Fair-Welcoming."
So carolling he trotted under lights and shadows
190 Of trembling woods, by waterfalls and sunny meadows,
And still he wandered, following where the water flows
To where, at the blue water's edge, a shrine arose
On marble pillars slender, with no wall between;
Through every arch the blueness of the sky was seen.
195 And underneath the fragile dome three narrow beds
Of lilies raised in windless air their silver heads.
Beside them sat a damosel, all clothed in bright,
Pale, airy clothes, and all her countenance filled with light,
And parted lips as though she had just ceased to sing.
200 Launcelot thinks he never has seen a fairer thing,
And checks his horse, saluting her. "God send you bliss,
Beautiful one! I pray you tell, what place is this?'
The damsel said, "The corseints[105] in the praise of whom
This tomb is built are yet far distant from the tomb.
205 Here, when the Wasted Country is no longer dry,
The three best knights of Christendom shall come to lie."
Launcelot remembers often to have heard them named
And guesses who is one of them: so half ashamed,
He asks her, with his eyes cast down, "What knights are these?'
210 And waits; and then lifts up his eyes again, and sees
No lady there: an empty shrine, and on the grass
No print of foot, where in grey dew the blackbirds pass.
Then came on high a disembodied voice and gave
Solitude tongue. "A grave for Bors," it cried, "A grave
215 For Percivale, a grave for Galahad:[106] but not
For the Knight recreant of the Lake, for Launcelot!"
Then came clear laughter jingling in the air like bells
On horses' manes, thin merriment of that which dwells
In light and height, unaging and beyond the sense
220 Of guilt and grieving, merciless with innocence.
    And presently he catches up his horse's head
And rides again, still following where the water led.
The sun rose high: the shadow of the horse and man
Came from behind to underneath them and began
225 To lengthen out in front of them. The river flowed

Wider and always slower and the valley road
Was soft with mud, and winding, like a worm, between
Wide swamps and warm entanglement of puddles green;
And multitude of buzzing and of stinging flies
230 Came round his sweated forehead and his horse's eyes;
The black turf squeaked and trembled at the iron hoofs.
  Then Launcelot looks and sees a huddle of flat roofs
Upon a little island in the steaming land,
A low, red, Roman manor-house; and close at hand
235 A lady, riding softly on a mule, who came
Towards him, and saluted him, and told her name,
The Queen of Castle Mortal; but to Launcelot
Somewhat like Morgan the enchantress,[107] and somewhat
Like Guinever, her countenance and talking seemed;
240 And golden, like a dragon's back, her clothing gleamed[108]
And courteously she prayed him, "Since the night is near
Turn now and take your lodging in my manor here."
"Lady, may God repay you" says the knight,[109] and so
Over the bridge, together, to the gate they go
245 And enter in. Young servitors enough he found
That kneeled before the lady, and came pressing round;
One took his helm, another took his spear, a third
Led off his horse; and chamberlains and grooms were stirred
To kindle fires and set him at the chimney side,
250 And clothe him in a long-sleeved mantle, soft and wide.
They go to dine. And presently her people all
Were gone away, he saw not where; and in the hall
He and the Lady sat alone. And it was night;
More than a hundred candles burned both still and bright.
255 His hostess makes great joy for him, and many a cup
Of strong wine, red as blood, she drinks; then rises up
And prays him bear her company and look on all
The marvels of her manor house. So out of hall,
Laughing, she leads him to the chapel-door: and when
260 That door was opened, fragrance such as dying men
Imagine in immortal countries, blown about
Heaven's meadows from the tree of life, came floating out.
No man was in the chapel, but he sees a light
There too of many hundred candles burning bright.
265 She led him in, and up into the choir, and there

He saw three coffins all of new cut stone, and fair
With flowers and knots, and full of spices to the brim
And from them came the odour that by now makes dim
His sense with deathly sweetness. But the heads of all
270 Those coffins passed beneath three arches in the wall.
On these he gazes; then on her. The sweet smell curls
About their brains. Her body is shaking like a girl's
Who loves too young; she has a wide and swimming eye;
She whispers him, "The three best knights of earth shall lie
275 Here in my house"; and yet again, "Lo, I have said,
The three best knights." But Launcelot holds down his head,
And will not speak. "What knights are these," she said. And "Nay,"
He answered. "If you name them not, I dare not say."
She laughed aloud—"A coffin for Sir Lamorake,
280 For Tristram;[110] in the third lies Launcelot du Lake."
He crossed himself and questioned her when these should die.
She answered, "They shall all be living when they lie
Within these beds; and then—behold what will be done
To all, or even to two of them, or even to one,
285 Had I such grace." She lifts her hand and turns a pin
Set on the wall. A bright steel blade drops down within
The arches, on the coffin-necks, so razor-keen
That scarce a movement of the spicey dust was seen
Where the edge sank. "Aï! God forbid that you should be
290 The murderer of good knights," said Launcelot. And she
Said, "But for endless love of them I mean to make
Their sweetness mine beyond recovery and to take
That joy away from Morgan and from Guinever
And Nimue and Isoud and Elaine,[111] and here
295 Keep those bright heads and comb their hair and make them lie
Between my breasts and worship them until I die."
(1930–33 [?]; 1969)

The Queen of Drum
A Story in Five Cantos

Canto I

I

(Quick! The last chance! The dawn will find us.[112]
Look back! How luminous that place
—We have come from there. The doors behind us
Swing close and closer, the last trace
5 Vanishes. Quick! Let no awaking
Wash out this memory. Mark my face,
Know me again—join hands—it's breaking—
Remember—wait!—know me . . .)

Remember whom?

Who is there? Who answered? Empty, the cold gloom
10 Before the daybreak, when the moon has set.
It's over. It was a dream. They will forget.

II

To the King of Drum,[113] at last, beyond pretence
Of sleep, the day returned, the inevitable sense
15 Of well known things around him: on the ceiling
The plaster-gilt rosettes crumbling, the lilies peeling.
Gentlemen, pages, lords, and flunkey things
In lace who act the nurse to lonely kings,
Tumbled his poor old bones somehow from bed.
20 Swallowing their yawns, whispering with louted head,
Passed him from hand to hand, tousled and grey
And blinking like an owl surprised by day,
Rubbing his bleary eyes, muttering between dry gums
"Gi' me my teeth . . . dead tired . . . my lords—'t all comes
25 From living in the valley. Too much wood.
Sleep the clock round in Drum and get no good."

III

Now half they had dressed the King, half made him dress.
And day's long steeplechase one jump the less
Unrolled ahead (night's pillows and the star
30 Of night no more immeasurably far).

Now the long[114] passage where the walls are thick
As in the Egyptian tombs, echoes his stick
Tapping the cold, grey floor. There, at his side,
With sharp, unlooked for sound, a door flung wide
35 As from impatient hands, and tall, between
The swing of the flung curtains, stepped the Queen.
—"So fast, Madam? Young limbs are supple, eh?
And easily get their rest. I'll dare to say
You have been abroad by night—not known your bed
40 More than an hour. Is it true?"

And when she said
Nothing at all, he tapped the ground, and nearing,
Knowingly, his big grey face to hers, and peering,
Screwed home the question, snarling. And she stood
45 And never spoke. She too was tired, the blood
Drained from her quiet cheek. Wind-broken skies
Had havocked in her hair, and in her eyes
Printed their reckless image. Coldest grey
Those eyes, and sharp[115] of sight from far away:
50 More bright a little, something steadier than
Man cares to meet with in the face of man
Or woman; alien eyes. For one unbroken
Big moment's silence, swift as rain, unspoken
Questions went to and fro, and edged replies
55 Flitting like motes from their embattled eyes
—(Out of the neighbouring past, an unlaid fear
Signals its fellows, calls 'I am here. I am here,"
Whispers the King, "Touch not, lest it should wake
The enormous tooth that once has ceased to ache")
60 Till with a shrug, turning, he first withdrew
His gaze, yet softly breathed, "You . . . Maenad, you!"

IV

That heavy day the servants had been late
Setting to rights the carven room of state
Where council met. Bucket and mop were there
65 Still, and the smell of soot was in the air,
And half-awakened, chilly footmen cursed
And jostled yet, as, one by one, the first
And youngest of the Notables of Drum
Came straggling in;[116] spiritless all, all dumb,

70 As men who with their first awakening yawn
Had sipped an added loathing for the dawn,
Thinking "The Council sits to-day."

And then,

—Long intervals between—the older men,
75 With more important frowns that seemed to claim
Business of state for pretext, drifting came
Down the long floor like arctic bergs afloat,
With rustling gowns, with clearing of the throat,
Bark of defiant cough, official sound
80 Of papers spread, and testy glance around.

V

Now at the long green board they are seated all
In the very old carved room, so thick of wall,
So narrow-windowed, here, an hour from noon,
Men work by lamplight in the month of June.
85 The oldest of them all play noughts and crosses,
A gambler reckons up his evening losses.
One trims his nails, one spreads his hands and lays
A bright, bald head between them on the baize.
The General, his big lips distended wide,
90 Fumbles with half a hand concealed inside,
Picking a tooth. The Chancellor, with head
Close to the paper and quick-moving lead,
Sketches and strokes all out and draws again
Angular pigs, straight trees, and armless men.
95 More peaceful far beside him in his place
The Lord Archbishop nods: a rosy face
Cherubically dimpled, settling down
Each moment further into beard and gown
—Into foamed, silvery beard and snowy bands;
100 Folded, on quiet breast, his baby hands
—Smooth, never-laboured hands, calm, happy heart,
Like sculptures monumentally at rest
On some cathedral tomb.
Then suddenly a[117] stir runs down the room,
105 —The crumpling of scrawled paper, and the shake
Hurriedly given to jog a friend awake,
Scraping of chairs, quick gabbled finishing
Of whispered tales. Men rise to meet the King.

VI

Heavily the hours, like laden barges passed
110 —Motion, amendment, order, motion. Now at last
The trickling current of the slow debate
Sets towards that ocean sea, where soon or late
Time out of mind their consultations come,
—The everlasting theme "What's wrong with Drum?"
115 When, marvellous to dull'd ears, elf-bright between
Two droning wastes of talk, one name—"The Queen"
Broke startling. And the scribbler dropped the pen
And sleepers rubbed their eyes and whispering men
Drew heads apart, watching.
120 Yes. Sure enough.
The Chancellor's on his feet and taking snuff
And writhing and grimacing with a bow
In the article of deprecation . . . Now,
Listen!
125 . . . "and also seen by vulgar eyes
In her most virtuous, yet, perhaps, unwise
Occasions" . . . "A King's house contains the weal
Of all. He is the axle of the wheel,
The root of the politic tree, the fountain's spring" . . .
130 "Nothing is wholly private in a King.
For what more private to each man alone
Than health, my lords? Yet, if the monarch groan,
The duteous subject" . . .
(Lost, once more, the thread . . .
135 Something like "fans the brow" and "fevered head,"
Then "rough affection")[118] . . . "dutifully rude,
Without offence, offending, must intrude."
And "Kings to their own majesty resign
The privacy, my lords, that yours and mine" . . .
140 (Hist! Now it's coming)
. . . "in a private woman
'Twere not convenient: for a queen, inhuman.
Thus to expose a teeming nation's care
And princes yet unborn, to the damp air
145 Of middle night, and fogs—the common curse
Of our low land—besides, my lords, what worse
May haunt such place and time. As well, you have heard,
All of you, how injuriously the word
Of these things runs abroad. The people know!

150 Always some chattering dame has seen her go
Past midnight, and on foot, beyond the gates
Out hill-wards, when the frost upon the slates
Winked to the moon . . . then, the same week, another
Has gossipped with a country girl, whose brother,
155 —Some forester—by night, in wind and rain,
Past three o'clock of the morn, time and again,
Plodding his homeward journey in the jaws
Of darkness, where the gust in dripping shaws
Blows out his lantern, swears he has often seen
160 Straight in his path, and like a ghost, the Queen,
—Scaring him: as he kneeled to kiss her hand
Brushing him by, so soft.
Cloud in the land
Nature has given enough: but this is cloud
165 Deeper than darkness, cold as death's own shroud,
Poisoning the people's thought. You must command
Where counsel fails. You, Sire, with sceptred hand,
With royal brow—stamp out the infected thing
. . . And merge, at last, the husband in the King."
170 But as he ended, from the lowest place
At the board's end, a screeching raw-boned boy
Jumps up, with hair like flax, and freckled face,
And knuckley fingers working with the joy
Of having found his tongue—"My lords, they say
175 Far more than this . . . and worse . . . they say . . . the sounds
And lights along the mountains far away
At night . . . and then she's on her hunting grounds
With all of those . . . they . . . you—you have fobbed them off
And lied to them . . ."
180 —but babble and loud cough,
Laughter and plucking hands and stare and frown
Had covered the boy's speech and pulled him down,
While lowly boomed the General, "Odds my life.
Damn nonsense. Have a wife and rule a wife.
185 Woman—they say—and dog—and walnut tree—
More you beat'm—better they be—"
When, gradually, a stir about the door,
A sense of things amiss, then more and more
A patch of silence, dimly felt,[119] that spread
190 In widening circles from the table's head,

Turned thither all their eyes, all ears to wait
The word of the King: who from his chair of state
Half rising (in his hand a paper shook)
Laboured, faltering, to speech, with shifty look
195 Settling towards blank dismay. "My lords—she's here—
My lords, the Queen—has something for your ear—
Craves entry."
And across those champions all
Change passed, as when the sunlight leaves the wall.

VII

200 And all at once the Queen was there,
A flash of eyes, a flash of hair,
Nostril widened, teeth laid bare,
Omens of her breathing, and
Robe caught breastward in one hand,
205 Tall mid their seated shapes: a hush
Of moments:[120] then the torrent rush
Of her speaking.
"What? All dumb
Conspirators? Now is your time. Now come,
210 You searchers of the truth, you diggers up
Of secrets, now come all of you,[121] the cup
Is full and brimming over and shall be poured
—You shall drink now. What? You—or you, my lord,
Forbid my wandering nights? Are you content
215 To lose your own? Will you, my lord, be pent
A prisoner every night within the wall,
You, General? Does one fetter bind us all?"
"Content?" he growled, "Why, Madam, who that's sane
And 's slept in starlight many a long campaign,
220 Would leave his bed by nights? What should I seek
Beyond my pillow, then?"—"Aye, Thus you speak,
Thus now you speak," she said, "When woods put on
Their daytime stillness, when the voice is gone
From rivers, and the cats of night lie curled
225 In sleep, and the moon moves beneath the world.
Fie! As if all that hear you did not know
The password, as yourself. Five hours ago
Where were you?—and with whom?—how far away?
Borrowing what wings of speed when break of day

230 Recalled you, to be ready, here, to rise
In the nick of time, and with your formal eyes
And grave talk, to belie that other face
And voice you've shown us in a different place?
What, mum as ever? Does the waking voice
235 So scare you on that theme? It is your choice
Not mine, to grub and drag the secret thence,
Where I've played fair . . . tho', faith, your long pretence
Has been my wonder; how you could return
Each morning to the mask and take concern,
240 Or seem to take concern, with toys—who's dead,
Whose[122] suit is gone awry and whose is sped,
Who's beautiful, and who grows past her prime—
As if it were there your heart lay! All the time
That flame to which your waking hours are ash,
245 Shining so near . . . one syllable too rash,
One glance unveiled, had let the secret out;
But always you slipped past and went about,
Skillfully—like conspirators who meet
Out of their lodge, and pass, and do not greet.
250 Oh fools! . . . if all the plotting brethren turn
Informers against one, shall that one burn
Or hang defenceless? All to keep his vow
Of silence? I have a tongue, and freedom now
To use it. The pact's off. I'll force you yet
255 To throw down all the cards: and where we met,
By night, and what we were, you shall recall.
Tho' limp as a dead man's your tongues should crawl
Unwilling to the word,—I'll make them speak,
Up, from your graves! You're shamming. You shall shriek
260 To split the clouds with truth, you shall proclaim
On housetops what your muttering dared not name
In corners. Or, as Lazarus' ghost, beneath
The cloths, back to its shrunk and emptied sheath
Wormed its way home, I'll force again to grow,
265 Under these masks you wear for daylight show,
The selves you are at night . . .
What? Nothing yet?
No answer? . . . can it be you do forget?
Did the gates shut so quick? Could you not bear
270 One small grain back to light and upper air?

Must I go down like Orpheus and retrace
The interdicted ford—out of that place,
Step by step, hand in hand, hail up what lies
Buried in you, and teach your waking eyes
275 To acknowledge it? I thought we had all known
What spends us in the dark, and why we groan
To feel the light return and the limbs ache,
Even in our slumber fighting not to wake . . .
I thought that you, being but the husks of men
280 All the drab day, remembered where and when
The ripe ear grows—where are the golden hills
It waves on, and the granaries it fills.
Call it again. Dive for it. Strain your sight,
Crack all your sinews, heaving up to light
285 What's under you. Thou sunken wreck, arise!
Sea-gold, sea-gems that fill the hollow eyes
Of admirals dead; out of thy smothering caves
Where colour is not, up, to where the waves
Turn emerald and the edge of ocean-cold
290 Is yielding,[123] and the fish go slashed with gold,
Up! 'gainst thy nature, up! put on again
Colour and form and be to waking men
Things visible. Heave all! Softly . . . it rears
Its dripping head. What, Lords? At last? Your ears
295 Remember now that song, those giant words,
Louder than woods that thundered, scattering birds
Like leaves along the sky, and whose the throats
Louder than cedars there whipt flat as oats . . .
Birds tumbled . . . the sky dipped . . ."
300 The Queen's voice broke.
Heavily, in that moment, like the stroke
Of an axe[124] falling, came the sight and sense
Of those about her: the long room, packed dense,
Her voice yet stirring echoes in the corners,
305 Dull, puzzled eyes, the patient smile of scorners,
Face behind unintelligible face,
Arms nudging and heads whispering in each place
Save where she looked. Then twice she made endeavour,
Grasped the great moment's virtue: gone forever:
310 Struggling to speak. Then (curses on the frame
Of woman!) her breast shook, and scalding came

Tears of deep rage. Bite thro' the lip, clench hand,
—All's vain. And now she saw the Archbishop stand
Beside her, whispering, "Daughter . . . come away,"
315 Heard the King's voice, "The Queen's not well[125] to-day."

Canto II

They dine at ten to three[126] in Drum;
At four the full decanters come
And, heavy with dark liquor, pass
Down the long tables polished smooth as glass,
5 In dark red rooms where the piled curtains sweep
Wine-coloured carpets[127] ankle deep.
(Outside, the thrush sings: unobserved, the flowers
Drop petals through those silent hours.)[128]
The King, too tired to drink his wine in state,
10 Was with the Chancellor *tête-a-tête.*
The Chancellor who with punctual sip
Raised his full glass to bloodless lip
A moment later than his master
In perfect time, now slow, now faster.
15 The tiptoe servants from the room
Stole reverently as from a tomb;
The door closed softly as the settling wing
Of pigeons in a wood. The King
Threw off his wig and wiped his glistening head
20 And, "Where's she now?" he said.

"The Queen, Sir? Since we left the Council board
I think she's mewed up somewhere with my lord
Archbishop."

"With old Daddy? Likely enough . . .
25 Do you suppose, now, he believes that stuff?"

"Daddy believe her? Oh Lord, Sir, not he!
Least of us all, Sir; less than you and me."

"Why, as for that—fill up, fill both the glasses.
Steenie, your health! you understand . . . what passes

30 Between us—mum's the word. We two together
Have come through many a storm and change of weather.
In confidence, now; tell me what you made
This morning of our loving wife's tirade?"

"Me, Sir? I think the Queen . . . has startled Drum
35 Excessively. She'll have her following; some
Will doubtless—"

"I'm not asking what she'll do
To others, man, but what she's done to you.
Your glass is empty."

40 "Well Sir, if you must
Thank you. No more! Your Majesty . . . I trust
I may be pardoned if I hesitate;
The failure of our plan . . . the whole debate
Turned upside down . . . has thrown me in such doubt,
45 I looked to your advice to lead us out."

"At least, you haven't passed it with a sneer
Like Daddy. You perceive there's . . . something . . . here?"

"Oh, not like Daddy, Sir. I'm humbler far.
These churchmen, in the bulk—"

50 "Why, there you are!
That's what I say. For if there were such things,
Some secret stairs and undiscovered wings
In the world's house, dark vacancies between
The rooms we know—behind the public scene
55 Some inner stage . . . if such things could be so,
The man who wears a mitre's paid to know
Or to invent it, eh? Of all men living
He's the least right to pass without misgiving."

"Oh very true. I see, Sir. After all,
60 We might in sleep be more than we recall
On waking?"

"Easy enough to talk at large
And laugh at her: but who'll refute the charge?
Like a puffed candle-flame at half past ten
65 My world goes out: at nine, perhaps, again
I find it . . ."

"Yes indeed. And in between
No one can tell us where or what we've been."

"Ah! There's the stickler, eh? We understand,
70 You and I, Steenie. Fill your glass. Your hand!
We don't remember."

"Yet . . . there's times, at waking,
One feels one has just failed in overtaking
Something . . . you can't say what . . . already, as your eyes
75 First catch it, shuffling on its day's disguise."

"I know, Steenie. Like on the hills, if one
White cotton-tail has flashed, the mischief's done;
Where you saw nothing, now you see the ground
Alive with rabbits half a mile around,
80 And all betrayed by one. So one queer thought
Peeps from the edge of sleep, and there you've caught
The implication of a thousand others,
And then . . . you're wide awake. Common sense smothers
The trail of the fugitives."

85 "But if one delves
As deep as that . . ."

"Speak out: only ourselves
Will hear you."

"Why . . . your Majesty has such a way!
90 I'm in an odd, confessing mood to-day.
I hardly know . . . it's strange we've never spoken
Of things like that . . . he-he! . . . I think the Queen has broken
Our dams all down—"

"What's that?"

95 "I said, the Queen
Had opened all the doors: that is, I mean—"

"That wasn't what you said."

"I said, the Queen
Had broken in the dams."

100 "Oh, very good!
Excellent . . . dykes in Holland . . . and the flood,
Disnatured for a hundred years, sighs-off the chain,
Easing its heart, and floods the land again.
I'll tell you what I feel . . . I think I know
105 How it would feel to be a man of snow
Set in the sunlight . . . yes: that's how I feel—
Deliciously soft liquefactions steal
Round the stiff corselet where we've frozen in
The fluid soul, so long . . . and drops begin
110 To hollow out warm caves and paths . . . but you,
You said, if one delved deep—?"

"Why, if you do,
Well, frankly—in such glances—well, by God!
I've fished up things that were extremely odd."

115 "I know the kind (come, drink about) and Daddy
Had reasons to ignore it."

"Reasons, had he?
You mean he knows?"

"He guesses well enough
120 That back there on the borderland there's stuff
Not marked on any map their sermons show
—They keep one eye shut just because they know—
Don't we all know?
At bottom?—that this World in which we draw
125 Our salaries, make our bows, and keep the law,
This legible, plain universe we use
For waking business, is a thing men choose
By leaving out . . . well, much; our editing,

(With expurgations) of some larger thing?
130 Well then, it stands to reason; go behind
To the archetypal scrawl, and there you'll find
. . . Well . . . variant readings, eh? And it won't do
Being over dainty there."

"That's very true.
135 Can't wear kid gloves."

"Once in a way, perhaps,
's pardonable—wholesome even—to relapse.
You never feel it, yet this keeping hold
Year after year . . . eh? . . . that's what makes us old.
140 Now when one was a boy . . . do you remember
(You'd have been twelve that year) one warm September
Under those laurels, with the keeper's dog
And the gypsy girl—the day we killed the frog?"

"Boys will be boys, Sir! By your leave again,
145 I'll fill your glass and mine. But now we're men
How can you reach . . . how does the Queen contrive
To keep the memory of her nights alive
Though we've forgotten?"
"Why—plague on her—she
150 Goes thither in the body."
"Didn't we?
I put a bold face on while she was making
Her speech this morning: but a knee-cap aching
And a bruised shin kept running in my head.
155 The devil!—how should knees get knocks in bed?"

"That's sympathetic magic . . . like Saint Francis . . .
Stigmata . . . when the Subtle Body dances
Ten miles away, you feel the palpitations.
. . . Like the wax doll for witches' incantations.
160 That fortune-telling man they whipped and branded,
What was his name?"

"Oh he was caught red-handed.
The floating lady and the flying tambourine . . .

All done by wires, Sir: Jesseran[129] you mean?
165 Why, if he's still alive, he's down below
Under the castle here. They loved him so
The people, and believed him; he was tried
In secret. But beyond all doubt he's died.
It's down to water level, under clay,
170 The dungeons of your father's father's day—
No one could live. The keepers hardly know
The way down; and it's twenty years ago."

"I'll dig him up, though. For our present game,
Living or dead, he might be much the same.
175 What?—never stare. I thought you understood.
Help me up, Steenie. So! I'm in the mood
For a frolic. Are those dams all down? Oh brave!
Trol-de-rol-trol! The emalgipated slave . . .
Wouldn't a lobster, now, feel more than well
180 If some kind friend unbuttoned 'm from 's shell!
That's how I feel. Hey, Steenie, watch your legs.
Let's have a song."

"This way, Sir. 'Ware the table.
I hold it, Sir, most seriously,
185 Both treasonous and treasonable,
Privatus homo, subjects such as me,
When Majesty is drunk, in contrariety
To flaunt an illegalical sobriety."

"Excellent! Have that in the statute book.
190 Steenie . . . my old, old friend . . . how beautiful you look.
We'll go to the dungeons, eh?"

"Absolutely deeper.
To the centre of the earth. We'll wake the sleeper.
Trumpets there!"

195 "We'll sing charms and ride on brooms
We'll fetch the dead men out of tombs,
We'll get with child the mountain hags
And ride the cruels of the crags . . .
How gardens love it when the gardener's eye

200 ’s wi’drawn a month, and ten feet high
The weeds foam round the cottage door . . .
Their dykes are down . . . the tide returns once more.
Liberty! Liberty! as the duchess says
Each night when they undo her stays.
205 Remember how the iambic goes?
ἐπιλελήσμεθ ἡδέως.[130]
Open the door there! Both! The other wing!
My lordge—The King is drunk; long live the King!”

Canto III

The dungeon stair interminably round and round
Draws on the King and Chancellor far underground
To his ancestral prison-house. And in the tower
The Queen and the Archbishop in her airy bower
5 Sit talking; the frail, slender tower that overlooks
Meadows and wheeling windmills and meandering brooks
Five miles towards the mountains of the spacious west.
The mountains swell towards them like a woman’s breast,
Their winding valleys, bountiful like opened hands,
10 Spread out their green embracement to the lower lands,
The pines on the peak’d ridges, like the level hair
Of racing nymphs are stretched on the clear western air.
Often she looked towards them and her eyes were brightened,
And her pulse quickened, her brow lightened;
15 And often at the old man’s voice she turned her head,
And each time more impatiently. “My lord,” she said,
“If you had laughed me down like all the rest,
I would have understood. But you’ve confessed
Such things may be. Then what we both believe
20 You’d keep a secret?”—“Lest I should deceive,”
Said he, “I hold my tongue. Truths may be such
That when they have cooled and hardened at the touch
Of language, they turn errors. So our speech
Fails us, and waking discourse cannot reach
25 The thing we are in dreams. Alas, my Queen,
What Spirit, while nature sleeps, has done or seen,
If told at morning, fades like fairy wealth,
And in its place the changeling comes by stealth,

The dapper lie, more marketable far
30 Than Truth, the maid. Daughter, I think you are
Willingly no deceiver. What you meant
To-day was truth; but all that truth was spent
Before you said ten words. What followed after
—All the wild tale you told of storm and laughter
35 And hunting on the hills—all this . . . (good now
On your salvation, never change your brow,
Soft! Softly! Quench those eyes)
All this, by a plain word, was it not lies?"

"How lies, my lord, when all the talk of Drum
40 Vouches my wanderings real? Play fairly. Come!
That I've gone there, is known; that I've met you
When you were also there, is that not true?"

"Have I been in that place? (We'll call it so
Though wrongly) . . . have I? . . . child, I do not know.
45 Sometimes I think I have. I am uncertain.
Ask me not. If a man could lift the curtain
The half-inch that's beyond all price—but none
Can tell, being wakened, what the night has done."

Her scorn leaped quickly at him. "If you know
50 Thus little of the lands to which I go,
How can you call my tale of them untrue?
Give me the lie who can! so cannot you."

"This is but baby's talk," he said, "Indeed
We cannot lift the curtain at our need,
55 It is immovable, but lights come through.
We know not—we remember that we knew."
And then he paused, and ruefully he smiled
Fondling his knee with thoughtful hand; and, "Child,"
He said, "How can it profit us to talk
60 Much of that region where you say you walk?
We are not native there: we shall not die
Nor live in elfin country, you and I.
Greatly I fear lest, wilfully refusing
Beauty at hand, you walk dark roads to find it,
65 Impatient of dear earth because behind it

You dream of phantom worlds, forever losing
What is more wonderful—too strange indeed
For you—too dry a flavour for the greed
Of uncorrected palates; this sweet form
70 Of day and night, the stillness and the storm,
Children, the changing year, the growing god
That springs, by labour, out of the turn'd sod."

"I have no child," she said. "What mockery is this,
What jailor's pittance offered in the prison of earth,
75 To that unbounded appetite for larger[131] bliss
Not born with me, but older than my mortal birth? . . .
When shall I be at home? When shall I find my rest?
My lord, you have lived happy and with cause have blessed
This world's habitual highway, where you walk at ease;
80 I walk not, but go naked upon bleeding knees.
And if this threadbare vanity of days, this lean
And never-ceasing world were all—if I must lose
The air that breathes across it from the land I've seen,
About my neck tonight I'd slip the noose
85 And end the longing. But it is not so;
And you—your words have half revealed—you know,
And will not tell. Oh pity, pity I crave
(This thirst will burn my body in the rotting grave).
Speak to me, father! tell me all the truth, confess!
90 Give me a plain No or an honest Yes.
Have you too found the way to such a place,
And in it have we all met face to face?"

"Peace, peace! Beware!"

"Of what should I beware?
95 What is the crucifixion that I would not dare,
To find my home? (When shall my rest be won?)
Why do you turn away: What have I done?"

"Almost crushed dead, I fear, on your own breast
With hot, rough, greedy hands what you love best.
100 It will not thus be wooed. You will not find
Your rest while such a storm is in your mind.
You may find something else."

"What do you mean?"

"Listen: there are two sorts of the unseen,
105 Two countries each from each removed as far
As the black dungeons of this castle are
From this green mountain and this golden sun.
And of the first, I say, we do not know;
But the other is beneath, where to and fro
110 Through echoing vaults continually chaos vast
Works in the cellarage of the soul, and things exiled,
And foolish giants howling from the ancestral past
Wander, and overweening Hopes, and Fears too wild
For this slow-ripening universe; chimeras, ghosts,
115 And succubi and cruelties. You are[132] more like,
Driven on by such a fury of desire, to strike
Those rocks than to make harbour on the happy coasts.
Wishing is perilous work."

"Go on," she said.
120 "What more?" the Bishop asked, and turned his head
Slowly away; "What more is there to tell?"
"You have described the downward journey well,
But of the realm of light, have you no word?"

"Nothing but that which all mankind have heard."

125 She turned away, she paced the floor,
She waited for the Bishop's word no more.
And he looked down, and more than once he passed
His hand across his face, and then at last
Spoke gently, as a man in much distress.
130 "Daughter," he said, "I see I must confess.
God knows I am an old, fat, sleek divine
—Lived easily all my life—far deeper skilled
In nice discriminations of old wine
Than in those things for which God's blood was spilled.
135 Enough of that. And now my punishment
Has found me and my time of grace is spent;
For now I must speak truth and find at need
My advocacy kills the cause I plead.
For if I say none knows, no man is sure

140 Of anything about that land, your eyes,
Seeing me thus world-ridden, thus impure,
How can they, if they would, judge otherwise
Than that my disallegiance from the laws
Of Spirit has dulled my edge and been the cause
145 Of this great ignorance I profess? How, then,
Believe me when I teach that holiest men
Are not less ignorant? (So I think, but I—
What do I know of saints or sanctity?)
But so I think; and so perforce I come
150 Into the court, though shamed, not daring to be dumb.
Hear, then, my tale.
I, who stand ignorant confessed,
Doctor of nescience, or, at best,
A plodding passman in the school
155 Meek Wonder and her maidens rule,
Who hold the brave world's blue and green
But for a magic-lantern screen
That enigmatically shows
The shadow of what no one knows;—
160 I yet believe (if such a word
Of these soiled lips be not absurd)
That from the place beyond all ken
One only Word has come to men,
And was incarnate and had hands
165 And feet and walked in earthly lands
And died, and rose. And nothing more
Will come or ever came before
With certainty. And to obey
Is better than the hard assay[133]
170 Of piercing anywhere besides
This mortal veil, which haply hides
Some insupportable abyss
Of bodiless light and burning bliss.
Hence, if you ask me of the way
175 Yonder, what can I do but say
Over again (as God's own Son
Seems principally to have done)
The lessons of your nurse and mother?
For all my counsel is no other
180 Than this, now given at bitterest need;

—Go, learn your catechism and creed.
Mark what I say, not how I live;
And for myself—may God forgive."

"I thought as much," she cried, "That pale,
185 Numbing, inevitable tale,
The deathbed of desire! Why do you cease?
Preach out your sermon, tell me now of peace
Of passions calmed with grey renunciation,
Longsuffering and obedience and salvation!
190 What is all this to me? Where is my home
Save where the immortals in their exultation,
Moon-led, their holy hills forever roam?
What is to me your sanctity, grave-clothed in white,
Cold as an altar, pale as altar candle light?
195 Not to such purpose was the plucking at my heart
Wherever beauty called me into lonely places,
Where dark Remembrance haunts me with eternal smart,
Remembrance, the unmerciful, the well of love,
Recalling the far dances, the far-distant faces,
200 Whispering me 'What does this—and this—remind you of?'
How can I cease from knocking or forget to watch—"

But other fingers now were on the latch
And with a swaggering stride a noisy, thin,
Hurried, portentous person had come in.
205 "Madam," he squeaked, "I've come to let you know
The Leader calls for both of you below."
Anger so stopped her heart and held her eyes
That, staring hard, she could not recognise
That pale face twisted with the uneasy thirst
210 Of looking more than even now it durst,
Hinting the tavern glance *en mousquetaire*[134]
Yet flinching, too, beneath her silent stare.
At last she knew—the ill-mannered boy, the same
Who at the council had bemired her name,
215 And at the door behind him she could see
Men with fixed bayonets standing, two or three.
And then she laughed—unsummoned laughter, light
And careless from the immeasurable height
Of unflawed youth, and said "What madness now?"

220 It was a world to see his reddening brow
And watch his venom'd fingers how they twist.
"Oh very fine! But that's all done," he hissed.
"And I'm no more your very humble dog.
Trust me, my lady, we have killed King Log
225 Under whose reign the license of your tongue
Has ladied it and laughed at us so long.
We have a Leader now, and you've a master.
Don't ask me who! You'll learn the story faster
Than you desire, perhaps: and you'll have leisure
230 To learn your duties and the Leader's pleasure.
For it's a new world now—and back to Drum
The days of our great ancestors are come.
The seven isles will tremble to the core,
And Terebinthia, when we go to war.
235 You shall behold the Leader when he comes
Riding the foremost of a thousand chargers
All white as milk, a conqueror, home to Drum,
Laden with pearls of Tessaropolis
And gold of Galma,[135] while in silver chains
240 The Emperor of the East attends his state
And Kings enslaved and many a captive isle.
Oh brave to be a Duce![136] brave to drink
The melted pearls of Tessaropolis
And burn the towers of many a captive isle
245 And to be called a Duce . . . but, meanwhile,
For both of you the Leader waits below."

And steel was at their backs. They had to go.

Canto IV

I

The Queen and the Archbishop and the Boy descend
Slowly by many stairways to the castle hall.
Often it seems a journey that will never end,
Often it seems a moment. They are silent all,
5 Thinking hard thoughts. The Bishop thinks them most of all.
For the Queen has heard a trumpet in her heart, and smiles;

She is buckling on her byrnie every step they go,
Ready to die or ready to use all her wiles
—Fierce Artemis[137] will help her. She has learned to know,
10 Long since, those pains and pleasures which the hunted know.
But he thinks how his Christendom is all to learn,
His soul to set and harden in the mould that makes
Eternal spirit, his leprosy to heal and turn
Fresh as the skin of childhood, in the time it takes
15 To reach the hall. (Incalculable time it takes;
The Watchers from beyond the world perceive each stair
Long with sidereal distances beyond all count,
A ladder of humility stretched up to where
The eternal forests tremble on the leavèd mount
20 Of Paradise. Up thither they behold him mount).
They reached the bottom of the bottom stair and passed
Into the hall. The General stood here, so vast,
With legs astride, so planted, that he seemed to bear
The weight of the whole house upon his shoulders square.
25 His red, full blood grandiloquently in his cheek
Spoke so that you could almost say his body shouted
And was his garish blazon ere his tongue could speak,
Saying, "I am the Leader, the event, the undoubted,
All-potent Fact, the firstborn of necessity,
30 I am Fate, and Force, and Führer, Worship me!"

II

The General at the council-board had heard
The Queen's harangue that day with scarce a word,
Indifferent first, and then amused, and then
Something within him in response had stirred.

35 All those nocturnal wanderings must be
A girlish dream, he thought, undoubtedly,
But if it came to dredging up one's dreams,
Well—he'd had curious nights as well as she.

He did not share the popular dismay.
40 No; if she wanted dreams to walk by day,
He was her man—only remained to see
If his or hers would bear the greater sway.

Perhaps, indeed, no conflict would arise;
The General thought he had a shrewd surmise
45 How hers would look when his experienced hand
Had eased them of their troublesome disguise.

For though this happened long before the name
Of Freud or his disciples rose to fame,
Men like the General, even then, had reached
50 (Empirically) doctrines much the same.

When Council rose, about his work he went,
And warnings to his gunmen all he sent,
And seized a press and moved some troops. He'd missed
His dinner, but the time had been well spent.

55 And so it came to pass, at five o'clock
The Jailor of the dungeons turned his lock
To let the King and Chancellor in. And down,
Singing, they went into the tunnelled rock.

At five past, he was visited again
60 —This time the General and a dozen men.
He clicked his heels. "How many entrances,"
The General asked "Lead down into that den?"

"Only this one, your honour," he replied.
"Good!" said the General, plucking from his side
65 His bunch of keys. And to his men, "Now boys,"
He said. They kicked the Jailor down inside.

They slammed and locked the door and turned away.
Inside, the Jailor heard the General say
"The keys? Oh throw them in the well. The fools
70 Chose to go down. I choose that they can stay."

And soon the castle was extremely still,
For all were killed whom they proposed to kill.
Servants with ashen face and hair on end
Came scampering at a call to do his will.

75 He said he liked his victuals with some taste;
He'd have a two-pint jug of porter, laced

With brandy, hot as hell, and devilled bones
And good strong cheese. And it was brought in haste.

He shovelled all these things inside his head,
80 And smacked his lips (large lips, and moist and red),
And belched a little, tapping with his whip
His booted calves. "Now for the girl!" he said.

III

The Bishop and the Queen arrived. He said,
"Madam, the King is both deposed and dead.
85 The Why and Wherefore of it's long to hear,
And politics are not a woman's sphere.
The King is dead—and your bereavement such
As you can bear without lamenting much
. . . Why! it's mere nature. If I made pretence
90 Of sympathy, it would insult your sense,
Aye, and your senses too—which never yet
Had anything from him you need regret.
Now listen—for you're neither prude nor dunce
And I can tell you my whole mind at once;
95 First, let me make it absolutely clear
That nobody has anything to fear
From me—provided that I get my way.
I'm always nice to people who obey,
Specially girls: and if you are kind to me
100 I will repay it double. Try! and see
How much more rich, more splendid and more gay
Your court will be than in the old King's day.
As for myself, I am not young, it's true,
At least, my dear, not quite so young as you;
105 But young at heart—and our blunt soldiers say
Old fiddles often are the best to play.
I'm not a jealous man: I'll leave you free
Except in one thing only. There must be
No more night wanderings nor no talk of them:
110 All that I most explicitly condemn . . .
It's nonsense too. Henceforth you must confine
Your limbs to bed o'nights—and that bed mine!"

No one could feel the quick of the Queen's heart
Except the Queen, and she had learned her part.

115 Just long enough she cast her look aside
And fluttered, then with silver voice replied,
"As for our consort, doubtless soon or late
The elderly must pay their debts to fate,
And young wives are aware they must submit
120 To widowhood—indeed they count on it.
Enough: the future is our chief concern.
Surely your Lordship has not now to learn
That his heroic deeds are eloquence
In female ears, admitting no defence.
125 In all ways irresistible you come,
Conqueror of things unconquered yet in Drum!
If I should play the girl and hang my head,
It would but show me rustic and ill-bred;
Yet, if I might demur, this time and place
130 Are hardly suitable in such a case.
These your heroic followers;—I am proud
To welcome them—but still, they make a crowd,
Nor can my answer be so full and clear
As your high dignity deserves—not here.
135 In Paphos,[138] Sir, not midst the watchful stars
Of public heaven, does Venus welcome Mars;
And, by your leave withdrawn into my tower,
I will await the Leader's private hour."

"Come!" said the General, "That's the sort of stuff!
140 Perhaps my methods were a trifle rough.
I am a plain, blunt soldier, as no doubt
You saw: but you have kindly helped me out.
Go to your tower, and I'll be there at six
But (in your ear, my lady) play no tricks!
145 Women are changeable! eh? no offence
But you shall have an escort with you hence.
Here! You!" (He called the raw-boned boy, whose name
I cannot give, for it is lost to fame)
"Go, follow to her bower the Queen of Drum,
150 And keep your eye upon her till I come.
If she escapes, you'd better face the devil
Than me: but if she finds you are uncivil,
By heaven I'll make you the first precedent
For eunuchs in my court. Now go!"
They went.

IV

155 The Leader takes a turn and rubs his hands,
Chuckling and murmuring "Who'd have thought it now?"
And then he comes where the Archbishop stands
And pulls the old man to him by the sleeve
Into a window, with a graver brow
160 Politically furrowed. "I believe
We know each other pretty well," said he,
"Experienced people seldom disagree.
You see there's been a change. I'm called to fill
The supreme office, by the people's will
165 Or, strictly, what the people will discover
To have been their will when all the shouting's over.
Now, in this new régime, of course your Grace
Must certainly retain his present place
And power and temporalities. Indeed,
170 If I might criticise, we rather need
Not less but more of what you represent;
For up till now—pray, take this as it's meant,
Kindly—a certain somnolence has come
To be the hall mark of the Church of Drum,
175 For several years. Henceforward that won't do;
And naturally I rely on you.
Faith—martyrdom—and all that side of things
Concerns Dictators even more than Kings.
Can you contrive a really hot revival,
180 A state religion that allows no rival?
You understand, henceforth it's got to be
A Drummian kind of Christianity—
A good old Drummian god who has always some
Peculiar purpose up His sleeve for Drum,
185 Something that makes the increase of our trade
And territories feel like a Crusade,
Or, even if neither should in fact increase,
Teaches men in my will to find their peace.
Those are the general principles. But now
190 The problem is (and you must show me how)
To deal with the late sovereign's disappearance.
I doubt if they'd believe in interference
From Heaven direct—a plain, Old Testament
Annihilation on the tyrant sent . . .
195 But, short of that, we either must produce

The corpse, or else some plausible excuse.
What do you think? The matter's in your line
And suited to your office more than mine."

The Bishop answered, "Any man in the world
200 Has more right to rebuke these words than I.
But I believe—I know you could not know
That I believed—in God. I dare not lie."

The General answered "I should hope you do;
I'm a religious man as well as you,
205 But now we're talking politics. You say
That you believe; the point is, so do they,
Which makes all doctrines easy to digest.
Come, now; I've made a very small request."

"I cannot tell them more than I believe.
210 I dare not play with such immeasurables.
I am afraid: yes, that's the truth, afraid,
Put it no higher. Fear would stop my tongue."

The Leader said, "Oh Lord, to have a fool
To deal with. God Almighty, keep me cool!
215 What do you fear? Have I not made it plain,
You and your Church have everything to gain?
Be loyal to the Leader and I'll build
Cathedrals for you, yes, and see them filled,
I'll give you a free hand to bait all Jews
220 And infidels. You can't mean to refuse?"

"I must: for He of whom I am afraid
Esteems the gifts that can promise me
Evil, or else of very small account."

"Silence!" The Leader said, "Silence, I say!
225 You never talked like this before to-day,
And now to make religion your pretence,
Frankly, I hold it sheer irreverence.
If you look down from such a starry height
As that, upon all earthly power and might,
230 Why, in God's name, have you not told us so

A year, or ten, or fifteen years ago?
Why was your other-worldliness so dumb
When every office went for sale in Drum,
When half the people had no bread to eat
235 Because the Chancellor'd cornered[139] all the wheat,
When the Queen played her witchery nights, and when
The old King had his women nine or ten?
All this you saw, unless you were asleep.
God! to sit still beside the course and keep
240 Your malice hid, till at the race's end
You dart your leg out to trip up a friend
Just at the goal. I'd counted upon you—
The thing so dangerous and my friends so few,
Would I have risked it if I thought the Church
245 Was going to turn and leave me in the lurch?
What? Silent still? Why then, damnation take you!
I've begged enough, I'll find a way to make you.
You've played a dirty trick, and now you'll rue it!"
He called his men and said, "Boys! Put him through it."

V

250 The raw-boned boy, meanwhile, was with the Queen.
She led him in the short way between
The great hall and her private tower,
—A little terrace, at that hour
A solitary place. And there
255 She knew that they would pass a stair
Down which she had scampered many a night
Into the garden by star-light,
Upon her arm she had a ring,
The bridal gift of the old King,
260 Hard, heavy gold that twists to take
The likeness of a tangled snake.
She works it downwards as they walk,
Little she heeds her jailor's talk.
She works it till that golden worm
265 Is round her knuckles and held firm.
And now they reached the stairway's head.
Never a word the lady said;
Out from her shoulder straight she flung
Her arm, so strong, so round, so young;

270 His wits were much too slow to save him—
It was a lovely blow she gave him.

Right in his mouth with all her strength
He got the gold. He sprawled his length,
Bloodied and blubbering; and when
275 He scrambled to his feet again,
He saw the wide, smooth lawn between
Himself and the swift-footed queen,
He saw her raiment flickering white
Against the hedge—then out of sight.

VI

280 The Leader's ruffians gather with great strokes
About the Bishop, with lead pipe and sticks,
As foresters about a tree with the axe,
With belts and bludgeons and with jibes and jokes.
His breath comes grunting under heavy shocks,
285 He pants so loud, they think that he still talks,
And rail upon him crying Plague and Pox!
Ever a bone breaks or a sinew cracks.
They beat upon his stomach till its wall breaks. Aoi!

In his imagination he seems to hang
290 Upon a cross and be tormented long,
Not nailed but gripping with his fingers strong.
With the toil thereof all his muscles are wrung,
Great pains he bears in shoulder, arm and lung.
He fears lest they should jolt the cross and fling
295 His body off from where he has to hang. Aoi!

Ever he calls to Christ to be forgiven
And to come soon into the happy haven.
Horrible dance before his eyes is woven
Of darkened shapes on a red tempest driven.
300 Unwearyingly the great strokes are given.
He falls. His sides and all his ribs are riven,
His guts are scattered and his skull is cloven,
The man is dead. God has his soul to heaven. Aoi!

Canto V

Wing'd with delight and fear, the Queen
Was running on the ridgy green.[140]
Up the first field that gently slopes
Towards the hills of all her hopes,
5 Happy the man who might have seen
The unripe breasts of that young Queen
So panting, and her face above
So flushed and eye-bright for his love,
As in this unregarding place
10 She breathed, she brightened, with the chase.
Up the long field in open view
Only to get her lead she flew,
But in the next she hugged the edge
Well hidden by the blackthorn hedge,
15 Then through the spinney chose a track
Still up, not daring to look back,
Then forty yards of sunken lane
Up hill, then to her left again,
Half level, and half losing ground
20 —For so she must to sidle round
A big ten-acre field where men
Were still at work, though even then
Looking with welcome in their eyes
To the slow-yellowing[141] western skies.
25 It was the hour when grass looks greener
And hay smells sweeter. None had seen her,
When up beyond the fields she came
Where three parts wild and one part tame
Old horses roll and donkeys bray
30 And geese in choleric cohorts stray
About the common land, that now
Springs steeply to the foot-hill's brow.
Here as she breasted the hot track
Baked with the sun, she first looks back
35 And sees the squat-built castle stand
Spider-like amid smooth Drum-land,
And from it, spreading like a fan,
The hunt she fled from—horse and man
Already dark and dwarf'd as ants

40 But creeping, nearing. While she pants,
Hard labouring up the stony ground
And slippery grass, above the sound
Of her blood hammering in her ears,
Music of baying dogs she hears.
45 Her wind is good, her feet are fast,
She knows how long they both will last,
On hounds and horses she has reckoned.
She gains that crest, and towards the second
Swifter she runs, yet not too swift.
50 Here the whole earth begins to lift
Its large limbs under robes of green
Higher, and deepening gaps between
Sink in warm shadow, and the sky,
Jostled with peaks, shows small and high.
55 The land of Drum is seen no longer,
The world is purer, the light stronger,
And streams and falls and everywhere
More streams sound on the quiet air.
Here well she knew her way, to turn
60 And find an amber-coloured burn
That musical with myriad shocks
Of water leaped its stair of rocks:
And up the stream from hold to hold
She clambered—the knife-edge of cold
65 Deliciously now reached her waist,
Now splashed her lips with earthen taste,[142]
(And now on the rock slabs her feet
Touch dry, warm moss and found it sweet.)
There wading, leaping in and out
70 She climbed to throw the trail in doubt,
And reached the head. High moorland lay
Before her, and peaks far away
And over them the broad sun sinking.
She stood to breathe a moment, thinking
75 Of many small things, many a place
Far from that evening's toil and chase,
Until the bloodhounds' noise behind
Came louder on a change of wind,
And quelled her spirit as she hearkened,
80 And drove her on.

The world was darkened.[143]
(Peak after peak, that had stood single
Stole from her tired eyes to mingle
And melt its fluid shape among
85 The notch-edged darkness whence it sprung;
And all one gloom the moorland grew
Save where some pool had caught the hue
Of the sky's deepening arch that spread
Pale and enormous overhead.)

90 And still she runs, but slowly now, and yet
More slowly, and pain burns her feet, and sweat
Tangles her hair on smarting eyes and brow;
And still she runs; only of running now
She thinks, not of the ending of the chase,
95 But always runs. There is a wretched place
Beyond the moor, right underneath the fells,
The last of homesteads, where a miser dwells—
A huddle of trees, a cottage under thatch,
A meadow and a cultivated patch.
100 Often in her night wanderings before
She had seen old Trap, and often from his door
He had shouted at her shadow "Witch!" and "Whore!"
Thither she ran and entered the low wood,
Sure-footed, silent as a beast pursued,
105 And from the covert, shaping both her lips
A way she knew, pressed with her finger tips,
Sent such a cry that no man in the dark
But would have sworn it was a vixen's bark.
It worked! Old Trap had poultry to defend;
110 That eldritch sound had hardly time to end
Before the miser with his gun was out
To shoot the varmint dead. But round about
The shadowy Queen had gone to his back door,
Lifted the latch and trod on his cool floor,
115 And in a trice his pan of creaming milk
Down her dry throat went travelling smooth as silk;
Two apples and a lump of his goat cheese
She snatched,[144] and laughed, and under darkening trees
Stole on—now let him guess what nightly fairy
120 Or catamountain has enjoyed his dairy!

And up his meadow grass she glided,
The last green place before the world of rocks,
And all the lives of darkness sided
With her: the veritable fox
125 Welcomed with joy his hunted sister,
The small things of the ditches bade her
Good fortune, glad that man had missed her,
The mountains spread their slopes to aid her;
The world was changing: night was waking
130 And mountain silence, all-estranging.

Now as she ran she saw the meadow
Darkened before her with her shadow,
Because the moon grew strong.[145] She turned;
Brittle and bright the crescent burned,
135 The thin and honey-coloured bow
Of the pure Huntress riding low.
Then to that sight her arm she raised,
Asking no favour, while she praised
The queen whose shafts destroy and bless
140 All wild souls of the wilderness,
Dark Hecate,[146] Diana chaste,
Virginal dread of woods and waste,
Titania,[147] shadowy fear and bliss
Of elf-spun night, great Artemis.
145 Deep her idolatry, for all,
Body and soul, beyond recall
She offered there: and body soon
Was filled all through with virtue of the moon,
That, like a spirit, in each tender vein
150 Flowed with nepenthe's power and eased all pain,
All weariness; and faster now she ran
Than when the toilsome chase began,
If it were running, for she seemed to glide
Over rough scree and rocky shelf
155 Smooth as a floating ship, through wide
And silvery lakes, or (like the moon herself,
Lapped in a motion which is also rest)—
To see the pale world's moonlit vest
Flit past beneath her—glimmering rocks
160 And tufts of grass like snowy locks,
Rivers of mercury, and towers

Of ebony, and stones like flowers.
Far over the piled hills, and past
The hills she knew, she travelled fast;
165 She found a valley like a cup
With moonshine to the brim filled up,
So pure a sweep of hollow ground,
Treeless, with turf so short around,
That not one shadow there could fall
170 But, smooth like liquid, over all,
Night's ghastly parody of day,
The lidless stare of moonlight lay.
Down into it, and straight ahead,
A single path before her led,
175 —A mossy way; and two ways more
There met it on the valley floor;
From left and right they came, and right
And left ran on out of the light.
And near that parting of three ways
180 She thought there was a silver haze,
She thought there was a giant's head
Pushed from the earth with whiteness spread
Of beard beneath and from its crown
Cataracts of whiteness tumbling down.
185 Then she drew near, tip-toed in awe,
And looked again; this time she saw
It was a thornbush, milky white
That poured sweet smell upon the night.
And nearer yet she came and then,
190 Bathed in its fragrance, looked again,
And lo! it was a horse and rider,
Breathing, unmoving, close beside her
More beautiful and larger
Than earthly beast, that charger,
195 Where rode the proudest rider;
—Rich his arms, bewitching
His air—a wilful, elfin
Emperor, proud of temper,
In mail of eldest moulding[148]
200 (And milkwhite cloak of silkworm,)
And sword of elven silver,
Smiling to beguile her;

A pale king, come from the unwintered country
Bending to her, befriending her, and offering white,
205 Sweet bread like dew, his handsel at that region's entry,
And honey pale as gold is in the moonlit night.
When his lips opened, poignant as the unripened note
Of early thrush at evening was his words' deceiving
The first few notes a-roving, then a silver rush
210 "Keep, keep," he bade her, "On the midmost moss-way,
Seek past the cross-way to the land you long for.
Eat, eat," he gave her of the loaves of faerie.
"Eat the brave honey of bees no man enslaveth.
Heed not the road upon the right—'twill lead you
215 To heaven's height and the yoke whence I have freed you;
Nor seek not to the left, that so you come not
Through the world's cleft into that world I name not.
Keep, keep the centre! Find the portals
That chosen mortals at the world's edge enter.
220 Isles untrampled by the warring legions
Of Heaven and Darkness—the unreckoned regions
That only as fable in His world appear
Who seals man's ear as much as He is able . . .
Many are the ancient mansions,
225 Isles His wars defile not,
Woods and land unwounding
The want whereof did haunt you;
Asked for long with anguish,
They open now past hoping
230 —All you craved, incarnate
Come like dream to Drum-land."

Warm was the longing, warm as lovers' laughter,
Strong, sweet, and stinging, that welled up to drift her
Away to the unwintry country, softer
235 Than clouds in clearest distance of Atlantic evening.
Warm was the longing; cold the dread
That entered after it. On her right hand
Descends[149] the insupportable. She turned her head,
But saw no more the air and moonlit land.
240 On all that side the world seemed falling,
From her own side the flesh seemed falling.
Dying, opening, melting, vanishing.

Yet to the sagging torment of that dissolution
She clung, contented with the vanishing
245 If only the fear'd moment never would arise
Of being commanded to lift up her eyes
And to see that whose dissimilitude
To all things, [150] (water, rocks, and air
And sap-green lives and the warm blooded brood,
250 With its aloofness) should, in the first stare
Of its aloofness,[151] make the world despair.
And that world was falling,
And her flesh was falling
And she was small; oh! were she small enough for crawling
255 Into some cranny under some small grass's root—
Rolled to a ball, dead-still beneath the Terror's foot;
To cover her face, close eyes, bury the closed eyes, and though
All hope to be unseen were madness, not to see,
Never to see, not to look up, never to know . . .
260 And all the world was falling
And her mind was falling.
Then, on a level with her own, there came
A face to which she could have given a name,
A face she had seen often (sinking down
265 Into foamed silvery beard and snowy gown),
And though it looked not as she thought the dead
Would look, she knew it spoke from among the dead,[152]
~~(A long way off. The small ancestral dread~~
~~Mixed with the world's and with her soul's falling,~~
~~Dread within dread. She heard it calling)~~

"Quick. The last chance. Believe not the seducing elf.
Daughter, turn back, have pity yet upon yourself
270 Go not to the unwintering land where they who dwell
Pay each tenth year the tenth soul of their tribe to Hell.
Hear not the voice that promises, but rather hear
His who commands, and fear. We have all cause to fear.
Oh draw not down the[153] anger, which is far away
275 And slow to wake. Turn homeward ere the end of day.
You would not see if you looked up out of your torment
That face—only the fringes of His outer garment
Run to it, daughter; kiss that hem." She answered, "No.
If you are with Him pray to Him that He may go,

280 Or pray that He may rend and tear me,
But go, go hence and not be near me."
And all the world was falling,
Spirit and soul were falling,
Body, brain and heart
285 Vanishing, falling apart;
Vacancy under vacancy
Shuddering gaped below;
"Go," was her prayer, "Go,
Go away, go away, away from me."
290 And the fear heightened
The command tautened;
Between her spirit and soul, dividing,
The razor-edged, ice-brook cold command was gliding,
Till suddenly, at the worst, all changed,
295 And like a thing far off, estranged,
Only remembered, like a mood,
That dread became. Her mortal blood
Flowed freely in the uncoloured calm,
Which woos[154] despair and is its balm.
300 Nothing now she will ever want again
But to glide out of all the world of men,
Nor will she turn to right or left her head,
But go straight on. She has tasted elven bread.
And so, the story tells, she passed away
305 Out of the world: but if she dreams to-day
In fairy land, or if she wakes in Hell,[155]
(The chance being one in ten) it doesn't tell.[156]
(1933–34 [?]; 1969)

Scholars' Melancholy

The mind too has her fossils to record her past,
Cold characters, immobile, of what once was new
And hot with life. Old papers, as we rummage through
Neglected drawers, still show us where the pen, fast, fast,
5 Ate up the sheets: and wondering, we remember vast
Designs and knowledge gathered, and intent to do
What we were able then to have done . . . something drew
A sponge across that slate. The ferly would not last.

Though Will can stretch his viaduct with level thrust
10 High above shagg'd woods, quaking swamp, and desert dust
Of changing times, yet he must dig for his material
In local quarries of the varying moment—must
Use wattle and daub in countries without stone, and trust
To basest matter the proud arches' form imperial.
(1933–34 [?]; 1934)

Notes

1. For the context of this poem, see Lewis's letter to Owen Barfield of summer [1927?], published in *Collected Letters of C. S. Lewis,* Volume 3: *Narnia, Cambridge, and Joy, 1950–1963* (hereafter, *CL* 3), ed. Walter Hooper (London: Harper Collins, 2006), 1623.

2. For the context of this poem, see Lewis's letter to Owen Barfield of June 8 [?, 1928?], *CL* 1:765.

3. In Norse mythology, a dwarf with a magic ring and the power to transform himself into a fish.

4. Odin is one of the chief gods in Norse mythology, who lived in Valhalla, in Asgard.

5. In Norse mythology, Balder is one of Odin's sons. See also note 28 on *Dymer,* in the chapter entitled "Poems 1926."

6. See Lewis's "Descend to Earth, Descend, Celestial Nine," in the chapter entitled "Poems 1907–1914," for affinities between the two poems.

7. This poem is found in an unpublished letter from Lewis to Owen Barfield of June 26, [1929?]. See the Bibliography of Poem Sources for additional information on the source of this poem.

8. For the context of this poem, see Lewis's letter to Owen Barfield of Oct. 21, 1929, *CL* 3 (supplement): 1512–13.

9. In his introduction to Lewis's *Collected Poems,* Hooper writes that "fourteen of [Lewis's] religious lyrics were sent to Owen Barfield during the summer of 1930 under the general title 'Half Hours with Hamilton,' and they are some of the most beautiful poems Lewis wrote. Most of these same poems were to appear a couple of years later in his semiautobiographical *The Pilgrim's Regress* (1933). They were always Lewis's favourites of his own poems" (xv). The

texts of the poems printed here are based on the first edition of *The Pilgrim's Regress* (London: J. M. Dent, 1933); hereafter, *PR*.

10. This poem appears in *PR*, 183–84.

11. Pheidias (490–430 B.C.) was an Athenian sculptor and the artistic director of the construction of the Parthenon. He created its most important religious images, leading many to believe that Pheidias had seen the exact images of the gods and revealed them to humankind.

12. This poem appears in *PR*, 187–88.

13. This poem appears in *PR*, 207–8.

14. This poem appears in *PR*, 227–28.

15. Revelation 8:10–11: "And the third angel sounded, and there fell a great star from heaven, burning as it were a lamp, and it fell upon the third part of the rivers, and upon the fountains of waters; And the name of the star is called Wormwood: and the third part of the waters became wormwood; and many men died of the waters, because they were made bitter." Ahriman was the evil spirit in the dualistic doctrine of Zoroastrianism; here, another name for Satan.

16. This poem appears in *PR*, 231.

17. This poem appears in *PR*, 234.

18. This poem appears in *PR*, 235–36.

19. A monad is the mathematical and/or philosophical name for an indivisible smallest material or spiritual constituent; the term is attributed to German philosopher Gottfried Wilhelm von Leibniz (1646–1716) who posited the "unwindowed" nature of monads, arguing that these smallest constituents of reality could have no causal interaction.

20. This poem appears in *PR*, 237–38. For an interesting gloss to this poem, see Lewis's letter to Arthur Greeves of Jan. 30, 1930, *CL* 1:877–78.

21. This poem appears in *PR*, 240–41.

22. This poem appears in *PR*, 243.

23. This poem appears in *PR*, 245–46. In Jewish folklore, Lilith was thought to be Adam's first wife; here Lewis's uses the name in the context of sexual seduction.

24. This poem appears in *PR*, 248–49.

25. *Druery* means "courtship; gallantry; love;" or "an object of love."

26. This poem appears in *PR*, 251–52.

27. A small thicket or wood.

28. *RESVRGAM* means "I shall rise again." *IO PAEAN* is a traditional opening for a Greek song of triumph or victory.

29. This poem appears in *PR*, 253–54.

30. Osiris was an ancient Egyptian god whose annual death and resurrection personified the self-renewing vitality and fertility of nature. *Antediluvian* means "before the deluge": in the Bible, that period of time between Adam's fall and Noah's flood.

31. This poem appears in *PR*, 255.

32. This poem appears in *PR*, 255–56. This is the last poem from *PR*.

33. *Grimalkin* is an archaic term for an old female cat, often with a bad-tempered or imperious nature.

34. In Greek mythology, Athene was the goddess of wisdom and war, noted for her virginity; here Lewis uses Athene as a metaphor for reason. Demeter was the goddess of the harvest and fertility, and the grieving mother of Persephone, who had been abducted and taken to Hades by Pluto; here Lewis uses Demeter as a metaphor for imagination.

35. This poem was a collaboration between Lewis and Owen Barfield.

36. Henri Bergson (1859–1941) was an important French philosopher perhaps best known for process philosophy, which rejected static values in favor of values of motion, change, and evolution.

37. Benedetto Croce (1866–1952) was an Italian philosopher known for what he termed "Absolute Idealism."

38. Frenchman René Descartes (1596–1650) is often referred to as the father of modern philosophy. He is best remembered for his statement, "I think, therefore I am."

39. Democritus was one of the two founders of ancient atomist theory, the other being his teacher, Leucippus.

40. This probably alludes to Pyrrho of Elis (360–270 B.C.), a Greek philosopher often thought to be the founder of skepticism.

41. German philosopher Johann Gottlieb Fichte (1762–1814) was one of the founders of German idealism.

42. Lewis wrote a footnote, the first of five he placed at the end of the poem: "Bentley *it's.*" I suspect it is an inside joke between Lewis and Barfield.

43. William Godwin (1756–1836) was the founder of philosophical anarchism and the father-in-law of English Romantic poet Percy Bysshe Shelley.

44. According to many philosophers, British empiricist David Hume (1711–1776) was the most important philosopher ever to write in English. Immanuel Kant (1724–1804) is the most significant of all modern philosophers, setting the terms (such as modern rationalism and empiricism) for much of nineteenth–and twentieth-century philosophy.

45. Lewis's second footnote to the poem comments: "Malone well suggests that this passage represents a series of scribal attempts to supply a hiatus in the archtype of MS."

46. For more on Leibniz, who was famous for his optimism, see note 19, above, to the poem "Because of Endless Pride."

47. George Santayana (1863–1952) was an important philosopher of naturalism as well as poet and cultural critic. Oswald Arnold Gottfried Spengler (1880–1936) was a German historian and philosopher of history who argued that the lifetime of a civilization is limited and will inevitably decay.

48. Thomas Aquinas (1225–1274) was an immensely influential philosopher and theologian in the tradition of scholasticism.

49. Lewis's third footnote to the poem states: "Dante. *Paradiso.* X. 79." The pertinent passage in *Paradiso* X (76–81) concerns St. Thomas Aquinus, who is first in a circle of twelve stars (renowned souls) forming a wreath around Beatrice and Dante: "So caroling, that ardent aureole / Of suns swung round us thrice their burning train, / As neigbouring stars swing round the steady pole; / Then seemed like ladies, from the dancing chain, / Not loosed, but silent as the measure's close" (Trans. Dorothy L. Sayers and Barbara Reynolds [London: Penguin, 1962]).

50. Lewis's fourth footnote to the poem states: "Ibid. X. 142." The pertinent passage in Dante's *Paradiso* X (139–48) draws a comparison between the circle of stars and the multiple mechanism of a chiming clock:

> Then, like the horloge, calling us to come,
> What time the Bride of God doth rise and sing,
> Wooing His love, her matins to her Groom,

Where part with part will push and pull, and ring,
Ding-ding, upon the bell sweet notes that swell
With love the soul made apt for worshipping,

E'en so I saw it move, the glorious wheel,
And voice with voice harmonious change and chime
Sweetness unknown, there only knowable

Where ever-present joy knows naught of time. (Trans. Dorothy L. Sayers and Barbara Reynolds [London: Penguin, 1962]).

51. Giovanni Battista Vico (1668–1744) argued that truth is verified through creation or invention and not through observation, thus placing him at odds with Descartes.

52. Pithecanthropus is a hypothetical genus of extinct primate postulated from bones found in Java in 1891.

53. Herbert George Wells (1866–1946) was a novelist, journalist, sociologist, and historian, best known for such his science-fiction novels *The Time Machine* and *The War of the Worlds.*

54. Xenophanes of Colophon was a Greek poet during the late sixth and early fifth centuries B.C., best remembered for his critique of anthropomorphism in religion.

55. Lewis's fifth and last footnote to the poem states: "MS. *As to Which fashioned which after which of Their images.* Keightley. *As to which fashioned Which after which of Their images.* Malone as above."

56. Zeno of Elea (490–430 B.C.) was a Greek philosopher best known for being the inventor of the dialectic and for his use of paradoxes.

57. In the holograph, the word *sail* is crossed out and *earth* is substituted.

58. In the holograph, the word *two* is crossed out and *to* is substituted.

59. In the holograph, the word *bright* is crossed out and *broad* is substituted.

60. In Greek mythology, the Titan Rhea was the daughter Uranus, the sky god, and Gaia, the earth goddess; after marrying her brother, Cronus, she gave birth to the six Olympian gods and goddesses, and is therefore known as "the mother of gods."

61. In the holograph, the words *scandal. Then* are crossed out and the phrase *shameful thing* is substituted.

62. In the holograph, the phrase *For life is loathed by* is crossed out and *Life is loathsome to* is substituted.

63. In the holograph, the word *bed* is crossed out and *bread* is substituted.

64. In the holograph, the word *drinking* is crossed out and *they drank* is substituted.

65. In the holograph, the word *dear* is used instead of *near.*

66. In the holograph, the word *brews* is crossed out and *draughts* is substituted.

67. In the holograph, an indecipherable word is crossed out and *liking* is substituted.

68. In the holograph before *grassy hill,* the word *the* is crossed out and *a* is substituted.

69. In the holograph, an indecipherable word is crossed out and *man* is substituted

70. In the holograph, an indecipherable phrase is crossed out and *Fear was informer* is substituted.

71. In the holograph, the phrase *among them* is crossed out and *for the stonemen* is substituted.

72. *Archon* means "ruler" or "lord."

73. In the holograph, the word *Of* is crossed out and *Over* is substituted.

74. In the holograph, the phrase *Deftly the dwarf* is crossed out and *The dwarf deftly* is substituted.

75. In the holograph, the word *before* is crossed out and *by* is substituted.

76. *Ferly* means "wonder."

77. In the holograph, the words *night sky* are crossed out and *darkness* is substituted.

78. In the holograph, the word *seeming* is crossed out and *gleaming* is substituted.

79. This conversation presages similar ones at the end of Lewis's *Perelandra* (London: Bodley Head, 1943) between Malacandra and Perelandra as well as between Tor and Tinidril.

80. The literal translation of this phrase is "he loved much." Lewis may be alluding to Luke 7:47 (AV): "Wherefore I say unto thee, Her sins, which are many, are forgiven; for she loved much: but to whom little is forgiven, the same loveth little."

81. In the holograph, the word *stealing* is crossed out and *fragrance* is substituted.

82. In the holograph, the phrase *Backward gazing* is crossed out and *Back oft I gazed* is substituted.

83. First published under the title *Launcelot* in *NP.*

84. Usk is a long valley in Wales.

85. Picts were an ancient warrior people living in eastern and northern Scotland during the Dark Ages, first described in Roman reports around A.D. 300.

86. The Sangrail is the Holy Grail.

87. Different version of the Arthurian legends variously identify Pelles as the Fisher King or as one of the keepers of the Holy Grail

88. In the holograph, Lewis crossed out the phrase *they say, this winter season, answered* and substituted *through all these winter days, gave answer.*

89. The holograph gives this word as *knights'; NP* gives this as *knight's.*

90. The holograph gives this word as *their; NP* gives it as *the.*

91. In some versions of the Arthurian legend, Mordred is both Arthur's son and his nephew.

92. In some versions of the Arthurian legend, Kai is noted for his acid tongue and boorish behavior.

93. The holograph gives this name as *Caliburn*; *NP* gives this as *Calburn*. In most versions of the Arthurian legend, Caliburn is another name for the Arthur's sword, Excalibur. Here Lewis lists Caliburn as one of Arthur's less noble knights.

94. In some versions of the Arthurian legend, Agravaine is called "the Arrogant" or "the Proud."

95. In the holograph, Lewis revised the lines *Stirred like a babe within her and woke; and wide, / Prospects of woe and pits of deep dismay, with tears* to *Stirred like a babe within her. Every nerve woke wide / To torture, with low-mourning pity of self, with tears.*

96. In the holograph, Lewis crossed out the word *and* and substituted *with.*

97. In the holograph, a five-line break follows this line.

98. In the holograph Lewis crossed out the words *on new-fashioned* and substituted *upon new-made.*

99. The word *overcast* is not followed by a period in the holograph, but is followed by a period in *NP.*

100. In the holograph, Lewis crossed out the word *open* and substituted *upon.*

101. In the holograph, this line is crossed out.

102. In the holograph, Lewis crossed out the phrase *Struck with the sun* and substituted *A respite in the.*

103. In the holograph, Lewis crossed out the word *on* and substituted *down.*

104. In the holograph Lewis crossed out the phrase *and down by winding* and substituted *by labyrinthine.*"

105. A corseint is a saint's body or a holy relic, or the shrine enclosing it.

106. In some versions of the Arthurian legend, Bors is the only knight to survive the quest for the Holy Grail and to return to Arthur's court. In other versions, Percivale (along with Bors and Galahad) is successful in his quest for the Holy Grail. In still others, Galahad, the illegitimate son of Launcelot, is successful in his quest for the Holy Grail, primarily because of his spiritual purity and remarkable bravery. After saying good-bye to Bors and Percivale, Galahad is taken up into heaven.

107. In most versions of the Arthurian legend, Morgan le Fay is both a wicked sorceress and the half-sister of Arthur.

108. In the holograph, Lewis crossed out the word *seemed* and substituted *gleamed.*

109. The holograph has this as *knight; NP* has this as *Knight.*

110. In some versions of the Arthurian legend, Lamorake was the son of King Pellinore and the brother of Percivale, and Tristan (also spelled Tristram), the Cornish knight, is one of Arthur's loyal supporters. For more on Tristan, see also note 40 to "Exercise on an Old Theme," in the chapter entitled "Poems 1915–1919."

111. In some versions of the Arthurian legend, Nimue is the Lady of the Lake, who gives Arthur Excalibur and enchants Merlin; Isoud (also spelled Isolde) is Tristan's adulterous lover (see also note 40 to "Exercise on an Old Theme," in the chapter entitled "Poems 1915–1919"); Elaine, who is King Arthur's niece, falls in love with Percivale.

112. After *Dymer, The Queen of Drum* is Lewis's most ambitious narrative poem. The text presented here follows the typescript Lewis sent to John Masefield, the poet laureate; the version printed in *NP* has also been consulted. Lewis often employs ellipses in the text, not to indicate missing text but for other purposes. In brief, the poem concerns a pompous old king whose young wife enjoys wandering at night through the realm, enjoying visions of faery and of transcendent beauty. Recalling similar themes in *SB, The Queen of Drum* insists faery exists and intimates that it has a beauty superior to any on earth; in the face of such beauty being denied, the poem argues that it is better to rebel and escape than to obey and acquiesce to life in the everyday world.

113. In the typescript, a written emendation in Lewis's hand substitutes the phrase *To the King of Drum*" for *To the guarded king.*

114. In the typescript, a written emendation in Lewis's hand substitutes the phrase *Now the long* for *The unending.*

115. In the typescript, a written emendation in Lewis's hand substitutes the word *sharp* for *clear.*

116. In the typescript, a written emendation in Lewis's hand substitutes the word *in* for *there.*

117. In the typescript following *suddenly,* a written emendation in Lewis's hand substitutes the word *a* for *the.*

118. This parenthetical passage appears in the text of the typescript but only as a footnote in *NP.*

119. In the typescript, a written emendation in Lewis's hand substitutes the phrase *dimly felt*" for "*felt not heard.*"

120. In the typescript, a written emendation in Lewis's hand substitutes the word *moments* for *moment.*

121. In the typescript, a written emendation in Lewis's hand substitutes the phrase *now*

come all of you for *ask your fill. Come all.*

122. The typescript and *NP* have this as *Who's.*

123. In the typescript, a written emendation in Lewis's hand substitutes the word *yielding* for *breaking.*

124. In the typescript, a written emendation in Lewis's hand substitutes the phrase *an axe* for *a sword.*

125. In the typescript, a written emendation in Lewis's hand substitutes the phrase *not well* for *is sick.*

126. In the typescript, a written emendation in Lewis's hand substitutes the phrase *ten to three* for *half-past two.*

127. In the typescript, *carpets* is substituted for *curtains.*

128. In the typescript, *those silent* is substituted for *that pause of.*

129. In the typescript, *Jesseran* is substituted for *Gesseran.*

130. This Greek phrase translates as "We forget sweetly."

131. In the typescript, *larger* is substituted for *longer.*

132. In the typescript following *You, are* is substituted for *and.*

133. In the typescript, *assay* is substituted for *essay.*

134. French phrase meaning "in musketeer."

135. In the typescript, *Galma* is substituted for *Calma.*

136. Italian word meaning "duke."

137. Artemis is the Greek goddess of the hunt, the moon, and virgins; Diana is the Roman equivalent.

138. Paphos is a coastal city in southwestern Cyprus long associated with the worship of the Greek goddess of sexual love, Aphrodite (equivalent to the Roman goddess Venus).

139. In the typescript, *cornered* is substituted for *corner.*

140. In the typescript, Lewis's handwriting directs that in canto v, lines 3 and 4 precede lines 1 and 2, as shown here; *NP* follows the same convention.

141. In the typescript, *slow-yellowing* is substituted for *slow-brightening.*

142. In the text of the typescript, the next two lines follow *earthen taste* as a parenthetical passage, but in *NP,* they appear only as a footnote.

143. In the text of the typescript, the next eight lines follow *darkened* as a parenthetical passage, but in *NP,* they appear only as a footnote.

144. In the typescript, *snatched* is substituted for *took.*

145. In the typescript, *grew strong* is substituted for *had risen.*

146. Hecate is the Greek goddess of witchcraft and sorcery, ghosts, the night, and the moon.

147. Titania is queen of the faery world in William Shakespeare's *A Midsummer Night's Dream.*

148. In the text of the typescript, the next line follows *moulding* as a parenthetical passage, but in *NP,* it appears only as a footnote.

149. In the typescript, *Descends* is substituted for *It came.*

150. In the text of the typescript, the following parenthetical passage appears after the word *things,* but in *NP,* it appears only as a footnote.

151. In the typescript, *aloofness* is substituted for *unlikeness.*

152. In the text of the typescript, the next three crossed-out lines follow *dead* as a parenthetical passage, but in *NP,* they appear only as a footnote.

153. In the typescript, *the* is substituted for *His.*

154. In the typescript, *woos* is substituted for *baits.*

155. In the typescript, an alternate rendering in Lewis's handwriting of this line as printed in *NP* is: *In fairy woods or dies and wakes in Hell.*

156. In the typescript, *it doesn't* is substituted for *I cannot* in *NP.*

Poems

1935–1949

The Examiner Sits into Quarrie

The examiner sits into Quarrie
Using the blude-red ink
"Now who ill tae fair Edinboro' gae
A' o'er the text to swink?"

5 Then up and spake child Blunden
Ane harper guid was he
"Oh I ill tae fair Edinboro' goe
Those manuscripts to see."[1]
(1935; 2006)

Where Reservoys Ripple

Where reservoys ripple
And sun-shadows stipple
The beard of the corn,
We'll meet and we'll kipple
5 We'll camp and then kipple
At Rudyard we'll kipple
From evening to morn.

And then we'll set off, yes!
Discussing your Orpheus
10 His meaning and myth,
Till fettered by Morpheus,
The leaden maced Morpheus,
Inaccurate Morpheus
At Chapel-en-le Frith.[2]
(1935; 2001)

The Planets

Lady LUNA, in light canoe,
By friths and shallows of fretted cloudland
Cruises monthly; with chrism of dews
And drench of dream, a drizzling glamour,
5 Enchants us—the cheat! changing sometime
A mind to madness, melancholy pale,
Bleached with gazing on her blank count'nance
Orb'd and ageless. In earth's bosom
The shower of her rays, sharp-feathered light
10 Reaching downward, ripens silver,
Forming and fashioning female brightness,
—Metal maidenlike. Her moist circle
Is nearest earth. Next beyond her
MERCURY marches;—madcap rover,
15 Patron of pilf'rers. Pert quicksilver
His gaze begets, goblin mineral,
Merry multitude of meeting selves,
Same but sundered. From the soul's darkness,
With wreathèd wand, words he marshalls,
20 Guides and gathers them—gay bellwether
Of flocking fancies. His flint has struck
The spark of speech from spirit's tinder,
Lord of language! He leads forever
The spangle and splendour, sport that mingles
25 Sound with senses, in subtle pattern,
Words in wedlock, and wedding also
Of thing with thought. In the third region
VENUS voyages . . . but my voice falters;
Rude rime-making wrongs her beauty,
30 Whose breasts and brow, and her breath's sweetness
Bewitch the worlds. Wide-spread the reign
Of her secret sceptre, in the sea's caverns,
In grass growing, and grain bursting,
Flower unfolding, and flesh longing,
35 And shower falling sharp in April.
The metal copper in the mine reddens
With muffled brightness, like muted gold,
By her finger form'd. Far beyond her
The heaven's highway hums and trembles,

40 Drums and dwindles, to the driv'n thunder
Of SOL's chariot, whose sword of light
Hurts and humbles; beheld only
Of eagle's eye. When his arrow glances
Through mortal mind, mists are parted
45 And mild as morning the mellow wisdom
Breathes o'er the breast, broadening eastward
Clear and cloudless. In a clos'd garden
(Unbound her burden) his beams foster
Soul in secret, where the soil puts forth
50 Paradisal palm, and pure fountains
Turn and re-temper, touching coolly
The uncomely common to cordial gold;
Whose ore also, in earth's matrix,
Is print and pressure of his proud signet
55 On the wax of the world. He is the worshipp'd male,
The earth's husband, all-beholding,
Arch-chemic eye. But other country
Dark with discord dins beyond him,
With noise of nakers, neighing of horses,
60 Hammering of harness. A haughty god
MARS mercenary, makes there his camp
And flies his flag; flaunts laughingly
The graceless beauty, grey-eyed and keen,
—Blond insolence—of his blithe visage
65 Which is hard and happy. He hews the act,
The indifferent deed with dint of his mallet
And his chisel of choice; achievement comes not
Unhelped by him;—hired gladiator
Of evil and good. All's one to Mars,
70 The wrong righted, rescued meekness,
Or trouble in trenches, with trees splintered
And birds banished, banks fill'd with gold
And the liar made lord. Like handiwork
He offers to all—earns his wages
75 And whistles the while. White-featured dread
Mars has mastered. His metal's iron
That was hammered through hands into holy cross,
Cruel carpentry. He is cold and strong,
Necessity's son. Soft breathes the air
80 Mild, and meadowy, as we mount further

Where rippled radiance rolls about us
Moved with music—measureless the waves'
Joy and jubilee. It is JOVE's orbit,
Filled and festal, faster turning
85 With arc ampler. From the Isles of Tin
Tyrian traders, in trouble steering
Came with his cargoes; the Cornish treasure
That his ray ripens. Of wrath ended
And woes mended, of winter passed
90 And guilt forgiven, and good fortune
Jove is master; and of jocund revel,
Laughter of ladies. The lion-hearted,
The myriad-minded, men like the gods,
Helps and heroes, helms of nations
95 Just and gentle, are Jove's children,
Work his wonders. On his wide forehead
Calm and kingly, no care darkens
Nor wrath wrinkles: but righteous power
And leisure and largess their loose splendours
100 Have wrapped around him—a rich mantle
Of ease and empire. Up far beyond
Goes SATURN silent in the seventh region,
The skirts of the sky. Scant grows the light,
Sickly, uncertain (the Sun's finger
105 Daunted with darkness). Distance hurts us,
And the vault severe of vast silence;
Where fancy fails us, and fair language,
And love leaves us, and light fails us
And Mars fails us, and the mirth of Jove
110 Is as tin tinkling. In tattered garment,
Weak with winters, he walks forever
A weary way, wide round the heav'n,
Stoop'd and stumbling, with staff groping,
The lord of lead. He is the last planet
115 Old and ugly. His eye fathers
Pale pestilence, pain of envy,
Remorse and murder. Melancholy drink
(For bane or blessing) of bitter wisdom
He pours for his people, a perilous draught
120 That the lip loves not. We leave all things
To reach the rim of the round welkin,

Heaven's hermitage, high and lonely.
(1934–35 [?]; 1935)

Sonnet

Dieu a établi la prière pour communiquer à ses creatures la dignité de la causalité.[3]
Pascal

The Bible says Sennacherib's campaign was spoiled
By angels:[4] in Herodotus it says, by mice—
Innumerably nibbling all one night they toiled
To eat his bowstrings piecemeal as warm wind eats ice.

5 But muscular archangels, I suggest, employed
Seven little jaws at labour on each slender string,
And by their aid, weak masters though they be, destroyed
The smiling-lipped Assyrian, cruel-bearded king.

No stranger that omnipotence should choose to need
10 Small helps than great—no stranger if His action lingers
Till men have prayed, and suffers their weak prayers indeed
To move as very muscles His delaying fingers,

Who, in His longanimity and love for our
Small dignities, enfeebles, for a time, His power.
(1935–36 [?]; 1936)

There Was a Young Person of Streatham

There was a young person of Streatham
Who said to his friends when he met 'em
"Old Lewis is dyin'
For *The Place of the Lion*[5]
5 But I *keep* people's books once I get 'em."

Ubi est leonis locus?
Caecilii lar et focus![6]
(1936; 2004)

Coronation March

Blow the trumpet! guardee tramp it!
Once to lord it thus was vulgar;
Then we could afford it; empire simpered,
Gold and gunboats were an ace of trumps.
5 Ranting poets then were plenty,
Loyalty meant royalties. Life is changing.
Now that bandogs mouth at random
Lion fallen into age and clawless,
Mid their snarling is the time for skirling
10 Pipes, and carefree scarlet. Therefore,
Rumble in the pageant drum-beat's magic,
Bunting wave on frontage bravely,
Grammar of heraldic rules unfolded
Spill forth gold and gules, and needling
15 Spire in floodlight pierce the midnight,
Pale as paper! Bright as any trumpet
Twinkle under taper gold of saintly
Crown of Edward; faintlier silver's
Elven gleam give female answer
20 With robe and globe and holiness of mitre.
Bray the trumpet, rumble tragic
Drum-beat's magic, sway the logic
Of legs that march a thousand in a uniform,
Flags and arches, the lion and the unicorn
25 Romp it, rampant, pompous tramping . . .
Some there are that talk of Alexander
With a tow-row-row-row-row-row.
(1936–37 [?]; 1937)

After Kirby's *Kalevala*[7]

Sound of weeping in slender grasses
Rose, a mourning in the pretty woodland.
Round him mourning were the tender grasses,
Flowers of leavèd glade were grieving,
5 Fading for the maiden's marring;
Woodland weeping for a mother's daughter.
In one place no grass was growing,

Flower-forsaken, earth was naked,
Where he had done the unholy thing,
10 Where maid had fallen and man stolen
Maidenhead of his mother's daughter.
Coolruff there, the son of Caleruff,
Drew the sword he had carried thither,
Stayed and turned the blade and eyed it,
15 Learned it over and tried it; asked it
A question now, man's word to metal,
Whether 'twere in its mind to slay him.
"Hungry art thou for flesh unholy,
Thirsty of blood that has offended?"
20 Sword perceived the mind of master,
Taskèd iron knew that asking,
Voice of sharpened edge gave answer,
"What should hinder, or what the wonder
If I taste of the flesh unholy,
25 Drink of the blood that has offended?
Blood of the faultless, flesh of guiltless
Eaten and drunk have I in plenty."
Coolruff then, the son of Caleruff,
Wearer of the heaven-blue buskins,
30 Set to the heath the sword-hilt firmly,
Wormlike thrusting it home: but upwards
Set the point to his breast, the sharpwork,
And flung his weight on the whetted iron.
That was his ending: few his winters.
35 Coolruff the mighty there the fated
Number of his days fulfilled. The exile
Spilled the spirit that fortune hated.
(1936–37 [?]; 1937)

Where Are the Walks?

Where are the walks? Where are the woods? Where is Wytham gone?[8]
Leisure and literature are lost under
The night's helmet as tho never they had been![9]
(1937; 2004)

The Future of Forestry

How will the legend of the age of trees
Feel, when the last tree falls in England?
When the concrete spreads and the town conquers
The country's heart; when contraceptive
5 Tarmac's laid where farm has faded,
Tramline flows where slept a hamlet,
And shop-fronts, blazing without a stop from
Dover to Wrath,[10] have glazed us over?
Simplest tales will then bewilder
10 The questioning children, "What was a chestnut?
Say what it means to climb a Beanstalk?
Tell me, grandfather, what an elm is.
What was Autumn? They never taught us."
Then, told by teachers how once from mould
15 Came growing creatures of lower nature
Able to live and die, though neither
Beast nor man, and around them wreathing
Excellent clothing, breathing sunlight—
Half understanding, their ill-acquainted
20 Fancy will tint their wonder-paintings
—Trees as men walking, wood-romances
Of goblins stalking in silky green,
Of milk-sheen froth upon the lace of hawthorn's
Collar, pallor on the face of birchgirl.
25 So shall a homeless time, though dimly
Catch from afar (for soul is watchful)
A sight of tree-delighted Eden.
(1937–38 [?]; 1938)

Chanson D'Aventure

I heard in Addison's Walk a bird sing clear,[11]
"This year the summer will come true, this year, this year.

"Winds will not strip the blossom from your apple-trees
This year, nor want of rain destroy the peas.

5 "This year time's nature will no more defeat you,
Nor all the promised moments in their passing cheat you.

"This summer will not lead you round, and back
To autumn, one year older, by the well-worn track.

"Often deceived, yet open once again your heart,
10 The gates of good adventure swing apart;

"This time, this time, as all these flowers foretell,
We shall escape the circle and undo the spell."

I said, "This might prove truer than a bird can know;
And yet your singing will not make it so."
(1937–38 [?]; 1938)

Experiment

Some believe the slumber
Of trees is in December
When timber's naked under sky
And squirrel keeps his chamber.

5 But I believe their fibres
Awake to life and labour
When turbulence comes roaring up
The land in loud October,

And plunders woods and sunders
10 And sends the leaves to wander,
And undisguises prickly shapes
Beneath the golden splendour.

Form returns. In warmer,
Seductive days, disarming
15 Its firmer will, the wood grows soft
And spreads its dreams to murmur.

Into earnest winter,
Like souls awaked, it enters;

The hunter Frost and the cold light
20 Have quelled the green enchanter.
(1937–38 [?]; 1938)

To Mr. Roy Campbell

Rifles may flower and terrapins may flame[12]
But truth and reason will be still the same;
Call them Humanitarians as you will,
The merciful are promised mercy still.
5 Loud fool! to think a nickname could abate
The blessing given to the compassionate.
Such ugly polysyllables may fright
Those Charlies on the Left of whom you write;[13]
No wonder—since it was from them you learned
10 How white to black by jargon can be turned;
For though your verse outsoars with eagle pride
Their spineless tunes (of which the old cow died).
Yet your bloodthirsty politics and theirs
Are two peas in a single pod, who cares
15 Which kind of shirt the murdering Party wears?
Oh Roy, repent: some feet of sacred ground,
A target to both gangs, may yet be found,
Sacred because, though now 'tis No-man's-land,
There stood your father's house: there you should stand.
(1938–39 [?]; 1939)

Hermione in the House of Paulina

How soft it rains, how nourishingly warm and green[14]
Is grown the hush'd solemnity of this low house
Where sunrise never enters, where I have not seen
The moon at night nor heard the footfall of a mouse,
5 Nor looked at any face but yours
Nor changed my posture in my place of rest
For fifteen years—oh how the quiet cures
My pain and sucks the burning from my breast.

It sucked out all the poison of my will and drew
10 All hot rebellions from me, all desire to break
The silence you commanded me . . . nothing to do,
Nothing to fear or wish for, not a choice to make,
Only to be; to hear no more
Cock-crowing duty calling me to rise,
15 But slowly thus to ripen, laid in store
In their dim granary near your watching eyes.

Pardon, great spirit, whose tall shape like a golden tower
Stands over me, or seems upon large wings to move,
Colouring with life my paleness, and with serene power,
20 By sober ministrations of severest love;
Pardon, that when you brought me here,
Still drowned in bitter passions, drugged with life,
I did not know . . . in faith, I thought you were
Paulina,[15] old Antigonus' young wife.
(1939–40 [?]; 1940)

How Can I Ask Thee, Father

How can I ask thee, Father, to defend
In peril of war my dearest friend to-day,[16]
As though I knew, better than Thou, the way,
Or with more love than thine desired the end?
5 When I, for the length of one poor prayer, suspend
So hardly for his sake my thoughts, that stray
And wanton, thrusting twenty times a day,
Clean out of mind the man I call my friend;
Who, if he had from thee, no better care
10 Than mine, were every moment dead. But prayer
Thou givest to man, not man to thee: thy laws
Suffering our mortal wish that way to share
The eternal will; at taste of whose large air
Man's word becomes, by miracle, a cause.
(1939–40 [?]; 1974)

Break, Sun, My Crusted Earth

Break, sun, my crusted earth,
Pierce, needle of light, within,
Where blind, immortal metals have their birth
And crystals firm begin.

5 To limbs and loins and heart
Search with thy chemic beam,
Strike where the self I know not lives apart
Beneath the surface dream.

For Life in secret goes
10 About his work. In gloom,
The mother helping not nor hindering, grows
The man inside the womb.
(1939–40 [?]; 1940)

The World Is Round

Naked apples, woolly-coated peaches
Swelled on that garden wall. Unbounded
Spicey odour of unmoving trees
Surrounded me, lying on the sacred turf,
5 Sweetened the sheltered air. The forest of trees,
Buoyed up in air like weeds in ocean
Grew without motion. I was the pearl,
Mother-of-pearl my nest. Milk-white the cirrus
Streaked the blue egg-shell of the distant sky,
10 Early and cool above the spicey forest.
Wise was the fangless serpent, drowsy.
I do not really remember that garden;
I remember the remembering, when first waking
I heard the golden gates behind me
15 Shut fast upon it. On a flinty road,
With east-wind blowing over the black frost,
I found my feet. Forth on a journey,
Gathering thin garment over aching bones,
I went. I wander still. But the world is round.
(1939–40 [?]; 1940)

Arise My Body

Arise my body, my small body, we have striven
Enough, and He is merciful: we are forgiven.
Arise, small body, puppet-like and pale, and go,
White as the bedclothes, into bed, and cold as snow.
5 Undress with cold, small fingers and put out the light,
And be alone, hush'd mortal, in the sacred night—
A meadow whipt flat under heavy rain, a cup
Emptied and clean, a garment washed and folded up,
Faded in colour, thinned almost to raggedness
10 By dirt and by the washing of that dirtiness.

Be not too quickly warm again. Lie cold; consent
To weariness and pardon's watery element.
Drink all the bitter water and the chilly death;
Soon enough comes the riot of warm blood and breath.
(1939–40 [?]; 1940)

The Floating Islands

The floating islands, the flat golden sky
At noon, the peacock sunset: tepid waves
With the land sliding over them like a skin:
The alien Eve, green-bodied, stepping forth
5 To meet my hero from her forest home,
Proud, courteous, unafraid; no thought infirm
Alters her cheek—
(1941 [?]; 1974)

Out of the Wound We Pluck

Out of the wound we pluck
The shrapnel. Thorns we squeeze
Out of the hand. Even poison forth we suck,
And after pain have ease.

5 But images that grow
Within the soul have life

Like cancer and, often cut, live on below
The deepest of the knife,

Waiting their time to shoot
10 At some defenceless hour
Their poison, unimpaired, at the heart's root,
And, like a golden shower,

Unanswerably sweet,
Bright with returning guilt,
15 Fatally in a moment's time defeat
Our brazen towers long-built;

And all our former pain
And all our surgeon's care
Is lost, and all the unbearable (in vain
20 Borne once) is still to bear.
(1941 [?]; 1964)

Epitaph

She was delicately, beautifully made,
So small, so unafraid,
Till the bomb came
(Bombs are the same,
5 Delicately, beautifully made).
(1942 [?]; 1942)

The Apologist's Evening Prayer

From all my lame defeats and oh! much more
From all the victories that I seemed to score;
From cleverness shot forth on Thy behalf
At which, while angels weep, the audience laugh;
5 From all my proofs of Thy divinity,
Thou, who wouldst give no sign, deliver me.

Thoughts are but coins. Let me not trust, instead
Of Thee, their thin-worn image of Thy head.

From all my thoughts, even from my thoughts of Thee,
10 O thou fair Silence, fall, and set me free.
Lord of the narrow gate and the needle's eye,
Take from me all my trumpery lest I die.
(1942 [?]; 1964)

To G. M.

If knowledge like a mid-day heat
Uncooled with cloud, unstirred with breath
Of undulant air, begins to beat
On minds one moment after death,

5 From your rich soil what life will spring,
What flower-unfolding paradise,
Through what green walks what birds shall sing;
What med'cinable gums, what spice.

Apples of what smooth gold! But fear
10 Assails me for myself. The noon
That nourishes earth, can only sear
And scald the unresponding moon.

Her ancient valleys have no soil,
Her needle-pointed hills are bare;
15 Water, poured on her rocks, would boil,
And noon lasts long, and long despair.
(1942 [?]; 1942)

The Admiral Stamped on the Quarter Deck

The Admiral stamped on the quarter deck [17]
Above the battle's wrack
And cried "Yo ho! From the mainmast yard
Suspend that useless quack!"
5 The officer of the bold marines
Salutes and answers back
And "Begging you pardon, Sir," says he,
"Where *is* that useless quack?"

“Oh shiver my timbers!” the admiral said.
10 “Marines are uncommon slack.
Come bustle about and quick find out
And arrest that useless quack.”
Then a matelot said (and he touched his head)
“If you please, I’ll show you his track.
15 In the round house there with your lady fair
I see’d that useless quack.”
They found the pair in the lily-white bed
And the lady cried “Alack.”
But over the side before they spied
20 Had leaped the useless quack
And he swam a league and a league again
And to England he swam back
And the First Lord said as he came to shore
“Why, there’s that useless quack!”
25 “My Lud” said Hump with a doleful dump
“We sailed through a U-boat pack.
At their first shell the admiral fell
But not the useless quack.
With their second shot the skipper they got
30 (I’m wearing the poor bloke’s mac’)
And the rest of the crew were soon polished off too
Except the useless quack.
But I sailed that ship and I fought that ship
From the Horn to the Skagerrak[18]
35 And the enemy thought ’twas a hundred men
When ’twas only the useless quack.
But she sank in sight of land, my lord,
And split with an awful crack,
Which is why you see none here save me,
40 At your service—the useless quack.”
“You’re a gallant lad,” the First Lord said
As he gave his shoulder a smack.
“Take a job on shore and sail no more,
But become a resident quack!”
(1943; 2014)

Awake, My Lute!

I stood in the gloom of a spacious room
 Where I listened for hours (on and off)
To a terrible bore with a beard like a snore
 And a heavy rectangular cough,
5 Who discoursed on the habits of orchids and rabbits
 And how an electron behaves
And a way to cure croup with solidified soup
 In a pattern of circular waves;
Till I suddenly spied that what stood at his side
10 Was a richly upholstered baboon
With paws like the puns in a poem of Donne's
 And a tail like a voyage to the Moon.
Then I whispered "Look out! For I very much doubt
 If your colleague is really a man."
15 But the lecturer said, without turning his head,
 "Oh, that's only the Beverage Plan!"[19]
As one might have foreseen, the whole sky became green
 At this most injudicious remark,
For the Flood had begun and we both had to run
20 For our place in the queue to the Ark.
Then, I hardly knew how (we were swimming by now),
 The sea got all covered with scum
Made of publishers' blurbs and irregular verbs
 Of the kind which have datives in–*um;*
25 And the waves were so high that far up in the sky
 We saw the grand lobster, and heard
How he snorted, "Compare the achievements of Blair[20]
 With the grave of King Alfred the Third,[21]
And add a brief note and if possible quote,
30 And distinguish and trace and discuss
The probable course of a Methodist horse
 When it's catching a decimal buss."
My answer was Yes. But they marked it N. S.,[22]
 And a truffle-fish grabbed at my toe,
35 And dragged me deep down to a bombulous town
 Where the traffic was silent and slow.
Then a voice out of heaven observed, "Quarter past seven!"
 And I threw all the waves off my head,
For that voice beyond doubt was the voice of my scout,[23]
40 And the bed of that sea was my bed.
(1943 [?]; 1943)

A Funny Old Man Had a Habit

A funny old man had a habit
Of giving a leaf to a rabbit.
  At first it was shy
  But then, by and by,
5 It got rude and would stand up to grab it.[24]
(1944; 1985)

The Salamander

I stared into the fire;[25] blue waves
Of shuddering heat that rose and fell,
And blazing ships and blinding caves,
Canyons and streets and hills of hell;
5 Then presently amidst it all
I saw a living creature crawl.

Forward it crept and pushed its snout
Between the bars, and with sad eyes
Into my quiet room looked out,
10 As men look out upon the skies;
And from its scalding throat there came
A faint voice hissing like a flame:

"This is the end, the stratosphere,
The rim of the world where all life dies,
15 The vertigo of space, the fear
Of nothingness; before me lies
Blank silence, distances untold
Of unimaginable cold.

"Faint lights that fitfully appear
20 Far off in that immense abyss
Are but reflections cast from here,
There is no other fire but this,
This speck of life, this fading spark
Existed amid the boundless dark.

25 “Blind Nature’s measureless rebuke
To all we value, I received
Long since (though wishes bait the hook
With tales our ancestors believed)
And now can face with fearless eye
30 Negation’s final sovereignty.”
(1944–45 [?]; 1945)

Best Quality Sackcloth & Ashes

Best quality Sackcloth & Ashes
in sealed packets
delivered in plain vans at
moderate charges
5 Messrs M. Cato and R. E. Morse.[26]
(1945; 2004)

From the Latin of Milton’s *De Idea Platonica Quemadmodum Aristoteles Intellexit*

Say, ye goddesses, guardians of the sacred grove,[27]
Say, oh Memory, mother of the Muses nine,
Tell, oh Eternity, who in thy immeasurable
Cave, lying leisurely, keepest the muniments[28]
5 (Far hence) and firm laws and decrees of Jupiter
And the gods’ journal and the heav’nly calendar,
Say who the First was, after whose exemplary
Feature and pattern Nature moulded humankind?
Ageless, the sky’s co-eval, incorruptible,
10 The model God worked by, universal, singular?
Not a mere notion in His mind, cerebrally
Twinn’d with maid Minerva[29] in divine fantasy.
No;—though in common to all men distributed,
He dwells apart, still one in singularity,
15 Nay—wilder miracle—bounded in locality.
Haply o’er-head, the planets’ fellow-traveller,
Through the ten spheres he marches on forever, or
Nearer Earth’s neighbourhood lurks in the Lunar globe;
Or, beside Lethe’s bank, drowsily he sits among

20 Souls yet waiting for weeds of flesh to animate;
Or far away in Earth's remotest wildernesses
Stalks—a stupendious[30] archëtypal giantship
Lifting to heav'n a head the gods would tremble at,
More huge than Atlas who upholds the universe.
25 *Him* neither that blind prophet, old Tiresias
(Whom loss of sight made visionary) e'er beheld,
Nor in the still night feather-footed Mercury
Ever revealed to his poetic followers.
No mage Assyrian found *Him,* though his memory
30 Track'd without faltering Ninus and his ancestors
Far back to Bel and to Osiris' progeny.[31]
Ev'n the Thrice Great, the glory of the Triple Name,
Ev'n Trismegistus left to Isis' worshippers[32]
No word of *Him,* though leaving many mysteries.[33]
(1945; 1945)

On the Death of Charles Williams

Your death sounds a strange bugle call, friend, and all becomes hard
To see plainly, describe truly. This new light imposes change,
Re-adjusts all a life's landscape as it thrusts down its probe from the sky
To re-arrange shadows, to change meadows, to erect hills and deepen vales;
5 I can't see the old contours; the slant alters. It's a bolder world
Than I once thought. I wince, caught in the shrill winds that dance on this ridge.
Is it the first sting of a world's waning, the great Winter? Or the cold of Spring?

I have lost now the one only friend wise enough to advise,
To touch deftly such problems. I am left asking. Concerning your death
10 With what friend now would it help much to spend words, unless it were you?
(1945; 1945)

This Literary Lion

This literary lion
Emulated Arion:[34]
When other holiday makers went golfin'
He rode his dolphin.
(1945 [?]; 2004)

Under Sentence

There is a wildness still in England that will not feed
  In cages; it shrinks away from touch of the trainer's hand;
Easy to kill, not easy to keep. It will not breed
  In a zoo for the public pleasure. It will not be planned.

5 Do not blame us too much if we, being woodland folk,
  Cannot swell the rejoicing at this new world you make;
We, hedge-hoggèd as Johnson, we unused to the yoke
  As Landor, surly as Cobbett (that badger), birdlike as Blake.[35]

A new scent troubles the air—friendly to you perhaps—
10 But we with animal wisdom understand that smell.
To all our kind its message is guns, ferrets, traps,
  And a Ministry gassing the little holes in which we dwell.
(1945; 1945)

On the Atomic Bomb (Metrical Experiment)

So; you have found an engine
Of injury that angels
Might dread. The world plunges,
Shies, snorts, and curvets like a horse in danger.

5 Then comfort her with fondlings,
With kindly word and handling,
But do not believe blindly
This way or that. Both fears and hopes are swindlers.

What's here to dread? For mortals
10 Both hurt and death were certain
Already; our light-hearted
Hopes from the first sentenced to final thwarting.

This marks no huge advance in
The dance of Death. His pincers
15 Were grim before with chances
Of cold, fire, suffocation, Ogpu,[36] cancer.

Nor hope that this last blunder
Will end our woes by rending
Tellus herself asunder—
20 All gone in one bright flash like dryest tinder.

As if your puny gadget
Could dodge the terrible logic
Of history! No; the tragic
Road will go on, new generations trudge it.

25 Narrow and long it stretches,
Wretched for one who marches
Eyes front. He never catches
A glimpse of the fields each side, the happy orchards.
(1945; 1945)

On Receiving Bad News

No; the sky will not break,
  And time will not stop.
Do not for the dregs mistake
  The first bitter drop.

5 When first the collar galls
  Tired horses know
Stable's not near. Still falls
  The whip. There's far to go.
(1945; 1945)

Consolation

Though beer is worse and dearer
And milk has got the blues,
Though cash is short and rations
Much shorter than the queues,
5 Though regular as strikes and crimes,
Each day before our eyes
As a sop to the Co-Octopus
Some little business dies;

Yet sing like mad that England
10 Is back to peacetime ways;
Not butter, eggs, or mutton,
Freedom or spacious days.
All those were non-essentials,
I've found a surer test—
15 If we thus caress the Muscovite,
England has turned to rest.

To ease my doubts Appeasement[37]
Returns. Peace must be here!
The tune of glorious Munich
20 Once more salutes my ear;
An ancient British melody—
We heard it first begin
At the court of shifty Vortigern[38]
Who let the Heathen in.
(1945 [?]; 1994)

The Birth of Language

How near his sire's careering fires
Does Mercury the planet run,
What wave of heat must lave and beat
That shining suburb of the Sun!

5 His burning flings supernal things
Like spindrift from his stormy crown,
He throws and shakes in rosy flakes
Intelligible virtues down.

And landing there in candent air
10 They muster thick as bees that swarm;
And each assumes both speech and plumes
And sandals wing'd and godlike form.

Due West—the sun's behest so runs—
They seek the wood where flames are trees.
15 'Neath crimson shade their limbs are laid
Beside the pure quicksilver seas;

Where thick with notes from liquid throats
The forest melody leaps and runs,
Till night lets robe the lightless globe
20 With darkness and with distant suns.

Awake they spring and shake the wing
And on the trees whose trunks are flames
They find like fruits, with rind and roots
And leaves of fire, their proper names.

25 At taste whereof with haste and love
They soar straight up the night's abyss.
Far, far below the arbours glow
Where first they knew Mercurial bliss.

They ache and freeze through vacant seas
30 Of night. Their nimbleness and youth
Turns lean and frore; their meaning more,
Their being, less. Life shrinks to truth.

They reach this Earth, where each has birth
Miraculous—a Word made breath;
35 Lucid and small, of use for all
Man's current need; and dry like death.

How dim below these symbols show,
Bony and abstract every one!
Yet if true verse once lift the curse
40 They feel in dreams their native sun.
(1945–46 [?]; 1946)

On Being Human

Angelic mind, they say, by simple intelligence
Perceive the forms of nature. They discern
Unerringly the archetypes, all the verities
Which mortals lack or indirectly learn.
5 Transparent with primordial truth, unvarying,
Mere Earthness and right Stonehood from that clear

High eminence are seen. Unveiled the seminal
Huge principles appear.

The Treeness of a tree they know; the meaning of
10 Arboreal life, how from earth's salty lap
The solar beam uplifts it, all the holiness
Enacted by leaves' fall and rising sap.
But never an angel knows the knife-edged severance
Of sun from shadow where the trees begin,
15 The blessèd cool at every pore caressing us—
For angels have no skin.

They see the Form of air. But mortals breathing it
Drink the whole summer down into the breast—
The lavish pinks, the new-mown field, the ravishing
20 Sea-smell, the wood-fire smoke that whispers *Rest;*
The tremor on the rippled pool of memory
Which from each scent in widening circle goes,
The pleasure and the pang—can angels measure it?
An angel has no nose.

25 The nourishing of life and how it flourishes
On death—and why—they utterly know; but not
The hill-born earthy spring, the dark, cold bilberries,
The ripe peach from the southern wall still hot,
Full-bellied tankards foamy-topped, or delicate
30 Half lyric lamb, a new loaf's billowy curves,
Nor porridge, nor the piercing taste of oranges,
For angels have no nerves.

Far richer they. I know the senses' witchery
Shields us, like air, from heavens too bright to see;
35 Imminent death to Man the barb'd sublimities
And dazzling edge of beauty unsheathed would be.
Yet here, and in this tiny charm'd interior,
This parlour of the brain, their Maker shares
With living men some secrets in a privacy
40 Forever ours, not theirs.
(1946; 1946)

Solomon

Many a column of cedar was in Solomon's hall,
Much jade of China on the inlaid wall.
Thrown aloft by the fountains with their soft foam,
A tremor of light was dancing in the emerald dome.

5 The popinjays on their perches, without stopping, praised
The unspeakable Lord; the flamingoes and the peacocks blazed.
Incense richly darkened the day. Princes stood
Waiting—a motley diapason of robes hotly hued.

At the King's entry on the dais there went round
10 Flash of diamonds, rustle of raiment, a sighing sound
From among his ladies. They were wrung with desire,
Enslaving the heart. Musicians plucked the grave wire.

Like the column of a palm-tree, like a dolomite tower,
Like the unbearable noon-day in the glare of its power,
15 So solemn and so radiant was Solomon to behold,
Men feared his immense forehead and his beard of gold.

Like thunder at a distance came from under his feet
The rumble of captive Jinn and of humbled Efreet.[39]
Column and foundation trembled. To Solomon's ring
20 Hell's abyss was obedient, and to the spells of the King.

By his bed lay crouching many a deadly Jinn;
He erected glory on their subjected sin.
By adamant will he was seeking the Adamite state
And flame-like monarchy of Man. But he came late.

25 He was wrong; it was possible no longer. Amid leaves
Bird-shaken, dew-scattering, it would have wakened Eve's
Maiden-cool laughter, could that lady have foretold
All his tragic apparatus—wives, magic, and gold.
(1946; 1946)

The True Nature of Gnomes

Paracelsus[40] somewhere in his writings tells us
    A gnome moves through earth like an arrow in the air,
At home like a fish within the seamless, foamless
    Liberty of the water that yields to it everywhere.

5 Beguiled with pictures, I fancied in my childhood
    Subterranean rivers beside glimmering wharfs,
Hammers upon anvils, pattering and yammering,
    Torches and tunnels, the cities of the dwarfs;

But in perfect blackness underneath the surface,
10 In a silence unbroken till the planet cracks,
Their sinewy bodies through the dense continuum
    Move without resistance and leave no tracks.

Gravel, marl, blue clay—all's one to travel in;
    Only one obstacle can impede a gnome—
15 A cave or mine-shaft. Not their very bravest
    Would venture across it for a short cut home.

There is the unbridgeable. To a gnome the air is
    Utter vacuity. If he thrust out his face
Into a cavern, his face would break in splinters,
20 Bursting as a man would burst in interstellar space.

With toiling lungs a gnome can breathe the soil in,
    Rocks are like a headwind, stiff against his chest,
Chief 'midst his pleasures is the quiet leaf mould,
    Like air in meadowy valleys when the wind's at rest.

25 Like sylvan freshness are the lodes of silver,
    Cold, clammy, fog-like, are the leaden veins
Those of gold are prodigally sweet like roses,
    Gems stab coolly like the small spring rains.
(1946; 1946)

The Meteorite

Among the hills a meteorite
Lies huge; and moss has overgrown,
And wind and rain with touches light
Made soft, the contours of the stone.

5 Thus easily can Earth digest
A cinder of sidereal fire,
And make the translunary guest
Thus native to an English shire.

Nor is it strange these wanderers
10 Find in her lap their fitting place,
For every particle that's hers
Came at the first from outer space.

All that is Earth has once been sky;
Down from the Sun of old she came,
15 Or from some star that travelled by
Too close to his entangling flame.

Hence, if belated drops yet fall
From heaven, on these her plastic power
Still works as once it worked on all
20 The glad rush of the golden shower.
(1946; 1946)

Pan's Purge

I dreamt that all the planning of peremptory humanity
Had crushed Nature finally beneath the foot of Man;
Birth-control and merriment, Earth completely sterilized,
Bungalow and fun-fair, had fulfilled our Plan,
5 But the lion and the unicorn were sighing at the funeral,
Crying at the funeral,
Sobbing at the funeral of the god Pan.

And the elephant was crying. The pelican in his piety
Struck his feathered bosom till the blood ran,

10 And howling at humanity the owl and iguanodon,
The bittern and the buffalo, their dirge began,
But dangerously, suddenly, a strange ecstatic shuddering,
A change that set me shuddering
Though all the wailful noises of the beasts ran.

15 No longer were they sorrowful, but stronger and more horrible,
It had only been a rumour of the death of Pan.
The scorpions and the mantichores and corpulent tarantulas
Were closing in around me, hissing *Long live Pan!*
And forth with rage unlimited the Northwind drew his scimitar,
20 In wrath with ringing scimitar
He came, with sleet and shipwreck, for the doom of Man.

And now, descending, ravening, loud and large, the avalanche,
And after it the earthquake, was loosed upon Man.
Towering and cloven-hoofed, the power of Pan came over us,
25 Stamped, bit, tore, broke. It was the end of Man;
Except where saints and savages were kept from his ravaging,
And crept out when the ravaging
Was ended, on an empty earth. The new world began.

A small race—a smiling heaven—all round the silences
30 Returned; there was comfort for corrected Man.
Flowered turf had swallowed up the towered cities; following
His flocks and herds where nameless, untainted rivers ran,
Leisurely he pondered, at his pleasure wandering,
Measurelessly wandering
35 Clear, on the huge pastures, the young voice of Man.
(1946–47 [?]; 1947)

The Romantics

Always the old nostalgia? yes;
We still remember times before
We had learned to wear the prison dress
And irons made our ankles sore.

5 Still, when we hear the train at night,
We envy the free travellers, whirled

In some few seconds past the sight
Of the blank walls that bound our world.

Escapists? yes; staring at bars
10 And chains, we think of files . . . and then,
Of wet night muffling moon and stars,
And luck befriending hunted men.

The turn-key (well he may) prefers
Our thoughts to have a narrower range.
15 The proper study of prisoners
Is prison, they tell us. Is that strange?

If lowering memory in our glance
Reveals its pride, they call it names
Like "fantasy" or "outworn romance."
20 So tireless propaganda tames

All but the strong whose hearts they break,
All but the few whose faith is whole.
Stone walls cannot a prison make[41]
Half so secure as rigmarole.
(1946–47 [?]; 1947)

Dangerous Oversight

By enemies surrounded, all venomously minded
  Against him to hound him to death, there lived a king
Who was great and merry-hearted; he ate and drank and sported;
  When his wounds smarted, he would dance and sing.

5 With gossiping and stories, with possets of canary,
  With goliards and glory, he made the time pass.
His merriment was heightened as his territories straitened,
  And his grip tightened on the stem of his glass.

When his foes assaulted he arose and exulted
10   Like a lover as he vaulted on his gaunt horse,
Sublime and elated. But each time he was defeated,
  For the lower gods hated him without remorse.

So his realm diminished; overwhelmed, it vanished,
He held at the finish but a small river-isle,
15 With his Queen, amid the saplings and the green rippling,
With his Fool and his Chaplain; held it for a while.

Till, breathing anger, the heathen in their hunger
Came with clangour to the river banks,
With their commissars and harlots, with their bombers and the skirling
20 Of their pipes, with their snarling and the rattle of their tanks.

And fast came the orders for the last king's murder.
From the reedy border the grey batteries spoke.
The long endeavor of those strong lovers
Relaxed forever amid stench and smoke.

25 From their fresh, unpolluted flesh there sprouted
A tree fair-fruited. Its smell and taste
Were big with Eden; every twig was laden
With gold, unheeded in the flowery waste.

Past the gossamer and midges, past the blossomy region
30 Of the bees, past the pigeon's green world, towards the blue,
Past the eagles' landings, many a league ascending
Above Alps and Andes, infallibly it grew.

And it cast warm joys upon vast horizons,
But its shadow was poison to the evil-eyed.
35 Yes. They ought to have felled it. They were caught unshielded.
Paralysed, they beheld it. They despaired and died.
(1947; 1947)

Call Him a Fascist? Thus the Rabbit

Call *him* a Fascist? Thus the rabbit,
Oblivious of their varying merits,
Takes all who share the simple habit
Of eating rabbit-pie, for ferrets.[42]
(1947; 2004)

The Small Man Orders His Wedding

With tambourines of amber, queens
In rose and lily garlanded
Shall go beside my noble bride
With dance and din and harmony,
5 And sabre clash and tabor crash
And lantern-light and torches flash
On shield and helmet, plume and sash,
The flower of all my armoury;

Till dawn at length by tawny strength
10 Of lions, lo! her chariot;
Their pride will brook no bridle—look,
No bit they bear, no farrier
Ere shod those feet that plod the street
Silent as ghosts; their savage heat
15 Is gentled as they draw my sweet,
New tamed herself, to marry me.

New swell from all the belfries tall,
Till towers reel, the revelry
Of iron tongue untiring swung
20 To booms and clangs of merriment!
While some prepare with trumpet blare
Before my gates to greet us there
When home we come; and everywhere
Let drum be rumbled steadily.

25 Once in, the roar and din no more
Are heard. The hot festivity
And blazing dies; from gazing eyes
These shadowy halls deliver her.
Yet neither flute nor blither lute
30 With pluck of amorous string be mute
Where happy maids their queen salute
And candle flames are quivering.

With decent stealth o'er fleecy wealth
Of carpets tripling soberly,

35 Depart each maid! Your part is played
And I to all her nobleness
Must mate my bare estate. How fair
The whole room has become! The air
Burns as with incense everywhere
40 Around, beneath, and over her.

What flame before our chamber door
Shines in on love's security?
Fiercer than day, its piercing ray
Pours round us unendurably.
45 It's Aphrodite's saffron light,
And Jove's monarchal presence bright
And Genius burning through the night
The torch of man's futurity.

For her the swords of furthest lords
50 Have flashed in fields ethereal;
The dynasts seven incline from heaven
With glad regard and serious,
And ponder there beyond our air
The infinite unborn, and care
55 For history, while the mortal pair
Lie drowned in dreaming weariness.
(1947 [?]; 1964)

Two Kinds of Memory

Oh still vacation, silver
Pause and relaxing of severer laws,
Oh Memory the compassionate,
Forever in the quiet pools of reverie
5 How you refresh the past, how you refashion it!

But iron Memory, tyrant
Importunate by night! whose lucid torture
Still back into the merciless,
Unalterable fact and choking halter of
10 The finished past, without appeal, coerces us.

Well did our fabling elders
Appoint two differing powers to rule with joint
Authority the underworld;
Persephone, the lost and found, the ineffable
15 Lady of spring and death, august and wonderful.

And Hades unevaded,
Stern and exact, whom neither prayers can turn
Nor lapse of years can mitigate;
On Orpheus when, the second time, he forfeited
20 Eurydice, he gazed, precise, unpitying.

His mercies even are cursed
Mockeries of life, cold, cold as lunar rock,
And all his famed Elysium
Worthless, if former joys in all their earthliness
25 Must there recur, mechanically, dizzily.

And round forever, bound for
No goal, caught in a circular rut, the soul
Re-lives her past—Orion on
His quarry and upon his foe the warrior
30 Ever pursuing and forever triumphing.

Thus hoarding and recording
He keeps the mummied past. In her it sleeps,
Dreams, stirs . . . then soft! the magical
Blendings and overgrowings, and the tenderness
35 Of budded spring makes green the graves of tragedies;

And joys remembered, poising
One moment on the past which was their home,
Spread wings, and then with arrowy,
Swift flight and airy song are off to light upon
40 The branches of the sun-shot woods of Paradise.

To call such magic falsehood
Is true—one sort of truth . . . what can you do
With men who say the merriment
And marvel and the full, rough ears at harvesting
45 Only tell lies about the corn-seed's burial?
(1947; 1947)

Le Roi S'Amuse

Jove gazed[43]
On woven mazes
Of patterned movement as the atoms whirled;
His glance turned
5 Into dancing, burning
Colour-gods who rushed upon the sullen world,
Ravaging, savaging, creating it anew—
Silver and purple, shrill-voiced yellow, turgid crimson, and virgin blue.

Jove stared
10 On overbearing
And aching splendour of the naked rocks;
Where his gaze smote
Hazily floated,
To mount like thistledown in countless flocks,
15 Fruit-loving, root-loving gods, cool and green
Of heather and orchard, feathery grasses, pollen'd lily, the olive and the bean.

Jove laughed;
Like cloven-shafted
Lightning, his laughter into brightness broke
20 From every dint
Where the severed splinters
Had scattered, a sylvan or a satyr woke—
Ounces came pouncing, dragon-people flew,
There was spirited stallion, squirrel unrespectful, clanging raven, and kangaroo.

25 Jove sighed;
The hoving tide of
Ocean trembled at the motion of his breath.
His sigh turned
Into white, eternal
30 Radiant Aphrodite, unafraid of death;
A fragrance, a vagrant unrest, on earth she flung.
There was bravery and building, and favouring and fondling,
and chuckling music and suckling of the young.

Jove thought;
35 He wove and wrought at

A thousand clarities. From his brows sprang
With earnest mien,
Stern Athene,
The cold armour on her shoulders rang.
40 Our sires at the fires of her lucid eyes began
To speak in symbols, to seek out causes, to name the creatures; we became Man.

World and Man
Unfurled their banner,
The blazing planets on the azure field;
45 Fresh-robed
In flesh, the ennobled
Spirits carousing in their myriads reeled;
There was frolic and holiday; Jove smiled to see
The abyss empeopled, his bliss imparted, the throng that was his and no longer he.
(1947; 1947)

Donkeys' Delight

Ten mortal months I courted
A girl with bright hair,
Unswerving in my service
As the old lovers were;
5 Almost she had learned to call me
Her dear love—and then
One moment changed the omens,
She was cold again,
For carelessly, unfairly,
10 With one glance of his eyes,
A gay, light-hearted sailor
Bore away the prize—
Unbought—which I had sought with
Many sonnets and sighs.

15 In stern desire I turned to
The Muses' service then
To seek how the unspeakable
Could be fixed by a pen,
Not to shrink though the ink that
20 I must use, they said,

Was my dearest blood, the nearest
    To my heart, the ripe-red.
I obeyed them, I made them
    Many a costly lay,
25 Till carelessly, unfairly
    A lad passed that way
Who set ringing with his singing
    All the woods and the lanes;
They gave him their favour,
30   Lost were all my pains.

I passed then to a Master
    Of a higher repute,
Trusting to find justice
    At the world's root;
35 With rigid fast and vigil,
    Silence and shirt of hair,
The narrow way to Paradise
    I trod with care;
But carelessly, unfairly,
40   At the eleventh hour there came,
Recklessly and fecklessly
    Without a single claim,
A ne'er-do-well, a dare-devil
    Who smelled of shag and gin;
45 Before me (and much warmer
    Was his welcome) he went in.

I stood then in the chill
    Of the great Morning,
Aghast, until at last
50   (Oh, I was late learning!)
I repented, I entered
    Into the excellent joke,
The absurdity; and my burden
    Rolled off as I broke
55 Into laughter—shortly after
    I had found my level;
With Balaam's ass[44] daily
    Out at grass I revel,
Now playing, now braying

60 Over the fields of light
Our soaring, creaking *Gloria,*
Our donkeys' delight.
(1947; 1947)

The End of the Wine

You think, if we sigh as we drink the last decanter,
We're sensual topers, and thence you are ready to prose
And read your lecture. But need you? Why should you banter
Or badger us? Better imagine it thus: we'll suppose

5 A man to have come from Atlantis[45] eastward sailing—
Lemuria[46] has fallen in the fury of a tidal wave;
The cities are fallen; the pitiless, all-prevailing,
Inhuman ocean is Numinor's[47] salt grave.

To Europe he comes from Lemuria, saved from the wreck
10 Of the gilded, loftily builded, countless fleet
With the violet sails. A phial hangs from his neck,
Holding the last of a golden cordial, subtle and sweet.

Untamed is Europe, unnamed—a wet desolation,
Unwelcoming woods of the elk, of the mammoth and bear,
15 The fen and the forest. The men of a barbarous nation,
On the sand in a circle standing, await him there.

Horribly ridged are their foreheads. Weapons of stone
Unhandy and blunt, they brandish in their clumsy grips.
Their females set up a screaming, their pipes drone,
20 They gaze and mutter. He raises his flask to his lips;

And it brings to his mind the strings, the flutes, the tabors,
How he drank with poets at the banquet, robed and crowned;
He recalls the pillared halls carved with the labours
Of curious masters (Lemuria's cities lie drowned).

25 The festal nights, when each jest that flashed for a second,
Light as a bubble, was bright with a thousand years
Of nurture—the honour, the virtue and the grace unreckoned
That sat like a robe on the Atlantean peers.

It has made him remember ladies and the proud glances,
30 Their luminous glances in Numinor and the braided hair,
The ruses and mockings, the music and the grave dances
(Where musicians played, the huge fishes goggle and stare).

So he sighs, like us; then rises and turns to meet
Those naked men. Will they make him their spoil and prey
35 Or salute him as god and brutally fawn at his feet?
And which would be worse? He pitches the phial away.
(1947; 1947)

Vitrea Circe

The name of Circe[48]
Is wrongly branded
(Though Homer's verses
Portrayed her right)
5 By heavy-handed
And moral persons
Misunderstanding
Her danger bright.

She used not beauty
10 For man's beguiling,
She craved no suitor;
Sea-chances brought
To her forest-silent
And crimson-fruited
15 And snake-green island
Her guests unsought.

She watched those drunken
And tarry sailors
Eat nectar-junket
20 And Phœnix-nests;
Each moment paler
With pride she shrunk at
Their leering, railing,
Salt-water jests.

25 They thought to pluck there
Her rosial splendour?
They thought their luck there
    Was near divine?
When the feast ended
30 She rose and struck them
With rod extended
    And made them swine.

No man with kisses
Or touch she tempted;
35 She scorned such blisses
    And toys, until
There came, undreamt of,
The tough Ulysses,
From fate exempted
40   By Pallas' will.

Then flashed above her
(Poor kneeling Circe,
Her snares discovered!)
    The Hero's blade.
45 She lay at mercy
His slave, his lover,
Forgot her curses,
    Blushed like a maid.

She'd none to warn her,
50 He hacked and twisted
The hedge so thorny,
    It let him pass.
Her awful distance,
Her vestal scorning,
55 Were bright as crystal,
    They broke like glass.
(1947; 1948)

Epitaph

From end to end of the bright, airy ward,
From end to end of the each delirious day,
The wireless whined or hammered, nagged or roared;
That was the pain no drugs could put away.
5 I asked for an hour of silence—half an hour
—Ten minutes to die sane. It wasn't granted.
Why should one prig, one high-brow, have the power
To stop what all those honest fellows wanted?
Therefore, oh God, if Paradise, as they tell,
10 Is full of music, oh in mercy save
For me one nook of silence, even in Hell;
And therefore, stranger, tiptoe by this grave,
And let posterity record of me,
"He died both for, and of, democracy."
(1948; 1948)

The Sailing of the Ark

The sky was low, the sounding rain was falling dense and dark,
And Noah's sons were standing at the window of the Ark.

The beasts were in, but Japhet said "I see one creature more
Belated and unmated there comes knocking at the door."

5 "Well, let him knock or let him drown," said Ham, "or learn to swim;
We're overcrowded as it is, we've got no room for him."

"And yet it knocks, how terribly it knocks," said Shem. "Its feet
Are hard as horns and O, the air that comes from it is sweet."

"Now hush!" said Ham. "You'll waken Dad, and once he comes to see
10 What's at the door it's sure to mean more work for you and me."

Noah's voice came roaring from the darkness down below:
"Some animal is knocking. Let it in before we go."

Ham shouted back (and savagely he nudged the other two)
"That's only Japhet knocking down a brad-nail in his shoe."

15 Said Noah "Boys, I hear a noise that's like a horse's hoof."
Said Ham "Why, that's the dreadful rain that drums upon the roof."

Noah tumbled up on deck and out he put his head.
His face grew white, his knees were loosed, he tore his beard and said

"Look, look! It would not wait. It turns away. It takes its flight—
20 Fine work you've made of it, my sons, between you all to-night!

O noble and unmated beast, my sons were all unkind;
In such a night what stable and what manger will you find?

O golden hoofs, O cataracts of mane, O nostrils wide
With high disdain, and O the neck wave-arched, the lovely pride!

25 O long shall be the furrows ploughed upon the hearts of men
Before it comes to stable and to manger once again,

And dark and crooked all the roads in which our race will walk,
And shrivelled all their manhood like a flower on broken stalk!

Now all the world, O Ham, may curse the hour that you were born—
30 Because of you the Ark must sail without the Unicorn."
(1948; 1948)

Late Summer

I, dusty and bedraggled as I am,
Pestered with wasps and weeds and making jam,
Blowzy and stale, my welcome long outstayed,
Proved false in every promise that I made,
5 At my beginning I believed, like you,
Something would come of all my green and blue.
Mortals remember, looking on the thing
I am, that I, even I, was once a spring.
(1948; 1964)

The Landing

The ship's stride faltered with a change of course, awaking us.
    Suddenly I saw the land (astern the East was red);
Budding like a flower amid pale and rippled vacancy,
    The island rose ahead.

5 All, then, was true! such lands in solid verity
    Dapple the last sea that laps against the sky;
Apple-gold, the headlands of the singing Hesperides[49]
    On glass-clear water lie.

Once before I'd seen it (but that was from Helicon)[50]
10 Clear and distinct in the circle of a lens,
Peering on tip-toes, one-eyed, through a telescope—
    Goddesses' country, never men's.

And now we were landing. Bright beasts and manifold
    Came like old familiars, nosing at our knees;
15 Nameless their kinds—Adam's naming of the animals
    Reached not those outer seas.

Up from the shore then, benumbed with hope, we went upon
    Danceable lawns and under gum-sweet wood,
Glancing ever up to where a green hill at the centre of
20 The hush'd island stood.

Reaching the top we looked over upon limitless
    Waters, untravelled, further West. But the three
Daughters of Hesperus were only carven images
    Hand-fast around a tree.

25 And instead of the Apples we found a golden telescope
    That burned our eyes there, flashing in the sun.
It was turned to the West (as once before on Helicon),
    We looked through it one by one.

There for the second time I saw, remote and perilous—
30 Bliss to behold it in the circle of the lens,
And this time surely the true one—the Hesperides'
    Country which is not men's.

Hope died . . . rose again . . . flickered and increased in us;
    Strenuous our longing; we re-embarked to find
35 That genuine and utter West. Far astern to East of us
    The false hope sank behind.
(1948; 1948)

The Turn of the Tide

Breathless was the air over Bethlehem; black and bare
    The fields; hard as granite were the clods;
Hedges stiff with ice; the sedge, in the vice
    Of the ponds, like little iron rods.
5 The deathly stillness spread from Bethlehem; it was shed
    Wider each moment on the land;
Through rampart and wall into camp and into hall
    Stole the hush. All tongues were at a stand.
Travellers at their beer in taverns turned to hear
10 The landlord—that oracle was dumb;
At the Procurator's feast a jocular freedman ceased
    His story, and gaped; all were glum.
Then the silence flowed forth to the islands and the north
    And it smoothed the unquiet river-bars,
15 And leveled out the waves from their revelling, and paved
    The sea with the cold, reflected stars.
Where the Cæsar sat and signed at ease on Palatine,
    Without anger, the signatures of death,
There stole into his room and on his soul a gloom,
20 Till he paused in his work and held his breath.
Then to Carthage and the Gauls, to Parthia and the Falls
    Of Nile, to Mount Amara it crept;
The romp and rage of beasts in swamp and forest ceased,
    The jungle grew still as if it slept.
25 So it ran about the girth of the planet. From the Earth
    The signal, the warning, went out,
Away beyond the air; her neighbours were aware
    Of change, they were troubled with doubt.

Salamanders in the Sun who brandish as they run
30 Tails like the Americas in size,
Were stunned by it and dazed; wondering, they gazed

Up at Earth, misgiving in their eyes.
In Houses and Signs the Ousiarchs divine[51]
Grew pale and questioned what it meant;
35 Great Galactic lords stood back to back with swords
Half-drawn, awaiting the event,
And a whisper among them passed, "Is this perhaps the last
Of our story and the glories of our crown?—
The entropy worked out?—the central redoubt
40 Abandoned?—The world-spring running down?"
Then they could speak no more. Weakness overbore
Even them; they were as flies in a web,
In lethargy stone-dumb. The death had almost come,
And the tide lay motionless at ebb.

45 Like a stab at that moment over Crab and Bowman,
Over Maiden and Lion, came the shock[52]
Of returning life, the start, and burning pang at heart,
Setting galaxies to tingle and rock.
The Lords dared to breathe, swords went into sheathes
50 A rustling, a relaxing began;
With rumour and noise of the resuming of joys
Along the nerves of the universe it ran.
Then, pulsing into space with delicate dulcet pace,
Came a music infinitely small,
55 But clear; and it swelled and drew nearer, till it held
All worlds with the sharpness of its call,
And now divinely deep, ever louder, with a leap
And quiver of inebriating sound,
The vibrant dithyramb shook Libra and the Ram,
60 The brains of Aquarius spun round[53]—
Such a note as neither Throne nor Potentate had known
Since the Word created the abyss.
But this time it was changed in a mystery, estranged,
A paradox, an ambiguous bliss.

65 Heaven danced to it and burned; such answer was returned
To the hush, the *Favete,* the fear
That Earth had sent out. Revel, mirth and shout
Descended to her, sphere below sphere,
Till Saturn laughed and lost his latter age's frost
70 And his beard, Niagara-like, unfroze;

The monsters in the Sun rejoiced; the Inconstant One,
  The unwedded Moon, forgot her woes;
A shiver of re-birth and deliverance round the Earth
  Went gliding; her bonds were released;
75 Into broken light the breeze once more awoke the seas,
  In the forest it wakened every beast;
Capripods fell to dance from Taproban to France,
  Leprechauns from Down to Labrador;
In his green Asian dell the Phœnix from his shell
80 Burst forth and was the Phœnix once more.

So Death lay in arrest. But at Bethlehem the bless'd
  Nothing greater could be heard
Than sighing wind in the thorn, the cry of One new-born,
  And cattle in stable as they stirred.
(1948; 1948)

The Prodigality of Firdausi

Firdausi[54] the tall cedar among Poets, lean of purse
And lean with age, had finished his august mountain of verse,
The great *Shah Nameh,* gleaming-glaciered with demon wars,
Bastioned with Rustem's bitter labours and Isfendiyar's,
5 Shadowed with Jamshid's ruin and splendour as with eagles' wings,
Its foot-hills dewy-forested with the amours of kings,
Echoing with rhymes that rushed like snow-fed torrents blue and cold.
The King commanded to be given him an elephant's burden of gold.

Firdausi the fierce Lion of the Poets of Iran
10 Was held in low esteem by government. The astute Divan
Extolled the King's munificence; but secretly they said
"Nay, send the old singer thirty thousand silver pounds instead,
The price of ten fat vineyards and a fine Circassian girl."
Therefore the Grand Vizier chose out a secretary, a churl,
15 A stretch-hemp without understanding and of base descent,
And bade him deliver their bounty. The man without shame arose and went.

He found the Apple of the Poets in the baths at ease
Discoursing with his friends. All honourable men were these,
Mathematicians, theologians, or warriors all,

20 Taking their wine and sugared rose-leaves in an airy hall,
Or lovers or astronomers. Like honey dropped their speech
Slowly with measure and decorum from the lips of each,
On roses and predestination and heroic wars
And rhetoric, and the brevity of the life of man, and the stars.

25 The Carbuncle of Poets courteously inquired his will.
The bearers laid the silver at his feet. The bath grew still,
The churl grew pale. Firdausi beckoned to the Nubian slave
Who dried their feet; to him the first ten thousand coins he gave.
Ten thousand more immediately he gave the captive boy
30 Who poured the wine. "My son," he said, "may Allah give you joy;
And in your grandson's house in unbelieving Frangistan
Make it your boast that you looked in the eyes of the Splendour of Iran."

Lastly the Flower of Poets to the churl himself returned
The remnant, saying, "Friend, you are pale. Undoubtedly you have earned
35 This trifle for your courtesy and for the heat of the day."
As if the pavement scorched his feet the pick-thank crept away.
The dogs growled as he passed, the beggars spat. Laughter and shame
Wait upon all his progeny; on him, Gehenna flame;
And instantly their discourse in the baths once more began
40 On the beauty of horses and women and the brevity of the life of man.
(1948; 1948)

Epitaph in a Village Churchyard

My grave my pillory, by this blabbing stone
    Forbidden to rest unknown,
I feel like fire my neighbours' eyes because
    All here know what I was.
5 Think, stranger, of that moment when I too
    First, and forever, knew.
(1949; 1949)

On a Picture by Chirico

Two sovereign horses standing on the sand.[55] There are no men,
The men have died, the houses fallen, a thousand years' war
Concludes in charnel, graves, and bones, and waves on a bare shore
  Are rolled in a cold evening when there is rain in the air.

5 These were not killed and eaten like the rest, they were too swift
And strong for the last stunted men to hunt in the great dearth.
Then they were already terrible. They inherit the large earth,
  The pleasant pastures, resonant with their stormy charge.

Now they have reached the end of land. They see for the first time,
10 Chilly in early March, the falling arches of the bay, vast
And empty in bitter sunset light, where once the ships passed.
  They halt smelling the salt in the air, and whinny with their lips.

These are not like the horses we have ridden; that old look
Of half-indignant melancholy and delicate alarm's gone.
15 Thus perhaps looked the breeding-pair in Eden when a day shone
  First upon tossing manes and glossy flanks at play.

They are called. Change overhangs them. Now their neighing is half speech.
Death-sharp across great seas, a seminal breeze from the far side
Calls to their new-crown'd race to leave the places where Man died—
20 The offer, is it? the prophecy, of a Houyhnhnm's land?[56]
(1949; 1949)

Adam at Night

Except at the making of Eve Adam slept
Not at all (as men now sleep) before the Fall.
Sin yet unborn, he was free from that dominion
Of the blind brother of death who occults the mind.

5 Instead, when stars and twilight had him to bed
And the dutiful owl, whirring over Eden, had hooted
A warning to the other beasts to be hushed till morning
And curbed their plays that the Man should be undisturbed,

He would lie, relaxed, enormous, under a sky
10 Starry as never since; he would set ajar
The door of his mind. Into him thoughts would pour
Other than day's. He rejoined Earth his mother.

He melted into her nature. Gradually he felt,
As though through his own flesh the elusive growth,
15 Hardening and spreading of roots in the deep garden,
In his veins, the wells re-filling with the silver rain;

And thrusting down far under his rock-crust,
Finger-like, rays from the sky that probed bringing
To bloom the gold and diamond in his dark womb;
20 The seething central fire moved with his breathing.

He guided his globe smoothly in the ether, riding
At one with his planetary peers around the sun;
Courteously he saluted the hard virtue of Mars
And Venus' prodigal glory as he spun between them.

25 Over Man and his Mate the hours, like waters, ran.
Then darkness thinned in the East; the treble lark
Carolling aroused the common people of Paradise
To yawn and scratch, to bleat and whinny in the dawn.

Collected now in themselves, human and erect,
30 Lord and lady walked on the dabbled sward,
As if two trees should arise, dreadfully gifted
With speech and motion. The Earth's strength was in each.
(1949; 1949)

Arrangement of Pindar

Pindar[57] stood with his chorus on a dancing floor. The stern poet
Uttered his dark warnings. Light as a flight of tumbling birds
Was the rising and falling, the wheeling and winding and pause of his words,
Gravely as virgins, young men of noble houses, trained and severe,
5 Strongly as if it were a battle, and resolutely danced his ode,
Their faces rigid, but their limbs and garments flowing like water.

"Excellence comes by nature, of itself. Some try for it by art
And rules; but if no hidden god have a finger in the work,
The fitting reward of their achievement is a perpetual silence;
10 For a soul's weight is born with her, and the laborious plodder,
Working in the dark, tries this and that, puddles and dabbles in a thousand
Attempted arts and virtues; never will his unfinished mind
Run a straight course to the winning post with undeflected pace.
For the gods themselves would not make bold to begin a feast or dance
15 In Heaven without the favour and consent of the solemn Graces;
For gods and men are of a single stock and came of the same womb
Though a force of utter separation is between them. We are nothing
And their unshakable, eternal floor is the firmament of brass.
We look at Delos, at an island: but the gaze of the happy gods from Olympos[58]
20 Looks down at a star, set in the dusky world's expanse, shining afar.

"We are tethered by Hopes that will say anything without blushing,
And the flowing water of foreknowledge is far away beyond our reach.
Therefore neither ashore nor in the hollow ships will praise be given
To a virtuous deed unless it endangers of the doer's life
25 (At Pindus the glory of the Dorian spear burst into flower),[59]
And we live for a day. What are we? What are we not? A man
Is a dream about a shadow. Only when a brightness falls from Heaven
Does human splendour expand and glow, and the days are soft.
"Not even to Kadmos, though a peer for gods, not to the Aiakid
30 Peleus, was there appointed a perfect, whole, unslippery life,[60]
Though these were fortunate, as men say, beyond all human bounds,
And heard the gold-wreathed Muses singing on their marriage day.
Over the mountain and to seven-gated Thebes the song
Drew near when deep-dark-eyed Harmonia became Kadmos' bride[61]
35 And Peleus took the sea-sage Nereus' daughter, the divine Thetis,[62]
And the gods came as guests. In golden chairs at his own table
Each saw the sceptred race of Kronos[63] and received their gifts,
And Zeus from all their former toils that day released them in joy.
But afterwards the sharp sorrow of his three daughters stripped
40 Kadmos' heart of comfort—even though the Father of the Sky
Had lain in Semele's desired bed and in her white embrace;[64]
And Peleus' only son whom the undying Thetis bore him
In Phthia, shot with an arrow at the Trojan war, was burnt
Upon a funeral pile and all the Danaans mourned about it.[65]
45 For we are men, our life is a day. He that will walk truth's way
Must take the blessing as it comes. Now from this quarter and now

From another the winged weathers ride forth. And not for long,
If it once grow heavy with goodness, will fortune remain good.

"Once his fate drove Herakles forth beyond Ister to the north
50 Following the doe with golden horns; on her horns one of the Pleiades[66]
Had written ARTEMIS, dedicating it to the huntress in her stead.[67]
Following quarry, that presently he came within sight of a land
Which is upon the other side of the cold northern wind;
And he stopped: he looked upon the trees of that country; he was seized
55 With sweet desire—oh for a sapling to plant in his own land!
But do not therefore imagine that either on foot or with sail and oar
You will ever find the miraculous way to the Hyperborean place.[68]
Of unattainable longings griding madness is the bitter fruit.

"But blessed is he who takes his journey into the grave, the hollow earth,
60 Having first seen the unspeakable sight at Eleusis;[69] for he knows
The meaning of life's ending and new beginning, the gift of Zeus.
There is an endless sunny equinox wherein good men receive
Life without toil far hence. The flower of their hand is never bruised
Wounding with oar or spade the earth or the salt water
65 For meager livelihood. Men such as loved to keep their word
Now dwell here, neighbouring the exalted gods, in a land with tears.
Those who have stood thrice over to their tackling and endured
Thrice in this and the other realm, keeping their hearts from evil,
There walk upon the road of Zeus the Father and arrive
70 At the tower of ancient Kronos. The sea's daughters, the landward breezes,
Blow always over the bless'd countries. Like burning gold the flowers
Hang in the island forests and others bloom in the bay, flowers of the foam.
The blessed ones weave them to bracelets for the arm, crowns for the head.
But the other sort have labour enough, hidden from the reach of our eyes.
75 And the voice of the Pierides[70] is hateful to all the enemies of Zeus.
Their melody that smooths the feathers of the eagle and seals its eyes
Till it nods, perched on his sceptre, in a delicious darkness and a trance,
Is an agony to those who lie in Tartarus.[71] Hundred-headed Typhon
Writhes under Etna when he hears it, vomiting lava and flame."[72]

80 Pindar sang. The heaven-descended nobles of the pure Dorian blood,
Not thinking that they understood it but silent in reverence for the god
And the stern poet, soberly attended and understood it all.
Tears stood in their eyes because of the beauty of the young men who danced.
(1949; 1949)

Epitaph

Here lies the whole world after one
Peculiar mode; a buried sun,
Stars and immensities of sky
And cities here discarded lie.
5 The prince who owned them, having gone,
Left them as things not needed on
His journey, yet with hope that he,
Purged by aeonian poverty
In Lenten lands, hereafter can
10 Resume the robes he wore as man.
(1949; 1949)

Conversation Piece: The Magician and the Dryad

MAGICIAN.
Out of your dim felicity of leaves, O Nymph appear:
Answer me in soft-showery voice, attempt the unrooted dance—
My art will sponsor the enormity. Now concentrate,
5 Arouse, where in your vegetative heart it drowses deep
In seminal sleep, your feminine response. *Conjuro te*
Per Hecates essentiam et noctis silentia,[73]
Breaking in Trivia's name your prison of bark.
Beautiful, awake!
10 DRYAD.
Risen from the deep lake of my liberty, into your prison
She has come, cruel commander.
MAGICIAN.
I have given speech to the dumb.
15 Will you not thank me, silver lady?
DRYAD.
Oh till now she drank
With thirst of myriad mouths the bursting cataracts of the sun
And drizzle of gentler stars, and indivisible small rain.
20 Wading the dark earth, made of earth and light, cradled in air,
All that she was, she was all over. Now the mask you call
A Face has come between her and the hemisphere's embrace;
Her sight is screwed into twin nodules of tormenting light;
Searing divisions tear her into five. She cannot hear,

25 But only see, the moon; earth has no taste; she cannot breathe
At every branch vibrations of the sky. For a dome of severance,
A helmet, a dark, rigid box of bone, has overwhelmed
Her hair . . . that was her lungs . . . that was her nerves . . . that kissed the air.
Crushed in a brain, her thought that circled coolly in every vein,
30 Turns into poison, thickens like a man's, ferments and burns.
She was at peace when she was in her unity. Oh, now release
And let her out into the seamless world, make her forget.
MAGICIAN.
Be free. Relapse. And so she vanishes. And now the tree
35 Grows barer every moment. The leaves fall. A killing air,
Sighing from the country of Man, has withered it. The tree will die.
(1949; 1949)

The Day with a White Mark

All day I have been tossed and whirled in a preposterous happiness.
Was it an elf in the blood? or a bird in the brain? or even part
Of the cloudily-crested, fifty-league-long, loud, uplifted wave
Of an unconcerned archangel's transit over and through my heart?

5 Reason kept telling me all day my mood was out of season.
It was too; all ahead is dark or splashed with hideous light.
My garden's spoiled; my holidays are cancelled; the omens harden;
The plann'd and the unplann'd miseries deepen; the knots draw tight.

Yet I—I could have kissed the very scullery taps. The colour of
10 My day was like a peacock's chest. In at each sense there stole
Ripplings and dewy sprinkles of delight that with them drew
Fine threads of memory through the vibrant thickness of the soul.

As though there were transparent earths and luminous trees should grow there,
And glimmering roots were visibly at work below one's feet,
15 So everything, the tick of the clock, the cock crowing in the yard,
Probing my soil, woke diverse buried hearts of mine to beat,

Recalling either adolescent heights and the inaccessible
Longings, the ice-keen joys that shook my body and turned me pale,
Or humbler pleasures, chuckling as it were in the ear, mumbling
20 Of glee as friendly animals talk in a children's tale.

Who knows if ever it will come again, now the day closes?
No one can give me—or take away—the key. All depends
On the elf, the bird, the angel. I question if the angel himself
Has power to choose when sudden heaven for me begins or ends.
(1949; 1949)

A Footnote to Pre-History

Faltering, with bowed heads, our altered parents
Slowly descended from their holy hill,
All their good fortune left behind and done with,
    Out through the one-way pass

5 Into the dangerous world, these strange countries.
No rumour in Eden has reached the human pair
Of shapes unlike yet like their own that wandered
    The earth beyond its walls.

But now they heard the mountains stirred and shaken,
10 All the heap'd crags re-echoing, the deep tarns
And caverns shuddering and the abysmal gorges
    With dismal drums of Dwarfs;

Or some prodigious night, waked by a thumping
Shock as of piles being driven two miles away,
15 Ran till the sunrise shone upon the bouncing
    Monopods at their heels;

Or held their breath, hiding, and saw their elders
The race of giants (the bulldozers' pace,
Heads like balloons, toad-thick ungainly torsos)
20   Dotting the plain like ricks.

They had more to fear once Cain had killed a quarter
Of human-kind and stolen away, and the womb
Of an unsmiling Hominid to the turncoat
    Had littered ominous sons.

25 A happy noise of liquid shapes, a lapping
Of small waves up and up the hills till all

Was smooth and silver, the clear Flood ascended,
    Ending that crew; but still

Memory, not built upon a skull at Piltdown,
30 Reaches us; we know more than bones can teach.
Eve's body's language, Seth within her quickening,
    Taught him the sickening fear.

He passed the word. Before we're born we have heard it.
Long-silenced ogres boom, voices like gongs
35 Reverberate in the mind; a Dwarf-drum rolls,
    Trolls wind unchancy horns.
(1949; 1949)

Notes

1. For the context of this poem, see Lewis's letter to Edmund Blunden of Mar. 26, 1935, *CL* 3:1526.

2. For the context of this poem, see Lewis's letter to Owen Barfield of Apr. 5, 1935, published in *Collected Letters of C. S. Lewis,* Volume 2: *Books, Broadcasts and the War, 1931–1949* (hereafter, *CL* 2), ed. Walter Hooper (London: Harper Collins, 2004), 158.

3. This quotation from Blaise Pascal's *Pensées* means "God has established prayer to communicate to his creatures the dignity of causality."

4. The defeat of the cruel Assyrian king Sennacherib is recorded in 2 Kings 19 and by the historian, Herodotus.

5. *The Place of the Lion* (London: Victor Gollancz, 1931) is a novel by Charles Williams.

6. "Where is 'The Place of the Lion'? / The home and hearth of Cecil!" For the context of these lines, see Lewis's letter to Cecil Harwood of July 1936, *CL* 2:200.

7. The *Kalevala* is a collection of folktales, considered by some to be the national epic of Finland. Lewis knew the *Kalevala* through the translation done by William Forsell Kirby, *Kalevala: The Land of Heroes* (1907).

8. This refers to Wytham Woods, an ancient, seminatural woodland to the west of Oxford.

9. For the context of this poem, see Lewis's letter to E. F. Carritt of Oct. 29, [1937], *CL* 2:220.

10. The port of Dover lies in Kent, on the southeastern coast of England, facing France across the Channel at its narrowest part; it is famous for its white chalk cliffs. Cape Wrath, in Scotland's Sutherland County, marks mainland United Kingdom's farthest northwesterly point.

11. The French title of this poem means "song of adventure." Addison's Walk, a well-known footpath within the grounds of Magdalen College, Oxford, was a favorite route of C. S. Lewis. A plaque bearing a version of this poem, "What the Bird Said Early in the year," now appears along Addison's Walk.

12. Ignatius Roy Dunnachie Campbell (1901–1957), of this poem's title, was a South African poet, with whose fascist political sympathies Lewis disagreed. "Rifles may flower and terrapins may flame," alludes to Campbell's first long poem, "The Flaming Terrapin" (1924), and to his later "Flowering Rifles" (1939).

13. The slang term *Charlies* means "idiots" or "fools."

14. The title of this poem refers to Hermoine, wife of Leontes, king of Sicily, in William Shakespeare's *The Winter's Tale;* after Leontes publicly and unjustly scorns her, the audience believes she has died of a broken heart. For Paulina, see note 15.

15. Paulina, Hermione's fiercely loyal friend, helps to hide her away and sixteen years later becomes the agent for her "resurrection."

16. The "dearest friend" referred to here is Lewis's brother, Warren.

17. In the holograph letter where this poem is found, Lewis's friend and doctor, Humphrey Havard, appended the following to the end of the poem: "By C. S. Lewis on my return from sea, Aug. 1943." For more on the source of this poem, see the Bibliography.

18. The Horn is probably a reference to the Cape of Good Hope, a rocky headland on the Atlantic coast of the Cape Peninsula, South Africa. The Skagerrak is a strait running between the southeast coast of Norway, the southwest coast of Sweden, and the Jutland peninsula of Denmark, connecting the North Sea and the Kattegat sea area, which leads to the Baltic Sea.

19. Perhaps a pun on William Henry Beveridge (1879–1963), a British economist and social reformer best known for his 1942 report, *Social Insurance and Allied Services,* more commonly known as the *Beveridge Report.*

20. Robert Blair (1699–1746) was a Scottish poet famed for his poem *The Grave.*

21. This probably refers to Alfred the Great (849–899), king of Wessex from 871 to 899.

22. This is the first of two footnotes by Lewis that appear at the end of the poem: "N. S. stands for *Non satis* (not enough), the mark given by Oxford examiners to a question on which the candidate has failed."

23. This is the second of Lewis's two footnotes appearing at the end of the poem : "A 'scout' is a college servant."

24. For the context of this poem, see Lewis's letter to Sarah Neylan of July 16, 1944, *CL* 2:619.

25. The word *salamander* comes from the Greek for "fire lizard." According to many legends, the salamander was believed to be a creature born in and able to exist in fire.

26. For the context of this poem, see Lewis's letter to Dorothy L. Sayers of July 6, 1945, *CL* 2:663.

27. The Latin title of Milton's poem (forming part of the title of Lewis's poem) is "On the Platonic Ideal as Understood by Aristotle." Immediately below the title of the poem, Lewis adds in brackets: "Milton's *De Idea Platonica* was probably intended as a mere academic squib; but genius sometimes laughs at authors' intentions. I hardly dare to hope that this version has preserved the goblin quality of the original: it will be enough if I send some readers to explore for themselves such a neglected and exquisite grotesque."

28. Documentary evidence by which one can defend a title to property or a claim to rights.

29. Minerva was the Roman goddess of wisdom.

30. On his use of the word *stupendious,* Lewis added this note at the end of the poem: "Milton, when writing English, prefers this form."

31. In Greek mythology, Ninus was king of Assyria and the founder of the city of Nineveh, which itself is sometimes called Ninus. The Assyrian/Babylonian Bel myth concerns a god who is slain and resurrected. In Egyptian mythology, Osiris was the king of Egypt who was resurrected as the King of the Dead.

32. Hermes Trismegistus was the supposed author of a series of ancient Greek sacred texts that form the basis of Hermeticism. Isis was an Egyptian goddess worshipped as the ideal mother and wife as well as the goddess of nature and magic.

33. Lewis added this note at the end of the poem: "By omitting the last five lines I cut the umbilical cord which, in the original, connects the fantasy with its scholastic occasion."

34. For the context of this poem, see Lewis's letter to Owen Barfield from Sept. 1945?, *CL* 2:669. Arion was an ancient Greek poet credited with inventing the dithyramb. He is chiefly remembered for the myth of his kidnapping by pirates and miraculous rescue by dolphins.

35. Lewis is referring to Samuel Johnson (1709–1784), Walter Savage Landor (1775–1864), William Cobbett (1763–1835), and William Blake (1757–1827).

36. The name of the Soviet secret police from 1923 to 1934.

37. In 1939, seeking to avoid Britain's involvement in another war, Prime Minister Neville Chamberlain met with German leader Adolf Hitler in Munich, returning to Britain with a settlement agreeing to Hitler's annexation of part of Czechoslovakia in return for the promise that Germany would stop there. Hitler's later annexation of the rest of Czechoslovakia and of Poland proved the failure of this policy of appeasement to Hitler's demands.

38. Vortigern was king of the Britons at the time of the arrival of the Saxons. He accepted the assistance of the Saxons in order to protect his kingdom against the Picts and Scots, granting them land as compensation. Later the Britons made war on the Saxons in their Kentish strongholds. After the death in battle of Vortigern's son, Vortemir, the *Historia Brittonum* records the massacre of the British nobles, and Vortigern's subsequent grant of Essex and Sussex to the Saxons.

39. In Arabian and Muslim folklore, jinns are ugly and evil demons with supernatural powers which they can bestow on persons able to summon them. Efreets are jinns with wings of fire, known for their strength and cunning.

40. Philippus Aureolus Theophrastus Bombastus von Hohenheim (1493–1541), known as Paracelsus, was a Renaissance physician, botanist, alchemist, astrologer, and general occultist.

41. This line is an allusion to the poem "To Althea, from Prison," by Richard Lovelace (1618–1657): "Stone walls do not a prison make, / Nor iron bars a cage; / Minds innocent and quiet take / That for an hermitage."

42. For the context of this poem, see Lewis's letter to Ruth Pitter of June 6, 1947, *CL* 2:780.

43. The title of this poem means "The King amuses himself."

44. For the story of Balaam's ass in the Bible, see Numbers 22:21–38.

45. Atlantis is a legendary island in the Atlantic Ocean, mentioned by Plato, that supposedly sank beneath the sea about 10,000 B.C.

46. Lemuria is a hypothetical lost continent first proposed by the nineteenth-century British scientist Philip Sclater to explain the presence of fossils related to lemurs in both India and Madagascar.

47. Numinor is Lewis's reference to a lost continent, actually spelled *Númenor,* created by his friend J. R. R. Tolkien for the fictional universe Tolkien explores in his trilogy, *The Lord of the Rings,* and other works.

48. The title of this poem comes from Horace's *Odes,* 1.17.20, and means "glittering Circe." In Greek legend, Circe was the witch who temporarily enchanted many of Odysseus's mariners, turning them into pigs, before giving them directions home.

49. In Greek mythology, the Hesperides were three nymphs who tended a rich, beautiful garden in a far western corner of the world.

50. The Helicon is a mountain in Boeotia, Greece, near the Gulf of Corinth; in Greek mythology, it was a site favored by the Muses, since two springs sacred to them were located there.

51. The Ousiarchs are planetary intelligences or spirits.

52. The four names given in these two lines refer to constellations: Crab is the English name of the constellation Cancer; Bowman, that of Sagittarius; Maiden, that of Virgo; and Lion, that of Leo.

53. The names in these two lines refer to three more constellations: Libra, the first, signifies "balance"; Ram is English name of Aries; and Aquarius signifies "water carrier."

54. Abul Kasim Mansur (940?–1020?), known as Firdausi, was the poet of the Persian national epic *Shah Nameh* (Book of Kings).

55. The title of this poem refers to a painting by Giorgio de Chirico (1888–1978), a Greek-born Italian artist; horses by the sea's edge, often near ruins, were a frequent subject of his work.

56. The Houyhnhnms were a race of intelligent horses described in the last part of Jonathan Swift's *Gulliver's Travels* (1726).

57. Pindar (518?–438? B.C.), the greatest lyric poet of ancient Greece, was a master of epinicia, a victory ode with this pattern: praise of the gods, reference to myth, and aphoristic moralizing. Pindaric odes were usually performed with a chorus and dancers.

58. In Greek mythology, the temple to Apollo was located at Delos. Mount Olympus was the home of the gods. *Olympos* is Lewis's variant spelling of *Olympus.*

59. Pindus is a range of mountains in Greece, of which the best known is Mount Parnassus. Dorians were a subgroup of the Greek people.

60. In Greek mythology, Kadmos was a Phoenician prince believed to have introduced the original alphabet to the Greeks. Peleus, the son of the king of Aegina, became king of the Myrmidons of Thessaly. Later he married the sea nymph Thetis and fathered the hero Achilles.

61. Harmonia was the goddess of harmony and concord.

62. The nereid (sea nymph) Thetis became the wife of Peleus after he captured her.

63. Kronos, the youngest of the Titans and god of time and the ages, especially time, was regarded as destructive and all-devouring. In fear of a prophecy that he would be overthrown by his own son, Kronos swallowed each of his children as soon as they were born. His wife, Rhea, saved their son Zeus by feeding Kronos a rock covered in swaddling clothes. Later Zeus forced Kronos to disgorge his other children and led them in a ten-year war that desposed Kronos and the other Titans.

64. Kadmos's daughters were Ino, Autonoë, Agave, and Semele. The mortal Semele bore Dionysus, her son by Zeus.

65. The Danaans were the most ancient tribe of the Greeks.

66. The Pleiades, the companions of Artemis, were the seven daughters of Atlas and the sea-nymph Pleione.

67. Lewis is alluding here to the third labor of Hercules, capturing the sacred stag of Artemis.

68. In Greek mythology, the Hyperboreans were a people who lived far to the north of Thrace, beyond Boreas, the north wind.

69. Eleusis was an ancient Greek city near Athens, sacred to the goddess Demeter and the site of the famous religious festival, the Eleusinian mysteries.

70. The Pierides is another name for the Muses, associated with Pieria, a region of Macedonia in Greece.

71. In Greek mythology, Tartarus was the great black pit beneath the earth.

72. In Greek mythology, Typhon was the monstrous immortal storm-giant who was defeated and imprisoned by Zeus in Tartarus. Mount Etna is the largest active volcano in Europe.

73. This Latin phrase translates as "I appeal to you, through the essence of Hecate and by the silence of the night."

Poems

1950–1963

As One Oldster to Another

Well, yes. The old bones ache. There were easier
Beds thirty years back. Sleep, then importunate,
Now with reserve doles out her favours.
Food disagrees. There are draughts in houses.

5 Headlong, the down night train rushes on with us,
Screams through the stations . . . How many more? Is it
Time soon to think of taking down one's
Case from the rack? Are we nearly there now?

Yet neither loss of friends nor an emptying
10 Future, nor England tamed and the ruin of
Long-builded hope thus far have taught my
Obstinate heart a sedate deportment.

Still beauty calls as once in the mazes of
Boyhood. The bird-like soul quivers. Into her
15 Flash darts of unfulfill'd desires and
Pierce with a bright, unabated anguish.

Armed so with anguish, Joy met us even in
Youth—who forgets? This side of the terminus,
Then, now, and always, thus and only
20 Thus were the doors of delight set open.
(1950; 1950)

A Cliché Came Out of Its Cage

You said "The world is going back to Paganism." Oh bright
vision! I saw our dynasty in the bar of the House
spill from their tumblers a libation to the Erinyes,[1]
and Leavis with Lord Russell wreathed in flowers,[2] heralded with flutes,
5 leading white bulls to the cathedral of the solemn Muses
to pay where due the glory of their latest theorem.
Hestia's fire in every flat,[3] rekindled, burnt before
the Lardergods.[4] Unmarried daughters with obedient hands
tended it. By the hearth the white-arm'd venerable mother
10 *domum servabat, lanam faciebat.*[5] Duly at the hour

of sacrifice their brothers came, silent, corrected, grave
before their elders; on their downy cheeks easily the blush
arose (it is the mark of freemens' children) as they trooped
gleaming with oil demurely home from the palaestra or the dance.[6]
15 Walk carefully, do not wake the envy of the happy gods,
shun ὕβρις;[7] the middle of the road, the middle sort of men,
are best: αἰδώς surpasses gold;[8] reverence for the aged
is wholesome as seasonable rain, and for a man to die
defending the city in battle is a harmonius thing.
20 Thus with magistral hand the puritan Σωφροσύνη[9]
cooled and schooled and tempered our uneasy motions;
heathendom came again, the circumspection and the holy fears . . .
you said it. Did you mean it? Oh inordinate liar, stop.[10]
(1950; 1950)

Not for Your Reading, Not Because I Dream

Not for your reading, not because I dream
To pay my debt for the still, ghostly beauty
Of yours: but as the clown brings fruit & cream
To a great lady, with his awkward duty.
(October 16, 1950; 2014)

Ballade of Dead Gentlemen

Where, in what bubbly land,[11] below
  What rosy horizon dwells to-day
That worthy man Monsieur Cliquot
  Whose widow has made the world so gay?[12]
5 Where now is Mr. Tanqueray?[13]
Where might the King of Sheba be
  (Whose wife stopped dreadfully long away)?
Mais où sont messieurs les maris?[14]

Say where did Mr. Beeton go[15]
10 With rubicund nose and whiskers grey
To dream of dumplings long ago,
  Of syllabubs, soups, and *entremets?*
  In what dim isle did Twankey lay
His aching head?[16] what murmuring sea

15 Lulls him after the life-long fray?
Mais où sont messieurs les maris?

How Mr. Grundy's cheeks may glow[17]
By a bathing-pool where lovelies play,
I guess, but shall I ever know?
20 Where—if it comes to that, *who,* pray—
Is Mr. Masham? Sévigné [18]
And Mr. Siddons and Zebedee[19]
And Gamp and Hemans,[20] where are they?
Mais où sont messieurs les maris?

25 Princesses all, beneath your sway
In this grave world they bowed the knee;
Libertine airs in Elysium say
Mais où sont messieurs les maris?
(1951; 1951)

The Country of the Blind

Hard light bathed them—a whole nation of eyeless men,
Dark bipeds not aware how they were maimed.
A long
Process, clearly, a slow curse,
5 Drained through centuries, left them thus.

At some transitional stage, then, a luckless few,
No doubt, must have had eyes after the up-to-date,
Normal type had achieved snug
Darkness, safe from the guns of heav'n;

10 Whose blind mouths would abuse words that belonged to their
Great-grandsires, unabashed, talking of *light* in some
Eunuch'd, etiolated,
Fungoid sense, as a symbol of

Abstract thoughts. If a man, one that had eyes, a poor
15 Misfit, spoke of the grey dawn or the stars or green-
Sloped sea waves, or admired how
Warm tints change in a lady's cheek,

None complained he had used words from an alien tongue,
No question'd. It was worse. All would agree.
20 "Of course,"
Came their answer. "We've all felt
Just like that." They were wrong. And he

Knew too much to be clear, could not explain. The words—
Sold, raped, flung to the dogs—now could avail no more;
25 Hence silence. But the mouldwarps
With glib confidence, easily

Showed how tricks of the phrase, sheer metaphors could set
Fools concocting a myth, taking the words for things.
Do you think this is a far-fetched
30 Picture? Go then about among

Men now famous; attempt speech on the truths that once,
Opaque, carved in divine forms, irremovable,
Dread but dear as a mountain—
Mass, stood plain to the inward eye.
(1951; 1951)

I Know Far Less of Spiders

I know far less of spiders than that poetess[21]
Who (like the lady in *Comus*[22] in the perilous wood)
Can study nature's infamies with secure heart . . . [23]
(1952; 2006)

Pilgrim's Problem

By now I should be entering on the supreme stage
Of the whole walk, reserved for the late afternoon.
The heat was to be over now; the anxious mountains,
The airless valleys and the sun-baked rocks, behind me.

5 Now, or soon now, if all is well, come the majestic
Rivers of foamless charity that glide beneath
Forests of contemplation. In the grassy clearings

Humility with liquid eyes and damp, cool nose
Should come, half-tame, to eat bread from my hermit hand.
10 If storms arose, then in my tower of fortitude—
It ought to have been in sight by this—I would take refuge;
But I expected rather a pale mackerel sky,
Feather-like, perhaps shaking from a lower cloud
Light drops of silver temperance, and clovery earth
15 Sending up mists of chastity, a country smell,
Till earnest stars blaze out in the established sky
Rigid with justice; the streams audible; my rest secure.

I can see nothing like all this. Was the map wrong?
Maps can be wrong. But the experienced walker knows
20 That the other explanation is more often true.
(1952; 1952)

Travellers! In Months without an R

Travellers! In months without an R
Beware the woods of Wongomar,
For then the resident bumble-bear
Booms all day through the thicket there.
5 Its face is round, as is its rump,
Its tail is a preposterous stump.
Its eyes are shut, its whiskers dense,
It lives on butterscotch and bats
And lines its nest with bowler hats
10 (Arranged in a volmonic plan).[24]
It cannot talk, but thinks it can,
And there it bumbles, there it hums,
It knocks you down: it rubs its eyes
Intending to apologise.
15 But when it sees it's laid you flat
It takes offence and steals your hat.[25]
(1952; 2006)

Interim Report

I merveill much that critiques doe complaine
Of books with scisers and with past compyld;
Certes who weenes this is a lesser payne
Then free invention is sore beguyld!
5 Witness myself who with sic labour vyld
Am oft so dased that I half repent
This great emprise, my fingers all defyld
With slimie stickphast foule and feculent
And deeme Dan Spenser self an easier journie went.[26]
(1952 [?]; 2006)

Vowels and Sirens

Chosen to seduce you,
Those dove-like vowels,
Deuro—kudos—Odusseus.
Opening the bay, his prow

5 Appeared. The air rang with
Sirens' voices.
The hero, bound, in anguish
Tried to retract his choice.

No word of solace
10 For a lover's longing
They breathed. Of vanished knowledge
Was their intemperate song;

Their music resembled
Some earlier music
15 That men are born remembering.
What all the gods refuse—

The backward journey
To the steep river's
High source, the great returning—
20 Those sirens feigned to give.

Cool voices, lying
  Words abuse him,
Cooing kudos Achaiôn,[27]
  Warbling their untrue news.
(1952; 1952)

Impenitence

All the world's wiseacres in arms against them
Shan't detach my heart for a single moment
From the man-like beasts of the earthy stories—
  Badger or Moly.

5 Rat the oarsman, neat Mrs. Tiggy Winkle,
Benjamin, pert Nutkin, or (ages older)
Henryson's shrill Mouse,[28] or the Mice the Frogs once
  Fought with in Homer.

Not that I'm so craz'd as to think the creatures
10 Do behave that way, nor at all deluded
By some half-false sweetness of early childhood
  Sharply remembered.

Look again. Look well at the beasts, the true ones.
Can't you see?. . . . cool primness of cats, or coney's
15 Half indignant stare of amazement, mouse's
  Twinkling adroitness.

Tipsy bear's rotundity, toad's complacence . . .
Why! they all cry out to be used as symbols,
Masks for Man, cartoons, parodies by Nature
20   Formed to reveal us

Each to each, not fiercely but in her gentlest
Vein of household laughter. And if the love so
Raised—it will, no doubt—splashes over on the
  Actual archtypes,

25 Who's the worse for that? Marry, gup! Begone, you
Fusty kill-joys, new Manichæans![29] Here's a

Health to Toad Hall, here's to the Beaver doing
Sums with the Butcher!
(1953; 1953)

March for Drum, Trumpet, and Twenty-one Giants

With stumping stride in pomp and pride
We come to bump and floor ye;
We'll tramp your ramparts down like hay
And crumple castles into clay
5 And, as we ramp and romp and play,
Our trump'll blow before us—
(*cresc.*) Oh trumpet, trumpet (tramp it, tramp it!),
trumpet blow before us!

We'll bend and break and grind and shake
10 And plunder ye and pound ye;
With trundled rock and bludgeon blow,
You dunder-heads, we'll dint ye so
You'll blunder and run blind, as though
By thunder stunn'd, around us—
15 (*ff.*) By thunder, thunder, thunder, thunder, thunder
stunn'd around us.

Oh tremble town and tumble down
And crumble shield and sabre!
Oh skimble-skamble counsels fail
20 And horses stumble and turn tail
And monarchs mumble and grow pale,
But rumble drum belaboured!
(*dim.*) Oh rumble, rumble, rumble, rumble, rumble
drum belaboured!
(1953; 1953)

D. H. Lawrence, Dr. Stopes

D. H. Lawrence, Dr. Stopes,[30]
Taught by you we fix our hopes
On that balmiest of dopes,
  Wholly earthly Luv.

5 Money-making calls for brains,
And of all our hard-won gains
After taxes what remains?
  No one taxes Luv.

Whisky, port, or gin-and-It
10 Harm the liver, sap the wit;
We can take (and yet keep fit)
  Lots and lots of Luv.

All the outdoor games we play
Fail us as years pass away:
15 Even the very old, they say,
  Still can manage Luv.

Even when toothless, blind, and hoar,
Able to perform no more,
Still in thought we fumble o'er
20 Dreams and drams of Luv.

Therefore let each film and book,
Every dinner that we cook,
Every tonic, garment, look,
  Nudge us on to Luv.
(1954; 2001)

Evolutionary Hymn

Lead us, Evolution, lead us
  Up the future's endless stair:
Chop us, change us, prod us, weed us.
  For stagnation is despair:
5 Groping, guessing, yet progressing,
  Lead us nobody knows where.

Wrong or justice in the present,
  Joy or sorrow, what are they
While there's always jam to-morrow,
10   While we tread the onward way?
Never knowing where we're going,
  We can never go astray.

To whatever variation
  Our posterity my turn,
15 Hairy, squashy, or crustacean,
  Bulbous-eyed or square of stern,
Tusked or toothless, mild or ruthless,
  Towards that unknown god we yearn.

Ask not if it's god or devil,
20   Brethren, lest your words imply
Static norms of good and evil
  (As in Plato) throned on high;
Such scholastic, inelastic,
  Abstract yardsticks we deny.

25 Far too long have sages vainly
  Glossed great Nature's simple text;
He who runs can read it plainly,
  "Goodness = what comes next."
By evolving, Life is solving
30   All the questions we perplexed.

On then! Value means survival—
  Value. If our progeny
Spreads and spawns and licks each rival,

That will prove its deity
35 (Far from pleasant, by our present
Standards, though it well may be.)
(1954; 1957)

To Mr. Kingsley Amis on His Late Verses

Why is to fight (if such be our fate)
Less "human" than to copulate,
When Gib the cat, I'll take my oath,
Wins higher marks than you for both?
(1954; 1954)

Ichabod

Brought up to date at last,[31] the English School
Accepts the *March of Progress* as her rule.
What though she has been compell'd to cast away
Some baggage valued in our grandam's day,
5 Pared down the *Middle Ages* to the quick,
Pruned bowery *Spenser* to a leafless stick,
And fobb'd great Milton off with such a share
As once had fall'n to *Hocclave, Hunt,* or *Blair?*[32]
Small is the loss; their works are out of touch
10 With *Life* (i.e., not read at Cambridge much);
Near *Fairy-land* too oft their Fancies stray,
"Breathing a lie through silver" as we say;
Or else their Muse embarrassingly sings
Of truth in Love or Loyalty to Kings,
15 Drags in Religion, praises feats of arms,
And hints a moral most where most she charms.
All this—as every Educator dreads—
Might only put ideas in pupils' heads,
Evoke *Nostalgia* (execrable shape);
20 And tempt to *Deviation* or *Escape.*
'Tis true, our novel programmes may astound
The wearied cab-horse of the weekly round,
The drudging *Tutor* on whose shoulders all
That pupils write or Boards prescribe must fall.

25 Therefore to him the wise decrees of Fate
Gave no preponderant voice nor extra weight;
Superior minds with less contracted views
Help to impose the task he might refuse.
Chair-borne, harmonious Brotherhood! we see
30 The *Professoriate* on Reform agree;
With these, in happy unison, a line
Of *Linguists* unexpectedly combine;
Who but admires the generous zeal they've shown
To sacrifice all subjects save their own?
35 (Their vertue soon may tempt us to a trial
Who can go furthest in in such self-denial).
Others support the scheme whose candid souls
No bias sways, no early love controls,
Detach'd, impartial, uncorrupted, cool,
40 Since they themselves have never read the School.
Thanks to all such! by whose officious aid
A life-time's labour is in ruins laid.
Now, moving with the Times, we must pursue
The record Mileage not the lingering view.
45 Born in an Age of Speed, 'tis Pace we seek;
Cram five, ten, twenty Authours in a week;
See Books and Periods with a Road-Hog's eye
In one continuous Blur go reading by—
Hints give the student all he needs to use
50 In Conversation or in glib Reviews.
Obey, ye Nymphs and Swains! Accept the Mode,
Step on the gas, devour th' affrighted road,
Drive, drive, like Nimshi's son—like mad—like Mr. Toad.[33]
(1954; 2014)

Odora Canum Vis: A defence of certain modern biographers and critics

Come now, don't be too eager to condemn[34]
Our little smut-hounds if they wag their tails
(Or shake like jellies as the tails wag them)
The moment the least whiff of sex assails
5 Their quivering snouts. Such conduct after all,
Though comic, is in them quite natural.

As those who have seen no lions must revere
A bull for Pan's *fortissimo,* or those
Who never tasted wine will value beer
10 Too highly, so the smut-hound, since he knows
Neither God, hunger, thought, nor battle, must
Of course hold disproportioned views on lust.

Of all the Invaders that's the only one
Even he could not escape; so have a heart,
15 Don't tie them or whip them, let them run.
So! Cock your ears, my pretties! Play your part!
The dead are all before you, take your pick.
Fetch! Paid for! Slaver, snuff, defile and lick.
(1954; 1954)

Cradle-song Based on a Theme from Nicolas of Cusa

Sky and stars,[35] sky and stars
Make us feel our prison bars.
(Dream and drowse) Man will try
To get out into the sky,
5 To escape, beyond the air,
From Down and Here to Up and There.

Suppose it done. Up there, outside,
Packed in a steel box we ride
Gazing out to see the vast
10 Heaven-scape rushing past.
Shall we? All that meets the eye
Is familiar; stars and sky.

Points of light with black between
Hang like a painted scene
15 Motionless, no nearer there
Than from Earth; everywhere
Equidistant from our ship.
Heaven has given us the slip.

Hush, my child. Outer space
20 Is a schema, not a place.

(Drowse and dream) where we are
Never can be sky or star.
The centre follows as we fly.
There's no way into the sky.
(1954; 1954)

Spartan Nactus

I am so coarse,[36] the things the poets see
Are obstinately invisible to me.
For twenty years I've stared my level best
To see if evening—any evening—would suggest
5 A patient etherized upon a table,[37]
In vain. I simply wasn't able.
To me each evening looks far more
Like the departure from a crowded yet a silent shore
Of a ship whose freight is everything, leaving behind
10 Gracefully, finally, without farewells, marooned mankind.

Red dawn splashed back from windows facing east
Never, for me, resembles in the least
A chilblain on a cocktail shaker's nose.
Waterfalls don't remind me of torn underclothes,
15 Nor glaciers of tin cans. I've never known
The moon look like a hump-backed crone—
Rather, a prodigy even now
Not naturalized, a riddle blazing in a Cyclops' brow,
Not to be trusted, showing us on what a place
20 We crawl and cling, a planet with no bulwarks, out in space.

Never has the white sun of a winter's day
Struck me as *un crachat d'estaminet.*[38]
I am like that odd man Wordsworth knew, to whom
A primrose was a yellow primrose, one whose doom
25 Retains him always in the class of dunces,
Compelled to offer Stock Responses,
Making the poor best that I can
Of dull things . . . peacocks, honey, the Great Wall, Aldebaran,[39]
Silver streams, cowslip wine, wave on the beach, bright gem,
30 The shape of trees or women, thunder, Troy, Jerusalem.
(1954; 1954)

Dear Dorothy, I'm Puzzling Hard

Dear Dorothy,[40] I'm puzzling hard
What underlies your cryptic card.
Are you the angel? and am I
The figure pointed at? Oh fie!
5 Or do you mean some timely warning
Well suited to Hangover morning?
If so, which allegorical sense
Am I expected to draw thence?
The lady with the mirror might
10 Be luxury and lewd Delight,
Or Venus rising from the foam,
Or (equally) the Church of Rome.
No matter, for I'm certain still
It comes to me with your good will;
15 Which, with my prayer, I send you back—
Madam, your humble servant, Jack.[41]
(1954; 2006)

On Another Theme from Nicolas of Cusa [*De Docta Ignorantia,* III. ix.]

When soul and body feed,[42] one sees
Their differing physiologies.
Firmness of apple, fluted shape
Of celery, or the bloom of grape
5 I grind and mangle as I eat,
Then in dark, salt, internal heat
Obliterate their natures by
The mastering act that makes them I.

But when the soul partakes of good
10 Or truth, which are her savory food,
By a far subtler chemistry
It is not they that change but she,
Who lets them enter with the state
Of conquerors her surrendered gate,
15 Or mirror-like digests their ray
By turning luminous as they.
(1954–55 [?]; 1955)

Legion

Lord, hear my voice; this present voice, I mean,
Not that which may be speaking an hour hence
When pride or pity of self or craving sense
Blunt the mind's edge, now momentarily keen.
5 Do not by show of hands decide between
My factions; condescend to the pretence
That what speaks now is I. In its defence
Dissolve my Lower House and intervene.

Thou wilt not, though we ask it, quite recall
10 Free will, once given. Yet to this moment's choice
Give unfair weight. Hold me to this. Oh strain
A point; use legal fictions. For, if all
My quarrelling selves must bear an equal voice,
Farewell—thou hast created me in vain.
(1955; 1955)

After Aristotle (Ἀρετὰ πολύμοχθε)

Virtue, thou whom men will toil[43]
Seek as their most precious spoil,
Gladly here in Greece for thy
Beauty, Virgin, men will die
5 And will live laborious days
And pass, unwearying, hard assays;
So arch-potent is thy touch
Upon mortal hearts, and such
Thy unfading fruit; by far
10 More esteemed than riches are;
Dearer than, and loved beyond,
Our father kind, our mother fond;
Dearer even that the deep-
Dark eyes of the god of Sleep.

15 Swift as hounds in chase of thee
Leda's twin-born progeny
And Heracles, whom Zeus begot,
To their last hour fainted not;
Following through labours long

20 Thee who mak'st thy lovers strong;
So for thee Achilles and
Aias[44] sought the silent land.

And now of late the nursling of
Atarneus[45] town for thy dear love
25 Thought it not much to throw away
The sunlight of our mortal day.
Therefore all the daughters nine
Of Mnemosyne[46] divine
Beyond the reach of death will raise
30 His name in song, nor from his praise
Disjoin the lauds of Zeus who best
Champions the truth of host to guest
And hallows the fine chords that tie
Friendship indissolubly.
(1956; 1956)

Who Knows if the Isolation, the Compact, the Firm-shaped

Who knows if the isolation, the compact, the firm-shaped
Dividual selving and peculium of blood and breath[47]
(Oh skull-roofed thought, oh rib-caged love!) can be escaped
By such an old, simple expedient as death?

5 How if this were the arena, not the prison? If here,
Focus'd at last, hence conquerable, hand to hand
That Retiarius[48] meets us with his net and spear,
And now's our chance to kill him, on this hot, dry sand?

Here he takes form; elsewhere he's a pervasive poison,
10 Masses compete; each flower is militant; the trees,
Lacking eyes, cannot cool their souls on the horizon;
Sap is dark will that works and neither loves nor sees,

And the grave, though not a fine, is a most private, place;[49]
Two bodies can't (all souls could) occupy all space.[50]
(1956; 2001)

Nan est Doctior Omnibus Puellis

Nan est doctior omnibus puellis,
Formidabilior fera Camilla,
Xanthippe magis impotens loquelae
Audax, garrula, pertinax, proterva,
5 Trux, torva, Eumenidum comes sororum,
Momi filia Zoilique mater,
Scribens horrida, χάϱδαμα βλέπουσα,
Per quam non licet esse neglegentem.[51]
(1956; 2006)

Epanorthosis (for the end of Goethe's *Faust*)

Solids whose shadow lay
Across time, here
(All subterfuge dispelled)
Show hard and clear.
5 Fondled impossibles
Wither outside;
Within, the Wholly Masculine
Confronts his bride.
(1956; 1956)

Experempment

There is a town seated in Bedfordshire
Or somewhere there—it doesn't matter greatly—
Where those who go, not knowing any better,
Can leave that station only if they've luck,
5 Can hope there only for a slow release,
Wander unending, as a nightmare does,
Through grey arcades, dark image of curved time.
I know my train will be a caterpillar.
So Job in ashes spent his misery
10 As I at Bletchley wait for my next train.
(1956; 2014)

Aubade

Somehow it's strange discovering,[52] dear,
That your given body has complete
As any woman's has, those sweet
And private things on which (too many a year)
5 Youth's casual act or more persistent thought
Unwearyingly, wearisomely, wrought;

As if, now raised to wealth, some boy
Who had tossed, and begged for, grimy pennies,
Allowed to bathe wrist-deep in guineas
10 Incredulous arms, should feel amid such joy
Some wonder that even these, so bright, clean, new
Were round and clinked and were a Queen's head too.
(1957; 2014)

Lords Coëval with Creation

Lords coëval with creation,
Seraph, Cherub, Throne and Power,
Pricedom, Virtue, Domination,
Hail the long-awaited hour!
5 Bruised in head, with broken pinion,
Trembling for his old dominion,
See the ancient dragon cower!
For the Prince of Heaven has risen,
Victor, from his shattered prison.

10 Loudly roaring from the regions
Where no sunbeam e'er was shed,
Rise and dance, ye ransomed legions
Of the cold and countless dead!
Gates of adamant are broken,
15 Words of conquering power are spoken
Through the God who died and bled:
Hell lies vacant, spoiled and cheated,
By the Lord of life defeated.

Bear, behemoth, bustard, camel,
20 Warthog, wombat, kangaroo,
Insect, reptile, fish and mammal,
Tree, flower, grass, and lichen too,
Rise and romp and ramp, awaking,
For the age-old curse is breaking.
25 All things shall be made anew;
    Nature's rich rejuvenation
    Follows on Man's liberation.

Eve's and Adam's son and daughter,
Sinful, weary, twisted, mired,
30 Pale with terror, thinned with slaughter,
Robbed of all your hearts desired,
Look! Rejoice! One born of woman,
Flesh and blood and bones all human,
One who wept and could be tired,
35   Risen from the vilest death, has given
    All who will the hope of Heaven.[53]
(1958; 2006)

An Expostulation (Against too many writers of science fiction)

Why did you lure us on like this,
Light-year on light-year, through the abyss,
Building (as though we cared for size!)
Empires that cover galaxies,
5 If at the journey's end we find
The same old stuff we left behind,
Well-worn Tellurian stories of
Crooks, spies, conspirators, or love,
Whose setting might as well have been
10 The Bronx, Montmartre, or Bethnel Green?[54]

Why should I leave this green-floored cell,
Roofed with blue air, in which we dwell,
Unless, outside its guarded gates,
Long, long desired, the Unearthly waits
15 Strangeness that moves us more than fear,
Beauty that stabs with tingling spear,

Or Wonder, laying on one's heart
That finger-tip at which we start
As if some thought too swift and shy
20 For reason's grasp had just gone by?
(1959; 1959)

Oh Doe Not Die

Oh doe not die, says Donne, *for I shall hate*
All women so. How false the sentence rings.
Women? But in a life made desolate
It is the joys once shared that have the stings.

5 To take the old walks alone, or not at all,
To order one pint where I ordered two,
To think of, and then not to make, the small
Time-honoured joke (senseless to all but you);

To laugh (oh, one'll laugh), to talk upon
10 Themes that we talked upon when you were there,
To make some poor pretence of going on,
Be kind to one's old friends, and seem to care,

While no one (O God) through the years will say
The simplest, common word in just your way.
(1960 [?]; 1964)

One Happier Look on Your Kind, Suffering Face

One happier look on your kind, suffering face,
And all my sky is domed with cloudless blue;
Eternal summer in a moment's space
Breathes with sweet air and glows and warms me through.

5 One droop of your dear mouth, one tear of yours,
One gasp of Faith half-strangled by its foe,
And down through a waste world of slag and sewers
And hammering and loud wheels once more I go.

Thus, what old poets told me about love
10 (Tristram's obedience, Isoud's sovereignty . . .)
Turns true in a dread mode I dreamed not of,
—What once I studied, now I learn to be;

Taught, oh how late! in anguish, the response
I might have made with exultation once.
(1960 [?]; 1964)

All This Is Flashy Rhetoric about Loving You

All this is flashy rhetoric about loving you.
I never had a selfless thought since I was born.
I am mercenary and self-seeking through and through:
I want God, you, all friends, merely to serve my turn.

5 Peace, re-assurance, pleasure, are the goals I seek,
I cannot crawl one inch outside my proper skin:
I talk of love—a scholar's parrot may talk Greek—
But, self-imprisoned, always end where I begin.

Only that now you have taught me (but how late) my lack.
10 I see the chasm. And everything you are was making
My heart into a bridge by which I might get back
From exile, and grow man. And now the bridge is breaking.

For this I bless you as the ruin falls. The pains
You give me are more precious than all other gains.
(1960 [?]; 1964)

Epitaph for Helen Joy Davidman

Here the whole world (stars, water, air,
And field, and forest, as they were
Reflected in a single mind)
Like cast off clothes was left behind
5 In ashes yet with hopes that she,
Re-born from holy poverty,
In Lenten lands, hereafter may

Resume them on her Easter Day.
(1960; 1960)

Dear Mr. Marshall, Thank You

Dear Mr. Marshall, thank you for your interesting letter,
I liked your kind remarks to me and liked your verses better.
You caught a glimpse of England and you counted it into rhyme.
But I regret to tell you that you caught it just in time
5 For day by day it vanishes—the woods are going down,
A horrible suburbia is linking town to town.
The narrow, winding roads grow broad and straight, the kindly earth
With contraceptive tarmac is forbidden to give birth;
The sorcerers of chemistry are poisoning the soil,
10 The bays and rivers are defiled with refuse and with oil,
And every day some liberty the subject once enjoyed
By order of the government is stealthily destroyed.[55]
(1963; 2006)

Re-Adjustment

I thought there would be a grave beauty, a sunset splendour
In being the last of one's kind: a topmost moment as one watched
The huge wave curving over Atlantis, the shrouded barge
Turning away with wounded Arthur, or Ilium burning.
5 Now I see that, all along, I was assuming a posterity
Of gentle hearts: someone, however distant in the depths of time,
Who could pick up our signal, who could understand a story. There won't be.
Between the new *Hominidae* and us who are dying, already
There rises a barrier across which no voice can ever carry,
10 For devils are unmaking language. We must let that alone forever.
Uproot your loves, one by one, with care, from the future,
And trusting to no future, receive the massive thrust
And surge of the many-dimensional timeless rays converging
On this small, significant dew drop, the present that mirrors all.
(1963 [?]; 1964)

1. In Greek mythology, the Erinyes, also known as the Furies, were goddesses of vengeance, perhaps three in number. Arising from the underworld, they would punish evildoers, particularly those committing unnatural crimes such as matricide or oathbreaking.

2. Frank Raymond (usually known as F. R.) Leavis (1895–1978) was a British literary critic and Cambridge University professor; he and Lewis had radically different view on the nature and value of literary criticism. Bertrand Arthur William Russell (1872–1970) was an eminent British intellectual, whose wide-ranging pursuits included philosophy, logic, mathematics, education, politics, history, social criticism. His *Why I Am Not a Christian* (1927) is philosophically as far from Lewis's *Mere Christianity* (1952) as Pluto is from the sun.

3. In Greek mythology, Hestia, an Olympian and a daughter of the Titans Cronos and Rhea, was virgin goddess of the hearth, and thus, by extension, of domestic and city life.

4. At the end of the poem Lewis offers this footnote regarding the Lardergods: "*Penates quasi a penu.*" The phrase is Latin for "the Household Gods from the food-storehouse, as it were."

5. This Latin phrase, meaning roughly " kept the house; spun the wool," is the traditional description of the attributes of a good wife used in Roman epitaphs. The proverbial good wife was Lucretia, who is seen at her housework when Sextus Tarquinius and Collatinus, her husband, arrive home unexpectedly (Livy *History of Rome* 1.57).

6. In ancient Greece, a palaestra was a school for sports, notably wrestling.

7. Greek for "hubris" or "arrogant pride."

8. Greek for "modesty" or "shame."

9. This Greek word, *sophrosyne,* means "temperance" or "soundness of mind." In Greek mythology, Sophrosyne was the goddess of temperance and restraint, of self-control, discretion, and harmonious balance.

10. This original version of "A Cliché Came Out of Its Cage" stops here. The following stanza was added when it was revised and published in C. S. Lewis, *Poems* (herafter, *P*), ed. Walter Hooper (New York: Harcourt Brace Jovanovich, 1964), and in *CP:*

Or did you mean another kind of heathenry?
Think, then, that under heaven-roof the little disc of the earth,
Fortified Midgard, lies encircled by the ravening Worm.
Over its icy bastions faces of giant and troll
Look in, ready to invade it. The Wolf, admittedly, is bound;
But the bond will break, the Beast run free. The weary gods,
Scarred with old wounds, the one-eyed Odin, Tyr who has lost a hand,
Will limp to their stations for the last defence. Make it your hope
To be counted worthy on that day to stand beside them;
For the end of man is to partake of their defeat and die
His second, final death in good company. The stupid, strong
Unteachable monsters are certain to be victorious at last,
And every man of decent blood is on the losing side.
Take as your model the tall women with yellow hair in plaits
Who walked back into burning houses to die with men,
Or him who as the death spear entered into his vitals
Made critical comments on its workmanship and aim.

Are these the Pagans you spoke of? Know your betters and crouch, dogs;
You that have Vichy-water in your veins and worship the event,
Your goddess History (whom your fathers called the strumpet Fortune).

11. Throughout this poem, Lewis appears to be alluding to husbands who have been overshadowed by domineering wives.

12. Veuve ("widow") Cliquot Ponsardin is a prestigious French champagne house founded in the eighteenth century and located in Reims. After Monsieur Cliquot died, his widow, Madame Barbe-Nicole Cliquot, née Ponsardin, oversaw the invention of riddling racks to facilitate removal of the lees, an innovation that changed champagne production.

13. Tanqueray is a famous brand of gin.

14. "But where have all the husbands gone?"

15. Samuel Beeton (1830–1877), a British Victorian publisher, is primarily known as the husband of Isabella Beeton (1835–1865), who collected recipes and articles on other aspects of running a household into a book, *The Book of Household Management,* that became enormously popular.

16. This probably refers to the hypothetical husband of Widow Twankey, a female character (played by a man) in the pantomime *Aladdin.* The Widow Twankey is a comic foil to Aladdin, her son, who is always played by an actress.

17. Mrs. Grundy, originally a priggish offstage character in Thomas Morton's eighteenth-century play *Speed the Plough,* has entered English as a term signifying a person of rigid respectability.

18. Samuel Masham was the husband of Abigail Masham (1670–1734) who was a favorite of Queen Anne and a cousin of Sarah Churchill, Duchess of Marlborough. Henri de Sévigné was married to the French intellectual Marie de Rabutin-Chantal, marquise de Sévigné (1626–1696), who was celebrated for her letters, especially those to her daughter. Henri was killed in a duel when Marie was only twenty-four. She never remarried.

19. William Siddons was the husband of Sarah Siddons(1755–1831), a Welsh actress who became famous in London for her Shakespearean roles, particularly her portrayal of Lady Macbeth. The Zebedee mentioned here may be John Zebedee, a character in an 1881 detective story by Wilkie Collins, *Who Killed Zebedee?* In this story, the newly wed Zebedee is murdered, ostensibly by his sleep-walking wife.

20. Mrs. Gamp was a character in Charles Dickens's novel *Martin Chuzzlewit,* a drunken nurse who would lay out the newly dead. About her own husband's laying out, she said: "Ah dear! When Gamp was summoned to his long home, and I see him a-lying in Guy's Hospital with a penny-piece on each eye, and his wooden leg under his left arm, I thought I should have fainted away. But I bore up." The Hemans mentioned here is probably Captain Alfred Hemans, husband of English romantic poet Felicia Dorothea Hemans (1793–1835); Felicia married the much older Alfred at age nineteen, but they separated seven years later, leaving her to raise their five sons alone. They never were together again.

21. This refers to the poet Ruth Pitter (1897–1992).

22. The masque *Comus* was written by John Milton in 1634.

23. For the context of this poem, see Lewis's letter of Apr. 16, 1952, to Ruth Pitter, *CL* 3:183.

24. In heraldry, a vol is a pair of outstretched bird's wings, connected at their shoulders but lacking a bird's body in the middle.

25. For the context of this poem, see Lewis's letter of June 20, 1952, to Genia Goelz, *CL* 3:204–5.

26. For the context of this poem, see Lewis's letter of June 22, 1952?, to William Borst, *CL* 3:206–7. Part of the fun in this poem is that its reference to Edmund Spenser (1552–1599) is underscored by Lewis's use of the Spenserian stanza (*ababbcbcc*).

27. The name Achaiôn, or Achaean, was used by Homer to mean Greeks in general, although later it came to mean specifically residents of the region of Achaea. Here it refers to Odysseus.

28. This refers to the little-known Scottish poet Robert Henryson (1430?–1506?) and his *Morall Fabillis of Esope the Phrygian* (1465?), particularly his *The Taill of the Lyoun and the Mous.*

29. The original Manichæans were followers of a Gnostic religion holding a doctrine of dualism—that everything derives from opposing principles such as good and evil or light and dark. Over time Manichæan became a pejorative name for anyone taking a simplistic stance of moral dualism and disdaining or rejecting the material world as evil. Here Lewis links the idea to those who belittle lovers of animal stories.

30. David Herbert Lawrence (1885–1930) was a celebrated English novelist, arguably the most important of the first third of the twentieth century. His novels, especially *Lady Chatterley's Lover* (1928), dealt frankly with human sexuality. Dr. Marie Stopes (1880–1958) was a leading advocate of birth control in England and played a major role in redefining female sexuality in the first half of the twentieth century.

31. The title of this poem, the Hebrew word *Ichabod,* means "the glory has departed." The occasion of the poem was Lewis's reaction to a proposed revision of the Oxford syllabus.

32. The English poet Thomas Hoccleve (1368?–1450?) was a contemporary and follower of Geoffrey Chaucer. James Henry Leigh Hunt (1784–1859) was a British poet, literary critic, and essayist. The Scottish poet Robert Blair (1699–1746) was known primarily for his long poem in blank verse, *The Grave.*

33. See 2 Kings 9:20 (AV): "And the watchman told, saying, He came even unto them, and cometh not again: and the driving *is* like the driving of Jehu the son of Nimshi; for he driveth furiously." The wealthy, lovable, but vain and irresponsible Mr. Toad—especially known for his reckless driving—is a character in Kenneth Grahame's novel, *The Wind in the Willows* (1908).

34. The title of this poem comes from Virgil's *Aeneid* and means "with keen-scented hunting dogs."

35. Nicholas of Cusa (1401–1464), referred to in this poem's title, was perhaps the most important German thinker of fifteenth century, and an ecclesiastical reformer, administrator, and cardinal.

36. The title of this poem means "Spartan having obtained."

37. This is an ironic allusion to the opening lines of T. S. Eliot's "The Love Song of J. Alfred Prufrock": "Let us go then, you and I, / When the evening is spread out against the sky / Like a patient etherized upon a table."

38. This French phrase means "a spittoon in a poor bar."

39. Aldebaran is the brightest star of the constellation Taurus.

40. Dorothy L. Sayers, the daughter of an Anglican clergyman and herself a Christian, was an English contemporary and friend of Lewis's. She was a scholar, translator, novelist, and poet.

41. For the context of this poem, see Lewis's letter of Dec. 27, 1954, to Dorothy L. Sayers, *CL* 3:548.

42. This poem alludes to Cusa's *De Docta Ignorantia,* "On Learned Ignorance" (1440). See also note 35, above.

43. The Greek phrase in the title may be translated as "won after much toil."

44. Aias was a Greek mythological hero, whose name in Latin translates to Ajax. The king of Salamis, he fought for the Greeks in the Trojan War and only his cousin Achilles surpassed him in strength and courage.

45. Atarneus was an ancient Greek city in what is now Turkey, known mainly as home to the young Aristotle after the death of his parents.

46. In Greek mythology, Mnemosyne was the personification of memory and the mother of the Muses.

47. The term *dividual* means "divided among or shared by several." In ancient Roman law, peculium was property or funds that a father or master allowed his wife, child, or slave to hold as his or her own.

48. In ancient Rome, a retiarius (from *rete,* "net") was a gladiator armed with a net and trident.

49. This is an allusion to lines in "To His Coy Mistress" by Andrew Marvell (1621–1678): "The Grave's a fine and private place, / But none I think do there embrace."

50. For the context of this poem, see Lewis's letter of Apr. 11, 1956, to Kathleen Raine, *CL* 3:734–35.

51. The final line of this poem is a direct quotation of Catullus, Poem 10.34. Following is an English translation of Lewis's poem by Nan Dunbar, found in Andrew Cuneo, "Selected Literary Letters of C. S. Lewis," 92, unpublished dissertation, in the Bodleian Library, Oxford, UK (hereafter, the Bodleian): MS. D.Phil. c. 16354:

> Nan is more learned than all the girls,
> More formidable than fierce Camilla;
> More unable to shut up than Xanthippe,
> Bold, garrulous, obstinate, aggressive,
> Fierce, grim comrade of the sister Furies,
> Momus's daughter, Zoilus's mother,
> Writing alarmingly, with watercress-sharp glare,
> She does not allow you to be careless.

52. An aubade is a morning love song.

53. For the context of this poem, see Lewis's letter of June 10, 1958, to Francis Turner, *CL* 3:955–56.

54. The Bronx is a borough of New York City; Montmartre is a district in north Paris; Bethnel Green is a district in East London.

55. For the context of this poem, see Lewis's letter of Feb. 16, 1963, to Blanchard Marshall, *CL* 3:1411.

Undated Poems

Poems First Published in Poems *(1964)*

The Ecstasy

Long had we crept in cryptic
Delights and doubts on tiptoes,
The air growing purer, clearer
Continually; and nearer
5 We went on to the centre of
The garden, hand in hand, finger on lip.

On right and left uplifted
The fountains rose with swifter
And steadier urgence, argent
10 On steely pillars, larger
Each moment, spreading foamy plumes
Thinner and broader under the blinding sun.

The air grows warmer; firmer
The silence grips it; murmur
15 Of insect buzz nor business
Of squirrel or bird there is not—
Only the fluttering of the butterflies
Above the empty lawns, dance without noise.

So on we fared and forded
20 A brook with lilies bordered,
So cold it wrung with anguish
Bitterly our hearts. But language
Cannot at all make manifest
The quiet centre we found on the other side.

25 Never such seal of silence
Did ice on streams or twilight
On birds impose. The pauses
In nature by her laws are
Imperfect; under the surface beats
30 A sound too constant to be ever observed.

From birth its stroke with equal
Dull rhythm, relentless sequence,
Taps on, unfelt, unaltered,
With beat that never falters—
35 Now known, like breathing, only when
It stopped. The permanent background failed our ear.

Said the voice of the garden, heard in
Our hearts, "That was the burden
Of Time, his sombre drum-beat.
40 Here—oh hard to come by!—
True stillness dwells and will not change,
Never has changed, never begins nor ends."

Who would not stay there, blither
Than memory knows? but either
45 Whisper of pride essayed us
Or meddling thought betrayed us,
Then shuddering doubt—oh suddenly
We were outside, back in the wavering world.

The Saboteuse

Pity hides in the wood,[1]
The years and tides,
The earth, the bare moon,
Death and birth,
5 The freezing skies, the sun
And the populous seas
Against her, one and all,
Are furiously incensed.

They have clashed spears to drown
10 The noise of her tears;
They have whetted swords. Still
They cannot forget.
Her faint noise in the wood
Destroys all,
15 A soul-tormenting treason
Threatening revolt.

They beat with clamorous gongs
  And din with hammers
To stun so light a noise.
20 They fear if once
Pity were heard aloud
  In the strong city,
Topless towers would fall,
  Engines stop.

25 Horribly alarmed, they have levied
  Their war and armed
All natural things against her.
  From horns and stings,
Mandibles, claws and paws
30 And the human hand,
From suns and ice, like a deer
  Pity runs;

Lest, if she wept in peace,
  While they slept,
35 (So they believe) the slow-
  Descending stream
Would grow to a pool, spread,
  Widen and overflow
And creep forth from the wood,
40 Grown strong and deep.

And they would wake at morning
  And find a lake
Lapping against their walls,
  Mining, sapping,
45 Patiently eating away
  The strong foundations
Of the towers of pain, rising
  An inch in an hour;

Till the compassionate water
50 Would ripple and plash
Far overhead, and the Powers
  Lay drowned and dead
Below, sharing the dark

With shark and squid
55 And the forgotten shapes
Of rotting wheels.

Therefore they woke destruction
Against her and invoked
The Needs of the Sum of Things
60 And the Coming Race
And the Claims of Order—oh all
The holiest names
Known in our hearts. They even
Included her own.

Prelude to Space: An Epithalamium

So Man, grown vigorous now,[2]
Holds himself ripe to breed,
Daily devises how
To ejaculate his seed
5 And boldly fertilize
The black womb of the unconsenting skies.

Some now alive expect
(I am told) to see the large,
Steel member grow erect,
10 Turgid with the fierce charge
Of our whole planet's skill,
Courage, wealth, knowledge, concentrated will;

Straining with lust to stamp
Our likeness on the abyss—
15 Bombs, gallows, Belsen camp,
Pox, polio, Thais' kiss
Or Judas,' Moloch's fires
And Torquemada's (sons resemble sires).[3]

Shall we, when the grim shape
20 Roars upward, dance and sing?
Yes: if we honour rape,
If we take pride to fling

So bountifully on space
The sperm of our long woes, our large disgrace.

On a Vulgar Error

No. It's an impudent falsehood. Men did not
Invariably think the newer way
Prosaic, mad, inelegant, or what not.

Was the first pointed arch esteemed a blot
5 Upon the church? Did anybody say
How modern and how ugly? They did not.

Plate-armour, or windows glazed, or verse fire-hot
With rhymes from France, or spices from Cathay,
Were these at first a horror? They were not.

10 If, then, our present arts, laws, houses, food
All set us hankering after yesterday,
Need this be only an archaising mood?

Why, any man whose purse has been let blood
By sharpers, when he finds all drained away
15 Must compare how he stands with how he stood.

If a quack doctor's breezy ineptitude
Has cost me a leg, must I forget straightway
All that I can't do now, all that I could?

So, when our guides unanimously decry
20 The backward glance, I think we can guess why.

Lines During a General Election

Their threats are terrible enough, but we could bear
All that; it is their promises that bring despair.
If beauty, that anomaly, is left us still,
The cause lies in their poverty, not in their will.
5 If they had power ("amenities are bunk"), conceive

How their insatiate gadgetry by this would leave
No green, nor growth, nor quietude, no sap at all
In England from The Land's-End to the Roman Wall.
Think of their roads—broad as the road to Hell—by now
10 Murdering a million acres that demand the plough,
The thick-voiced Tannoy[4] blaring over Arthur's grave,
And all our coasts one Camp till not the tiniest wave
Stole from the beach unburdened with its festal scum
Of cigarette-ends, orange-peel, and chewing-gum.
15 Nor would one island's rape suffice. Their visions are
Global; they mean the desecration of a Star;
Their happiest fancies dwell upon a time when Earth,
Flickering with sky-signs, gibbering with mechanic mirth,
One huge celestial charabanc, will stink and roll
20 Through patient heaven, subtopianized from pole to pole.

You Do Not Love the Bourgeoisie

You do not love the Bourgeoisie. Of course: for they
Begot you, bore you, paid for you, and punched your head;
You work with them; they're intimate as board and bed;
How could you love them, meeting them thus every day?
5 You love the Proletariat, the thin, far-away
Abstraction which resembles any workman fed
On mortal food as closely as the shiny red
Chessknight resembles stallions when they stamp and neigh.

For kicks are dangerous; riding schools are painful, coarse
10 And ribald places. Every way it costs far less
To learn the harmless manage of the wooden horse
—So calculably taking the small jumps of chess.
Who, that can love nonentities, would choose the labour
Of loving the quotidian face and fact, his neighbor?

Dear Roy—Why Should Each Wowzer on the List

Dear Roy[5]—Why should each wowzer on the list [6]
Of those you damn be dubbed Romanticist?
In England the romantic stream flows not

From waterish Rousseau but from manly Scott,[7]
5 A right branch on the old European tree
Of valour, truth, freedom, and courtesy,
A man (though often slap-dash in his art)
Civilized to the centre of his heart,
A man who, old and cheated and in pain,
10 Instead of snivelling, got to work again,
Work without end and without joy, to save
His honour, and go solvent to the grave;
Yet even so, wrung from his failing powers,
One book of his would furnish ten of ours
15 With characters and scenes. The very play
Of mind, I think, is birth-controlled to-day.
It flows, I say, from Scott; from Coleridge too.[8]
A bore? A sponge? A laudanum-addict? True;
Yet Newman[9] in that ruinous master saw
20 One who restored our faculty for awe,
Who re-discovered the soul's depth and height,
Who pricked with needles of the eternal light
An England at that time half numbed to death
With Paley's, Bentham's, Malthus' wintry breath.[10]
25 For this the reigning Leftist cell may be
His enemies, no doubt. But why should we?
Newman said much the same of Wordsworth too.
Now certain critics, far from dear to you,
May also fondle Wordsworth. But who cares?
30 Look at the facts. He's far more ours than theirs;
Or, if we carve him up, then all that's best
Falls to our share—we'll let them take the rest.
By rights the only half they should enjoy
Is the rude, raw, unlicked, North Country boy.

Infatuation

Body and soul most fit for love can best
Withstand it. I am ill, and cannot rest,
Therefore I'm caught. Disease is amorous, health
At love's door has the pass both in and out.
5 Want cannot choose but grub with needy snout
In ravenous dreams, let temperance wait on wealth.

Don't think of her tonight . . . the very strain
Wears the will down; then in she comes by stealth.

How am I made that such a thing can trouble
10 My fancy for a day? Her brain's a bubble,
Her soul, a traveller's tale. Her every thrust
And trick I understand . . . the mould so mean,
And she the thousandth copy, comes between
My thoughts and me . . . unfrank, unfit for trust,
15 Yet ignorant in her cunning, a blind tool,
When nature bids her, labouring as she must.

Back to my book. Read. Read. Don't think upon her,
Where every thought is hatred and dishonour.
I do not love her, like her, wish her well.
20 Is it mere lust? But lust can quench his thirst
In any water; rather, at the first,
There was one moment when I could not tell
The thing she surely is. I stood unarmed
That moment, and the stroke that moment fell.

25 She stood, an image lost as soon as seen,
Like beauty in a vision half-caught between
Two aimless and long-lumbering dreams of night.
The thing I seek for was not anywhere
At any time on earth. That huntress air
30 And morning freshness was not hers by right.
She spoke, she smiled; put out what seemed the flame,
Left me the cold charred sticks, the ashes white.

And from these sprang the dream I dare not chase,
Lest, the long hunt being over, I embrace
35 My shadow. (Furies wait upon that bed)
It plucks me at the elbow . . . "love can reach
That other soul of hers . . . charity teach
Atrophied powers once more to raise the head,
Sweet charity." But she can never learn;
40 And what am I, whose voice should wake the dead?

How could she learn, who never since her birth
Looked out of her desires and saw the earth

Unshadowed by herself. She knows that man
Has whimsies, and will talk, and take concern
45 With wonderings and desires that serve no turn
Of woman. She would ape (for well she can),
The rapt disciple at her need, till mask
Was needless . . . And all ends where it began.

Her holiest moods are gaudy desecrations
50 Of poor half holy things: her exaltations
Are frothed from music, moonlight, wine and dance;
Love is to her a dream of bridal dresses,
Friendship, a tittering hour of girl's caresses,
Virtue, a steady purpose to advance,
55 Honoured, and safe, by the old well-proven roads,
No loophole left to passion or to chance.

I longed last night to make her know the truth
That none of them has told her. Flushed with youth,
Dazed with a half-hour triumph, she held the crowd.
60 She loved the boys that buzzed on her like flies,
She loved the envy in the women's eyes,
Faster she talked. I longed to cry aloud,
"What, has no brother told you yet, with whom
With what, you share the power that makes you proud?"

65 Could she have looked so noble, and no seed
Of spirit in her at all? But mother-greed
Has linked her boy-like splendour to the yoke.
Venus infernal taught such voice and eyes
To bear themselves abroad for merchandise . . .
70 Horrible woman-nature, at one stroke
Making the beauty, bending beauty down
To ruthless tasks, before the spirit awoke.

Thank heaven, though I were meshed and made secure,
Its odds, she'd never have me. I am poor . . .
75 Thank heaven, for if she did, what comes behind!
Can I not see her now, marked with my name,
Among my friends (shame not to hide my shame),
And her glib tongue runs on and rambles blind
Through slippery paths, revealing and revealing,
80 While they for my sake cover it and are kind.

Kind? Let them look at home. Which of them all
Knows how his act or word next hour may fall?
Into them, too, this might have come, unbidden,
Unlooked for. For each one of us, down below
85 The cauldron brews in the dark. We do not know
By whom, or on what fields, we are reined and ridden.
There are not acts; spectators of ourselves
We wait and watch the event, the cause is hidden.

All power in man is mummery: good report
90 A fable: this apparent mind, the sport
For mumbling dynasts old as wind and tide.
Talk, posture, gild it over . . . still the motion
That moves us is not ours, but in the ocean
Of hunger and bleak fear, like buoys we ride,
95 And seem to move ourselves, and in the waves
Lifting and falling take our shame and pride.

Aubade

Eight strokes sound from within. The crowd, assembled
Outside, stare at the gate (it disregards them).
What lure brings them so early, under driving
Smoke-grey cloud with a hint of rain, before their
5 Day's work? Might pity draw them? Was the motive
Self-pleased—say, Pharisaical—delight in
Earth's old *lex talionis?*[11] Easy answers,
Yet both short of the truth perhaps. The sharpest
Cause might be that amid the swirl of phantoms—
10 Film, broadcast, propaganda, picture-thinking—
Death, like cancer or crime or copulation,
Stands out real; and the soul with native hunger
(Called *sensationalism* in cultured circles)
Seeks food ev'n in the dingiest of quarters.
15 I, snugged down in a bed, in warm refinement,
Dare not judge what attraction called and kept them,
Packed thus, waiting an hour or so to see the
Jail's black flag running up between the chimneys.

To Andrew Marvell

Marvell,[12] they say your verse is faint
Beside the range of Donne's;[13]
Too clear for them, too free from taint
Of noise, your music runs.

5 Their sultry minds can ill conceive
How godlike power should dwell
Except where lungs with torment heave
And giant muscles swell.

The better swordsman with a smile
10 His cool *passado*[14] gives;
Smooth is the flooding of the Nile
By which all Egypt lives.

Sweetness and strength from regions far
Withdrawn and strange you bring,
15 And look no stronger than a star,
No graver than the spring.

Lines Written in a Copy of Milton's Work

Alas! the happy beasts at pasture play
All, all alike; all of one mind are they;
By Nature with indifferent kindness blessed,
None loves a special friend beyond the rest;
5 No sparrow lacks a friend with whom to roam
All day for seeds till evening bids them home;
Whom if with cunning beak the cruel kite
Or peasant's arrow snatch from him tonight,
With a new friend next day, content, he wings his flight.
10 Not so is Man, who in his fellows finds
(Hard fate!) discordant souls and alien minds!
To him, though searching long, will scarce be shown
One heart amidst a thousand like his own;
Or if, at last relenting, fate shall send
15 In answer to his prayer, the authentic friend,
Him in some unsuspected hour, some day

He never dreaded, Death will snatch away
And leave behind a loss that time can ne'er allay.

Who now can charm to rest each eating care?
20 Who now the secrets of my bosom share?
Who now can while away with the delight
Of his discourse the livelong winter night,
When cracking nuts and hissing apples roast
Upon the hearth and from his southern coast
25 The wet wind in the elm-tree branches roars
And makes one vast confusion out of doors?

Alone I walk the fields and plains, alone
The dark vales with dense branches overgrown.
Here, as day fades, I wait, and all around
30 I hear the rain that falls with sullen sound.

Through Our Lives Thy Meshes Run

Through our lives thy meshes run
Deft as spiders' catenation,
Crossed and crossed again and spun
Finer than the fiend's temptation.

5 Greed into herself would turn
All that's sweet: but let her follow
Still that path, and greed will learn
How the whole world is hers to swallow.

Sloth that would find out a bed
10 Blind to morning, deaf to waking,
Shuffling shall at last be led
To the peace that knows no breaking.

Lechery, that feels sharp lust
Sharper from each promised staying,
15 Goes at long last—go she must—
Where alone is sure allaying.

Anger, postulating still
Inexcusables to shatter,
From the shelter of thy will
20 Finds herself her proper matter.

Envy had rather die than see
Other's course her own outflying;
She will pay with death to be
Where her Best brooks no denying.

25 Pride, that from each step, anew
Mounts again with mad aspiring,
Must find all at last, save you,
Set too low for her desiring.

Avarice, while she finds an end,
30 Counts but small the largest treasure.
Whimperingly at last she'll bend
To take free what has no measure.

So inexorably thou
On thy shattered foes pursuing,
35 Never a respite dost allow
Save what works their own undoing.

Such Natural Love Twixt Beast and Man

Such natural love twixt beast and man we find
That children all desire an animal book,
And all brutes, not perverted from their kind,
Woo us with whinny, tongue, tail, song, or look:
5 So much of Eden's courtesy yet remains.
But when a creature's dread, or mine, has built
A wall between, I think I feel the pains
That Adam earned and do confess my guilt.
For till I tame sly fox and timorous hare
10 And lording lion in my self, no peace
Can be without; but after, I shall dare
Uncage the shadowy zoo and war will cease;
Because the brutes within, I do not doubt,
Are archetypal of the brutes without.

When the Grape of the Night Is Pressed

When the grape of the night is pressed
Nearly dry, and the trains rest
And roads are empty and the moon low,
Out of my body's breast I go,
5 Insecure, as a child escaped,
Animula[15] flittering in the night unshaped;
Lacking wings; but I leap so high
It wants but a little more to fly.
Down I swoop with a seven-league stride
10 From church's spire to river side,
There scarce touching the ground, and then
Up to the elm-tree tops again;
Rising higher each leap and still
Sinking lower again, until
15 Lured to venture at last too much
I dream of flying indeed—no touch
Of earth between; then, holding breath
I poise on a perilous edge. But faith
All goes out of my soul—too late!
20 Air is emptiness: man has weight.
Unsupported I drop like lead
To where my body awakes in bed
Screaming-scared—and yet glad, as one
Who, after vain pretence, has done
25 With keeping company too great
For his lean purse and low estate.

Till Your Alchemic Beams Turn All to Gold

Till your alchemic beams turn all to gold
There must be many metals. From the night
You will not yet withdraw her silver light,
And often with Saturnian tints the cold
5 Atlantic swells at morning shall enfold
The Cornish cliffs burnished with copper bright;
Till trained by slow degrees we have such sight
As dares the pure projection to behold.
Even when Sol comes ascendant, it may be

10 More perfectly in him our eyes shall see
All baser virtues; thus shall hear you talking
And yet not die. Till then, you have left free,
Unscorched by your own noon's intensity
One cool and evening hour for garden walking.

These Faint Wavering Far-travell'd Gleams

These faint wavering far-travell'd gleams
Coming from your country, fill me with care. That scent,
That sweet stabbing, as at the song of thrush,
That leap of the heart—too like they seem
5 To another air; unlike as well
So that I am dazed with doubt. As a dungeoned man
Who has heard the hinge on the hook turning
Often. Always that opened door
Let new tormentors in. If now at last
10 It open again, but outward, offering free way,
(His kind one come, with comfort) he
Yet shrinks, in his straw, struggling backward,
From his dear, from his door, into the dark'st corner,
Furthest from freedom. So fearing, I
15 Taste not but with trembling. I was tricked before.
All the heraldry of heaven, holy monsters,
With hazardous and dim half-likeness taunt
Long-haunted men. The like is not the same.
Always evil was an ape. I know.
20 Who passes to paradise, within that pure border
Finds there, refashioned, all that he fled from here.
And yet . . .
But what's the use? For yield I must,
Though long delayed, at last must dare
25 To give over, to be eased of my iron casing,
Molten at thy melody, as men of snow
In the solar smile. Slow-paced I come,
Yielding by inches. And yet, oh Lord, and yet,
—Oh Lord, let not likeness fool me again.

The Phoenix Flew into My Garden

The Phoenix flew into my garden and stood perched upon
  A sycamore; the feathered flame with dazzling eyes
Lit up the whole lawn like a bonfire on midsummer's eve.
  I ran out, slipping on the grass, reeling beneath
5 The news I bore: "The Sole Bird is not fabulous! Look! Look!"
  The dark girl, passing in the road, heard me. Her eyes
Lit up (I saw her features flood-lit in those golden rays)
  So that I called, or else the Bird called, and we went
Over the wet lawn—shadows for our train—towards the Wonder.
10 Then, looking round, I saw her eyes . . . could it be true?
Was I deceived? . . . oh, say I was deceived . . . I thought her eyes
  Had all along been fixed on me, not on the Bird.

Thrice-honoured Lady, make not of your spoon your meat, for silver
  (How much less, tin or wood?) contains no nourishment.
15 I will be all things, any thing, to you, save only that.
  Break not our hearts by telling me you never saw
The Phoenix, that my trumpery silhouette, thrusting between,
  Made an eclipse. For I had dreamed that I had caught
For His own beak a silver, shining fish such as He loves,
20 And, having little of my own to offer Him,
Was building much on this miraculous draught. If the line breaks,
  Oh with what empty hands you send me back to Him!

The Nativity

Among the oxen (like an ox I'm slow)
I see a glory in the stable grow
Which, with the ox's dullness might at length
    Give me an ox's strength.

5 Among the asses (stubborn I as they)
I see my Saviour where I looked for hay;
So may my beastlike folly learn at least
    The patience of a beast.

Among the sheep (I like a sheep have strayed)
10 I watch the manger where my Lord is laid;

Oh that my baa-ing nature would win thence
    Some woolly innocence!

Love's as Warm as Tears

Love's as warm as tears,
    Love is tears:
Pressure within the brain,
Tension at the throat,
5 Deluge, weeks of rain,
Haystacks afloat,
Featureless seas between
Hedges, where once was green.

Love's as fierce as fire,
10   Love is fire:
All sorts—infernal heat
Clinkered with greed and pride,
Lyric desire, sharp-sweet,
Laughing, even when denied,
15 And that empyreal flame
Whence all loves came.

Love's as fresh as spring,
    Love is spring:
Bird-song hung in the air,
20 Cool smells in a wood,
Whispering "Dare! Dare!"
To sap, to blood,
Telling "Ease, safety, rest,
Are good; not best."

25 Love's as hard as nails,
    Love is nails:
Blunt, thick, hammered through
The medial nerves of One
Who, having made us, knew
30 The thing He had done,
Seeing (with all that is)
Our cross, and His.

Yes, You Are Always Everywhere

Yes, you are always everywhere. But I,
Hunting in such immeasurable forests,
Could never bring the noble Hart to bay.

The scent was too perplexing for my hounds;
5 Nowhere sometimes, then again everywhere.
Other scents, too, seemed to them almost the same.

Therefore I turn my back on the unapproachable
Stars and horizons and all musical sounds,
Poetry itself, and the winding stair of thought.

10 Leaving the forests where you are pursued in vain
—Often a mere white gleam—I turn instead
To the appointed place where you pursue.

Not in Nature, not even in Man, but in one
Particular Man, with a date, so tall, weighing
15 So much, talking Aramaic, having learned a trade;

Not in all food, not in all bread and wine
(Not, I mean, as my littleness requires)
But this wine, this bread . . . no beauty we could desire.

Stephen to Lazarus

But was I the first martyr,[16] who
Gave up no more than life, while you,
Already free among the dead,
Your rags stripped off, your fetters shed,
5 Surrendered what all other men
Irrevocably keep, and when
Your battered ship at anchor lay
Seemingly safe in the dark bay
No ripple stirs, obediently
10 Put out a second time to sea
Well knowing that your death (in vain
Died once) must all be died again?

Five Sonnets

1

You think that we who do not shout and shake
Our fists at God when youth or bravery die
Have colder blood or hearts less apt to ache
Than yours who rail. I know you do. Yet why?
5 You have what sorrow always longs to find,
Someone to blame, some enemy in chief;
Anger's the anaesthetic of the mind,
It does men good, it fumes away their grief.
We feel the stroke like you; so far our fate
10 Is equal. After that, for us begin
Half-hopeless labours, learning not to hate,
And then to want, and then (perhaps) to win
A high, unearthly comfort, angel's food,
That seems at first mockery to flesh and blood.

2

There's a repose, a safety (even a taste
Of something like revenge?) in fixed despair
Which we're forbidden. We have to rise with haste
And start to climb what seems a crazy stair.
5 Our consolation (for we are consoled,
So much of us, I mean, as may be left
After the dreadful process has unrolled)
For one bereavement makes us more bereft.
It asks for all we have, to the last shred;
10 Read Dante, who had known its best and worst—
He was bereaved and he was comforted
—No one denies it, comforted—but first
Down to the frozen centre, up the vast
Mountain of pain, from world to world, he passed.

3

Of this we're certain; no one who dared knock
At heaven's door for earthly comfort found
Even a door—only smooth, endless rock,
And save the echo of his cry no sound.
5 It's dangerous to listen; you'll begin
To fancy that those echoes (hope can play

Pitiful tricks) are answers from within;
Far better to turn, grimly sane, away.
Heaven cannot thus, Earth cannot ever, give
10 The thing we want. We ask what isn't there
And by our asking water and make live
That very part of love which must despair
And die and go down cold into the earth
Before there's talk of springtime and re-birth.

4

Pitch your demands heaven-high and they'll be met.
Ask for the Morning Star and take (thrown in)
Your earthly love. Why, yes; but how to set
One's foot on the first rung, how to begin?
5 The silence of one voice upon our ears
Beats like the waves; the coloured morning seems
A lying brag; the face we loved appears
Fainter each night, or ghastlier, in our dreams.
"That long way round which Dante trod was meant
10 For mighty saints and mystics not for me,"
So Nature cries. Yet if we once assent
To Nature's voice, we shall be like the bee
That booms against the window-pane for hours
Thinking that way to reach the laden flowers.

5

"If we could speak to her," my doctor said,
"And told her, 'Not that way! All, all in vain
You weary out your wings and bruise your head,'
Might she not answer, buzzing at the pane,
5 'Let queens and mystics and religious bees
Talk of such inconceivables as glass;
The blunt lay worker flies at what she sees,
Look there—ahead, ahead—the flowers, the grass!'
We catch her in a handkerchief (who knows
10 What rage she feels, what terror, what despair?)
And shake her out—and gaily out she goes
Where quivering flowers stand thick in summer air,
To drink their hearts. But left to her own will
She would have died upon the window-sill."

Now that Night Is Creeping

Now that night is creeping
O'er our travail'd senses,
To Thy care unsleeping
We commit our sleep.
5 Nature for a season
Conquers our defences,
But th' eternal Reason
Watch and ward will keep.

All the soul we render
10 Back to Thee completely,
Trusting Thou wilt tend her
Through the deathlike hours,
And all night remake her
To Thy likeness sweetly,
15 Then with dawn awake her
And give back her powers.

Slumber's less uncertain
Brother soon will bind us
—Darker falls the curtain,
20 Stifling-close 'tis drawn:
But amidst that prison
Still Thy voice can find us,
And, as Thou has risen,
Raise us in Thy dawn.

Lady, to This Fair Breast I Know but One

Lady, to this fair breast I know but one
Fair rival; to the heart beneath it, none.

Have You Not Seen that in Our Days

Have you not seen that in our days
Of any whose story, song, or art
Delights us, our sincerest praise
Means, when all's said, "You break my heart?"

Strange that a Trick of Light and Shade Could Look

Strange that a trick of light and shade could look
So like a living form that, first, I gave
The shadow mind and meaning; then, mistook
His will for mine; and, last, became his slave.

If We Had Remembered

If we had remembered earlier our Father's house
Where we grew together, and that old kindness,
You would not now be dying, oh my sister, my spouse,
Pierced with my sword in the battle's heat and the blindness.

Spirit? Who Names Her Lies

. . . Spirit? Who names her lies.
Who cares for a bodiless ghost without any eyes
Or feet to run with at all, or ear for the call
Of the rushing rain, and the crack of the opening skies?
5 But I'd have a body, a bird's fleet body that flies.

All Things

All things (e.g. a camel's journey through
A needle's eye) are possible, it's true.
But picture how the camel feels, squeezed out
In one long bloody thread from tail to snout.

Lady, a Better Sculptor Far

Lady, a better sculptor far
Chiseled those curves you smudge and mar,
And God did more than lipstick can
To justify your mouth to man.

Erected by Her Sorrowing Brothers

Erected by her sorrowing brothers
In memory of Martha Clay.
Here lies one who lived for others;
Now she has peace. And so have they.

Here Lies One Kind of Speech

Here lies one kind of speech
That in the unerring hour when each
Idle syllable must be
Weighed upon the balance, she,
5 Though puzzled and ashamed, I think,
To watch the scales of thousands sink,
Will see with her old woodland air
(That startled, yet unflinching stare,
Half elf, have squirrel, all surprise)
10 Hers quiver and demurely rise.

Other Undated Poems

An Age Will Come

1. A possible metre:

An age will come
 When England has no trees;
Her plains be dumb
 In loudest breeze,
5 No nymphs shall hide
 In the discovered land.
The arboricide
 Rules from sand to sand.
Andred is down,
10 Sherwood is laid low,
Bare cliffs frown
 Where Dean was used to grow.
Gone is Arden,
 Now no squirrel
15 When the nuts harden
 Hoards in Wirrall;
The heather blue
 Now feels the wind alone
Where trees once grew
20 In Caledon.[17]

2. The same metre with the internal rhyme removed and so spelled that you can imagine it has final–e:

An age schal come when Englonde hath no trees,
His playnes be stille in lowdesta breeze
Ne goddesse hyde in þe discouerd lande
The cruell aire rules from sande to sande.
5 Andred is slayne, Sherewode is layd lowe
Bare cleves are wher Dene did use to growe.
Gone is Ardene, now no squirrele
Whan þe nottes waxen stoores in wirrele
Þise herbes so blewe now ranketh al alone
10 Wher trees did stonde in Caledon.

3. The same as we might read it edited into the appearance of decasyllables:

An age schal cum when Englonde hath no trees

His playnës [schal] be stille in lowdeste breeze,
Ne goddesse hyde in þe discouerd lande
The cruell aire ruleth from sand to sande.
5 Andred is slayne [and] Sherwoode is layd lowe.
Bare clevës are wher Dene did use to growe:
[Y-]gone is Ardenë, now no squirrele
When nottës waxen stooreth in Wirrele,
Þise herbës blewë ranketh al alone
10 Wher [herde] trees did stonde in Caledon.
(2014)

As Long as Rolling Wheels Rotate

As long as rolling wheels rotate
Each on its fixèd Havender,
Or gray-haired colonels gravitate
Towards their favorite Clavender,
5 So long my lyre will celebrate
O'er every other Pavender
The Lamb where lodged of late
—*Of late.* Aye, there's the Ravender!
Its form will spring immaculate
10 From Memory's washing-Tavender,
As fresh and sweet as snowy sheet
That long hath lain in Lub.
(2014)

But in All Dialects

But in all dialects save Wessex
Long ĒA's, mutated, turned to Ē's: ex-
amples, wessex HIERAN : HERAN
Elsewhere: instead of CIERAN, CERAN.
(2001)

Fidelia Vulnera Amantis

Two wings upbear the eternal shadow's flight;[18]
One whirs us into sleep, the other wakes,
One steals with downy theft, one heavily breaks
Our hearts. And *False Security* the right
5 Is called; but the sinister *Gloating Fright*,
Which evil first for power, then power mistakes
For greatness, and in shuddering worship slakes
Masochist thirst at the fat dugs of night.

How often I have been the fool of the first,
10 Strutting heroics where the true brave durst
No battle, you well know. Let it not stand
For insolence if I too show the curs'd
Black-vaulted wave behind you, ripe to burst;
For faithful are the wounds of a friend's hand.
(2014)

Finchley Avenue

We're proud of Finchley Avenue; it's quiet there,
High up and residential and in wholesome air,
With views out over London, and both straight and wide,
Shaded with copper beeches upon either side
5 Growing in grass, and corporation seats between.
There, as you walk, the houses can be hardly seen;
Such living walls of laurel and of privet stand,
Or sometimes rhododendron, upon either hand,
And once a wooden paling; and, above all these,
10 The amateurs and idlers of the world of trees—
Acacia and laburnum or such coloured things
As buzz and trill with birdsong and with insect wings.
Or else there may be banks of grass that steeply climb
Up to the hedge—reminders of the vanished time
15 When between fields this roadway ran of old the same
Straight course, and farmers called it by some different name.
Even at the wooden gates if you look in you see
But little, for the drives are twisted cunningly.
A gravelled sweep, a shrubbery, a slope of grass,

20 A gable-end, is all they show you as you pass.
But you and I are privileged and, if we please,
May enter. We were cradled in such homes as these.
Dating from nineteen-hundred or from nineteen-six,
They are steep-roofed, unstuccoed, and reveal their bricks;
25 By now they are out of fashion, and their very shape
And Tudorish graces damned with the black word Escape;
The bird-bath and the rockery and the garden seat
Scorned as a craven bourgeoisie's unearned retreat,
Whose privacy confesses a dim sense of guilt;
30 But all that looked so different when they were built!
These are your true antiquities. That garden lawn
Is the primordial fountain out of which was drawn
All you have since imagined of the lawn where stood
Eve's apple tree, or of the lands before the flood.
35 That little clump of trees (for it looks little now)
Is your original forest and has taught you how
To think of the great wilderness where trees go on
For ever after trees up the wild Amazon.
In that suburban attic with its gurgling sound
40 Of water pipes, in such a quiet house, you found
In early days the relics of still earlier days,
Forgotten trumpery worn to act forgotten plays,
Old books, then first remembered, calling up the past
Which then, as now, was infinitely sweet and vast.
45 There first you felt the wonder of deep time, the joy
And dread of Schliemann standing on the grave of Troy.[19]
The Avenue is full of life from nine till ten;
The owners of these houses are all hurrying then
To catch their trains. They catch them, and when these are gone,
50 By ones and twos the tradesmen in their vans come on;
The bread-man and the butcher and the man from Gee's
Who brings you soap and Rinso and a pound of cheese.
But even these come rarely after twelve, and soon
We sink to the dead silence of the afternoon.
55 No countryside can offer so much solitude.
I have known the world less lonely in a winter wood,
For there you hear the striking of a village clock
Each hour, or the faint crowing of a distant cock.
But here is nothing. Nobody goes past. No feet
60 But mine. I doubt if anyone has used this seat,

Here in the shade, save only me. And here I sit
And drink the unbroken silence and reflect on it.
    What do they do? Their families have all gone hence,
Grown up. The whole long avenue exhales the sense
65 Of absent husbands, housework done, uncharted hours . . .
Is it a painful emptiness that dully lowers
Over unhappy women—or a blessed state
Of truancy wherein they darkly celebrate
Rites of some *Bona Dea*[20] which no man may see?
70 I am sure they are all virtuous, yet it seems to me
Almost an eerie rashness to possess a wife
And house that go on living with their different life,
Forever inaccessible to us, all day;
For, as we knew in childhood, if the fathers stay
75 At home by chance, that whole day takes a different tone,
Better, or worse, it may be; but unlike its own.
(1986)

Go Litel Tugge upon thes Watres Shene

Go litel tugge upon thes watres shene [21]
To see thes shipmen and his wise werkes,
Go Alisaundre and lady Maudalene,
Don Barfield and the maister of his clerkes
5 That of his countenaunce spruce and derke is!
O boisterous Tames lay adoun the rage
Till we be comen hoom from thilk vyage![22]
(2014)

If with Posterity Good Fame

If with posterity good fame
I cannot have, then let my name
Become at least a friendly joke
That where men congregate to smoke
5 My bathos and my rimes absurd
With laughter may be sometime heard
But with a friendly feeling still
For where they laugh they'll think no ill.

With Bozzy, Bavius, Blackmore be
10 Room for the Vorticists and me.[23]
For tho long dead I'll love the earth
And have no shame to mend their mirth.
(2001)

Laertes to Napoleon

Oh all day long wave out the banners.
My ears are full of roaring guns,
The culverin cracks the eldritch spanners
And both are tight—are these the ones

5 That later, when night turns the heaven
Sweep far out from the shore? Then lo,
The corslet eased, unstrapped the sweven,[24]
And the aftermath one lubric glow.[25]
(2001)

Lines to Mr. Compton Mackenzie

Good heavens, Sir, will you condemn us[26]
To talk of Rōmulus and Rĕmus[27]
And Vĕnus—or perhaps Wĕnoos?
Each language has its native use,
5 And words like Sāturn are abōm-
inable here, if nòt at Rome.
Man, were you never taught at school
The genuinely English rule?
Antepenultimatis[28] with us
10 For the most part are shortened. Thus
Crīme, crĭminal, and *rāre,* but *rărity*
(It rhymes in Thomas Hood with *charity*)[29]
It's English, which you claim to love,
You're mangling in the interests of
15 A long-dead alien form of speech.
Learn your own tongue before you teach,
And leave us meanwhile for our share
"The freedom of oure ain vulgaire."[30]
(1998)

Of This Great Suit Who Dares Foresee the End?

Of this great suit who dares foresee the end?
Perhaps, when the Bench speaks, praise will be mine
For having held my post while sage and friend
And all went straggling towards the opposer's line;

5 Perhaps in his just notes it stands appointed
Already, though the black cap and the frown
Delay, that having mocked the heaven's anointed,
Depth below depth, self-judged, I must sink down;

Either shall but write large what stood before
10 In cursive on my front. Placed high or low,
I must not glory nor complain, no more
Than streams that to their proper levels go.

Which way the Judge sums up, let that be best,
For only in his will can either rest.[31]
(2014)

That Was an Ugly Age

That was an ugly age. There was a wind rising
Black enough to blow out all the lamps of the world,
Loud enough to roar down both the dance tune and the hymn.
Goths were coming. It was the beginning of the end.
5 They pulled Rome out from the castle of cards
Which history had been building. The whole thing collapsed,
Athens, Cnossus, Mycenae, immemorial Khan
Ur and Babylon. It was the very end.
(2001)

The Goodly Fair

The goodly fair
    In the temple yonder—
I saw her there.
    It made me wonder
5 How God above
    With His wisdom all
Could make my love
    So celestial,
So like a dream
10 On earth to appear;
For with the beaming
    Of her eyes so clear,
I am for-wounded
    Even to the heart
15 That from my death
    Away I cannot start.
(2014)

To Mrs. Dyson, Angrie

These inky firmaments and flaws of rain,[32]
The wet weed swaying on the fallows dun,
How falsely our philosophers explain!
These neither spot i' the sun
5 Nor anticyclone from the western main
Hath made to be. No! with unkindly charm
The mortal *Pearl* such mischief hath us done,[33]
Choosing to "arme
Those lookes, the heav'n of mildnesse with Disdain."[34]
10 Since, lady, in your face
Daunger the giant hath meek *Pity* slain,
Mist drapes our woods and gusts of anger chace
Leaves (like our hearts) from every rivelled tree.
Yet, sure, in such a gentle heart a place
15 For mercy too should be.
If but the power were equal to the will,
I would speed hence, a suppliant, to your bowers;

Scarce would I stay to fill
Some pearly chariot with dim Syrian flowers,
20 To gild for such a progress the pale horns
Of some poor ten or twenty unicorns,
—To harness some thrice happy hippogriff,[35]
—To load with gifts of frankincense the hands
Of seven dusky legions, if—sad if—
25 (There is no other rhyme for hippogriff)
Power jumped with will. But jealous fate withstands.
So to your queenly self, so to your lord
(If such a style accord
With any mortal; as great Venus' groom,
30 Anchises old,[36] tho' declined to the tomb
Was honoured for the sea-born goddess sake)
Excuse your slave, for even the humblest take
Free pardon from necessity; and make,
Smiling, our autumn skies put off their gloom.
(1998)

Tu Silentia Perosus

Tu silentia perosus
Mea? Tu qui otiosus,
Vacuus ad omnes horas,
Sauerkrautias devoras.
5 Et, cervisus amaris
Delectatus, evagaris,
Expers omnium laborum.
Per popinas barbarorum?
At me tristis influenza
10 (Declinatur quasi Mensa)
Angit, exoletis nervis:
Me pupillorum catervis
Mane tenant relegatum
Durae leges et stipatum;
15 Deinde, dum per sociorum
Vagor hortum nuper, florum
Captus cum amoenitate.
Stupidus securitate,

Limen horte transituro
20 Mihi, maximo et duro
Portae pondere pertundo
Digitum, cruorque fundo
Herbas multum per novellas,
Edo luridas querellas,
25 Blasphematico errore
Aves fugo cum terrore—
"Non innoxia" (ut Maro
Dixit) "verba," ore amaro.
Hinc, cum opus, cumque morbus
30 Ne tenant, musarum orbus
Quid scribam: Tu peregrine,
Anthroposophe, divine
Tu poeta, oughtas writere
Letteras quae quenunt dilightere.[37]
(2014)

YAH!

YAH !
"When Banquo saw the witches he remarked,[38]
"What rhubarb, senna, or purgative drug
has spoiled my reason?"

5 You will laugh when I tell you that I
read yours *twice*, much mystified, before
I saw what it was.[39]
(2001)

Notes

The poems in this chapter comprise those for which no date of composition is known. Those in the first section were all published for the first time in 1964 in C. S. Lewis, *Poems.* The dates following those in the second section are their dates of first publication, if any.

1. In the title of this poem, *saboteuse* is the feminine form of *saboteur.*

2. An epithalamium is a poem written for a bride on her way to the marital chamber.

3. Belsen (or Bergen-Belsen), located in northwestern Germany, was one of the most horrific of the Nazi concentration camps of World War II. Thais was a Greek courtesan, the lover of Ptolemy, who is held to have encouraged Alexander the Great to burn the palace at Persepolis in the fourth century B.C. In the Bible, Moloch was a god of the Canaanites, to whom children were sacrificed by being burned alive. Tomás de Torquemada (1420–1498), a Dominican prior who became confessor to Spain's monarchs, Ferdinand II and Isabella, was appointed first Grand Inquisitor of the Inquisition, a tribunal set up to enforce conformity to a "purified" Catholicism. His use of torture and burning of heretics has linked his name with religious bigotry and fanaticism.

4. A Tannoy is a loudspeaker for public addresses.

5. This refers to South African poet Ignatius Roy Dunnachie Campbell (1901–1957). For more on him, see note 12 to the poem "To Mr. Roy Campbell" in the chapter entitled "Poems 1935–1949."

6. A wowzer is a puritanical enthusiast or fanatic.

7. Jean-Jacques Rousseau (1712–1778) was a French philosopher. Walter Scott (1771–1832) was a Scottish poet and novelist.

8. Samuel Taylor Coleridge (1772–1834) was an English critic and poet.

9. John Henry Newman (1801–1890) was the most important religious leader of Victorian England. Initially a High Church Anglican clergyman, he later converted to Catholicism and became a cardinal.

10. William Paley (1743–1805) was an English Anglican clergyman and theologian and a proponent of utilitarianism. The English philosopher and social reformer Jeremy Bentham (1748–1832) was the founder of modern utilitarianism. Thomas Robert Malthus (1766–1834), a Cambridge graduate and scholar of political economy, was the author of the influential "Essay on the Principle of Population," which contended that human population growth would invariably be checked by disease and famine.

11. The principle or law of retaliation.

12. Andrew Marvell (1621–1678) was an English metaphysical poet, a satirist, and a member of Parliament. He was also a friend of John Milton.

13. John Donne (1572–1631), like Marvell a generation later, was an English metaphysical poet, a satirist, and a member of Parliament. Despite being raised Catholic, he became an Anglican clergyman in later life.

14. In fencing, a *passado* is a forward thrust with the weapon while advancing with one foot.

15. The Latin word *animula,* literally "little life," means "a small soul or spirit."

16. In the Bible, see Acts 7 and John 11.

17. The place-names in this poem are those of ancient forests in the British Isles. Andred, or Andredes weald, the Saxon name for "the forest of Andred," is an ancient area in southeastern England now known merely as the Weald, once thickly forested. The royal forest of Sherwood,

in the southwestern county of Nottinghamshire, is reputed to have been the refuge of Robin Hood. The forest of Dean, in Gloucestershire in southwestern England, is an ancient area of mixed woodland that served as a royal hunting reserve in the Tudor era and a source of timber in the age of sail. The Forest of Arden, once located in the central county of Warwickshire and mentioned by Shakespeare in *As You Like It*, has virtually disappeared, although scattered ancient trees remain. The Wirrall (from Saxon words for "myrtle" and "corner" or "slope"), is a small peninsula in Cheshire and Merseyside in northwestern England, bounded on three sides by the rivers Mersey and Dee and the Irish Sea. Lewis uses Caledon as a shortened form of Caledonian Forest, the name of a forest covering much of Scotland's southern uplands in the Roman era; one medieval history claims that the legendary King Arthur fought a battle there.

18. This poem, whose Latin title means "Faithful are the wounds of one who loves," appears in an unpublished and undated letter to Owen Barfield; title translation by A. J. Reyes. See Bibliography of Poem Sources for more on sources.

19. Heinrich Schliemann (1822–1890) was the German archaeologist whose excavations at the archeological site of at Hisarlik, Turkey, in 1871 confirmed the theory, put forward by Charles Maclaren in 1822, that it was the site of ancient Troy.

20. In ancient Roman religion, *Bona Dea*—the Good Goddess—was associated with chastity in women and with fruitfulness both in humans and in nature generally.

21. In using the phrase "Go litel tugge" Lewis may be making a playful nod in the direction of the many writers who have used the "Go little book" motif, including, perhaps most famously, Geoffrey Chaucer, who wrote at the end of *Troilus and Criseyde*: "Go, little book, go, little myn tragedye, / Ther God thy makere yet, er that he dye, / So sende might to make in some comedye! / But little book, no making thou n'envie, / But subgit be to alle poesye." The references to Alisaundre and Maudalene are probably to Barfield's son, Alexander, and wife, Maud.

22. This poem appears in an unpublished and undated letter to Owen Barfield. See Bibliography of Poem Sources for more on sources.

23. Bozzy was the nickname given the eighteenth-century Scottish writer and lawyer James Boswell (1740–1795) by Samuel Johnson, whom he immortalized in his famous biography. Boswell also remains known for his frank and lively journals. Bavius was an ancient Roman critic who attacked the writings of others, particularly Virgil and Horace; his name has come to mean any critic jealous of artists who are superior to him. Richard Blackmore (1654–1729) was an English writer and critic ridiculed by his fellow writers, among them Alexander Pope, for the dullness of his own poetry. Vorticism was a short-lived modernist movement in art and poetry at the turn of the twentieth century that condemned Victorian sentimentality and celebrated the energy of industrialization.

24. This is Lewis's footnote, which appears at the end of the poem: "Sweven is here used to mean a knapsack."

25. This poem appears in an unpublished and undated letter to Owen Barfield. See Bibliography of Poem Sources for more on sources.

26. Edward Montague Compton Mackenzie (1883–1972), addressed in the title of this poem, was a prolific Scottish novelist, poet, essayist, critic, and historian, as well as a nationalist who helped found the Scottish National Party.

27. Romulus and Remus were the twin brothers central to Rome's foundation myth.

28. *Antepenultimatis* means "that which is two before the last in a series."

29. Thomas Hood (1799–1845) was a British poet and publisher. Chiefly remembered for his comic verse, he also wrote biting poems protesting social conditions.

30. Lewis use a similar phrase in his preface to *English Literature in the Sixteenth Century, Excluding Drama:* "As I write 'French,' not *Français,* I have also written 'Scotch,' not *Scottish;* aware that these great nations do not so call themselves, but, claiming the freedom of 'my ain vulgaire'" (v).

31. This poem appears in an unpublished and undated letter to Owen Barfield. See Bibliography of Poem Sources for more on sources.

32. This poem to Margaret Mary Bosworth Dyson, née Robinson, wife of Lewis's friend Hugo Dyson, appears to be a playful apology by Lewis for an unintended slight or missed appointment such as a dinner engagement

33. Lewis may be punning on the name Margaret, since it means "pearl."

34. An allusion to John Milton's *Paradise Lost* where Satan, in the form of a serpent, speaks to Eve: "Wonder not, sovran Mistress, if perhaps / Thou canst, who are sole Wonder, much less arm / Thy looks, the Heav'n of mildness, with disdain" (book 9, 532–34).

35. A hippogriff is a mythical winged beast, a cross between a griffin and a mare, having the head and foreparts of a griffin and the body and back legs of a horse.

36. In Greek mythology, the mortal Anchises was a lover of the goddess Aphrodite (Venus), by whom she bore a son, the Trojan hero Aeneas.

37. Translation of the Latin text by A. J. Reyes:

You, insulted by my silence?
You, who with ample leisure
And no distractions, into all hours
Are devouring sauerkraut-dishes,
And who, in beers and bitters
Delighting, wander
Free from all cares,
Round foreign taverns?
But me, sadly, the 'flu
(As if a table to be bent)
Has grabbed hold, my muscles wasting away;
I, fettered by pupils,
From early in the morning, am held in confinement,
Crushed as well by harsh statutes;
Moreover, while I was wandering
Recently through the Fellows' Garden,
Enchanted by the pleasantness of the flowers,
Like a fool without a care,
As I was about to cross the garden threshold,
On the very large, rough,
And heavy door, I cut
My finger and poured
A lot of blood on the young grass;
I gave voice to ghastly complaints,
And by this blasphemous error,
I made the birds flee in terror—
"Spells not harmless" (As Virgil

said) from my bitter tongue.
And so, since work and since sickness
Are keeping me bereft of the Muses,
What could I write? But you,
Wanderer, anthroposophist, divine poet,
You ought to write
A letter which can bring delight.

38. Macbeth's friend and later imagined rival in William Shakespeare's play *Macbeth*.

39. This poem appears in an unpublished and undated letter to Owen Barfield. It is prefaced by: "From a paper." See Bibliography of Poem Sources for more on sources.

Appendix

Early Poems

The status of the literary corpus of C. S. Lewis's prose has largely been resolved. At the same time, the status of Lewis's unpublished poetry remains unresolved.[1] Specifically, in the preface to the 1986 reprint of C. S. Lewis's *Spirits in Bondage* (1919), Walter Hooper reviewed the initial publication history of that volume, Lewis's first published work. He did this primarily by drawing on Warren Lewis's notes in "The Lewis Papers: Memoirs of the Lewis Family, 1850–1930."[2] Warren's careful assessment of the development *SB* includes reference to an early collection of poems entitled "The Metrical Meditations of a Cod":

> It would be during this [Easter 1915] visit to Little Lea that Clive wrote the first poetry which he himself considered worthy of preservation so late as 1917. In the two years intervening between Easter 1915 and Easter 1917, he wrote fifty-two poems which he copied carefully into an old Malvern Upper Fifth Divinity note book, prefixing them with a chronological list of titles. The whole is entitled "The Metrical Meditations of a Cod."[3]

Hooper then noted that the "Metrical Meditations" were lost, perhaps, according to Warren, in a fire since "Jack himself burnt all documents therein transcribed [in "LP"], including his own diaries, in or soon after 1936."[4]

Accordingly, scholars of Lewis's poetry have assumed that the "Metrical Meditations" were destroyed. However, as I neared the end of research for my book, *C. S. Lewis Poet: The Impulse of His Poetic Legacy*, I came across a curious holograph notebook purported to be in the hand of Arthur Greeves, Lewis's lifelong friend and the person to whom Lewis had entrusted the "Metrical Meditations" at various times, particularly when Lewis was serving in France during World War I.[5] The title page of this holograph notebook, "Early Poems," reads: "English Verses Made By—Clive Staples Lewis:—and Copied by His Friend—Joseph Arthur Greeves:—Belfast in the Year 1917." Fifty-two poems are listed in chronological order in the table of contents.[6] What caught my eye was the number fifty-two, since this is the identical number

Warren refers to as having comprised "Metrical Meditations." I contend that "Early Poems" is in fact a draft of the supposedly lost "Metrical Meditations."[7] This essay will briefly review the evidence for this contention and explore the relationship between "Early Poems" (and by association "Metrical Meditations") and *SB*.[8]

Lewis's letters indicate that Greeves was intimately involved in the development of his earliest lyrical poems. On June 29, 1915, Lewis writes Greeves: "I am glad to hear that you are keeping up the 'illustrative' side of your art, and shall want you to do some for my lyric poems. You can begin a picture of my 'dream garden' where the 'West wind blows.' As directions I inform you it is 'girt about with mists,' and is in 'the shadowy country neither life nor sleep,' and is the home of 'faint dreams.'"[9] Undoubtedly Lewis is referring to passages in the heretofore unpublished poem "My Western Garden" that appears as the first poem in "Early Poems":

> I know a garden[10] where the West-Winds blow;
> Far hence it lies, and few there be that know,
> And few that tread the road that leads thereto.
>
> Its gladsome glades are girt about with mists,
> And o'er its sward a slumberous streamlet twists,
> Flowing like Lethe, soundless.
>
> No chart will guide thee to that twilit land,
> Nor mariner hath reached that Ocean's strand,
> For space it knoweth not, nor Time's rough hand.
>
> But to the home of those faint dreams that keep,
> The shadowy country, neither Life nor Sleep,
> Which parts full wakening from the voiceless deep.[11]

Before long, Greeves is requesting that Lewis send him copies of his poems, and in his replies Lewis often alludes to poems appearing in "Early Poems." The first mention of this kind occurs in a letter Lewis wrote Greeves on July 11, 1916, a passage that again refers to "My Western Garden": "I am very flattered that you remember that old line about the 'garden where the west wind' all these months, and will certainly copy out anything that is worth it if you can find me a shop in dear Belfast where I can buy a decent MS book" (*CL* 1:209–10).

The second mention occurs two weeks later, in a letter of July 25, 1916, when Lewis informs his friend that he is "writing at present a rather lengthy (for me that is) poem about Hylas, which you shall see if it is a success" (*CL* 1:221). "Early Poems" contains a previously unpublished poem entitled "Hylas," which begins:

Surely by now I must be dead:
It seems so very long ago
When by the sedgy bank I fled
And heard the cold green river flow
With summer murmuring o'er his bed.
I fell. A horrid gloom of night
Covered my eyes, and in my head
There came a singing. . . . [12]

The third example comes from a letter dated September 18, 1916, when Lewis wrote Greeves about the poem "Star Bath": "I was very much interested in your description of those lakes [near Portsalon in County Donegal], tho' I must say that considering my eager desire to see them, both this year and last, it was particularly kind of you to go just after I had left . . . I can quite imagine how fine it must have been—rather like the 'Star Bath' as I picture them" (*CL* 1:222). At about this same time, Warren Lewis notes in "The Lewis Papers" that a version of the "Star Bath" was added to "Metrical Meditations."[13] References to poetry in Lewis's correspondence to Greeves are absent for almost nine months after this, in part because Lewis was earnestly studying to win an Oxford scholarship; this intense study was rewarded when he matriculated at University College, Oxford, on April 29, 1917.[14]

The last two references to "Early Poems" (or "Metrical Meditations") in Lewis's correspondence to Greeves appear in the summer of 1918. On June 3, 1918, Lewis asks: "By the way, haven't you got a reddy-brown MS. book of mine containing 'Lullaby' and several other of my later poems? I wish you would send it here, as I have decided to copy out all my work of which I approve and get it typed as a step toward possible publishing. Even if nobody will have them a complete typed copy would be a great convenience" (*CL* 1:378). "Early Poems" contains two poems entitled "Lullaby." The first, "Lullaby" (Summer 1916), is actually a draft of the poem that later appears as "Night (IX)" in *SB* (16–17); the second, "Lullaby! Lullaby!" (undated), is a draft of the poem that later appears as "Lullaby" in *SB* (70–71).[15]

The last reference to "Early Poems" (or "Metrical Meditations") appears when Lewis writes Greeves about the progress of his *SB* manuscript, culminating in his joyful announcement on September 12, 1918: "The best of news! After keeping my MS. for ages Heinemann has actually accepted it. . . . Mr. Heinemann . . . writes to say that he 'will be pleased to become its publisher.'" He adds that it may be well to re-consider the inclusion of some of the pieces 'which are not perhaps on a level with my best work'" (*CL* 1:397).[16]

A review of the contents of "Early Poems" makes clear its links with *Spirits in Bondage*.[17] Below I list the table of contents of "Early Poems" and note which of the poems listed there have versions that appear in either *Spirits in Bondage* or *Collected Poems*.

My Western Garden (Easter 1915)
A Death Song (Easter 1915)
The Hills of Down (Easter 1915); in *CP*, 229–30[18]
Against Potpourri (Summer 1915); in *CP*, 231–32
To the Gods of Old Time (Summer 1915)
The Town of Gold (Summer 1915)
The Wood Desolate (Summer 1915)
Anamnesis (Summer 1915)
A Prelude (Summer 1915); in *CP*, 233–34[19]
Ballade of a Winter Morning (Christmas 1915); in *CP*, 234–35
Sonnet—to John Keats (Christmas 1915)
Yet More of the Wood Desolate (Christmas 1915)
The Wind (Christmas 1915)
Sonnet (Christmas 1915); appears in *SB* as "Sonnet" (XX), 33
New Year's Eve (Christmas 1915)
Noon (Christmas 1915); appears in *SB* as "Noon" (XVIII), 31[20]
Night (Easter 1916); appears in *SB* as "Night" (XXIX), 55–56
Ad Astra (Easter 1916); appears in *SB* as "Victory" (IV), 7–8
A Hymn (Easter 1916); appears in *SB* as "To Sleep" (X), 18
The Roads (Easter 1916); appears in *SB* as "The Roads" (XXXIV), 63–64
Laus Mortis (Easter 1916); appears in *CP* as *Laus Mortis,* 236–37
In His Own Image (Easter 1916)
Sonnet [The clouds are red behind us and before] (Easter 1916)
Loneliness (Easter 1916)
The Little Golden Statuette (Easter 1916)[21]
Sonnet [I have not bowed in any other shrine] (Summer 1916)[22]
The Satyr (Summer 1916); appears in *SB* as "The Satyr" (III), 5–6
The Star Bath (Summer 1916); appears in *SB* as "The Star Bath" (XXXVI), 67
Sonnet—to Sir Philip Sydney (Summer 1916); in *CP*, 237
Lullaby (Summer 1916); appears in *SB* as "Night" (IX), 16–17
Exercise on an old Theme (Summer 1916)
The Autumn Morning (Summer 1916); appears in *SB* as "The Autumn Morning" (XXI), 34–35[23]
Of Ships (Christmas 1916); in *CP*, 238
Couplets (Christmas 1916); in *CP*, 240–41
Hylas (Christmas 1916)
The Ocean Strand (Christmas 1916); appears in *SB* as "The Ocean Strand" (XVII), 29–30
Hesperus (Christmas 1916); appears in *SB* as "Hesperus" (XXXV), 65–66
How I saw Angus the God (Christmas 1916); appears in *SB* as "How He Saw Angus the God" (XXXIII), 61–62

Decadence (Christmas 1916)[24]
Milton Read Again (Easter 1917); appears in *SB* as "Milton Read Again" (XIX), 32
Ballade Mystical (Easter 1917); appears in *SB* as "Ballade Mystique" (XXVIII), 53–54
L'Apprenti Sorcier (Easter 1917); appears in *SB* as "L'Apprenti Sorcier" (XXII), 39–40
ΜΗΔΕΝ ΑΓΑΝ (Easter 1917)
Irish Nocturne (Easter 1917); appears in *SB* as "Irish Nocturne" (V), 9–10
Ballade on a certain pious gentleman (Easter 1917)
Circe—a fragment (Easter 1917); in *CP,* 241
Song of the Pilgrims (Easter 1917); appears in *SB* as "Song of the Pilgrims" (XXV), 47–49
Exercise (Easter 1917); in *CP,* 242
The Philosopher (Easter 1917); appears in *SB* as "The Philosopher" (XVI), 27–28[25]
Ode; contains versions of lines 1–13, 43–46, 14–21, and 22–25 of "Ode for New Year's Day" (VIII), in *SB,* 13–15
Venite; title only, no poem.
My Own Death Song; appears in *SB* as "Death in Battle" (XL), 74–75[26]

In addition, the following poems or titles, numbered up to fifty-eight, are included in "Early Poems" but are not listed in the table of contents. They appeared to have been added later. However, poem 51, "Venite," consists of the title only with no poem, while 53 is missing entirely: no title nor poem exists in the holograph. In fact, the "Early Poems" actually holds fifty-six poems. Of this last group, three have versions that later appear in *SB,* while one, "Tho' it's truth they tell, Despoina," contributes several lines to a poem in *SB.*

53. [Both title and poem missing.]
54. Lullaby! Lullaby!; appears in *SB* as "Lullaby" (XXXVIII), 70–71
55. Tho' it's truth they tell, Despoina; contains versions of lines 26–42 of "Ode for New Year's Day" (VIII) in *SB,* 13–15
56. If men should ask; appears in *SB* as "Apology" (VII), 12
57. Oh there is a castle built; appears in *SB* as "World's Desire" (XXXIX), 72–73
58. Despoina, bear with me

In sum, of these fifty-six poems actually appearing in "Early Poems, twenty-five appear later, in whole or part, in revised form in *SB.*[27]

Notes

This appendix reproduces in emended form the first part of an article I originally published as "Lost but Found: The 'Missing' Poems of C. S. Lewis's *Spirits in Bondage*," *Christianity and Literature* 53 (Winter 2004): 163–201.

1. For more on this, see my article "Glints of Light: The Unpublished Short Poetry of C. S. Lewis" (hereafter, "Glints"), *SEVEN: An Anglo-American Literary Review* 15 (1998): 73–96, and my book *C. S. Lewis, Poet: The Legacy of His Poetic Impulse* (Kent, Ohio: Kent State Univ. Press, 2001).

2. This eleven-volume typescript (hereafter, "LP") is available in the Wade Center. Used by permission. Warren's complete description of the relationship between "Metrical Meditations" and *SB* is fascinating reading and can be found in "LP," volumes 4 and 5.

3. This passages goes on:

> It is perhaps not irrelevant to explain here the Ulster word "cod," from which Clive formed for himself the diminutive "Kodotta" which appears so frequently in his letters. Patterson in his Glossary defines cod as, (1) "a silly, troublesome fellow," and (2) v. "to humbug or quiz a person; to hoax; to idle about. 'Quit your coddin.'" It has however a third meaning, namely an expression of humourous and insincere self depreciation; an Ulsterman will say of himself, "Am'nt I the quare oul' cod to be doin' so and so," and it is in this latter sense that it is to be understood in this context. ("LP" 4:306)

4. Cited by Walter Hooper in his preface to *SB*, xii.

5. The original copy of the notebook is at the Linen Hall Library, Belfast. A photocopy of it is available in the Wade Center, CSL/MS-41/X; all subsequent references to "Early Poems" are to this notebook. Used by permission.

6. However, the notebook actually holds five more poems, not listed in the table of contents but numbered fifty-four through fifty-eight; no poem or title numbered fifty-three exists in the notebook. See more on this below.

7. I first raised the issue of this notebook in *C. S. Lewis, Poet*, 308–10. In making this claim I realize that there is no way to prove that Lewis, rather than Greeves, wrote these poems, particularly the twenty-one unpublished poems. However, given Greeves's obvious devotion to Lewis and the internal evidence found in the notebook itself, I have no doubt the poems are in fact the work of the young Lewis. After the table of contents, the following phrase in French appears: "At the well-worn path that leads to Mt. Parnasse" (De Ronsard).

8. Ten poems included in the holograph notebook "Early Poems" have been published in Lewis's "A Miscellany of Additional Poems" in *CP*. Because he apparently did not know about "Early Poems," however, Hooper did not use the versions of these ten poems that appear in the holograph notebook for the "Miscellany"; instead, he used versions of these poems found in "LP."

9. Lewis, *CL* 1:134.

10. In his preface to the 1950 edition of *Dymer* (reprinted in *Narrative Poems*), Lewis writes about the importance of the "western garden" motif in his early imaginative life, particularly his desire for *Sehnsucht*: "From at least the age of six, romantic longing—*Sehnsucht*—had played an unusually central part in my experience. Such longing is in itself the very reverse

of wishful thinking: it is more like thoughtful wishing. But it throws off what may be called systems of imagery. One among many such which it had thrown off for me was the Hesperian or Western Garden system, mainly derived from Euripides, Milton, Morris, and the early Yeats" (4). In a review of an early draft of this essay, David C. Downing wrote: "This poem may be the young Lewis's first attempt to set down in words a master motif in his imagination, the one which shows up as a mystical vision in *The Pilgrim's Regress* and the paradisal setting of *Perelandra.*" Lewis includes a related poem, "Hesperus," in *SB* (65–66).

11. A month later, in a letter of July 24, 1915, Lewis wrote Greeves that he was "determined to teach you to like poetry" (*CL* 1:138).

12. Hylas was servant to Heracles and accompanied him on the voyage of the *Argo,* captained by Jason. After Heracles's oar broke at Cius, Hylas, who had been sent to fetch water for supper, inadvertently came to a fountain inhabited by Naiads. They were so taken with his beauty that they pulled him into the water to be their companion. Although this is not a particularly lengthy poem and may not be the one Lewis is referring to in his letter to Greeves, it provides clear evidence Lewis wrote a poem under this name.

13. The holograph notebook "Early Poems" contains a version of "The Star Bath" that is almost exactly the same as that included by Warren in "LP" (5:122–23). The version of the "Star Bath" eventually published in *SB* (67) contains moderate revisions, including changes of words, the deletion of one line, and a shift in ending from a question to a declarative.

14. On June 8, 1917, Lewis joined the army and was billeted at Keble College; two days later, he writes Greeves about his continuing efforts at verse: "I am in a strangely productive mood at present and spend my few moments of spare time in scribbling verse. When my 4 months course in the cadet battalion is at an end . . . I propose to get together all the stuff I have perpetrated and see if any kind publisher would like to take it" (*CL* 1:321). Later that fall, on Oct. 28, 1917, in a veiled but obvious reference to either "Early Poems" or "Metrical Meditations," Lewis writes Greeves: "Better not send the MS. book till we're sure where I'll be" (*CL* 1:340). Moreover, on New Year's Eve 1917, writing from the trenches in France, Lewis advises Greeves to "send on my MS. book—the Metrical Meditations one—to Ravenswood Rd—I have yielded to oft repeated suggestions that it should go there" (*CL* 1:350). In addition, almost six months later, writing on May 23, 1918, from the Liverpool Merchants Mobile Hospital, Etaples, where he was recovering from battle wounds, Lewis sends Greeves "a little song I wrote the other day, which I hope you will approve" (*CL* 1:372). He encloses in that letter "Song [Fairies must be in the woods]." This poem does not appear in "Early Poems" but a version does appear in *SB* (50). The important thing about these letters is that they clearly reveal that Greeves was holding a manuscript of Lewis's poetry. Consequently, it is reasonable to assume that Greeves may have taken it upon himself to transcribe Lewis's poems into the holograph notebook "Early Poems."

15. On July 17, 1918, Lewis writes Greeves:

> I am truly sorry to have left you so long without a letter. My best excuse is that already "my hand aches and my eyes grow weary" with writing, for I am at present busily engaged in copying out the final version of my poems: in a few days the new MS. will be ready for the typist and when it returns thence it will begin the round of the publishers . . . Of course the book is now very different from the one you have, by the insertion of several new pieces and the alteration or omission of some of the old. The arrangement I find particularly difficult and besides I am beginning to grow nervy and distrust my own

judgement. It is hard to know whether you are improving or spoiling a thing . . . When I have got the MS. off (it used to be my love but is now becoming more my tyrant!) I will write you a longer and better letter. (*CL* 1:389–90)

This letter suggests that as Lewis worked on "copying out the final versions of [his] poems" that later appeared in *SB*, he may have performed revisions on the two "Lullaby" poems from "Early Poems" that eventually became "Night (IX)" and "Lullaby" in *SB*.

16. See also Lewis's letters to Greeves, all in *CL* 1, dated Aug. 7, 1918 (392); Oct. 13, 1918 (406); Nov. 2, 1918 (412–13); Mar. 2, 1919 (440); and June 2, 1919 (453–54). Heinemann's dissatisfaction with some of the poems in the original *SB* manuscript may imply that it contained poems from "Early Poems" (or "Metrical Meditations"). As we follow the story, Lewis tells Greeves (in the same Sept. 12, 1918, letter discussed above) that he has sent Heinemann "5 new poems." Apparently, however, Heinemann still was not satisfied. On Oct. 8, 1918, Heinemann wrote Lewis:

> I have read through your "Spirits in Prison" [the original manuscript title] again, in its revised form, and suggest that the following numbers might with advantage be ommitted [*sic*], partly because they do not strengthen the book as a whole, partly because they are less original perhaps than the bulk of your work:
> 5.) To Sir Philip Sydney
> 7.) Ballade on a certain pious gentleman.
> 14.) Sonnet.
> 22.) Retreat.
> 24.) In Venusberg. ("LP" 6:49)

According to Hooper in the preface to *SB*, Lewis sent Heinemann "'Our Daily Bread,' 'The Autumn Morning,' 'Alexandrines,' 'Tu Ne Quæsieris,' and 'Spooks' [to replace the] five poems in the original manuscript" (xxxiv). I have not been able to verify Hooper's assertion, but if it is accurate this means that these five poems most likely date to some time during or after Oct. 1918, since Heinemann's letter to Lewis is dated Oct. 8, 1918. A version of "The Autumn Morning" appears in "Early Poems."

Heinemann's letter and the text of "Early Poems" provide us insight into one of the few times where we can infer Lewis's revision process. First, we know that the poem "To Sir Philip Sidney" that Heinemann directed Lewis to drop from what came to be *SB* was, according to Warren Lewis, originally a part of "Metrical Meditations," and that a version of it, "Sonnet—to Sir Philip Sydney" (Summer 1916) appears in "Early Poems." Hooper later published this poem in *CP* as "Sonnet—to Sir Philip Sydney" (Autumn 1916) (*CP*, 237).

Second, a version of "Ballade on a Certain Pious Gentleman" that Heinemann similarly disliked appears in "Early Poems" (where it is dated Easter 1917) and was almost certainly a part of "Metrical Meditations." Third, the inclusion of five other sonnets in "Early Poems" in addition to "Sonnet—to Sir Philip Sydney," makes it more difficult to determine which of these five remaining sonnets Heinemann was recommending that Lewis drop. We can narrow the field by one, since one of these five in "Early Poems," "Sonnet [The stars come out; the fragrant shadows fall]" (Christmas 1915), is a version of "Sonnet" (XX) that appears in *SB* (30); accordingly, it is reasonable to contend that this sonnet may be a version of one that originally appeared in "Metrical Meditations."

The sonnet that Heinemann wanted Lewis to drop seems likely, therefore, be one of the four remaining sonnets in "Early Poems": "Sonnet—to John Keats" (Christmas 1915); "Sonnet [The clouds are red behind us and before]" (Easter 1916); "Sonnet [I have not bowed in any other shrine]" (Summer 1916); and "ΜΗΔÈΝ 'ÁΓΑΝ" (Easter 1917). Unfortunately, lacking any other textual clues, we cannot surmise with any certainty which of these four Heinemann wanted Lewis to drop from the original manuscript of *SB*—if, in fact, the sonnet to which he referred was not another sonnet entirely that has not survived. Lastly, neither "Retreat" nor "In Venusburg" appear in "Early Poems," and so far as I can ascertain no versions of them have survived. It is possible, however, that "A Death Song" (Easter 1915), which begins "I am weary of Summer weather," may be linked to "Retreat" and that the missing "Venite" may be linked to "In Venusberg."

17. In addition, ten poems in "Early Poems" that do not appear in *SB* have been subsequently published in the section entitled "A Miscellany of Additional Poems" of *CP*: "The Hills of Down" (Easter 1915), "Against Potpourri" (Summer 1915), "A Prelude" (Summer 1915), "Ballade of a Winter's Morning" (Christmas 1915), "*Laus Mortis*" (Easter 1916), "Sonnet—To Sir Philip Sydney" (Autumn 1916), "Of Ships" (Christmas 1916), "Couplets" (Christmas 1916), "Circe—A Fragment" (April 1917), and "Exercise" (April 1917). As these ten poems appear so long after the publication of *SB*, I will not focus on them here; however, the versions in *CP* contain only very minor changes from those in "Early Poems." I have written extensively about them in *C. S. Lewis Poet*, 27–51.

18. In "LP," Warren Lewis offers powerful evidence that "Early Poems" is an early draft of "Metrical Meditations." His discussion of the historical development of "Metrical Meditations," including specific reference to when certain poems were written, illustrates an almost one-for-one correspondence between the poems in "Early Poems" and those he asserts were in "Metrical Meditations." In my listing of those found in "Early Poems," I show this by grouping the poems according the time Warren Lewis says they were written and by footnoting his specific reference to this in "LP." For instance, of the first three poems, he writes in "LP": "Of the poems included in the 'Metrical meditations,' three are marked as having been written in Easter 1915. Of the three, one was subsequently published, and does not therefore concern us at the moment; of the remaining two we select the following specimen [what follows is 'The Hills of Down,' now in *CP*, 229–30]" (4:306). In this particular case, I think Warren Lewis is mistaken when he says "one was subsequently published," because he confuses "A Death Song" (2 in "Early Poems") for "My Own Death Song" (52 in "Early Poems"), which was published in *SB* as "Death in Battle" (74–75).

19. In "LP," after one of his letters dated Aug. 20, 1915, Warren Lewis writes: "We turn again to Clive's 'Metrical Meditations.' In view of what he has previously said to Arthur Greeves about the difficulty of writing at Gastons, we may presume that the six poems in the MS. volume dated 'Summer 1915' were written at Little Lea in Aug. [1915]. I select the two which follow for reproduction" (5:14). The two Warren Lewis selects are "Against Potpourri" and "A Prelude," now in *CP*, 231–34.

20. In "LP," after an entry dated Jan. 1916 and the poem "Noon," Warren Lewis writes: "In all, [C. S. Lewis] added seven poems to his 'meditations' under the general date 'Christmas 1915.' 'Noon' was subsequently to be published. This which follows is doubtless reminiscent of mornings spent with Arthur Greeves either at Little Lea or Bernagh" (5:46). Warren Lewis then reproduces "Ballade of a Winter's Morning," now in *CP*, 234–35.

21. In "LP," after an entry from W. T. Kirkpatrick to Albert Lewis dated Apr. 1, 1916, Warren Lewis writes: "Clive, arrived at home, turns his attention once more to poetry, and in this

Easter holiday nine more poems were added to his 'Metrical Meditations.' Of these, three were subsequently published. Of those unpublished, I select the following" (5:72). What follows is an early version of 'Night,' now in *SB*, 55–56, and 'Laus Mortis,' now in *CP*, 236–37.

22. This poem has appeared in print once before. See *C. S. Lewis, Poet,* 321–22.

23. In "LP," after a letter from C. S. Lewis to Greeves dated Sept. 18, 1916, Warren Lewis writes:

> During the holidays which are now nearly at an end, Clive, in spite of a visit with his friend Arthur to Donegal, had found time to add seven poems to his 'Metrical meditations.' Of these two were subsequently published, one as it stands in the MS., and another with some alteration. The first of these, the Star Bath, had possibly been suggested by Arthur Greeves' account of the lakes near Port Salon, which town he had apparently visited in the previous year, and we reproduce it, both for its intrinsic worth, and for the sake of the author's reference. My other selection from this holiday's harvest was probably drafted at Bookham while he was reading Sydney's "Arcadia." (5:122)

What follows this passage in "LP" is an early version of "The Star Bath," now in *SB*, 67, and "Sonnet—To Sir Philip Sydney," now in *CP*, 237.

24. In "LP," after a letter from Kirkpatrick to Albert Lewis dated Dec. 22, 1916, Warren Lewis writes: "Clive is now back again at Little Lea, where he once more turns to his 'Metrical Musing.' In the Christmas holidays of 1916 he added another seven poems to his collection; of these three were afterwards published. It is a little surprising that we hunt in vain in these seven poems for any hint of the impression which a first sight of the beauty of Oxford might have been expected to make on such a sensitive and receptive nature. Of the unpublished poems, the following two seem to me to be well worthy of preservation" (5:170). What follows are "Of Ships," now in *CP*, 238–39, and "Couplets," now in *CP*, 240–41.

25. In "LP," Warren Lewis quotes from Albert [Lewis's] pocket diary: "Sunday 25th. March [1917]. Before lunch, usual. Walk 4 to 6. Supper cold bacon and Moselle-agreed" (5:196). Then he adds: "This entry suggests to me that Clive had failed to get home by 'the Sunday,' and was detained in Oxford until the 26th. We know from Clive's own pocket book that he 'went up' for the first time on the 26th of April. In the month which he spent at Little Lea he was more than usually occupied with his 'Metrical Meditations' to which he added no fewer than ten pieces; of these four were published as then written, two more were published in an altered form, and four remain unpublished. From the latter four I select the two following" (5:197). What follows are "Circe—A Fragment," now in *CP*, 241, and "Exercise," in *CP*, 242.

26. In "LP," Warren Lewis reproduces "Death in Battle" (6:99–100); this appears in *SB*, 74–75.

27. That "Early Poems" served as a primary source for *SB* is significant for several reasons. First, although elsewhere I have documented extensively Lewis's visceral aspiration to achieve acclaim as a poet through the 1920s, these twenty-five poems, most written between Easter 1915 and Easter 1917, while he was living in Bookham and being tutored by W. T. Kirkpatrick, provide additional evidence of his passion for poetry and shed further light on his poetic maturation. For a detailed account of Lewis's early aspirations to achieve acclaim as a poet, see King, *C. S. Lewis, Poet,* 1–26.

Second, of the seventeen other poems in *SB* (including the "Prologue"), I would argue that ten of them are almost certainly "battlefield" poems; that is, they are poems Lewis wrote while serving in the trenches in France during World War I, as each contains thematic connections to wartime experiences. These ten are "Satan Speaks" (I), "French Nocturne," "Spooks," "In Prison," "De Profundis," "Satan Speaks" (XIII), "Dungeon Grates," "Alexandrines," "Oxford," and "Song" (the last of which was written shortly before a letter Lewis sent to Greeves on May 23, 1918; see *CL* 1:372–73). Furthermore, because we know Lewis sent Heinemann "Our Daily Bread" and "Tu Ne Quæsieris" sometime after Oct. 8, 1918, as replacements for poems Heinemann disliked, it is reasonable to surmise they, too, are battlefield poems. Of the remaining five, I suggest "Prologue" was written shortly before the publication of *SB* in 1919, while "The Witch" may have connections to the lost "Medea" (one version ran to twelve hundred lines), a poem Lewis began working on as early as July 11, 1916. See *CL* 1:209; 277–78; 282; 460; 465–66, 467, and 653. "In Praise of Solid People" gives evidence of having been written while Lewis was studying with Kirkpatrick (between Sept. 19, 1914, and Mar. 20, 1917). "The Ass" and "Hymn (For Boy's Voices)" are difficult to date, although the former opens with "I woke and rose and slipt away / To the heathery hills in the morning gray," strongly hinting at the Hills of Down, and thus its being written at Little Lea during a school holiday.

Third, these twenty-five poems offer partial insight into Lewis's revision process. Seven of the poems in "Early Poems" that later appear in *SB* give evidence of only minor revisions: a word change or other insubstantial modification here or there. For instance, line 5 in "Sonnet [The stars come out; the fragrant shadows fall]" from "Early Poems" reads "And twinkling glow-worms round about me crawl," while the same line from "Sonnet" (XX) in *SB* reads "And twinkling glow-worms all about me crawl." Likewise the last stanza of "Ad Astra" in "Early Poems" reads "Though often bruised beneath a heavy a rod / Yet, like the phoenix, from each fiery bed / Higher the dauntless spirit lifts its head / And higher—till this beast become a god," while in "Victory" from *SB* it is modified to read "Though often bruised, oft broken by the rod, / Yet, like the phoenix, from each fiery bed / Higher the stricken spirit lifts its head / And higher—till the beast become a god." Other poems reflecting only minor changes between the version in "Early Poems" and that found in *SB* are "Noon," "The Roads," "The Ocean Strand," "How I Saw Angus the God," and "Song of the Pilgrims."

Sixteen poems from "Early Poems" later appearing in *SB* reflect moderate revisions, including significant alterations in word choice and added or deleted lines and stanzas. In addition to the moderate changes already noted above regarding "The Star Bath," the diction in "The Satyr" from "Early Poems" is extensively modified in "The Satyr" from *SB*. For example, the former poem opens:

When the white hands of the spring
First their showering blossoms fling
    O'er the world, then down the vallies
Comes the satyr caroling;

Far he roams the windy shore,
Shadowy glen and mountain hoar
    Where an oread chores rallies,—
    Making music evermore.

The latter, however, gives these lines as:

When the flowery hands of spring
Forth their woodland riches fling,
  Through the meadows, through the valleys
Goes the satyr carolling.

From the mountain and the moor,
Forest green and ocean shore
  All the faerie kin he rallies
  Making music evermore.

While the tone and theme of the poems remain unchanged, the alterations in diction indicate how seriously Lewis practiced the craft of poetry; the version published in *SB* is more poetic, reflecting an artist's concern with sound, rhythm, and pace. The poem titled "The Autumn Morning" in both works provides another example of moderate revisions. While the diction used in the "Early Poems" version is very similar to that used in the *SB* version, the former contains three addition stanzas that do not appear in the published version. Similarly, while lines 1–19 in "Oh there is a castle built" from "Early Poems" are largely repeated in "World's Desire" from *SB*, the latter version contains an additional ten lines to conclude the poem. Other poems reflecting moderate revisions are "Night," "A Hymn," "Lullaby," "Hesperus," "Milton Read Again," "Ballade Mystical," "L'Appreniti Sorcier," "Irish Nocturne," "The Philosopher," "My Own Death Song," "If men should ask," "Oh there is a castle built," and "Lullaby! Lullaby!"

Two poems from "Early Poems" are heavily revised by the time they appear in *SB;* indeed, Lewis actually combines the two poems into one. "Ode" from "Early Poems" contains thirty-six lines that are a mixture of couplets and alternate rhyme. Its first thirteen lines are essentially repeated in lines 1–13 of "Ode for New Year's Day" from *SB;* in addition, lines 16–20 from "Ode" appear, largely unchanged, as the last four lines, 43–46, in *SB*'s "Ode for New Year's Day," while lines 21–28 and 33–36 from the earlier version of the poem appear as lines 14–21 and 22–25 respectively of the published version. However, "Ode for New Year's Day" of *SB* also incorporates the poem "Tho it's truth they tell" from "Early Poems." The earlier version consists of eighteen lines—also a mixture of couplets and alternate rhyme—that appear with only minor changes as lines 26–42 of "Ode for New Year's Day." While it would be fascinating to discover the steps that led Lewis to combine these two poems into "Ode for New Year's Day," the record of these extensive revisions has not survived.

Introductory Letter to *Collected Poems*

The following document appears in holograph in "Young King Cole and Other Pieces," by C. S. Lewis, identified there as "Fellow of Magdalen College, Oxford," in the Bodleian, Dep. c. 883. It is signed but not titled or dated by Lewis. In *Collected Poems of C. S. Lewis*, edited by Walter Hooper (London: Fount, 1994), it appears after Hooper's introduction under the title "Introductory Letter of 1963 by C. S. Lewis."

Dear Madam (or Sir)—Spectacles made for one man will suit another only by a lucky accident; and since there was no thought of pleasing you when the pieces in this volume were written it is a hundred to one against your finding it any pleasure to read them. This letter, well-used, will enable you to write a very passable review without that laborious preliminary.

You may safely and even truly say that the author is out of touch with all the dominant trends of contemporary literature. If you don't think the word too *usé,*[1] you can call him an escapist. From what or into what or why he is escaping, I think you had better not discuss; your readers don't expect it and that sort of thing may easily land one in difficulties.

Poetic Diction[2] and even archaism ought certainly to be among the charges you bring. But I wouldn't line the author up with other archaists unless you have really read them. And remember that "Wardour Street,"[3] beside being a bit stale, is an expression that has strings attached to it.

This, with a quotation or so—you can choose them blind, for I assure you there is no part of the book you will dislike much more than another—would almost do for a short notice. If, however, you are paid by the inch or your employer for any reason wants to fill up space, you could say that the author seems mainly interested in phonetic patterns: consonances, assonances, internal or inbedded rhymes, and all that. An internal rhyme is a thing like "exCEPT at the making of Eve Adam SLEPT":[4] an inbedded rhyme, one like "In CRIMSon shade their LIMBS are laid."[5] If you are short of matter this distinction should be good for a hundred and odd words. You may trot it out as your own if you like, for I won't give you away and those who read your review will obviously not be likely to read the book. A reference to Skaldic metres[6] might come in at this point. There are, to be sure, people who really know about them, but they again will not be among your readers.

I wouldn't, however, go on to say anything of your own about metres. Your education has been neglected on that side and you would probably mistake for *vers libre*[7] the pieces which are really in the strictest and most complicated metres of all. Anyway, your public has no interest in the subject.

For safety's sake don't embark on an imaginary history of how, when or why the things were written.[8] Keep that for dead authors. When you apply it to the living there are people who know whether the results are right or wrong. I have never once known them to be right.

For the same reason I'd avoid *Quellenforschung*.[9] It involves biographical, and indeed literary, knowledge which you don't possess. But though you should keep clear of the thing there is no reason why you shouldn't use the word. For example, it would be quite effective—on the basis of this very passage—to say, "Lewis, for reasons not hard to conjecture, deprecates *Quellenforschung*." This sentence, by the way, has the advantage that if there is any confusion in the printing-house (or elsewhere) between *deprecate*[10] and *depreciate*,[11] it won't really matter. Whichever turns up in print, you can defend it.

I mean, of course, defend it against your own kind. You needn't bother about defending it against me, for I have one great virtue as an author—I never answer criticism. Falsehoods about matter of fact (if they meet my eyes) I do;[12] and it is only fair to your profession to say that no one whom I caught lying about me ever lied about me again. Of my dead friends you had better be more careful than of me. I have been thought to have a pretty vein in spurgalling[13] a ghoul.

With myself, on the other hand, you can be (barring fact) pretty free. The psychological and sociological line in denigration is generally the most reliable.[14] Why not invent a new group to which you can assign me—say, The Angry Old Men? Though I may not be so angry—not, anyway, with things in general—as the Young Men,[15] I have perhaps a better claim to Age than some of them to Youth. But whatever line you take, have a good time, please your own fancy, and don't waste any pains trying to find out the particular types of mud you think I would most dislike. I don't belong to a presscutting concern and consequently I see reviews of my own work only by accident. It would be a shame if any carefully concocted venom thus went to waste.

It is of course just possible that some one critic who reads this letter may be of quite a different sort from those I have been trying to help: may love and understand what I have attempted and may be concerned not at all with me as a person or a type but solely with diagnosing and exhibiting the kind and degree of my failure or success. That is the critic whose praise I covet and whose censure I fear but will never resent. There is no need to elaborate the point. We understand one another.

For the rest—for you, the far more probable critic—I have a kindlier feeling than

you may suppose. Wilfred Shadbolt[16] in the comic opera had not become an assistant tormentor because he liked assistant tormenting. You are not a reviewer for the fun of a thing, and if you rose much above the orthodox contemporary type of work in this kind you would probably lose your job. Your trade is dreadful as gathering samphire[17] and I wish you the speedy chance of a better one with all my heart.
Yours etc.
C. S. Lewis

Notes

1. Lewis may be employing *usé* in the sense of "overused."

2. Lewis may be alluding to ideas and principles in Owen Barfield's *Poetic Diction: A Study in Meaning* (London: Faber and Gwyer, 1928), a book Barfield dedicated to "Clive Hamilton ('Opposition is true friendship')." Chapter 10 of the book is entitled "Archaism."

3. The expression *Wardour Street* implies the use of near-obsolete words for effect.

4. This is first line of Lewis's poem "Adam at Night," first published in *Punch* 216 (May 11, 1949): 510.

5. The line *'Neath crimson shade their limbs are laid* appears in Lewis's poem "The Birth of Language," first published in *Punch* 210 (Jan. 9, 1946): 32.

6. The predominate meter in skaldic poetry—from ancient Scandinavian and Norse literature—is known as *dróttkvætt;* it consists of a series of strict alliterations and rhyme patterns, with lines divided up into couplets so that the alliterations and rhyme patterns deal with the pairs of lines.

7. Free verse.

8. Lewis writes at length on his distaste for this kind of literary criticism in several essays, most notably in "Modern Theology and Biblical Criticism," in *Christian Reflections,* ed. Walter Hooper (Grand Rapids, Mich.: Eerdmans, 1967). The essay was first read at Westcott House, Cambridge, on May 11, 1959.

9. German for "source investigation."

10. *Deprecate* means "to plead earnestly against."

11. *Depreciate* means "to lessen the value of."

12. For an example, see Lewis's letter to the editor, *English* 14 (Summer 1962): 75, where he corrects the mistaken assumption that his book *An Experiment in Criticism* (Cambridge, UK: Cambridge Univ. Press, 1961) was a veiled personal attack on F. R. Leavis.

13. Literally, "to gall a horse or other animal with a spur while riding"; here Lewis uses the word more generally in the sense of injuring or disabling.

14. For Lewis's thoughts about this kind of criticism, see his essays "Psycho-Analysis and Literary Criticism," *Essays and Studies* 27 (1942), and "The Anthropological Approach," in *English and Medieval Studies Presented to J. R. R. Tolkien on the Occasion of his Seventieth Birthday,* ed. Norman Davis and C. L. Wrenn (London: George Allen and Unwin, 1962). Both essays are reprinted in C. S. Lewis, *Selected Literary Essays,* ed. Walter Hooper (Cambridge, UK: Cambridge Univ. Press, 1969).

15. Lewis may have in mind here the "angry young men," a group of British novelists and playwrights emerging in the 1950s whose work was characterized by disdain for and frustration

with the established social order, particularly England's class system. Writers often regarded as belonging to this group included John Wain, for his novel *Hurry on Down* (1953); Kingsley Amis, for his novel *Lucky Jim* (1954) and his play *Look Back in Anger* (1956); and John Osborne, for his play, *The Entertainer* (1957).

16. Wilfred Shadbolt was the "head jailer and assistant tormentor" in Gilbert and Sullivan's Savoy opera, *The Yeomen of the Guard; or, The Merryman and His Maid* (1888).

17. Samphire is a fleshy edible plant native to Europe's coastal areas and salt marshes.

Bibliography of Poem Sources

The poems appearing in this volume have been drawn from holdings in Oxford University's Bodleian Library in Oxford, UK, and in the Marion E. Wade Center at Wheaton College, Wheaton, Ill., and from notebooks held by Walter Hooper, as well as the following manuscripts, articles, and books.

Manuscripts, Articles, and Books

Adams, Richard, ed. *Occasional Poets: An Anthology.* Harmondsworth, Middlesex, UK: Penguin Books, 1986.

Fear No More: A Book of Poems for the Present Time by Living English Poets. Cambridge, UK: Cambridge Univ. Press, 1940. While all the poems in this volume are published anonymously, six copies contain an additional leaf giving the names of the authors of the poems (including Lewis), and one of these is in the Bodleian.

Gilbert, Douglas, and Clyde S. Kilby. *C. S. Lewis: Images of His World.* Grand Rapids, Mich.: Eerdmans, 1973.

Green, Roger Lancelyn, and Walter Hooper. *C. S. Lewis: A Biography.* London: Collins, 1974.

Hardie, A. M., and K. C. Douglas, eds. *Augury: An Oxford Miscellany of Verse and Prose.* Oxford: Blackwell, 1940.

King, Don W. *C. S. Lewis, Poet: The Legacy of His Poetic Impulse.* Kent, Ohio: Kent State Univ. Press, 2001.

———. "Glints of Light: The Unpublished Short Poetry of C. S. Lewis" (hereafter, "Glints"). *SEVEN: An Anglo-American Literary Review* 15 (1998): 73–96.

———. "Lost but Found: The 'Missing' Poems of C. S. Lewis's *Spirits in Bondage*" (hereafter, "Lost but Found." *Christianity and Literature* 53 (Winter 2004): 163–201.

Lewis, C. S. *Collected Letters of C. S. Lewis.* Volume 1: *Family Letters 1905–1931* (hereafter, *CL* 1). Edited by Walter Hooper. London: Harper Collins, 2000.

———. *The Collected Letters of C. S. Lewis.* Volume 2: *Books, Broadcasts and the War, 1931–1949* (hereafter, *CL* 2). Edited by Walter Hooper. London: Harper Collins, 2004.

———. *The Collected Letters of C. S. Lewis.* Volume 3: *Narnia, Cambridge, and Joy, 1950–1963* (hereafter, *CL* 3). Edited by Walter Hooper. London: Harper Collins, 2006.

———. *The Collected Poems of C. S. Lewis* (hereafter, *CP*). Edited by Walter Hooper. London: Fount, 1994.

———. *Dymer.* London: J. M. Dent, 1926. Also consulted was the reprinted edition with an introduction by Lewis (London: J. M. Dent, 1950).
———. "Early Poems: English Verses Made by Clive Staples Lewis and Copied by His Friend Joseph Arthur Greeves: Belfast in the Year 1917" (hereafter, "Early Poems"). Holograph. The original is held by the Linen Hall Library, Belfast, Ireland. A photocopy of the original available in the Wheaton College's Wade Center, CSL / MS-41 / X.
———. "Half Hours with Hamilton or Quiet Moments" (hereafter, "Half Hours with Hamilton"). Holograph versions available in the Wade Center, CSL / MS-53, and the Bodleian, MSS. Facs. c. fols. 143–152. The manuscript bears this epigraph: "It is hoped that this little selection from my works, from which all objectionable matter has been carefully excluded, will be found specially suitable for Sunday and family reading, and also to the higher forms of secondary schools."
———. *Letters to Malcolm: Chiefly on Prayer.* London: Geoffrey Bles, 1964.
———. *Narrative Poems* (hereafter, *NP*). Edited by Walter Hooper. New York: Harcourt Brace Jovanovich, 1969.
———. *The Pilgrim's Regress* (hereafter, *PR*). London: J. M. Dent, 1933.
———. *Poems* (hereafter, *P*). Edited by Walter Hooper. New York: Harcourt Brace Jovanovich, 1964.
———. *Selected Literary Essays.* Edited by Walter Hooper. Cambridge, UK: Cambridge Univ. Press, 1969.
——— [Clive Hamilton, pseud]. *Spirits in Bondage: A Cycle of Lyrics* (hereafter, *SB*). London: Heinemann, 1919. Reprint, with an introduction by Walter Hooper, New York: Harcourt Brace Jovanovich, 1984.
———. "Young King Cole and Other Pieces by C. S. Lewis, Fellow of Magdalen College, Oxford." Typescript and holograph available in the Bodleian, Dep. c. 883–84.
Lewis, Warren H., ed. "The Lewis Papers: Memoirs of the Lewis Family, 1850–1930" (hereafter, "LP"). 11 volumes. Unpublished typescript available in the Warren H. Lewis Papers, Wade Center.

Other Sources by Specific Poem or Collection

"Abecedarium Philosophicum." Written in collaboration with Owen Barfield, this poem was first published in the *Oxford Magazine* 52 (Nov. 30, 1933): 298. A partial draft appears in "LP" 9:164–65.

"Adam at Night." First published (under N. W.) in *Punch* 216 (May 11, 1949): 510. Revised and retitled "The Adam at Night" in *P*, 45, and *CP*, 59. Holograph versions available in the Wade Center, CSL / MS-45, and in the Bodleian, MSS, Facs. c. 54, fol. 121.

"Admiral Stamped on the Quarter Deck, The." Published here for the first time. Found in an unpublished letter to Humphrey Havard, Aug. 1943; Havard appends the following to the end of the poem: "By C. S. Lewis on my return from sea, Aug. 1943." Holograph version available in the Wade Center, CSL / MS-1.

"After Aristotle (Ἀρετὰ πολύμοχθε)." First published (under N. W.) in the *Oxford Magazine* 74 (Feb. 23, 1956): 296. Reprinted in *P*, 80, and *CP*, 94. Holograph version available in the Wade Center, CSL / MS-2. Typescript version available in the Bodleian, Dep. c. 884.

"After Kirby's *Kalevala*." First published (under N. W.) in the *Oxford Magazine* 55 (May 13, 1937): 595. Holograph versions available in the Wade Center, CSL / MS-32, and in the Bodleian, MSS. Facs. c. 54, fol. 141.

"Against Potpourri." From "Early Poems." First published in *CP,* 231.

"Age Will Come, An." Published here for the first time. Holograph version available in the Wade Center, CSL / MS-144.

"Alexandrines." From *Spirits in Bondage.*

"All Things." First published as "Epigrams and Epitaphs 8" in *P,* 134; reprinted in *CP,* 148. Holograph version available in the Bodleian, Dep. c. 884.

"All This Is Flashy Rhetoric about Loving You." First published as "As the Ruin Falls" in *P,* 109; reprinted in *CP,* 123. Holograph versions available in the Bodleian, Dep. c. 883 and MSS. Facs. c. 54, fol. 104.

"Anamnesis." From "Early Poems." First published in King, "Lost but Found."

"And After This They Sent Me to Another Place." First published in King, "Glints," 80–81. See also "LP" 3:262–63.

"Apologist's Evening Prayer, The." First published in *P,* 129; reprinted in *CP,* 143. An early draft of this poem appears in a letter to Sister Penelope, July 29, 1942, published in *CL* 2:527. Holograph versions available in the Wade Center, CSL / MS-137/B, and in the Bodleian, Dep. c. 883.

"Apology." From *Spirits in Bondage.*

"Arise My Body." First published in *Fear No More,* 89. Revised and retitled "After Prayers, Lie Cold," in *P,* 130, and *CP,* 144. Holograph version available in a notebook Hooper holds.

"Arrangement of Pindar." First published in *Mandrake* 1, no. 6 (1949): 43–45. Revised and retitled "Pindar Sang" in *P,* 15, and *CP,* 29. Holograph versions available in the Wade Center, CSL / MS-6, and in the Bodleian, MSS, Facs. c. 54, fols. 137–38.

"Artless and Ignorant Is Andvāri." Found in an unpublished letter to Owen Barfield, June 26, [1929?]. First published in King, *C. S. Lewis, Poet,* 294. Holograph versions available in the Wade Center, CSL / MS-7, and in the Bodleian, MSS. Facs. c. 54, fol. 127.

"As Long as Rolling Wheels Rotate." Published here for the first time. Holograph version available in the Wade Center, CSL / MS-84.

"As One Oldster to Another." First published (under N. W.) in *Punch* 218 (Mar. 15, 1950): 294–95. Revised and reprinted in *P,* 41, and *CP,* 55. Holograph and typescript versions available in the Bodleian, Dep. c. 833–34.

"Ass, The." From *Spirits in Bondage.*

"Aubade [Somehow it's strange discovering, dear]." Found in an unpublished letter to Owen Barfield, July 12, 1957. Published here for the first time. Holograph versions available in the Wade Center, CSL / MS-9, and in the Bodleian, MSS. Facs. c. 54, fol. 109.

"Aubade [Eight strokes sound from within]." First published in *P,* 78; reprinted in *CP,* 92. Holograph version available in the Bodleian, Dep. c. 884.

"Autumn Morning, The." From *Spirits in Bondage.*

"Awake, My Lute!" First published in the *Atlantic Monthly* 172 (Nov. 1943): 113, 115. Reprinted in *CP,* 246.

"Ballade Mystique." From *Spirits in Bondage.*

"Ballade of a Winter's Morning." From "Early Poems." First published in *CP,* 234.

"Ballade of Dead Gentlemen." First published (under N. W.) in *Punch* 220 (Mar. 28, 1951): 386. Reprinted in *P,* 42, and *CP,* 56.

"Ballade on a Certain Pious Gentleman." From "Early Poems." First published in King, "Lost but Found."

"Because of Endless Pride." First published in *PR.* Revised and retitled "Posturing" in *P,* 89, and *CP,* 103. Holograph versions available in "Half Hours with Hamilton," and in the Bodleian, MSS, Facs. c. 54, fol. 80.

"Best Quality Sackcloth & Ashes." Found in a letter to Dorothy L. Sayers, July 6, 1945. First published in *CL* 2:663.

"Birth of Language, The." First published (under N. W.) in *Punch* 210 (Jan. 9, 1946): 32. A later draft appears in a letter to Ruth Pitter, July 24, 1946, published in *CL* 2:725–26. Revised and reprinted in *P,* 10, and *CP,* 24. Holograph versions available in the Wade Center, CSL / MS-12, CSL / MS-13/B, and CSL / MS-165/B, and in the Bodleian, MSS, Facs. c. 54, fols. 90–91.

"Break, Sun, My Crusted Earth." First published in *Fear No More,* 72. Substantially revised and retitled "A Pageant Played in Vain," in *P,* 96, and *CP,* 110. Holograph versions available in the Wade Center, CSL / MS-131, and in the Bodleian, MSS. Facs. c. 54, fol. 94.

"But in All Dialects." Found in an unpublished letter to Owen Barfield (n.d.). First published in King, *C. S. Lewis, Poet,* 293. Holograph version available in the notebook "Including author manuscript of poems undated" in the Wade Center, and in the Bodleian, MSS. Facs. c. 54, Fol. 118.

"Call *Him* a Fascist? Thus the Rabbit." Found in a letter to Ruth Pitter, June 6, 1947. First published in *CL* 2:780. Holograph available in the Wade Center, CSL / MS-43/B.

"Carpe Diem." First published in *C. S. Lewis: Images of His World,* ed. Douglas Gilbert and Clyde Kilby (Grand Rapids, Mich.: Eerdmans, 1973), 113; this version appears as a holograph and is dated Oct. 13, 1913. It is the version I publish here. A slightly different version was included in a letter Lewis sent his father, postmarked Oct. 19, 1913 (see "LP" 4:87–90). When Warren Lewis reproduces the poem in "LP," he titles it "Carpe diem after Horace. In the metre of 'Locksley Hall.'" Tennyson's "Locksley Hall" is written in lines of eight-stressed catalectic trochaic meter. In his unpublished biography of his brother, Warren Lewis quotes W. T. Kirkpatrick's comment on this poem after receiving a copy of it from Albert Lewis: "The verse translation takes my breath away. It is an amazing performance for a boy of his age—indeed for a boy of any age" (see the Warren H. Lewis Papers in the Wade Center, 29). The poem was probably written with the encouragement of Henry Wakelyn Smith (a.k.a. Smugy or Smewgy), Lewis's first great teacher. Lewis writes about Smith in Surprised by Joy (hereafter SJ) and devotes part of the narrative poem "And After This They Sent Me to Another Place" to him. Lewis used Horace's "Aequam Memento Rebus" (Book II, Ode iii) as his model, though he slightly shifted the sober, at times depressing Horatian tone to an upbeat, seize-the-day affirmation. This is most apparent in a comparison of the final stanzas. Horace says: "Omnes eodem cogimur, omnium / Versatur urna serius ocius / Sors exitura et nos in aeternum / Exsilium impositura cumbae." This Latin text is found in *Horace: The Odes and Epodes,* ed. C. E. Bennett (Cambridge, Mass.: Univ. of Massachusetts Press, 1914), 114. A translation, by J. H. Deazeley, follows. See *The Complete Works of Horace,* ed. Caspar Kraemer Jr.; trans. J. H. Deazeley (New York: Modern Library, 1936), 186.

One bourne constrains us all; for all
The lots are shaken in the urn,
Whence, soon or late, will fall our turn
Of exile's barge without recall.

"Carpet Rises in the Draught, The." First published in King, "Glints," 85. See "LP" 11:251, where Warren Lewis says his brother dated the poem "probably 1922–23."

"Chanson D'Aventure." First published (under N. W.) in the *Oxford Magazine* 56 (May 19, 1938): 638. Revised and retitled as "What the Bird Said Early in the Year" in *P,* 71, and *CP,* 85. Holograph and typescript versions available in the Bodleian, Dep. c. 883–84.

"Circe—A Fragment." From "Early Poems." First published in *CP,* 241.

"Cliché Came Out of Its Cage, A." First published in *Nine: A Magazine of Poetry and Criticism* 2 (May 1950): 114. Revised (with new second stanza) and reprinted in *P,* 3, and *CP,* 17. Holograph versions available in the Wade Center, CSL / MS-28 / X, and in the Bodleian, Dep. c. 883.

"Consolation." First published in *CP,* 249. Holograph version available in the Bodleian, Dep. c. 884. Hooper dates the poem as sometime in 1945.

"Conversation Piece: The Magician and the Dryad." First published (under N. W.) in *Punch* 217 (July 20, 1949): 71. Revised and retitled "The Magician and the Dryad" in *P,* 8, and *CP,* 22. Holograph and typescript versions available in the Bodleian, Dep. c. 883–84.

"Coronation March." First published (under N. W.) in the *Oxford Magazine* 55 (May 6, 1937): 565. Revised and reprinted in *P,* 67, and *CP,* 81. Holograph versions available at the Wade Center, CSL / MS-32, and in the Bodleian, MSS, Facs. c. 54, fol. 141.

"Country of the Blind, The." First published (under N. W.) in *Punch* 221 (Sept. 12, 1951): 303. Reprinted in *P,* 33, and *CP,* 47.

"Couplets." From "Early Poems." First published in *CP,* 240.

"Cradle-song Based on a Theme from Nicolas of Cusa." First published in the *Times Literary Supplement,* June 11, 1954, 375. Revised and retitled "Science-Fiction Cradlesong" in *P,* 57, and *CP,* 71. Holograph version available in the Bodleian, Dep. c. 883.

"Dangerous Oversight." First published (under N. W.) in *Punch* 212 (May 21, 1947): 434. A later draft appears in a letter to Ruth Pitter, July 6, 1947, published in *CL* 2:792–94. Revised and retitled "Young King Cole" in *P,* 19, and *CP,* 33. Holograph versions available in the Wade Center, CSL / MS-38/B, and in the Bodleian, Dep. c. 884.

"Day with the White Mark, The." First published (under N. W.) in *Punch* 217 (Aug. 17, 1949): 170. Revised and reprinted in *P,* 28, and *CP,* 42. Holograph and typescript versions available in the Bodleian, Dep. c. 883–84.

"Dear Dorothy, I'm Puzzling Hard." In a letter to Dorothy L. Sayers, Dec. 27, 1954. First published in *CL* 3:548.

"Dear Mr. Marshall, Thank You." In a letter to Blanchard Marshall, Feb. 16, 1963. First published in *CL* 3:1411.

"Dear Roy—Why Should Each Wowzer on the List." First published as "To Roy Campbell," in *P,* 66; reprinted in *CP,* 80. Holograph version available in the Bodleian, Dep. c. 884.

"Death in Battle." From *Spirits in Bondage.*

"Death Song, A." From "Early Poems." First published in King, "Lost but Found."

"Decadence." From "Early Poems." First published in King, "Lost but Found."

"De Profundis." From *Spirits in Bondage.*

"Descend to Earth, Descend, Celestial Nine." First published in King, *C. S. Lewis, Poet,* 245–65; for a brief discussion of the poem, see 28–34. See also "LP" 3:321–36, where Warren Lewis notes that the poem was written "between the summers of 1912 and of 1913" (321).

"Despoina, Bear with Me." From "Early Poems." First published in King, "Lost but Found."

"D. H. Lawrence, Dr. Stopes." In a letter to Dorothy L. Sayers, Mar. 4, 1954. First published in King, *C. S. Lewis, Poet,* 296. See also *CL* 3:436–37. In Lewis's follow-up letter to Sayers of Mar. 9, 1954, he offered to alter the opening lines to: "D. H. Lawrence, Sigmund Freud, / Taught by you we now avoid, / All restraints that once destroyed / Wholly earthly Lerv" (437). Holograph version available in the Wade Center, CSL / MS-36.

"Donkeys' Delight." First published (under N. W.) in *Punch* 213 (Nov. 5, 1947): 442. Revised and reprinted in *P,* 29, and *CP,* 43. An early draft appears in a letter to Ruth Pitter, July 6, 1947, published in *CL* 2:790–92. Holograph versions available in the Wade Center, CSL / MS-37, and in the Bodleian, MSS, Facs. c. 54, fol. 133.

"Dungeon Grates." From *Spirits in Bondage.*

Dymer. London: J. M. Dent, 1926 (under pseudonym Clive Hamilton); reprinted 1950 (under Lewis's own name) with a preface by Lewis. Except for holograph rough drafts of cantos 6, 7, 8, and 9 in a notebook held by Walter Hooper (with copies held at the Wade Center), there are no other holographs of *Dymer.* Hooper dates the drafts as composed in 1924–25 (preface to *SB,* x). Lewis himself offers a chronological history of the writing of *Dymer* (see the note at the end of canto 11). To my knowledge no copy of the original typescript survives. The text presented here is based on the first edition.

"Early Poems: English Verses Made by C. S. Lewis." I have offered a careful analysis of "Early Poems" in my essay "Lost but Found: The 'Missing' Poems of C. S. Lewis's *Spirits in Bondage,*" *Christianity and Literature* 53 (Winter 2004): 163–201. Rather than reproduce the entire article in this volume, I have excerpted an emended version of the first portion of the essay as an appendix to this volume; it includes a discussion of how "Early Poems" relates to *Spirits in Bondage,* a list of all the poems appearing in "Early Poems," and the date of each poem. Another important source of information regarding some of the poems in this collection is "LP," since eleven of the poems appear there: "The Hills of Down," "Against Potpourri," "A Prelude," "Ballade of a Winter's Morning," "Laus Mortis," "Sonnet—To Sir Philip Sydney," "Of Ships," "Couplets," "Circe—A Fragment," "Exercise," and "Ballade Mystical" (published as "Ballade Mystique" in *SB*). While I have consulted the versions in "LP," unless otherwise noted the texts published here are from "Early Poems." After the table of contents of "Early Poems," the following phrase in French appears: "Au chemin frayé qui conduit sur Parnasse" (At the well-worn path that leads to Mt. Parnasse) (De Ronsard). "Early Poems" also contains a title page for the poem "Venite," but does not provide the text of the poem.

"Ecstasy, The." First published in *P,* 36; reprinted in *CP,* 50. Holograph and typescript versions available in Bodleian, Dep. c. 883–84.

"End of the Wine, The." First published (under N. W.) in *Punch* 213 (Dec. 3, 1947): 538. Revised and retitled "The Last of the Wine" in *P,* 40, and *CP,* 54. Holograph and typescript versions available in the Bodleian, Dep. c. 883–84.

"Epanorthosis (for the end of Goethe's *Faust*)." First published (under N. W.) in the *Cambridge Review* 77 (May 26, 1956): 610. Revised and retitled "Epigrams and Epitaphs 15" in *P,* 136, and *CP,* 150. Typescript version available in the Bodleian, Dep. c. 884.

"[Epigraph]." From *Spirits in Bondage.*

"Epitaph [From end to end of the bright, airy ward]." First published in the *Spectator* 181 (July 30, 1948): 142. Revised and retitled "Epigrams and Epitaphs 14" in *P,* 135, and *CP,* 149. Holograph and typescript versions available in the Bodleian, Dep. c. 883–84.

"Epitaph [Here lies the whole world after one]." First published in the *Month* 2 (July 1949): 8. Revised and retitled "Epigrams and Epitaphs 17" in *P,* 137, and *CP,* 151. Holograph and typescript versions available in the Bodleian, Dep. c. 883–84.

"Epitaph [She was delicately, beautifully made]." First published in *Time and Tide* 23 (June 6, 1942): 460. Revised and retitled "Epigrams and Epitaphs 11" in *P,* 135, and *CP,* 149. Holograph versions available in the Wade Center, CSL / MS-127/B, and in the Bodleian, Dep. c. 883.

"Epitaph for Helen Joy Davidman." This is a re-working of "Epitaph (Here Lies the Whole World after One)," which was first published in the *Month* 2 (July 1949): 8 and was revised and retitled "Epigrams and Epitaphs, No. 17" in *P,* 137, and *CP,* 151. It serves as Davidman's memorial marker at the Oxford Crematorium. First published in this form in *C. S. Lewis:*

Images of His World, by Douglas Gilbert and Clyde S. Kilby (Grand Rapids, Mich.: Eerdmans, 1973), 65. Also appears in *CL* 3:1172 and in *CP,* 252. Holograph versions available in the Bodleian, Dep. c. 883.

"Epitaph in a Village Churchyard." First published in *Time and Tide* 30 (Mar. 19, 1949): 272. A later draft appears in a letter to Ruth Pitter, Aug. 24, 1949, published in *CL* 2:972. Retitled "Epigrams and Epitaphs 16" in *P,* 136, and *CP,* 150. Holograph and typescript versions available in the Bodleian, Dep. c. 883–84.

"Erected by Her Sorrowing Brothers." First published as "Epigrams and Epitaphs 10" in *P,* 134; reprinted in *CP,* 148. Holograph and typescript versions available in the Bodleian, Dep. c. 883–84.

"Essence." First published in *Fear No More,* 4. Reprinted in *CP,* 248. Holograph versions appear in "Half Hours with Hamilton" and in the Bodleian, MSS, Facs. c. 54, fol. 105.

"Examiner Sits into Quarrie, The." In a letter to Edmund Blunden, Mar. 26, 1935. First published in *CL* 3:1526.

"Exercise." From "Early Poems." First published in *CP,* 242.

"Exercise on an Old Theme." From "Early Poems." First published in King, "Lost but Found."

"Experempment." Published here for the first time. Holograph version, dated Oct. 5, 1956, available in the Wade Center, CSL / MS-46.

"Experiment." First published in the *Spectator* 161 (Dec. 9, 1938): 998. Revised and retitled as "Pattern" in *P,* 79, and *CP,* 93. An early draft of this poem appears in a letter to Owen Barfield, Sept. 6, 1938, published in *CL* 2:230. Holograph versions available at the Wade Center, CSL / MS-110, and in the Bodleian, MSS, Facs. c. 54, fol.123.

"Expostulation (Against too many writers of science fiction), An." First published in the *Magazine of Fantasy and Science Fiction* 16, no. 6 (June 1959): 47. Reprinted in *P,* 58, and *CP,* 72.

"Evolutionary Hymn." First published (under N. W.) in the *Cambridge Review* 79 (Nov. 30, 1957): 227. Reprinted in *P,* 55, and *CP,* 69. An early draft appears in a letter to Dorothy L. Sayers, Mar. 4, 1954, published in *CL* 3:435–36. Holograph version available in the Wade Center, CSL / MS-67.

"Fidelia Vulnera Amantis." Found in an unpublished letter to Owen Barfield [n.d.]. Published here for the first time. Holograph versions available in the Wade Center, CSL / MS-138, and in the Bodleian, MSS. Facs. c. 54, fol. 52.

"Finchley Avenue." First published in Adams, *Occasional Poets,* 102–4. Reprinted in *CP,* 250. Holograph version available in the Bodleian, Dep. d. 809, fols. 64–65.

"Five Sonnets." First published in *P,* 125; reprinted in *CP,* 139. Holograph and typescript versions available in the Bodleian, Dep. c. 883–84 and MSS. Facs. c. fols. 139–40. Another holograph is available in the Wade Center, CSL / MS-95, where sequence is titled "Quantum est quo veneat Omne?" This is a quotation from *Manilius: Astronomica,* Book 4, line 406. A. T. Reyes notes the Latin text for lines 406–7: "quid caelo dabimus? quantum est, quo veneat omne? / impendendus homo est, deus esse ut possit in ipso." G. P. Goold translates this passage as "What then shall we give for heaven? What is the worth of that, with which we may purchase all? / Man must expend his very self, before God can dwell in him." See G. P. Goold, ed. and trans., *Manilius: Astronomica* (Cambridge, MA: Harvard Univ. Press, 1977).

"Floating Islands, The." First published in Green and Hooper's *C. S. Lewis: A Biography,* 171. Holograph version available in a notebook Hooper holds.

"Footnote to Pre-History, A." First published (under N. W.) in *Punch* 217 (Sept. 14, 1949): 304. Revised and retitled "The Adam Unparadised" in *P,* 43, and *CP,* 57. Holograph versions available in the Wade Center, CSL / MS-48, and in the Bodleian, MSS, Facs. c. 54, fol. 130.

"French Nocturne." From *Spirits in Bondage.*

"From the Latin of Milton's *De Idea Platonica Quemadmodum Aristoteles Intellexit.*" First published in *English* 5, no. 30 (1945): 195. Lewis refers to a draft of this poem in a letter to Owen Barfield, July 12, 1945, published in *CL* 2:664.

"Funny Old Man Had a Habit, A." Found in a letter to Sarah Neylan, July 16, 1944. First published in *C. S. Lewis: Letters to Children,* ed. Lyle W. Dorsett and Marjorie Lamp Mead (London: Collins, 1985), 21. Also in *CL* 2:619.

"Future of Forestry, The." First published (under N. W.) in the *Oxford Magazine* 56 (Feb. 10, 1938): 383. Revised and reprinted in *P,* 61, and *CP,* 75. Holograph versions available in the Wade Center, CSL / MS-32, and the Bodleian, MSS, Facs. c. 54, fols. 141–42.

"God in His Mercy Made." First published in *PR.* Revised and retitled "Divine Justice" in *P,* 98, and *CP,* 112. Holograph versions available in "Half Hours with Hamilton" and in the Bodleian, MSS, Facs. c. 54, fol. 97.

"Go Litel Tugge upon Thes Watres Shene." Found in an unpublished letter to Owen Barfield, [n.d]. Published here for the first time. Holograph versions are available in the Wade Center, CSL / MS-51, and in the Bodleian, MSS. Facs. c. 54, fol. 89.

"Goodly Fair, The." Published here for the first time. Holograph version available in the Wade Center, CSL / MS-146.

"Have You Not Seen that in Our Days." First published as "Epigrams and Epitaphs 2" in *P,* 133; reprinted in *CP,* 147. Holograph and typescript versions available in the Bodleian, Dep. 883–84.

"Heart-breaking School." First published in King, "Glints," 79–80. See also "LP" 3:41–42.

"Hedgehog Moralised, The." First published in King, *C. S. Lewis, Poet,* 293. Appears in an unpublished letter to Owen Barfield, [1927–1928?]. Holograph versions available in the Wade Center, CSL / MS-139, and in the Bodleian, MSS. Facs. c. 53, fol. 210; the holograph includes a heading with the word *PURCPINABILIA,* several drawings by Lewis of porcupine-like creatures on top of someone in a bed who is saying "'TS ABSURB," the phrase "URCHINS / Shall for that vast of night that they may work / All exercise on thee," and another drawing of a porcupine-like creature blowing a horn with the phrase "URCHIN blasts (and mildew power)."

"Here Lies One Kind of Speech." First published as "Epigrams and Epitaphs 13" in *P,* 135; reprinted in *CP,* 149. Holograph and transcript versions are available in the Bodleian, Dep. c. 883–84.

"Hermione in the House of Paulina." First published in *Augury: An Oxford Miscellany of Verse and Poetry,* ed. A. M. Hardie and K. C. Douglas (Oxford: Blackwell, 1940), 28. Revised and reprinted in *P,* 18, and *CP,* 32. Holograph versions are available in the Wade Center, CSL / MS-56, and in the Bodleian, MSS, Facs. c. 54, fol. 119.

"Hesperus." From *Spirits in Bondage.*

"He Whom I Bow To." First published in *PR.* Revised and retitled "Footnote to All Prayers" in *P,* 129, and *CP,* 143. Holograph versions available in "Half Hours with Hamilton" and in the Bodleian, MSS, Facs. c. 54, fol. 126.

"Hills of Down, The." From "Early Poems." First published in *CP,* 229.

"How Can I Ask Thee, Father?" First published in Green and Hooper, *C. S. Lewis: A Biography,* 183. Holograph version available in a notebook Hooper holds.

"How He Saw Angus the God." From *Spirits in Bondage.*

"Hylas." From "Early Poems." First published in King, "Lost but Found."

"Hymn (For Boys' Voices)." From *Spirits in Bondage.*

"I Am not One that Easily Flits Past in Thought." First published in *PR.* Revised and retitled "When the Curtain's Down" in *P,* 97, and *CP,* 111. Holograph version appears in "Half Hours with Hamilton."

"Ichabod." Published here for the first time. This poem was found in unpublished correspondence between Lewis and Max Beloff, the editor of the *Oxford Magazine,* in May 1954. After initially submitting the poem (under N. W.) to Beloff, Lewis withdrew it. Beloff pressed Lewis to reconsider, but Lewis wrote: "Impossible! You see my party won: which leaves me (as a satirist) undone. I even may let the embittered numbers flow, but only cads insult a beaten foe." Holograph versions available in Wade Center, CSL / MS-183/B, and in the Bodleian, Dep. c. 773 fols. 235–38 (title by Lewis).

"If We Had Remembered." First published as "Epigrams and Epitaphs 5" in *P,* 133; reprinted in *CP,* 147. Holograph version available in the Wade Center, CSL / MS-127/B (there it Lewis entitled it "Any Soul to Any Soul"); holograph and typescript versions available in the Bodleian, Dep. c. 883–84.

"If with Posterity Good Fame." First published in King, *C. S. Lewis, Poet,* 297. Holograph version available in the Bodleian, Dep. c. 884.

"I Have Come Back with Victory Got." First published in *PR.* Revised and retitled "Dragon-Slayer" in *P,* 94, and *CP,* 108. Holograph version appears in "Half Hours with Hamilton."

"I Have Scraped Clean the Plateau." First published in *PR.* Revised and retitled "Virtue's Independence" in *P,* 88, and *CP,* 102. Holograph versions available in the Bodleian, Dep. c. 884.

"I Know Far Less of Spiders." In a letter to Ruth Pitter, Apr. 16, 1952. First published in *CL* 3:183.

"I Know Not, I." First published in *PR.* Revised and retitled "Angel's Song" in *P,* 107, and *CP,* 121. Holograph and typescripts versions available in the Bodleian, Dep. c. 883–84.

"Impenitence." First published (under N. W.) in *Punch* 225 (July 15, 1953): 91. Reprinted in *P,* 2, and *CP,* 16.

"In a Spring Season I Sailed Away." This poem, which Hooper entitled "The Nameless Isle" and dated to Aug. 1930, was first published in *NP,* 105–27. A holograph version of this poem appears in a notebook held by Walter Hooper and includes an introductory note by Lewis. The text presented here follows the holograph version and the version printed in *NP.* In brief, "In a Spring Season I Sailed Away" reflects Lewis's love of Old English alliterative verse, with each line divided into half lines where one sound bridges the halves to connect the whole. In the opening line of the poem, for instance, the first half line, "in a *s*pring *s*eason," bridges to the second, "I *s*ailed away," by the *s* sound, which alliterates and creates the bridge; with few exceptions, this alliterative pattern is repeated throughout. The 742 lines of alliterative verse tell a fast-paced story of a shipwrecked mariner and his adventures on a magic island. Although Lewis did not divide it into cantos, the poem can be broken into four parts. Part 1, covering the first 226 lines, concerns the shipwreck and the mariner's subsequent encounter with a beautiful enchantress who commissions him to find and release her daughter from the spell of an evil wizard. Part 2, lines 226–373, shows the mariner on his quest, where he discovers an abandoned flute and a comically grotesque dwarf who offers to assist him. Part 3, lines 374–593, describes the mariner's meeting with the wizard and the release of the enchantress' daughter. Part 4, lines 594–742, presents the reconciliation of the enchantress and the wizard, as well as the mariner's idyllic voyage back to England.

Lewis's introductory note follows:

Every verse contains two half-verses. Each half-verse contains two beats or accents: and two dips which may consist of any number of unaccented syllables. The dips and beats may be arranged:

a. In falling rhythm (—u—u) (—uu—uu) (—u—uu), etc.

e.g. Éarly at évening

Máster máriner

b. In rising rhythm (u—u—) (uu—uu—) (u—uu—), etc.

e.g. of the mén was I

While fást and fáir

c. In clashing rhythm (uu——uu) (u——u), etc.

e.g. In a spríng seáson

Over our shíp scúdding

d. As beat-dip-beat, without a second dip, if the single dip contains a syllable so strong that it nearly equals a beat (—´—u—) (—´—´uu—).

e.g. Eíghtéen in áll

wítch-heárted quéen

The reader should read all with its natural accent and carefully avoid the artificial accents of syllabic verse

e.g. Óf thĕ *sea's rísing*

not, as it would be in the heroic line

Óf the sea's rísing múch he spoke in vain.

There may be either two or three alliterations in the verse, of which only one can fall in the second half verse.

All vowels alliterate together.

More on Lewis's ideas about alliterative verse can be found in his essay "The Alliterative Metre," in *Selected Literary Essays,* ed. Walter Hooper (Cambridge, UK: Cambridge Univ. Press, 1969), 15–26.

"Infatuation." First published in *P,* 73; reprinted in *CP,* 87.

"In His Own Image." From "Early Poems." First published in King, "Lost but Found."

"In Praise of Solid People." From *Spirits in Bondage.*

"In Prison." From *Spirits in Bondage.*

"Interim Report." In a letter to William Borst, June 22, [1952?]. First published in *CL* 3:206–7.

"In Winter When the Frosty Nights Are Long." First published in King, "Glints," 75. See "LP" 4:121, where Warren Lewis says this fragment dates from winter 1913 to spring 1914.

"Irish Nocturne." From *Spirits in Bondage.*

"Iron Will Eat the World's Old Beauty Up." First published in *PR.* Revised and retitled "Deception" in *P,* 90, and *CP,* 104.

"I Will Write Down the Portion that I Understand." Appears in a letter to Owen Barfield, May 6, 1932, published in *CL* 2:77–78; in the letter Lewis writes: "I send . . . the opening of the poem. I am not satisfied with any part I have yet written and the design is ludicrously ambitious. But I feel it will be several years anyway before I give it up." In *C. S. Lewis: A Biography,* Green and Hooper write: "In the spring of 1932 [Lewis] had another go at writing the story of Joy leading on to conversion. This, like the first attempt, was to be in the form of a long narrative poem. Only 34 lines of it have survived" (127). Hooper and Green then quote the first twelve lines. The complete text of these thirty-four lines of rhyming alexandrine couplets was first published in King, "Glints," 86–87. Holograph version available in the Wade Center, CSL / MS-141.

"I Woke from a Fool's Dream, to Find All Spent." First published as "Epigrams and Epitaphs 3" in *P,* 133; reprinted in *CP,* 147. This poem appears in variant holographs in "Half Hours with Hamilton," in a notebook Hooper holds, and in the Bodleian, MSS. Facs. c. fol. 144.

"Joy." First published (under the pseudonym Clive Hamilton) in the *Beacon* 3, no. 31 (May 1924): 444–45. Reprinted in *CP,* 243.

"Lady, a Better Sculptor Far." First published as "Epigrams and Epitaphs 9" in *P,* 134; reprinted in *CP,* 148. Holograph version available in the Bodleian, Dep. c. 884.

"Lady, to This Fair Breast I Know but One." First published as "Epigrams and Epitaphs 1" in *P,* 133; reprinted in *CP,* 147. Holograph and typescript versions available in the Bodleian, Dep. c. 883–84.

"Laertes to Napoleon." In an unpublished letter to Barfield, [n.d.]. First published in King, *C. S. Lewis, Poet,* 292. Holograph versions available in the Wade Center, CSL / MS-54, and in the Bodleian, MSS. Facs. c. 54, fol. 124.

"Landing, The." First published (under N. W.) in *Punch* 215 (Sept. 15, 1948): 237. Revised and reprinted in *P,* 27, and *CP,* 41. Holograph and typescript versions available in the Bodleian, Dep. c. 883–84.

"L'apprenti Sorcier." From *Spirits in Bondage.*

"Late Summer." First published in *P,* 104; reprinted in *CP,* 118. A draft of the last line of this poem appears in a letter to Ruth Pitter, Aug. 31, 1948, published in *CL* 2:875. Holograph versions are available in the Bodleian, Dep. c. 883 and in a notebook Hooper holds.

"Laus Mortis." From "Early Poems." First published in *CP,* 236.

"Legion." First published in the *Month* 13 (Apr. 1955): 210. Revised and reprinted in *P,* 119, and *CP,* 133. Holograph versions available in the Wade Center, CSL / MS-72, and in the Bodleian, MSS. Facs. c. 54, fol. 100.

"*Le Roi S'Amuse.*" First published (under N. W.) in *Punch* 213 (Oct. 1, 1947): 324. Revised and reprinted in *P,* 23, and *CP,* 37. Holograph versions available in the Wade Center, CSL / MS-66, and in the Bodleian, Dep. c. 883.

"Lines During a General Election." First published in *P,* 62; reprinted in *CP,* 76. Two holograph versions are available in the Bodleian, Dep. c. 883; in one holograph version, the title is "Government."

"Lines to Mr. Compton Mackenzie." First published in King, "Glints," 90–91. Holograph versions available in the Wade Center, CSL / MSS-166, B, and in the Bodleian, MS. Eng. lett. c. 861, fol. 69.

"Lines Written in a Copy of Milton's Work." First published in *P,* 83; reprinted in *CP,* 97.

"Little Golden Statuette, The." From "Early Poems." First published in King, "Lost but Found."

Loki Bound. See "LP" 4:218–20. First published in King, *C. S. Lewis, Poet,* 265–69. The poem was written sometime before June 5, 1914, since Lewis writes Arthur Greeves on that date: "Of course, take the 'Loki Bound' MS over to Bernagh [Greeves's home, directly across the street from Lewis's home, Little Lea, in Belfast] anytime you feel inclined to compose a little operatic music" (*CL* 1:59). In a letter to Greeves dated Oct. 6, 1914, Lewis proposes they collaborate on the poem with an eye toward making it an opera, Wagner's influence and his own experience writing "Descend to Earth" obviously operating upon his imagination. Lewis offers a detailed synopsis of this "would-be tragedy" in the letter; for its entire text, see *CL* 1:75–78. Warren Lewis says this poem "occupies thirty two pages of a folio notebook, and is elaborately written, in black ink, with the characters names, episode headings etc. in red. The volume bears for title, 'LOKI BOUND and other poems' by C. S. Lewis" ("LP" 4:217). Unfortunately, Warren Lewis preserved only four fragments of the poem, consisting respectively of eighty-three lines, eight lines, sixteen lines, and twelve lines. He also explains how the manuscript containing *Loki Bound* was destroyed: "Jack himself burnt all documents therein transcribed [in "LP"], including his own diaries, in or soon after 1936" (cited by Walter Hooper in his preface to *Spirits in Bondage,* xii).

"Loneliness." From "Early Poems." First published in King, "Lost but Found."

"Long at Lectures." In a letter to Owen Barfield, Oct. 21, 1929. First published in King, *C. S. Lewis, Poet,* 294–95. Also published in *CL* 3 (supplement): 1512–13.

"Lord Is a Jealous God—A Careful Shepherd, The." In a letter to Owen Barfield, Summer (1927?), first published in *CL* 3:1623.

"Lords Coëval with Creation." In a letter to Francis Turner, June 10, 1958, first published in *CL* 3:955–56.

"Love's as Warm as Tears." First published in *P,* 123; reprinted in *CP,* 137. Holograph version available in the Bodleian, Dep. c. 883.

"Lullaby." From *Spirits in Bondage.*

"March for Drum, Trumpet, and Twenty-one Giants." First published in *Punch* 225 (Nov. 4, 1953): 553. Revised and reprinted as stanza 2 of "Narnian Suite," in *P,* 7, and *CP,* 21. Here is stanza 1:

March for Strings, Kettledrums, and Sixty-three Dwarfs

With plucking pizzicato and the prattle of the kettledrum
We're trotting into battle mid a clatter of accoutrement;
Our beards are big as periwigs and trickle with opopanax,
And trinketry and treasure twinkle out on every part of us—
(Scrape! Tap! The fiddle and the kettledrum).

The chuckle-headed humans think we're only petty poppetry
And all our battle-tackle nothing more than pretty bric-a-brac;
But a little shrub has prickles, and they'll soon be in a pickle if
A scud of dwarfish archery has crippled all their cavalry—
(Whizz! Twang! The quarrel and the javelin).

And when the tussle thickens we can writhe and wriggle under it;
Then dagger-point'll tickle 'em, and grab and grip'll grapple 'em,
And trap the trick'll trouble 'em and tackle 'em and topple 'em
Till they're huddled, all be-diddled, in the middle of our caperings—
(Dodge! Jump! The wriggle and the summersault).

When we've scattered 'em and peppered 'em with pebbles from our catapults
We'll turn again in triumph and by crannies and by crevices
Go back to where the capitol and cradle of our people is,
Our forges and our furnaces, the caverns of the earth—
(Gold! Fire! The anvil and the smithying).

Holograph versions available in the Bodleian, Dep. c. 883.

"Meteorite, The." First published in *Time and Tide* 27 (Dec. 7, 1946): 1183. Lewis also published a variant version (with very small differences), in *Miracles: A Preliminary Study* (London: Geoffrey Bles, 1947). Hooper reprinted the *Time and Tide* version in *P*, 99, and *CP*, 113. Holograph version available in the Bodleian, Dep. c. 884.

"ΜΗΔÈΝ ἌΓΑΝ." From "Early Poems." First published in King, "Lost but Found."

"Milton Read Again." From *Spirits in Bondage.*

"My Heart Is Empty." First published in *PR*. Revised and retitled "The Naked Seed" in *P*, 117, and *CP*, 131. Holograph versions available in the Wade Center, CSL / MS-78, and in the Bodleian, MSS, Facs. c. 54, fol. 154.

"My Western Garden." From "Early Poems." First published in King, "Lost but Found."

"Nan est Doctior Omnibus Puellis." In a letter to Nan Dunbar, Apr. 20, 1956. First published in *CL* 3:740.

"Nativity, The." First published in *P*, 122; reprinted in *CP*, 136. Holograph versions available in the Bodleian, Dep. c. 883 and MSS. Facs. c. 49, fol. 103.

"Nearly They Stood Who Fall." First published in *PR*. Revised and retitled "Nearly They Stood" in *P*, 102, and *CP*, 116. Holograph versions available in "Half Hours with Hamilton" and in the Bodleian, MSS, Facs. c. 54, fol. 97.

"New Year's Eve." From "Early Poems." First published in King, "Lost but Found."

"Night [After the fret and failure of this day]." From *Spirits in Bondage.*

"Night [I know a little Druid wood]." From *Spirits in Bondage.*

"Nimue." In a letter to Arthur Greeves, Sept. 18, 1919. First published in *They Stand Together: The Letters of C. S. Lewis to Arthur Greeves,* ed. Walter Hooper, (London: Collins, 1979), 261. Also published in *CL* 1:466. In the letter, Lewis writes that he has given up writing his "Medea" and instead is turning to make his "Nimue" from a monologue into a narrative: "This is the first stanza, do you think it any good?" No other stanzas of the poem survive.

"Noon." From *Spirits in Bondage.*

"Not for Your Reading, Not Because I Dream." Published here for the first time. This poem appears in holograph on the inside cover of Ruth Pitter's copy of *Dymer* (London: J. M. Dent & Sons Ltd.; New York: MacMillian, 1926, 1950). Above the poem is the inscription: "Ruth Pitter from C. S. Lewis 16/10/50." This copy of *Dymer* is available in the Bodleian, Arch H. e. 144.

"Now that Night Is Creeping." First published as "Evensong" in *P*, 128; reprinted in *CP*, 142. Holograph version available in the Bodleian, Dep. c. 884.

"Ocean Strand, The." From *Spirits in Bondage.*

"Ode for New Year's Day." From *Spirits in Bondage.*

"*Odora Canum Vis:* A defence of certain modern biographers and critics." First published in the *Month* 11 (May 1954): 272. Revised and reprinted in *P*, 59, and *CP*, 73.

"Of Ships." From "Early Poems." First published in *CP*, 238.

"Of This Great Suit Who Dares Foresee the End?" Found in an unpublished letter to Owen Barfield, [n.d.]. Published here for the first time. Holograph versions available in the Wade Center, CSL / MS-85, and in the Bodleian, MSS. Facs. c. 54, fol. 108.

"Oh Doe Not Die." First published as "Joys That Sting" in *P*, 108; reprinted in *CP*, 122. Holograph versions available in the Wade Center, CSL / MS-83, and in the Bodleian, Dep. c. 883 and MSS. Facs. c. 54, fol. 103.

"Oh That a Black Ship." Appears in a letter to Leo Baker, [Aug. 14? 1920], published in *CL* 1:506.

"Old Grey Mare, The." Warren Lewis writes: "[This] poem I judge from internal evidence to be the earliest of Clive's attempts in verse which survives" (166). He judges the poem dates from as early as 1907 and as late as 1909. See "LP" 3:166–67. Revised and first published in *Puffin Post* 4, no. 1 (1970): 14–15.

"Old Kirk, Like Father Time Himself." First published in King, "Glints," 82–83. See "LP" 4:64–65.

"On Another Theme from Nicolas of Cusa [*De Docta Ignorantia,* III. ix.]." First published in the *Times Literary Supplement,* Jan. 21, 1955, 43. Revised and retitled "On a Theme from Nicolas of Cusa" in *P,* 70, and *CP,* 84. Holograph versions available in the Wade Center, CSL / MS61, and in the Bodleian, MSS. Facs. c. 54, fol. 102.

"On a Picture by Chirico." First published in the *Spectator* 182 (May 6, 1949): 607. Revised and reprinted in *P,* 69, and *CP,* 83. Holograph and typescript versions available in the Bodleian, Dep. c. 883–84.

"On a Vulgar Error." First published in *P,* 60; reprinted in *CP,* 74. Holograph versions available in the Bodleian, Dep. c. 883.

"On Being Human." First published (under N. W.) in *Punch* 210 (May 8, 1946): 402. A later draft appears in in a letter to Ruth Pitter, July 24, 1946, published in *CL* 2:727–28. Revised and reprinted in *P,* 34, and *CP,* 48. Holograph versions available in the Wade Center, CSL / MS-127/B, and in the Bodleian, Dep. c. 883.

"Once the Worm-laid Egg Broke in the Wood." First published in *PR.* Revised and retitled "The Dragon Speaks" in *P,* 92, and *CP,* 106. Holograph version appears in "Half Hours with Hamilton"; holograph and typescripts versions available in the Bodleian, Dep. c. 883–84.

"One Happier Look on Your Kind, Suffering Face." First published as "Old Poets Remembered" in *P,* 109; reprinted in *CP,* 123. Holograph version available in the Bodleian, Dep. c. 883.

"On Receiving Bad News." First published in *Time and Tide* 26 (Dec. 29, 1945): 1093. Revised and retitled "Epigrams and Epitaphs 12" in *P,* 135, and *CP,* 149. Holograph versions available in the Wade Center, CSL / MS-121, and in the Bodleian, MSS. Facs. c. 54, fol. 122.

"On the Atomic Bomb (Metrical Experiment)." First published in the *Spectator* 175 (Dec. 28, 1945): 619. Reprinted in *P,* 64, and *CP,* 78. An early draft appears in a letter to Owen Barfield, Dec. 19, 1945, published in *CL* 2:688–89. Holograph versions available in the Wade Center, CSL / MS-8, and in the Bodleian, MSS, Facs. c. 54, fol. 132.

"On the Death of Charles Williams." First published in *Britain Today* no. 112 (Aug. 1945): 14. Revised and retitled "To Charles Williams" in *P,* 105, and *CP,* 119. Holograph versions available in the Wade Center, CSL / MS-159/Xt, and in the Bodleian, Dep. c. 883.

"'Our Daily Bread.'" From *Spirits in Bondage.*

"Out of the Wound We Pluck." A version of stanza 5 appears in a letter to Sister Penelope, Nov. 9, 1941, in *CL* 2:495. First published as "Relapse" in *P,* 103; reprinted in *CP,* 117. Holograph version available in a notebook Hooper holds.

"Ovid's 'Pars estis pauci.'" First complete publication appears in King, "Glints," 77–78. See "LP" 4:191–92. In a letter to his father dated June 22, 1914, Lewis writes: "I enclose a few verses in imitation of Ovid, which were top of the form last week and well-spoken of by Smugy. Do you care for that metre? There are a great many rhymes in it, which makes it difficult; but the thing that I want to learn is "to move easily in shackles" (*CL* 1:62). Stanzas 1 and 3 appear in Green and Hooper, *C. S. Lewis: A Biography,* 138.

"Oxford." From *Spirits in Bondage.*

"Pan's Purge." First published (under N. W.) in *Punch* 212 (Jan. 15, 1947): 71. Reprinted in *P,* 5, and *CP,* 19. Holograph version available in the Bodleian, Dep. c. 883.

"Passing To-day by a Cottage, I Shed Tears." First published in *PR*. Revised and retitled "Scazons" in *P,* 118, and *CP,* 132. Holograph versions available in "Half Hours with Hamilton" and in the Bodleian, MSS, Facs. c. 54, fol. 125.

"Philosopher, The." From *Spirits in Bondage.*

"Phoenix Flew into My Garden, The." First published as "The Phoenix" in *P,* 121; reprinted in *CP,* 135. Holograph version available in the Bodleian, Dep. c. 884.

"Pilgrim's Problem." First published in the *Month* 7 (May 1952): 275. Reprinted in *P,* 119, and *CP,* 133.

"Planets, The." First published in *Lysistrata* 2 (May 1935): 21–24. Revised and reprinted in *P,* 12, and *CP,* 26. Holograph version available in a notebook Hooper holds.

"Prelude, A." From "Early Poems." First published in *CP,* 233.

"Prelude to Space: An Epithalamium." First published in *P,* 56; reprinted in *CP,* 70. Holograph version available in the Bodleian, Dep. c. 883.

"Prodigality of Firdausi, The." First published (under N. W.) in *Punch* 215 (Dec. 1, 1948): 510. Revised and reprinted in *P,* 21, and *CP,* 35. Typescript version available in the Bodleian, Dep. c. 884.

"Prologue." From *Spirits in Bondage.*

"Quam Bene Saturno." Lewis's first published poem, it appeared in the July 1913 issue of *Cherbourg School Magazine,* toward the end of his time at Cherbourg House, Malvern, where he was a student between Jan. 1911 and July 1913. See "LP" 4:51–52; there the poem is dated July 29, 1913. Holograph and typescript versions available in the Bodleian, Dep. c. 884.

Queen of Drum, The. First published in *NP,* 129–75. In *NP,* Hooper dates it to 1933–34, although he suggests Lewis may have worked on analogues as early as 1918, including "The Silence of the Night." No complete holograph version of the poem exists, although holograph fragments of the opening stanza of Canto I are available in the Bodleian, MSS. Facs. c. 54, fols. 116–18; in addition, a copy of fol. 117 is available in the Wade Center, CSL / MS-98. Furthermore, "Spirit! Who Names Her Lies," titled "Epigrams and Epitaphs 7" in *P,* 134, and *CP,* 148, is drawn from the opening lines of fol. 117. Lewis sent a typescript version to John Masefield, the poet laureate, who offered comments in four undated letters to Lewis (see *NP,* 177–78).

"Quick! The Black, Sulphurous, Never Quenched." First published in *PR*. Revised and retitled "Forbidden Pleasure" in *P,* 116, and *CP,* 130. Holograph versions available in "Half Hours with Hamilton," and in the Bodleian, MSS. Facs. c. 54, fol. 116.

"Re-Adjustment." First published in *Fifty-Two: A Journal of Books and Authors* 14 (Autumn 1964): 4. Reprinted in *P,* 102, and *CP,* 116. Holograph and typescript versions available in the Bodleian, Dep. c. 883–84.

"Roads, The." From *Spirits in Bondage.*

"Romantics, The." First published in the *New English Weekly* 30 (Jan. 16, 1947): 130. Revised and retitled "The Prudent Jailer" in *P,* 77, and *CP,* 91. Holograph and typescript versions available in the Bodleian, Dep. c. 883–84.

"Saboteuse, The." First published in *P,* 38; reprinted in *CP,* 52. Holograph and typescript versions available in Bodleian, Dep. c. 883–84.

"Sailing of the Ark, The." First published (under N. W.) in *Punch* 215 (Aug. 11, 1948): 124. Revised and retitled "The Late Passenger" in *P,* 47, and *CP,* 61. Holograph versions available in the Wade Center, CSL / MS-108, and in the Bodleian, MSS, Facs. c. 54, fol. 136.

"Salamander, The." First published in the *Spectator* 174 (June 8, 1945): 521. Revised and reprinted in *P,* 72, and *CP,* 86. Holograph versions available in the Wade Center, CSL / MS-105, and in the Bodleian, MSS, Facs. c. 54, fol. 129.

"Satan Speaks [I am Nature, the Mighty Mother]." From *Spirits in Bondage.*

"Satan Speaks [I am the Lord your God, even he that made]." From *Spirits in Bondage.*

"Satyr, The." From *Spirits in Bondage.*

"Save Yourself. Run and Leave Me. I Must Go Back." First published as "6" in "Epigrams and Epigraphs" in *P,* 134; reprinted in *CP,* 148. This poem is available in "Half Hours with Hamilton," Wade Center, CSL / MS-53, and in holographs and typescript in the Bodleian, Dep. c. 883–84.

"Scholars' Melancholy." First published (under N. W.) in the *Oxford Magazine* 52 (May 24, 1934): 734. Reprinted in *P,* 84, and *CP,* 98. Holograph version available in a notebook Hooper holds.

"Set on the Soul's Acropolis the Reason Stands." First published as "Reason" in *P,* 81. Although the poem has never been dated, I believe it was written shortly before, during, or after Lewis worked on the poems that appear in *PR*. I make this argument based on the appearance of a female character in *PR* named Reason. See *PR,* 70–87. Holograph version available in a notebook Hooper holds.

"Shortest Way Home, The." First published (under N. W.) in the *Oxford Magazine* 52 (May 10, 1934): 665. Revised and retitled "Man is a Lumpe Where All Beasts Kneaded Be" in *P,* 68, and *CP,* 82. Holograph versions available in "Half Hours with Hamilton," the Wade Center, CSL / MS-62, and in the Bodleian, MSS, Facs. c. 54, fol. 120.

"Silence of the Night, The." First published in King, *C. S. Lewis, Poet,* 271–75. See "LP" 8:164–67.

"Small Man Orders His Wedding, The." First published in *P,* 31; reprinted in *CP,* 45. Holograph versions available in the Wade Center, CSL / MS-109, and in the Bodleian, MSS. Facs. c. 54, fols. 115–16 and Dep. c. 883. A slightly different holograph, with the title "An Epithalamium for John Wain feigned to be spoken in his person giving orders for his wedding" signed "C.S.L., June 1947," is available in the Bodleian, MS. Eng. C. 2724, fol. 55.

"Solomon." First published (under N. W.) in *Punch* 211 (Aug. 14, 1946): 136. Revised and reprinted in *P,* 46, and *CP,* 60. Holograph versions available in the Wade Center, CSL / MS-127/B, and in the Bodleian, Dep. c. 883.

"Song." From *Spirits in Bondage.*

"Song of the Pilgrims." From *Spirits in Bondage.*

"Sonnet [I have not bowed in any other shrine]." From "Early Poems." First published in King, *C. S. Lewis, Poet,* n. 53 to chapter 2.

"Sonnet [The Bible says Sennacherib's campaign was spoiled]." First published (under N. W.) in the *Oxford Magazine* 54 (May 14, 1936): 575. A later draft, dated Oct. 26, 1949, appears in *CL* 2:989–90. Revised and reprinted in *P,* 120, and *CP,* 134. Holograph versions available in the Wade Center, CSL / MS-111, and in the Bodleian, MSS, Facs. c. 54, fol. 128.

"Sonnet [The clouds are red behind us and before]." From "Early Poems." First published in King, "Lost but Found."

"Sonnet [The stars come out; the fragrant shadows fall]." From *Spirits in Bondage.*

"Sonnet to John Keats." From "Early Poems." First published in King, "Lost but Found."

"Sonnet to Sir Philip Sydney." From "Early Poems." First published in *CP,* 237.

"Spartan Nactus." First published (under N. W.) in *Punch* 227 (Dec. 1, 1954): 685. Revised and retitled "A Confession" in *P,* 1, and *CP,* 15. Holograph version available in the Bodleian, Dep. c. 883.

"Spirit? Who Names Her Lies." First published as "Epigrams and Epitaphs 7" in *P*, 134; reprinted in *CP*, 148. Holograph versions available in the Wade Center, CSL / MS-113, and in the Bodleian, MSS. Facs. c. 54, fols. 117–18.

"Spooks." From *Spirits in Bondage.*

"Star Bath, The." From *Spirits in Bondage.*

"Stephen to Lazarus." First published in *P*, 125; reprinted in *CP*, 139. Holograph version available in the Bodleian, Dep. c. 883.

"Strange that a Trick of Light and Shade Could Look." First published as "Epigrams and Epitaphs 4" in *P*, 133; reprinted in *CP*, 147. Holograph version available in a notebook Hooper holds.

"Such Natural Love Twixt Beast and Man." First published as "Eden's Courtesy" in *P*, 98; reprinted in *CP*, 112. Holograph version available in a notebook Hooper holds.

"Tale of Psyche Is Unjustly Told, The." First published in King, *C. S. Lewis, Poet,* 269–71. See "LP" 8:163–64.

"That Was an Ugly Age." First published in King, *C. S. Lewis, Poet,* 297. Holograph versions available in the Bodleian, Dep. c. 884.

"There Was a Young Person of Streatham." In a letter to Cecil Harwood, July 1936. First published in *CL* 2:200.

"These Faint Wavering Far-travell'd Gleams." First published as "Sweet Desire" in *P*, 114; reprinted in *CP*, 128. Holograph versions available in the Wade Center, CSL / MS-120, in the Bodleian, MSS. Facs. c. 54, fol. 82, and in a notebook Hooper holds.

"They Tell Me Lord, that When I Seem." Early drafts appear in a letter to Owen Barfield, June 19, 1930, published in *CL* 1:903–4, and in a letter to Dom Bede Griffiths, Apr. 4, 1934, published in *CL* 2:137. First published in Lewis's *Letters to Malcolm,* 92–93. Revised and retitled "Prayer" in *P*, 122, and *CP*, 136. Holograph versions available in "Half Hours with Hamilton" and in a notebook Hooper holds.

"This Literary Lion." In a letter to Owen Barfield [Sept. 1945?], published in *CL* 2:669. Holograph available in the Wade Center, CSL / L-Barfield, 58, W. The holograph also contains a drawing by Lewis of a man playing a harp and singing "Ancient fortifications / Sleet behind!"

"Thou Only Art Alternative to God." First published in *PR*. Revised and retitled "Wormwood" in *P*, 87, and *CP*, 101. Holograph versions available at the Wade Center, CSL / MS-122, and in the Bodleian, MSS, Facs. c. 54, fol. 83.

"Through Our Lives Thy Meshes Run." First published as "Deadly Sins" in *P*, 91; reprinted in *CP*, 105. Holograph version available in a notebook Hooper holds.

"Thus Æ to Ě." In a letter to Owen Barfield, June 8?, 1928?, published in *CL* 1:765. In the letter, Lewis prefaces the poem with: "I am writing a great new poem—also a Mnemonic rime on English sound changes in octosyllabic verse."

"Till Your Alchemic Beams Turn All to Gold." First published as "Noon's Intensity" in *P*, 114; reprinted in *CP*, 128. Holograph versions available in the Wade Center, CSL / MS-124, in the Bodleian, MSS. Facs. c. 54, fol. 81, and in a notebook Hooper holds.

"To Andrew Marvell." First published in *P*, 82; reprinted in *CP*, 96. Holograph versions available in the Wade Center, CSL / MS-126, and in the Bodleian, MSS. Facs. c. 54, fol. 106.

"To G. M." First published in the *Spectator* 169 (Oct. 9, 1942): 335. A later draft appears in a letter to Ruth Pitter, July 24, 1946, published in *CL* 2:726–27. Revised and retitled "To a Friend" in *P*, 104, and *CP*, 118. Holograph versions (titled "To–") available in the Wade Center, CSL / MS-125, and in the Bodleian, MSS, Facs. c. 54, fol. 85.

"To Mr. Kingsley Amis on His Late Verses." First published in *Essays in Criticism* 4 (Apr.

1954): 190. Lewis's poem is a response to Kingsley Amis's "Beowulf," *Essays in Criticism* 4 (Jan. 1954): 85.

"To Mr. Roy Campbell." First published (under N. W.) in the *Cherwell* 56 (May 6, 1939): 35. Revised and retitled "The Author of *Flowering Rifle*" in *P*, 65, and *CP*, 79. Holograph version available in the Bodleian, Dep. c. 883.

"To Mrs. Dyson, Angrie." First published in King, "Glints," 89. Holograph version available in the Bodleian, MS. Eng. lett. c. 220/7, fols. 2–3.

"To Sleep." From *Spirits in Bondage.*

"To the Gods of Old Time." From "Early Poems." First published in King, "Lost but Found."

"Town of Gold, The." From "Early Poems." First published in King, "Lost but Found."

"Travellers! In Months without an R." In a letter to Genia Goelz, June 20, 1952, first published in *CL* 3:204–5.

"True Nature of Gnomes, The." First published (under N. W.) in *Punch* 211 (Oct. 16, 1946): 310. Reprinted in *P*, 9, and *CP*, 23.

"Tu Ne Quæsieris." From *Spirits in Bondage.*

"Turn of the Tide, The." First published (under N. W.) in *Punch* 215 (Nov. 1, 1948). Revised and reprinted in *P*, 49, and *CP*, 63. Holograph versions available in the Wade Center, CSL / MS-26, and in the Bodleian, MSS, Facs. c. 54, fols. 134–35.

"Tu Silentia Perosus." Published here for the first time. Holograph versions available in the Wade Center, CSL / MS-128, and in the Bodleian, MSS. Facs. c. 54, fols. 111–12. On the top margin of the holograph is the following: "I had written (from Germany) complaining of his not writing to me. O[wen] B[arfield]." At the end of poem there is a drawing by Lewis of a man in a Biergarten sitting at a table reading a German newspaper surrounded by dachshunds and a note by Lewis: "These are dachshunds—not dragons as you might suppose."

"Two Kinds of Memory." First published in *Time and Tide* 28 (Aug. 7, 1947): 859. Two early drafts appear in a letter to Ruth Pitter, Feb. 2, 1947, published in *CL* 2:758–61. Revised and reprinted in *P*, 100, and *CP*, 114. Holograph versions available in the Wade Center, CSL / MS-86/B, and in the Bodleian, MSS, Facs. c. 54, fol. 114.

"Under Sentence." First published in the *Spectator* 175 (Sept. 7, 1945): 219. Revised and retitled "The Condemned" in *P*, 63, and *CP*, 77. Holograph versions available in the Wade Center, CSL / MS-31, and in the Bodleian, MSS, Facs. c. 54, fol. 88.

"Victory." From *Spirits in Bondage.*

"Vitrea Circe." First published (under N. W.) in *Punch* 214 (June 23, 1948): 543. An early draft appears in a letter to Ruth Pitter, July 6, 1947, published in *CL* 2:794–95. Revised and reprinted in *P*, 25, and *CP*, 39. Holograph versions available in the Wade Center, CSL / MS-38/B, and in the Bodleian, Dep. c. 883.

"Vowels and Sirens." First published in the *Times Literary Supplement,* Special Autumn Issue (Aug. 29, 1952), xiv. Revised and reprinted in *P*, 76, and *CP*, 90. Holograph versions available in the Wade Center, CSL / MS-27, and in the Bodleian, Dep. c. 883 and MSS. Facs. c. 54, fol. 99.

"West Germanic to Primitive Old English." This mnemonic poem of fifteen lines was first published in Walter Hooper's preface to Lewis's *Selected Literary Essays,* xv; there he suggests the poem was composed sometime in 1925. Holograph available in a notebook Hooper holds.

"When Lilith Means to Draw Me." First published in *PR*. Revised and retitled "Lilith" in *P*, 95 and *CP*, 109. Holograph version appears in "Half Hours with Hamilton." Another version of this poem appears in a letter to Greeves, Apr. 29, [1930?], published in *CL* 1:895–96. Yet another holograph version is available in the Bodleian, MSS, Facs. c. 54, fol. 107.

"When the Grape of the Night Is Pressed." First published as "After Vain Pretence" in *P,* 106; reprinted in *CP,* 120. Holograph versions available in the Wade Center, CSL / MS-133, in the Bodleian, MSS. Facs. c. 54, fol. 95, and in a notebook Hooper holds.

"When the Year Dies in Preparation for the Birth." This poem, which Hooper entitled "Launcelot" and dates to the early 1930s, was first published in *NP,* 95–103, with the text following the holograph manuscript, available at the Bodleian, Dep. d. 809, fols. 2–8. The text presented here follows the holograph manuscript and the version printed in *NP.* In brief, "When the Year Dies in Preparation for the Birth" is a narrative fragment of 296 lines of alexandrine couplets. The poem, heavily influenced by Lewis's reading of Malory's *Morte D'Arthur* and, to a lesser degree, of Tennyson's *Idylls of the King,* is set within the context of a Sangrail quest by the knights of Arthur's court. Though Gawain is mentioned early, the poem essentially concerns Launcelot's quest, Guinevere's distress while he is gone, her subsequent anger at his delay in coming to her after his return, and the story he tells about his quest.

"Where Are the Walks?" First published in a letter to E. F. Carritt, Oct. 29, [1937], published in *CL* 2:220.

"Where Reservoys Ripple." In a letter to Owen Barfield, Apr. 5, 1935. First published in King, *C. S. Lewis, Poet,* 295. Also published in *CL* 2:158. Holograph version available in the Wade Center, CSL / MS-142.

"Who Knows if the Isolation, the Compact, the Firm-shaped." In a letter to Kathleen Raine, Apr. 11, 1956. First published in King, *C. S. Lewis, Poet,* 295–96. Also published in *CL* 3:734–35. Holograph versions available in the Wade Center, CSL / MS-134/B, and in the Bodleian, Dep. C. 884.

"Wind, The." From "Early Poems." First published in King, "Lost but Found."

"Witch, The." From *Spirits in Bondage.*

"Wood Desolate (near Bookham), The. From "Early Poems." First published in King, "Lost but Found."

"World Is Round, The." First published in *Fear No More,* 85. Revised and retitled "Poem for Psychoanalysts and/or Theologians" in *P,* 113, and *CP,* 127. Holograph version available in a notebook Hooper holds.

"World's Desire." From *Spirits in Bondage.*

"YAH!" Found in an unpublished letter to Owen Barfield, [n.d.]. First published in King, *C. S. Lewis, Poet,* 292–93. Holograph version available in the Wade Center, CSL / MS-54, and in the Bodleian, MSS. Facs. c. 54, fol. 124.

"Yes, You Are Always Everywhere." First published as "No Beauty We Could Desire" in *P,* 124; reprinted in *CP,* 138. Holograph versions available in the Bodleian, Dep. c. 883.

"Yet More of the Wood Desolate." From "Early Poems." First published in King, "Lost but Found."

"You, Beneath Scraping Branches." Titled "Leaving For Ever the Home of One's Youth," this poem was first published in Adams, *Occasional Poets,* 101. Warren Lewis dates it to around June 19, 1930, and provides the text in "LP" 11:79–80. Holograph version available in the Bodleian, Dep. c. 883.

"You Do Not Love the Bourgeoisie." First published as "The Genuine Article" in *P,* 63; reprinted in *CP,* 77. Holograph version available in a notebook Hooper holds.

"You Rest Upon Me All My Days." First published in *PR.* Revised and retitled "Caught" in *P,* 115, and *CP,* 129. Holograph versions available in "Half Hours with Hamilton" and in the Bodleian, MSS, Facs. c. 54, fol. 98.

Index of Titles

Index of First Lines